The New York Times

Book of Science Literacy,

Volume II

T I M E S **T** B O O K S

R A N D O M   H O U S E

The New York Times
Book of Science Literacy,
Volume II

The Environment from Your Backyard to the Ocean Floor

By the writers of
Science Times
Edited by Nicholas Wade,
Cornelia Dean, and William A. Dicke

Library of Congress Cataloging-in-Publication Data

The New York Times book of science literacy : the environment
  from your backyard to the ocean floor / by the writers of The
  science times ; edited by Nicholas Wade, Cornelia Dean, and William A. Dicke — 1st ed.
        p.   cm.
    ISBN 0-8129-2215-8
    1. Environmental education—North America. 2. Environmental
  education—South America. 3. Pollution—North America.
  4. Pollution—South America. I. Wade, Nicholas. II. Dean, Cornelia.
  III. Science times.
  GE90.N7N48   1994
  363.7—dc20   93-41260

Manufactured in the United States of America
9   8   7   6   5   4   3   2   1
First Edition

CONTENTS

Section 1: The Texture of Nature

Section 2: Rips in the Fabric

Section 3: Courting Disaster

Section 4: Saw, Fire, and Leaf

Section 5: Disturbing the Atmosphere

Section 6: Diapers to Lawn Mowers

Section 7: Economists Consider Ecology

Section 8: Priorities and Reassessments

Section 9: Repairing the Tapestry

CONTRIBUTORS

NA   Natalie Angier
EMB   Emily M. Bernstein
NB   Nina Bick
CB   Celestine Bohlen
JEB   Jane E. Brody
EHB   Elizabeth Heilman Brooke
JB   James Brooke
MWB   Malcolm W. Browne
CD   Catherine Dold
COD   Cornelia Dean
NDK   Nicholas D. Kristof
JRL   Jon R. Luoma
NCN   Nathaniel C. Nash
PP   Peter Passell
JP   Jane Perlez
DES   David E. Sanger
KS   Keith Schneider
PS   Philip Shabecoff
MS   Marlise Simons
MIS   Michael Specter
WKS   William K. Stevens
WS   Walter Sullivan
JT   John Tagliabue
PET   Patrick E. Tyler
MAU   Mark Uhlig
MLW   Matthew Wald
SWD   Sheryl WuDunn
CKY   Carol Kaesuk Yoon

INTRODUCTION

IF ONE age of innocence ended when Adam and Eve were expelled from Eden, another surely came to a close when their progeny grew numerous and wasteful enough to destroy the planet's natural balances. Modern economies have reached such a scale that they can overwhelm even the resilient fabric of nature unless carefully restrained. Governments, in other words, must either protect nature or accept the consequences of degrading it.

But protecting nature is an onerous duty. It raises the cost of most mining, manufacture, and agriculture. It provokes the vehement opposition of groups who have assumed the free right to clear forests, drain marshlands, graze cattle, or discharge wastes.

Amid the fierce controversy engendered by most environmental issues, it is often hard for bystanders to judge where the truth lies and what remedies are just. It can be hard for the experts, too, since the seriousness of many threats must often be assessed with only partial information in hand.

The United States has seen two decades of vigorous environmental legislation, with sweeping laws to safeguard air, soil, and water, and to avert specific threats ranging from the greenhouse effect to radon seeping into homes. Abroad, America has subscribed to international treaties intended to protect the ozone layer, stabilize the climate, conserve endangered species, and ban ocean dumping.

This array of complicated laws and regulations is broadly supported, but has also stimulated a sharp anti-environmental backlash, marked by a stream of books charging that the threats were exaggerated and the responses excessive. Some of this revisionist literature may be well founded. Those who press for new environmental legislation do not usually understate the danger they seek to avert. New information has made some threats seem less pressing and their remedies disproportionately costly. Abandoned dumps of toxic chemicals are probably one such example. The dumps need to be cleared up sometime, but the burden of illness in communities living around them has been small so far. Other parts of the revisionist thesis, including suggestions that the threat to the ozone layer is a hoax or the greenhouse effect an illusion, are less convincing.

The purpose of this book is to provide readers a thorough and well-rounded understanding of current environmental issues and controversies. It focuses on the science that provides, or should provide, the framework for political discussion. Unlike the formal approach of a textbook, the articles on which this book is based were prompted by the need to explain current events. Most originally appeared in the Science Section that is part of every Tuesday's *New York Times*, and were written by the paper's science writers led by William K. Stevens. Another group of articles, contributed to the paper's international news pages, were written by our foreign correspondents, in particular Marlise Simons. The articles all appeared during a period from January 1990 to October 1993, except for an especially important series written by Marlise Simons from the Brazilian rain forests in 1988 and 1989.

Though much newspaper writing, almost by definition, is ephemeral, the items selected for this book are mostly feature articles, and are more explanatory in nature than those tied directly to the day's news. They benefit from being grouped together here and presented in a logical order rarely obtainable in a daily newspaper.

The argument of the book is straightforward. Animals and plants depend on each other in many intimate ways, so that a change to one organism in an ecology may affect others even far down the food chain (Section 1). Many valuable and important species are already being driven to the brink of extinction (Section 2). In some parts of the world, even whole ecologies have been put under stress by human activities (Section 3). Forests in particular, both the tropical forests and the temperate zone forests of the United States and Europe, are under relentless pressure from developers (Section 4).

Besides the worldwide loss of habitats and species, two other global concerns have arisen, the thinning of the protective ozone layer in the stratosphere, and the possibility of climate change triggered by industrial waste gases (Section 5).

But not everything is bad. Countries like the United States, having tackled the major sources of pollution, are now dealing for the most part with second-order problems (Section 6). They have also begun to experiment with market-based incentives to curb pollution, as economists' views on environmental issues become more influential (Section 7).

Some threats, when revisited, seem less serious than at first appeared (Section 8). And a new school of environmentalists is turning its attention to trying to restore vanished ecologies (Section 9).

The idea for this collection came from Steven Wasserman of Times Books. The unseen hands that commissioned or helped shape many of the articles are those of my colleagues Cornelia Dean, until recently deputy science editor, and William Dicke, who edits the environmental page in *Science Times*. To the *New York Times*'s reporters belongs the credit for such insights, instruction, and diversion as this book may offer.

Nicholas Wade
Science Editor

The New York Times

Book of Science Literacy,

Volume II

The Texture of Nature

THE INTERWOVENNESS OF LIVING THINGS

OVER MILLIONS of years of evolution, the acacia trees of the Amazon forest have developed a special relationship with certain species of ant. The acacias produce hollow thorns for the ants to live in and special protuberances that ants find tasty. In return, the ants defend their tree vigorously against the many creatures that would try to eat its leaves.

Not all relationships in nature are as close as this symbiosis, but few if any organisms live in complete isolation from their surroundings. A web of dependencies links one organism with another and ties their fates together. Biologists call these linked assemblages of plants and animals an ecological system. Though nature is robust, these links can be a source of weakness that allows a pollutant to penetrate deep through an ecology. The pesticide DDT was absorbed first by soil organisms, then by mice, then by birds of prey like peregrine falcons. The chemical made the eggshells so thin that the young birds failed to hatch and the falcon was driven to the edge of extinction. Radiation from the explosion of the Chernobyl power plant in Ukraine spread over the tundra of Scandinavia and was absorbed by grazing reindeer, which became so radioactive they had to be destroyed.

The chapters in this section focus on some especially rich links in the fabric of nature. Tropical forests teem with life, but much of the diversity is to be found up high in the forest canopy. Despite the heavy rains in the tropics, the canopy is rather dry. Important sources of water are the aerial ponds formed by a special family of plants called bromeliads. Forming a tight cup with their leaves, the tree-dwelling bromeliads catch rain-

water, and the pools they form give shelter and sustenance to many species of the canopy.

Nature rewards animals that find special niches,
and some of these niches are odd indeed. Scarabs are a
family of beetles that specialize in disposing of dung,
which they bury underground as food for their larvae.
Their activities clear waste and fertilize the soil, stimulating plant life and the dependent communities of animals. Like the bromeliads of the forest canopy, scarabs
are key organisms on which many others depend.

The diversity of species in tropical forests may be
related to the long periods of relative stability during
which species have had time to evolve complicated relationships with one another. The cradle of life on earth
is not the forests, however, but the oceans. The sea is
where life first began to flourish, and it holds a far
greater variety of life forms.

Why should any species or ecosystem not make way
if some human society needs its space? What country
can afford to preserve every last species of obscure beetle
in its most distant forests? The more that people come

to understand the intricacy of nature's tapestry, perhaps the less willing they will be to see any piece of it carelessly destroyed.

AT HOME IN THE POOLS OF THE SKY

A VISITOR who glances upward into the canopy of a New World tropical rain forest will be struck by the sight of spiny, succulent plants that festoon the tree branches and trunks, making a constellation of star-shaped silhouettes against the sky. This large family of plants, called bromeliads, is well known to plant enthusiasts and is most familiar to Americans in the form of its domesticated relative, the pineapple. As biologists invade the upper reaches of the forest canopy, a habitat that some see as the last frontier of the tropics, they are discovering that these air plants are the hub of much of the canopy's activity. Researchers say these abundant plants are being recognized as a vital source of nutrients and of diversity in the rain forest, much more important than anyone had previously suspected. Dr. Brian M. Boom, vice president for botanical science at the New York Botanical Garden, says the plants have undergone "an evolutionary explosion" in the tropics of the Americas.

The bromeliads, through an unusual feature of their architecture, are miniature, self-contained ecosystems, central to the lives of many creatures in this upper stratum of the jungle, where some biologists say nearly half of the earth's species live. With the signing of the biodiversity treaty at the Earth Summit in Rio de Janeiro in 1992, the world has taken a first step toward protecting species like bromeliads and the diverse canopy habitats that they help support. "It's a very exciting time," said Dr. Nalini Nadkarni, a professor of biology at the Evergreen State College in Olympia, Washington, who has worked in the Monteverde Cloud Forest Reserve in Costa Rica. "It's exciting to get to the plants in this upper part of the forest that nobody knows anything about."

Anyone who does manage the task of scaling a tree to look into a bromeliad will find the secret to its importance. Bromeliads hold a pool of rainwater deep inside, the centerpiece in their tight rosette of leaves. A paradoxically rare resource in the lush rain forest, the water in the bromeliads' coveted pools allows the plants to survive in this otherwise rather arid habitat and at the same time lures all manner of creatures to share in the watery riches.

Tropical birds, like the orange-bellied trogon, fly in to sip from the pools, which are called tanks, while poison dart frogs, with flattened bodies and spindly legs perfect for maneuvering through the bromeliads' leaves, bathe, hunt, and raise their young in the aerial pools. One tree frog is so well adapted to these plants that it can swivel its head to block off the entire tank, preventing evaporation as well as the entrance of other animals.

Bromeliads are home to many other small animals, including many still unnamed species of beetle and ants, some so tree-loving that their feet never touch the earth. Less charismatic but still numerous are the tank's many worms, microbes, and protozoans. Examinations of these plants have yielded as many as 300 different species. "If you take a bromeliad and you plunge it out into a petri dish and look under a dissecting scope, it's just a zoo," Dr. Nadkarni says.

Dr. David Benzing, the Robert S. Danforth Professor of Biology at Oberlin College, says: "What we discovered in a cloud forest in Venezuela was that the diversity of animal life, mostly invertebrates, in these tanks in the canopy equaled that on the ground, which is a phenomenal discovery. It indicates that these bromeliad tanks are providing a major resource for life in the canopy and the tropical forest. Wet forest canopy is probably the most species-rich of all the terrestrial communities in the world, and bromeliads are really a pivotal part of the whole system."

The more biologists learn, the more they find that the lives of the bromeliads and their animal entourages are intricately entwined. Researchers have discovered many animals and even some predaceous plants that depend entirely upon the bromeliad as a home and breeding place. They have also found that the tree-dwelling bromeliads, perched far from the rich resources below, depend on their animal associates for their own survival in the forests' penthouse.

Although some bromeliad species live in the soil, at least half of the species are air plants that grow on trees. Air plants use their roots only to hold themselves in place. Perched in the trees, these bromeliads must get all their water from clouds and fog and from the rainwater they have managed to store in their tanks.

As for the nutrients that other plants get from the soil, the bromeliad fosters the generation of its own fertilizer. In a happy mutualism, the animals swimming in a bromeliad's tank excrete wastes, while bacteria and insects help decompose and digest leaves and dead bodies that have fallen into the water, making a rich organic soup. Scientists have discovered that the bromeliad then feeds from its leafy tureen, using specialized hairs to strain out what it needs. These hairs, called trichomes, can grow on the outer leaves as well, enabling the plant to gather moisture from the cloud forest's humid air.

Tank bromeliads can range from three inches across to as large as three feet. No matter what the size, their complex architecture provides a range of habitats, from open water in the center to leaves holding pockets of humus at the edges, making the plants suitable for a correspondingly wide array of creatures.

Trails of tree-dwelling ants lead out from the edges of the bromeliad, where they have made their nests in the dry shade of the older, outer leaves. Some ant species are so fond of bromeliads that when they build their huge mound nests in the trees, they plant their own seeds.

In among the leaves or in the tank itself, the colors of a fluorescently patterned poison dart frog may flash, as tiny inch-long males grapple for dominance or sing for a mate. Named for the poisonous secretions in their skin, which they use to deter predators but which humans use to tip deadly blow darts, these frogs are colored in black and bright yellows and greens and reds, some with patterns of dots or stripes on their bodies and spindly limbs.

Some species of poison dart frog have been seen only in bromeliads, their lives revolving entirely around the resources of the plant. Although the habits of many species remain obscure, scientists continue to patch together pieces of the bizarre poison dart frog story. They have tracked mother frogs as they hop from bromeliad to bromeliad visiting each nursery pool where they have left a tadpole or two. The mother frog lowers herself in to feed her offspring a nutritious meal of unfertilized eggs.

Although creatures as different as frogs and crabs and beetles clamber around the spiny leaves of bromeliads where they raise their young, they all seem to have one thing in common. As they compete for space in the aquatic nursery in this crowded habitat, they work hard to protect their young from the many dangers to be found there, whether by reducing the time spent in the water or fighting off predators coming to eat them.

"The idea is that there are lots of awful nasty predators in the water, and anything you can do to reduce your time in the water the better," says Dr. Maureen Donnelly, a researcher at the American Museum of Natural History who has studied the poison dart frogs.

Scientists have seen poison dart frogs in Panama laying their eggs in the dangerously dry leaf litter, presumably to protect them from the hazards of predation in pools. And in the newest study of the curious habits of the bromeliad entourage, a German researcher published a description in June of 1992 of bromeliad crab mothers in Jamaica carefully clearing tanks of predatory insects before laying their larvae in the water. In the weeks that their tender young develop, these tiny guardians, less than an inch across, watch over them by ridding the tanks of young damselfly nymphs and other dangerous hunters.

Bromeliads are also hosts to other plants. Some are home to algae, others to tiny predaceous plants. The insectivorous plants sunk in the pools are hard to spot, Dr. Benzing says, except when they flower and their blooms jut through the surface of the water. When small, unsuspecting insects in the tank swim by the plant, they trigger a bladder, which pops open, sucking in the nearby water and usually the unfortunate prey. The insect caught in this tiny trap, which is about one fifth of an inch long, is soon digested.

Seen from below, the forest canopy is all undersides of leaves, with windows of light between the shadows and silhouettes of branches and their bromeliads. From above, the canopy appears as a richly patterned carpet woven of moss and tree plants that coat the spreading branches.

According to Dr. Nadkarni, who has spent many hours observing air plants and their animal visitors from a cot set high in the canopy, it is a different world from above. "It's beautiful," she says. "It looks like a packed garden of plants."

Biologists who study the highly successful bromeliads, of which there are 2,000 to 3,000 species, are finding that they often comprise a surprising bulk of the rain forest's mass. So rich are these arboreal gardens that in a single tree in Costa Rica the air plants weighed more than 300 pounds.

Dr. Benzing says that in a recent study, he and his colleagues found that life in the canopy seemed to mirror life below it. "In fact, the canopy contains a lot of organisms very similar to those on the ground, sometimes with the same species," he says, adding that even when the species are different the ecological roles are the same. For many researchers studying this habitat, so dominated by air plants and their associates, the real challenge will be the unraveling of the web of interactions that link the distinct but connected worlds of terrestrial and canopy ecosystems. Dressed like mountaineers, casting ropes up into the treetops, biologists will continue to explore the complex world that stretches out in parallel to the one so far below it.

[CKY, JUNE 1992]

THE SCARAB, A PEERLESS RECYCLER

IN the vast world of beetles, scarabs have the stamp of nobility, their heads a diadem of horny spikes, their bodies sheathed in glittering mail of bronze or emerald or cobalt blue. The ancient Egyptians so worshipped the creatures that when a pharaoh died, his heart was carved out and replaced with a stone rendering of the sacred beetle. But perhaps the most majestic thing about the group of insects known romantically as scarabs, and more descriptively as dung beetles, is what they are willing and even delighted to do for a living. Dung beetles venture where many beasts refuse to tread, descending on the waste matter of their fellow animals and swiftly burying it underground, where it then serves as a rich and leisurely meal for themselves or their offspring.

Each day, dung beetles living on the cattle ranches of Texas, the savannas of Africa, the deserts of India, the meadows of the Himalayas, the dense undergrowth of the Amazon—anyplace where dirt and dung come together—assiduously clear away billions of tons of droppings, the great bulk of which comes from messy mammals like cows, horses, elephants, monkeys, and humans. Scientists have long appreciated dung beetles as nature's indispensable recyclers, without which the planet would be beyond the help of even the most generous Superfund cleanup project. But only recently have they begun to understand the intricacies of the dung beetle community and the ferocious inter-beetle competition that erupts each time a mammal deposits its droppings on the ground. Researchers are learning that every dung pat is a complex microcosm unto itself, a teeming habitat not unlike a patch of wetland or the decaying trunk of an old redwood, although in this case the habitat is thankfully short-lived. For scarabs, it may be said that waste makes haste, and entomologists have discovered that as many as 120 different species of dung beetles and tens of thousands of individuals will converge on a single large pat of dung as soon as it is laid, whisking it away within a matter of hours or even minutes. "If it weren't for dung beetles," says Dr. Bruce E. Gill, a scarab researcher at Agriculture Canada, a government agency in Ottawa, "we'd be up to our eyeballs in you-know-what."

The diversity of beetles that will flock to a lone meadow muffin far exceeds what ecologists would have predicted was likely or even possible, and scientists are being forced to rethink a few pet notions about how animals compete for limited goods and what makes for success or failure in an unstable profession like waste management. They are learning that beetles have evolved a wide assortment of strategies to get as much dung as possible as quickly as possible, to sculpt it and manipulate it for the good of themselves and their off-spring, and to keep others from snatching away their valuable booty. Researchers are also realizing that chance and good fortune play a far greater role than they had thought in determining who reaches a prized resource first and who is able to make the most of it.

The knowledge they are gleaning about the dung beetle community also applies to their understanding of how species compete for more conventional resources, including plants or prey animals. "I'm fascinated by the enormous diversity of dung beetles that you can see in one dung pat," says Dr. Ilkka Hanski of the University of Helsinki in Finland. "I don't know of any other insect community where such large numbers could be seen in such a small area. It is extraordinary." Many of the latest findings have been gathered into a book, *Dung Beetle Ecology*, edited by Dr. Hanski and Dr. Yves Cambefort of the Natural History Museum in Paris. The book is intermittently technical and arcane, but it nevertheless transforms a beetle that one might have preferred not to dwell on at all into an insect of such worthiness, respectability, and even charm that one would like to immediately order a few hundred thousand to help clean up the streets of one's hometown.

Dung beetles, it turns out, are among humanity's greatest benefactors. Not only do they remove dung from sight, smell, and inadvertent footstep, but they add fertilizing nitrogen to the soil by burying whatever they do not immediately eat. "Experiments have shown that by burying the dung underground, the beetle increases the amount of nitrogen getting from the dung and into the soil, as opposed to being lost in the atmosphere," says Dr. Gill. Like earthworms, the beetles also churn up and aerate the ground, making it more suitable for plant life. Dung beetle larvae consume parasitic worms and maggots that live in dung, thus helping to cut back on microorganisms that spread disease. "They revitalize the soil, they eliminate noxious wastes we don't like, they keep pastures clean," says Dr. Brett C. Ratcliffe, curator and professor at the University of Nebraska State Museum in Lincoln. "They do so many beneficial things, but if you ask a person on the street what they've heard about dung beetles, they'll look at you like you're crazy."

As beetles go, scarabs are exceptionally sophisticated. In Africa and South America, where some species are the size of apricots, the beetles may couple up like birds to start a family, digging elaborate subterranean nests and provisioning them with dung balls that will serve as food and protection for their young. And these dung balls, called brood balls, are not slapdash little marbles. With a geometric artistry befitting the sculptor Jean Arp, the beetles use their legs and mouthparts to fashion freshly laid dung into huge spherical or pear-shaped objects that may be hundreds of times the girth of their creators. Some beetles even coat the balls with clay, resulting in orbs so large, round, and firm they look machine-made. "When they were first found by expeditions in India and Africa," says Dr. Ratcliffe, "people thought they were cannonballs." Still working as a duo, the beetles then roll each ball away from the dung pat and down into the underground nest. The female lays a single egg in each brood ball; among the largest species, there may be only one ball and thus one baby per couple. Safe within its round cocoon, the larva feasts on the fecal matter. As the infant develops over a period of months, the mother stays nearby and tends to the brood balls with exquisite care, cleaning away poisonous molds and fungi and assuring that her young will survive to emerge from its incubator as an adult. That sort of maternal devotion is almost unheard-of among beetles, which normally lay their eggs in a mindless heap and lumber away.

Other scarabs are superspecialists, their habits streamlined to harvest the ordure of one type of mammal alone. Such beetles may cling to the rump fur of a kangaroo, for example, or a wallaby or a sloth, awaiting the moment when the final stage of mammalian digestion is complete and then leaping onto the droppings in midair. Some beetles dine solely on giraffe waste, others on the excretions of wild pigs. Some Panamanian beetles will fly each morning up to the treetop canopies where howler monkeys sleep. They wait for the primates to awake and do their morning business, quickly latching onto the released flotsam and sailing with it one hundred feet to the ground, where they then can bury it. But the majority of dung beetles are generalists rather than specialists, able to make a meal and outfit a nest with any droppings they can find. "One of the interesting things about the dung beetle family is how some are very species-specific, and some will use any kind of dung they can get their feet on," said Dr. Bernd Heinrich of the University of Vermont in Burlington.

Of keenest interest to the beetles are the generous patties provided by large herbivores, which by the nature of their digestive system must void themselves frequently. The average cow produces ten to fifteen large pats per day. Elephants will provide about four pounds of waste every hour or so, and it is an elephant pat that can become a pulsating Manhattan of beetles, with different species exhibiting a huge variety of tactics. Big scarabs will roll huge balls of it to their nests several yards away, sometimes pushing the balls over logs and boulders; smaller dung-rolling species will shove off with more modest portions. Another class of beetles, called tunnelers, will inter big hunks of dung right beneath the pat, while other, pin-sized beetles will live within the pat itself, munching on it even after it has begun to dry up and be of little use to the larger, more aggressive scarabs. Robber beetles will try to sneak in and pilfer balls painstakingly shaped by others. Joining the fray are many species of dung-eating flies. "It's like a fast-food outlet, with everybody heading toward it to get a piece of the action," says Dr. Gill. A dung heap is also a sort of singles bar, where beetles in search of mates can meet and begin the joint effort of gathering the goods for their nest. Some of the larger beetles use dung in their courtship dances, the male lifting a deftly rolled bit of dropping and shaking it provocatively in the face of a female. All of which means that little dung will go to waste. One research team in Africa reported counting 16,000 beetles on a single elephant dung pat; when the scientists returned two hours later, the pat had disappeared.

The incentive to move quickly is great. Not only does every beetle want to get away with the biggest slice of the pie, but while it is scavenging in an exposed heap of dung, it is itself extremely tempting as prey to many insectivores. "You'll see birds, mongooses, monkeys, and other small predators picking around in elephant dung," says Dr. Jan Krikken of the Rijksmuseum of Natural History in Leiden, The Netherlands. To counteract predation, some beetles have evolved persuasive disguises. One species that frequents elephant dung resembles an undigested stick of the type commonly found in the herbivore's droppings.

Behind the diversity of dung beetles is the resource they live on. Hard though it is to fathom, dung is an exceedingly appealing resource. Most mammals digest only a fraction of the food they eat, and whatever they discard is rich in proteins, nutrients, bacteria, yeast, and other sources of nourishment. Best of all, dung is easy. Animals fight back against would-be predators, and plants generate poisons to ward off herbivores, but dung does not bother defending itself against consumption. "It's available, everyone defecates, and it's the line of least resistance," says Dr. Robert D. Gordon of the Department of Systematics Entomology at the Agricultural Research Service in Washington.

Dung beetles may prefer the droppings of the biggest mammals, but the insects originated more than 350 million years ago, before the appearance of such mammals. Scientists speculate that dung beetles may have fed on dinosaur waste, but no beetle fossil has ever been found in the midst of petrified dinosaur dung. With the rise and spread of the great mammals around the world, dung beetles likewise began to diversify and multiply. Indeed, the two events occurred in parallel, and some researchers have suggested that large mammals may never have reached the population densities seen in places like the African savanna without the aid of beetles to clean up their waste, thus allowing the plants they feed on to keep growing. "They're key organisms in the environment," said Dr. Heinrich. "Small beetles may allow a large diversity of herbivores to exist where otherwise a smaller density would have to be."

From the dawn of agriculture and the domestication of waste-heavy livestock animals, human beings also have recognized the incalculable value of the beetles, the ancient Egyptians taking their admiration to the greatest lengths. Dr. Cambefort of the Natural History Museum in Paris has proposed that the Egyptians' tradition of mummifying their kings and burying them in pyramids was modeled after the burial of a beetle larva in a dung ball. Just as a beetle rises from dirt to a new life, Dr. Cambefort suggests, so the Egyptians believed their pharaohs would be reborn from their interred cocoons. In other words, he says, the Great Pyramids of Giza may be nothing more than glorified dung pats.

The benefits of scarab beetles have not gone unnoticed in our own time. *Dung Beetle Ecology* recounts the ambitious and largely successful effort by the Australian government to import thousands of exotic dung beetles to help reduce the mountains of dung generated by cattle and sheep. Those livestock animals had themselves been brought to the continent within the past two centuries, and indigenous Australian dung beetles, accustomed to moderate bits of kangaroo and koala dung, were unable to handle the foreign animals' enormous output. By the 1960s, the fecal problem had reached crisis proportions, and the dread native bush flies, which breed in excrement, had reached levels pestilent enough to give birth to the famed "Australian salute," a brush of the hand across the face to swipe away flies. "If you had a barbecue outside in western Australia, you'd have so many flies on the meat that you wouldn't be able to see it on your plate," says Dr. Bernard M. Doube of the Commonwealth Scientific and Industrial Research Organization, a government agency in Adelaide. But with the successful introduction of two dozen species of beetles from Asia, Europe, and Africa, the dung problem has begun to subside. In the past two or three years, many parts of southern and western Australia have been almost entirely freed of the dung-breeding flies, and pastures that once were coated with a carapace of cattle dung have been restored to useful verdancy. "What we've done is one of the most ambitious programs for biological control ever undertaken in the world," says Dr. Doube. But, he adds, the program may have been too effective for its own good: "People tend to forget things that aren't there to bother them anymore," he says. "So now they underrate what we've done." The United States government has also imported beetles from Africa and Asia to help recycle cattle waste in Florida and South Texas.

On a more theoretical scale, ecologists have also learned much from the insects. Scientists historically believed that more than one species could not coexist in the same ecosystem without showing some differences in their use of resources. "The general rule was that one competitor would eventually prevail over the other," says Dr. Hanski. "There were mathematical equations showing that it must be true." But given the diversity of dung beetles living on a single resource, nature obviously was not obeying the equations, he says. Entomologists investigating the beetles have realized that dung as a resource has a few distinguishing characteristics. It is far more ephemeral than, say, a patch of flowers or a burrow of rodents, being here today and gone today. And its distribution in the environment is exceedingly random, with no easily defined rules about when or where it is likely to appear. To most animals, everywhere and anywhere is a potential lavatory. Therefore, Dr. Hanski says, a strong element of happenstance must be figured into any calculation of the dynamics of the dung beetle community. As it turns out, randomness fosters the survival of many competing species. Some of the larger dung beetles may be inherently better than others at monopolizing prodigious quantities of dung once they get to the pat, he says. But because a smaller, weaker beetle is as likely to be close to the site of miraculous presentation as is a larger and more aggressive beetle, the weaker species will always have a shot at a food source, and the superior scarab will not be able to systematically outcompete it. "The randomness of the distribution of dung adds a crucial element of chance to survival," he says, "and that element incidentally favors the coexistence of many species."

He said that whereas dung is an extreme example of an unpredictable resource, other types of ecosystems are likely to be riddled with random fluxes that affect the balance of species and that have yet to be identified. In nature's casino, fortune as well as fitness determines survival. [NA, DECEMBER 1991]

A CORNUCOPIA OF LIFE, BARELY EXPLORED

DEEP in the ocean, where only the faintest glimmers of light penetrate the frigid waters, there lives a creature that for more than a century has eluded the most diligent scientific pursuers, even though it is believed to be as large as a city bus. One of the earliest records of the monster, a giant squid, dates to the 1870s, when a group of Newfoundland fishermen presented a tentacle, "the horn of a big squid," to the Reverend Dr. Moses Harvey, a biologist from St. John's, Newfoundland, who developed a keen interest in the giant. The "horn," actually the tip of a giant tentacle, had been hacked off the squid with an axe in a battle in which the fishermen were trying to pull it up and the creature seemed to be pulling them down. Since then, dead and dying squid have washed ashore, but despite all efforts, no one has ever succeeded in seeing the sixty-foot-long *Architeuthis* (pronounced ark-e-TOOTH-iss), which is Greek for chief squid, swimming in its natural habitat far below the ocean's surface. For marine biologists this elusive squid has become a symbol of how little is known about the creature-filled seas compared with knowledge of life on land.

As scientists chip away at the task of finding the sea's undiscovered creatures, many of which lurk hidden in the depths, they are finding at every turn a surprising abundance of new and previously unknown animals. Some scientists say this great pageant of marine life is so impressive that it puts the meager offerings of the land to shame. But as intriguing as recent finds have been, biologists who try to explore life on the ocean bottoms continue to be stalled by the difficulties of working there. With their study of ocean creatures restricted by short stays of manned and unmanned submersibles on just a few spots of the ocean floor or by the dredging of the ocean bottom with boxes and scoops, scientists find their limited view of deep sea life growing at an achingly slow pace. Marine scientists say if the land were studied as spottily as the sea, many of its most impressive creatures, like elephants, anacondas, and tigers, would be as elusive as the giant squid. "It's unlikely that a beast as long as a city bus would escape notice in any terrestrial habitat for long," said Dr. Sylvia Earle, adviser to the administrator of the National Oceanic and Atmospheric Administration, speaking at a 1992 conference at Cornell University at which researchers discussed marine biology and conservation. "Yet it's been possible for giant squids to elude even highly motivated scientists."

Unlike terrestrial habitats, the seas teem with a seemingly endless array of creatures, some so bizarre that years after their discovery they defy classification even into phyla, the principal groups for related types of life forms. And the deeper the ocean is, marine scientists say, the stranger and more diverse its fauna become. Indeed, perhaps the greatest number of unknown sea creatures waiting to be discovered are lurking in the sea's deepest abyssal plains, a region once thought to be entirely devoid of life. Dr. J. Frederick Grassle, director of the Institute of Marine and Coastal Sciences at Rutgers University, listed the phyla that he and colleagues recently pulled from the depths off New Jersey and Delaware. Some are familiar, like the Cnidaria, a group that includes jellyfish, anemones, and corals, and the Mollusca, the family of snails and clams. But besides these are a multitude of unusual animals like lamp shells, peanut worms, moss animals, ribbon worms, beard worms, and many others that lack common names. Dr. Grassle and a colleague, Dr. Nancy Maciolek, of the ocean sciences unit of Battelle Memorial Institute in Duxbury, Massachusetts, published the study in February 1992 in *The American Naturalist*. "You name any kind of odd group that you've ever heard of or seen," Dr. Grassle says, "and they're there in the deep sea."

Dr. Frank Talbot, a marine ecologist and director of the National Museum of Natural History at the Smithsonian Institution, has sampled the life at the deep sea bottom. "I found that one drag would bring up glass fibers, which come from the glass rope sponge. You'd have great bundles of this stuff and a whole set of one kind of animals. And the next time you'd go down and you'd come up with the ooze from the bodies of many small skeletons looking like concrete with stones rafted from Antarctica, a big concretelike mix. If you take one grab after the next, each grab has very little overlap with the one before."

Dr. Grassle said that in their recent study covering an area of the deep sea no bigger than two tennis courts, he and colleagues found an abundance of 90,677 individuals representing more than fourteen different phyla, a feat impossible to match in any terrestrial habitat. Although counts vary slightly from scientist to scientist, there are estimated to be no more than eleven phyla in all terrestrial habitats combined, only one of which, the onychopora, an obscure group of tropical wormlike creatures, is restricted to land. The sea, on the other hand, is home to twenty-eight phyla, thirteen of which are found nowhere else, neither on land nor in fresh water. Even the tally of eleven terrestrial phyla tends to overstate the land's diversity. Most species belong to just a few of its eleven phyla. The myriad species of insects and spiders all belong to the single giant phylum of the arthropods. All mammals, fish, birds, amphibians, and reptiles belong to another single phylum, known to zoologists as the chordates. "We have been enormously overemphasizing biodiversity on land," says Dr. Elliott A. Norse, chief scientist at the Center for Marine Conservation, "in contrast to the biodiversity where it is, in the sea."

The sea has not only more phyla than the land but also, scientists are finding, more species within these phyla. In the same deep sea study from which Dr. Grassle and colleagues documented an abundance of marine phyla, researchers found many new species as well. The study yielded 798 species, 460 of which had never before been seen. "What we're finding is, our real conclusion is, that we can't estimate the total number of species in the deep sea," Dr. Grassle says. "There are just enormous numbers." In shallower waters, like those over a continental shelf, each new sample of an area brings up fewer new species, he notes. "That tells you you've found most of what's there. In the deep sea you don't get that feeling at all. Every sample seems to bring up something different."

The sea has greater diversity of habitats, too, says Dr. Norse. "The land has a film of life that mostly extends from 100 feet above the ground level and then a few into the ground," he says. "The sea is occupied by living things from its surface all the way down to the bottom of the sea, sometimes as much as 36,000 feet." The heterogeneity of sea environments, some scientists say, contributes to the great diversity of life in the seas. Scientists once believed that the ocean floor was rather uniform. Because in the deep sea there is no light to enable plants to grow and to serve as food, the detritus that rains down from above is the only source of nutrients. "Because there isn't a lot of food getting to the bottom, everywhere there is a patch of food, it makes it very different from the surrounding area," Dr. Grassle says. "It's that kind of heterogeneity that allows species to diversify."

But biologists say that the most important reason that the ocean's life forms are so richly diverse may be that it is the birthplace of life. Humans tend to think of the seas as remote and foreign environments, but from the grand perspective of evolutionary history it is actually life on land that is the curious exception. "There are only a small number of organisms that have evolved the basic tricks of living outside the ocean," Dr. Norse says. "Life on land is really a remarkable series of variations on a few themes."

The greater range of life's variations, even in the dark and near-freezing waters of the deep sea, provides sights so strange that they seem to be of another world. Scientists who sink down to the sea floor in submersibles, or who view the deep sea through the eyes of remotely deployed cameras, may be assailed by the strangest of sights, like the graceful dancelike movements of the cirrate or hooded octopus, its pink arms swaying in the deep sea currents, or great herds of sea cucumbers, grazing the nutrient-rich sediments as they march in the slow motion so characteristic of this eerie world.

Scientists exploring these deep sea pastures have rediscovered creatures that were known only from fossils and thought to have become extinct millions of years ago. Some of these living fossils, like the sea lilies, have been placidly passing the aeons in the watery darkness since long before the dinosaurs ruled. The sea lilies were quickly recognized as kin to their closest living relatives, which in fact are not lilies but starfish. But other living fossils like Paleodictyon, first seen in photographs from the mid-Atlantic ridge, seemed so strange to the eyes of researchers that they were assumed to be the result of a photographic problem and not living creatures at all. A Chinese checkerboard of dots, this creature baffled expert biologists and was instead identified by paleontologists. It now shares the name given to similarly patterned life forms seen in sedimentary muds that hardened into rock hundreds of millions of years ago.

Scientists estimate that less than one tenth of 1 percent of the deep sea has been surveyed. Given these estimates, it is perhaps not surprising that a giant squid could defy pursuit for so long. Scientists concede that other creatures, perhaps even larger and stranger than the monstrous Architeuthis, may continue to defy discovery in their vast watery refuges. It is no wonder, then, that many of the sea's rarer creatures are less likely to be seen in the flesh than in the form of fossils that perished in seas that disappeared millions of years ago. One reason for that is the extreme difficulty biologists face in exploring the deep oceans, and scientists say much work is still conducted in nineteenth-century style, dredging up the bottom. "It's analogous to flying over the surface of the land at night with a couple of strong lights and throwing down a sampling device off the airplane and seeing what you get," Dr. Norse says. "It's very hard to put together a picture when that's the way you have to sample."

The deep sea, as remote as it is, has not remained impervious to the human presence. Curious and intrepid scientists who have risked their lives to explore the deepest ocean canyons have sometimes completed their journey only to find at the bottom of the abyss a carpet of cigarette tins, burnt coal, beer cans, license plates, and other urban refuse. "There's no doubt that we've managed to clutter up some portions of the deep sea floor, particularly along shipping lanes," Dr. Talbot says. But, he added, "most of the ocean floor is really pristine."

If so, there is still a chance of protecting the deep oceans before they suffer the same degradation inflicted on tropical forests. Scientists warn that life in the cold, dark regions of the oceans progresses so slowly that any wound will take far longer to heal than in more productive areas like the tropics.   [CKY, JUNE 1992]

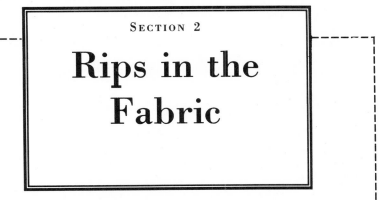

Rips in the Fabric

THREATS TO SPECIES

THE BOOK of nature has many pages, more than have yet been counted. But the pages are being destroyed faster than anyone can read them. Throughout the world, thousands of species of animals and plants slide toward the precipice of extinction as settlers clear new ground, developers drain wetlands, and loggers fell forests.

Most of these lost and disappearing species are unknown. They perish before biologists can tag them with Latin names and enter them in their catalogs. A lot are drab plants or small beetles, perhaps of no use to anyone.

But that has yet to proved. Among them are surely treasures like the single species of periwinkle that provides two anticancer drugs, vincristine and vinblastine.

The plight of well-known animals therefore must stand as surrogate for the millions of anonymous species being driven into precarious existence. The articles in this section describe the reasons for the predicament of several major species. The magnificent bluefin tuna fetches too much as sushi to be let alone. The rhinoceros is losing ground in most parts of the world to poachers who prize its horn. Parrots are victims of the cruel trade in tropical birds; the lemurs of Madagascar are driven from their forests or shot on sight, not for money but for superstitious beliefs.

Many people would argue that species have a right to existence regardless of their economic worth. The gaudy, poisonous monarch butterfly is of no use to anyone, yet the world would be the poorer without it. That loss may come soon. All the monarchs that roam the United States east of the Rockies are dependent on a handful of oyamel fir groves in Mexico where they spend the winter. Should loggers continue to erode these habitats, the annual monarch migration, an ancient natural wonder, will finally cease.

The world has many books, diligently preserved in libraries for future scholars and historians even if they seem of little use to contemporary readers. Many people would agree that not a title should be lost from the archives, since each is part of our written heritage. Should we not be equally pained to lose any part of our natural heritage?

A BUTTERFLY'S FRAGILE JOURNEY

EVERY December in the fir-covered mountains of southern Mexico, hundreds of millions of monarch butterflies packed in tight, brilliant clusters settle in for their winter rest after completing one of nature's most extraordinary feats. Each year, the insects migrate as far as 2,500 miles between their summer breeding grounds in the northern United States and Canada and their winter retreats in Mexico.

This splendid natural phenomenon can no longer be taken for granted. The butterfly's special wintering sites in thirteen Mexican mountain enclaves—and in certain "monarch groves" in coastal California where a smaller, separate cohort spends the winter—are threatened by logging and development. Vigorous conservation efforts in Mexico may have helped secure the monarch's refuges there. And voters in Pacific Grove, California, approved the $2 million purchase of a privately owned monarch grove to save it from development. But the battle is far from won, scientists and conservationists say. "With a small amount of human negligence, everything could disappear," said Carlos Gottfried, the chairman of the board of Monarca, a nonprofit organization based in Mexico City that has been spearheading a vigorous effort to preserve the Mexican wintering grounds. And Dr. Lincoln P. Brower of the University of Florida, an expert on the monarch, fears that despite the Mexican conservation campaign, "we could lose the whole migration to Mexico in the next decade or so."

What makes the monarchs' migration so special is that the butterflies successfully navigate their path to wintering grounds they have never seen: the butterflies that leave the Mexican winter retreats to head back northward in the spring are the great-grandparents of those that return in the fall. Catching rides from Canada to Mexico on winds and spiraling columns of warm air, these expert little gliders in orange-and-black finery set their course unerringly toward faraway destinations. Birds routinely migrate such long distances, but no other insects are known to do so. The returning monarchs, each born in the north, rely solely on navigational instructions programmed genetically into one of the tiniest of nervous systems.

"If you've ever looked inside the brain of a butterfly, it's about the size of a pinhead," says Dr. Brower, "and yet the minicomputer inside that pinhead has all the necessary information to get them to Mexico without having been there before." How this guidance system works is a mystery, and the prospect of someday understanding such a "complex neuronal control system" is reason enough in itself to preserve the monarch migrations, Dr. Brower says.

Scientists do know that the annual flight of the monarchs is part of an ecological relationship among the butterflies, their habitat, and the climate that is as fragile as the tissue-winged insects themselves. Conservationists wish to preserve the whole ecological framework because it is what makes possible the natural wonder of the migration. The monarch would disappear from almost all of North America if the migration ceased, although nonmigrating populations would continue to exist in southern Florida and parts of the tropics.

Fortunately for the conservation effort, the monarch migration is beginning to acquire a mystique akin to that of the great whales and the African elephant. Growing numbers of tourists flock to marvel at the quivering masses of monarchs that festoon the trees in the wintering areas. Residents of those areas invest the monarchs with a pride that sometimes borders on reverence. In Pacific Grove, they are the biggest thing in town. Motels are named for them. Children dressed in monarch costumes parade through the town each fall when the butterflies appear.

In Mexico, the insects' arrival at the beginning of November coincides with a religious observance in which the butterflies, according to a mythology going back to pre-Columbian days, are seen as the returning souls of the dead. And in the United States, the monarch is a front-runner, along with the honeybee, in a continuing campaign to name a national insect.

The monarch's glamour, in the view of some conservationists, makes it an ideal test of the willingness of North Americans to care for an ecological treasure. "If the people can and will save their monarchs, perhaps they will be ready to think about other beneficial insects; only then will we see a true popular campaign for biological diversity," Robert Michael Pyle wrote in 1989 in the journal of the Xerces Society, an international organization dedicated to the preservation of invertebrate habitats. The society has been active in the campaign to preserve monarch habitats in California.

While the conservation effort goes on, a small band of scientists continues to tease out the details of the migration itself. Its origins of migration lie in the monarch's dependence on the milkweed plant and in the inability of the insect, as a tropical creature, to withstand cold weather. In ancient times, scientists believe, the milkweed plant moved up from its home in the tropics to colonize North America, and the monarchs followed their food plant northward.

Milkweed contains bitter poisons, called cardiac glycosides, that originally evolved as a defense mechanism to protect the plants from insect predators. The monarchs not only adapted to defeat the poison but converted it to a chemical weapon for their own defense. The monarch's caterpillars feed on the plants, storing the toxic chemicals in their bodies as they grow. The adult butterflies retain the poisons, which make predators throw up. A bird that has tasted one monarch never tries another. Scientists believe that the distinctive orange-and-black markings of the insect serve as a warning signal that birds observe. Another North American butterfly, the viceroy, has evolved markings similar to the monarch's, and this mimicry helps protect it even though it lacks the monarch's chemical defenses.

Two species of birds have adapted to the poison and feast on the butterflies. So has a mouse that gorges on the somnolent bodies of monarchs passing the winter in Mexico. So far these predators have not significantly reduced the monarch's numbers.

The United States enjoys two different populations of monarchs, one to the east of the Rockies and one to the west. The western monarchs spend the winter in the groves of California. Monarchs east of the Rockies are the offspring of butterflies that overwintered in Mexico. The winter refuge, discovered in 1974, consists of thirteen compact wintering sites scattered in a small seventy-five-by-thirty-five-mile area in the mountains seventy-five miles west of Mexico City.

The sites are ideal, said Dr. Brower, because they maintain a climate that is just right for the monarchs at a time when their highest priority, aside from survival, is to conserve energy for the return migration in the spring. The wintering area is just south of the Tropic of Cancer and its temperature is relatively stable. The butterflies roost in mountainside fir trees within a narrow altitude band ranging from

9,500 to 11,000 feet, their gaudy bodies sometimes festooning a tree so thickly that neither branch nor needle can be seen.

At that altitude, the air is warm enough to keep the butterflies from freezing but cool enough so that they do not burn up calories unnecessarily. They fly around when warmed, wasting energy. The high mountains also capture moisture that bathes the butterflies and prevents water loss. A similarly suitable microclimate exists on the California coast, where the wintering sites of the western monarchs are situated.

At the end of their autumn flight from colder climes, the monarchs arrive in Mexico robust, virginal, and celibate, their brilliance as fresh as if they had just emerged from the chrysalis. They are superbutterflies with a nine-month life span, living longer than any others. In the spring, they awaken from their winter dormancy as feverish, single-minded lovers, rushing pell-mell to where the first milkweeds are coming up along the United States Gulf Coast.

"We don't know too much about their flight north, but we do know one thing—they're in more of a hurry" than on the fall return flight, said Dr. David Gibo, a biologist at the University of Toronto who has studied the monarchs' flight habits. "It's a race to the milkweed."

Because of their haste, he said, the butterflies appear to use up much of their energy in powered flight, so heavily that although millions leave Mexico, relatively few reach the United States. Those that do arrive come in low, almost on the deck, males searching for females and both sexes searching for milkweeds. "A male hangs around these milkweed patches, and if a female comes through, he'll just go after her like a pursuit ship," says Dr. Brower. "If there are lots of males around, they'll harass the female, who has lots of ways of evading them. She might fly through the branches of a tree, and the male gets lost. Then she goes and lays her eggs." This furious expenditure of energy drains the parent butterflies of life. Their offspring fly off northward, following the milkweed as it appears, and by summer have dispersed across the northern half of the United States east of the Rockies, ranging as far north as North Dakota, southern Ontario, and Maine.

The western migration is smaller and less dramatic. In the spring, the butterflies leave their refuges on the California coast. Their first new generation is born on the slopes of the Sierras, and subsequent movement takes the monarchs into Idaho, Nevada, Utah, and as far south as Phoenix. Dr. Brower and colleagues in Florida in November 1990 confirmed that the first generation born in the East appears in the Gulf states rather than farther north. They did so by analyzing the kinds of poisons contained in butterflies' bodies. Some species of milkweed grow only in certain parts of the country, and the poisons vary in a way that provides a "fingerprint" by which it is possible to identify which species of milkweed nourished the butterfly—and, therefore, in what part of the country the butterfly was born.

East of the Rockies, three or four more generations of butterflies are born after the group born on the Gulf Coast flies to its northern range. Each of these generations lives for about three weeks, except the one tapped by nature to complete the cycle by heading south once again. In August, the reproductive organs of this generation become dormant. Its members lose interest in sex, but they become very gregarious and irresistibly attracted to flowers and each other. They cloak goldenrods, daisies, and other composite flowers in what Dr. Brower calls "social drinking groups," sucking up nectar to nourish them on their journey. In contrast to the urgent flight of their great-grandparents from Mexico in the spring, Dr. Gibo says, these southward-flying monarchs take it relatively easy. He has studied their flight tactics, tracking them from his glider and with ground radar. He has found that the butterflies expertly exploit ascending spirals of warm air, called thermals, then glide downwind until hitching onto another thermal. Glider pilots, Dr. Gibo says, have seen monarchs circling as high as three quarters of a mile. If a crosswind interferes with their course, the monarchs can somehow correct for it, to keep on course southwestward to Mexico. Faced with a headwind, the monarchs simply drop to earth and look for nectar. When they arrive in southern Texas and northern Mexico, they go on a feeding binge designed to see them through the winter. "By the time they get to the overwintering site," Dr. Brower says, "they're literally butterballs."

Conservationists concerned about threats to the butterflies' overwintering places are encouraged by a 1990 vote in Pacific Grove, California, to protect the town's monarch site. "I'm really proud of them," Dr. Brower said. "They had to get 67 percent of the vote and they got 69 percent." Still, the butterflies remain in a precarious position in both California and Mexico, said Curtis Freese, vice president for regional programs of the World Wildlife Fund, which is aiding the Mexican conservation project. With just a few small wintering sites serving the entire population, he said, "one can never feel entirely easy, can never rest." Dr. Brower expressed doubt that the Mexican preservation efforts would be wholly successful. In 1986, the Mexican government banned logging in the overwintering areas. But since then, Dr. Brower said, he has seen loggers cutting trees "right in the butterfly colonies." He said loggers had also cut empty trees used by monarchs in previous years and to which they might have returned in the future.

Mexico has turned one of its thirteen wintering sites into a tourist attraction, and plans to convert a second, in hopes that local people will make money off the tourist trade and perceive protection of the roosting trees to be in their own interest. Some 70,000 tourists visited the first site in 1989, said Mr. Gottfried of Monarca, the Mexican conservation organization, and the number is steadily growing. Mr. Gottfried, who has been fighting the battle to preserve the monarch migration for thirteen years, said he believed that the Mexican government and public were giving the monarch issue serious attention. Mr. Gottfried said that during a recent field trip to the thirteen sites, "I was very pleased with what I saw. There's been no cutting this year in the core area," he said. "This is the first year I can say that with total conviction."

Dr. Brower responded: "I hope they've stopped the cutting, but I strongly doubt they have. Sometimes the loggers don't get going till the height of the dry season in February. The Mexicans seem to respect the butterflies." But until it is clear that cutting has stopped, he said, there is danger of "a catastrophe that's going to spell the end of monarch butterflies in eastern North America."

[WKS, DECEMBER 1990]

WHERE HAVE ALL THE MONARCHS GONE?

EVERY fall millions of reddish-brown and black monarch butterflies move southward across the United States to the lush fir forests in Mexico, where they spend the winter. But in 1992 some of the normally crowded migration routes are nearly empty. Although the monarchs were relatively plentiful from the Appalachians west to the Continental Divide, biologists say that the number in the East fell 90 percent from the record high in 1991.

As researchers begin to seek the reasons for the decline, conservationists warn that the lack of monarchs in the summer of 1992 in some areas may be a sign of things to come for the species, whose habitat is threatened in both the United States and Mexico. "It's the canary taking its first gasp as the methane comes in telling us we are approaching a major explosion," says Dr. Lincoln P. Brower, a leading monarch authority from the University of Florida.

Dick Walton, a founder of the Monarch Migration Association of North America, watches each year for monarchs as they migrate south past the Cape May Bird Observatory in New Jersey. "Last year around this time, in fifteen minutes I saw over 700 butterflies moving past a point on the dune at the beach," he said in 1992. "Last night I found no monarchs in the roost. This morning our volunteers on the beach said they saw one."

Ann Swengel and Dr. Paul Opler coordinate a nationwide butterfly survey for the Xerces Society, an insect conservation group. Ms. Swengel is in contact with many volunteers who count butterflies each year around the Fourth of July. "In the Northeast, people have seen almost no monarchs," she said. Although researchers can use the survey to document a 90 percent decrease in counts from last year in the East, it is difficult to say what that means in terms of absolute numbers, since the one-day survey only measures relative abundances.

Dr. Dave Wagner, a biologist involved in the Xerces count in Connecticut, said: "We checked 200 to 300 plants and found no caterpillars, and that's phenomenal. I've been plagued by kindergarten and elementary schoolteachers calling to ask why they can't find any for their classes to raise."

Researchers say the decline could be a result of the devastating winter of 1991 at the butterflies' roosting sites in the mountains of Mexico. During that winter, Dr. Brower and his colleagues estimated that as many as 80 percent of the monarchs died there. He attributed much of the mortality to wood harvesting in and around the areas where the butterflies roost. Not only the roosting trees themselves are being cut, but also the surrounding firs are being taken, exposing the butterflies to excessive wind and cold.

Ms. Swengel said that the remainder of the monarch butterflies that migrate into Mexico, those breeding west of the Appalachians to the Continental Divide, seemed to fare much better during the summer of 1992. In fact, Midwestern populations did remarkably well considering that these monarchs are also thought to spend the winter in the Mexican sites where so many butterflies previously died. The puzzle has prompted some biologists to suggest that perhaps the Midwest was repopulated by monarchs that spent the winter in undiscovered roosts somehow hidden from human destruction.

Dr. Chip Taylor, a biologist at the University of Kansas, got his first glimpse of the 1992 monarch situation in the spring in Linares, Mexico, as he waited along a flyway the monarchs use to enter the United States. In 1991, he saw hundreds of thousands of monarchs migrating through in the first week of April, but in 1992, he said, he saw only three monarchs in three weeks. "I picked up on information later that they'd made it back quite nicely to Wisconsin, Minnesota, and Michigan," Dr. Taylor said. "And I thought, Hey, they got around me somehow. Then I heard that quite a lot of monarchs had been seen migrating north farther west, west of San Antonio."

Although many questions remain about monarch movements, Dr. Taylor believes there may be two separate flyways into Mexico. In addition to the known track east of the Sierra Madre, where he waited in vain, he said that mounting anecdotal evidence from the summer pointed toward another, more westerly track that could have fed the Midwest from undiscovered, protected sites.

Dr. Brower said he also believed that there might be undiscovered sites. But he noted that monarchs prefer to spend the winter in very wet, lush fir forests. Because in Mexico these forests are found only in a restricted habitat known as the summer fog belt, he said, the possibilities for such new sites were quite limited. And he noted that other hypotheses might equally well explain the differences in the monarchs' success across the country. For instance, Dr. Brower suggested that in 1992 the butterflies might simply have shrunk their range back to their ancestral limits. Whereas milkweed plants, the caterpillar's food plant, can now be found by roadsides and in fields across the country, the plant was once largely confined to the Plains. "What we may be seeing, in fact, is that the monarchs have been really hit so hard that they just didn't make it into New England," Dr. Brower said.

Whatever the explanation, conservationists emphasize that unless this most spectacular of insect migrations is protected, the world may never find out. "Here's the best-known butterfly in the world," Dr.

Brower said, "and we still know so little about it, and that's good reason to save it in Mexico. It's like going into a library and picking up a fantastic novel and having the back of the book torn out if they succeed in killing it off." [CKY, OCTOBER 1992]

THE AYE-AYE, A BIZARRE AND ENDANGERED PRIMATE

THE aye-aye is a creature that can be described only by comparing it piecemeal with other things. It is the size of a cat, has the ears of a bat, the snout of a rat, a tail like a witch's broom, and a long, knobby middle finger that would look just fine on that same witch's hand. Its teeth are as tough as a beaver's and its eyes bulge out from its skull like a tree frog's. And when a baby aye-aye cries, it sounds like a squeezed rubber duck—particularly when it is being held with exceptional clumsiness by a visitor attempting neither to hurt the little beast nor to be hurt herself. This is, after all, the first aye-aye to be born in captivity outside Madagascar, its native home, and its birth signals a possible turnaround in the fate of the animal considered the world's most endangered primate. Thus, it is an honor to be allowed to pick up the three-week-old baby and feel its coarse fur, its writhing, protesting muscles, its tiny heart thumping in fear and fury.

At the same time, the researchers at the Duke University Primate Center in Durham, North Carolina, where the aye-aye was born early in April 1992, have spoken graphically of the baby's efforts to bite its handlers, and of how an aye-aye's teeth can pop the top off a coconut in moments. As the twelve-ounce creature eeps shrilly and squirms its head this way and that, one wonders if the little darling would be injured too badly were it to be dropped on the floor. "Well, I'd say Blue Devil is ready to return to his mother," says Dr. Elwyn L. Simons, a primatologist who runs the center at Duke and who named the baby after the university's championship basketball team. "I think he's had enough excitement for one day." Yes, please.

Dr. Simons is a rotund man who speaks slowly, pads about as quietly as a panther, and can imitate with delightful precision the gestures of the endangered primates he cares for. "Watch this, this is how an aye-aye drinks," he said, and then jerked his middle finger rapidly back and forth, back and forth, from an imaginary source of liquid and up to his mouth, slurping ever so slightly for effect. Later, when he bit into a banana, he grinned slyly, fully aware of the portrait he presented as he ate. More often, however, Dr. Simons appears quite serious, and with reason. He and his colleagues at the primate center, as well as other scientists at zoos and universities, are struggling to save the aye-aye and other lemurs from extinction. The thirty species of lemurs alive today are limited almost exclusively to Madagascar, an island off the coast of East Africa that is one and a half times the size of California. And because the forests of Madagascar are dwindling to the vanishing point, as an impoverished and rapidly swelling human population slashes and burns the forests simply to survive, all thirty species are considered endangered.

Dr. Simons and his colleagues are trying to breed the lemurs in captivity, with the hope of eventually reintroducing at least some of the species back into national reserves on Madagascar. They are also striving to learn everything possible about lemur desires, habits, and appetites, and any other insights that can be used to better the animals' chances for survival in the wild. As a group, lemurs have been much less intensively studied than, for example, chimpanzees and orangutans. A Yale University doctoral student recently completed the first long-term study of aye-ayes on Madagascar, and even after eighteen months of extremely difficult research she has only just begun to understand their social structure, courtship rituals, and other basic questions.

Although lemurs are prosimians, or pre-monkeys, and in brain size and other features are more primitive than the so-called higher primates, they are extraordinarily vivid, some with faces like quizzical little monks, others with the shocking blue eyes of Paul Newman. The tiniest species, the mouse lemur, is six inches long and is the world's smallest primate, whereas the biggest lemur, the indri, is almost three feet long. The primate center has been extremely successful at rearing lemurs, and it now has more than 400 representatives of fifteen species scampering about in large cages or through sixty-five acres of open-air enclosures in the North Carolina woods. Researchers from the United States and Europe come to the center to study lemur behavior as the primates squabble, forage, mate, raise their young, groom each other with their comblike teeth, and otherwise carry on in conditions that approximate wilderness, although the outdoor enclosures are fenced with wires that will deliver a very mild shock should a lemur develop undue wanderlust.

Some primatologists are particularly interested in the lemur as a kind of living fossil, a creature that survived through the lucky accident of its geographic isolation on Madagascar. Elsewhere lemurs became extinct, displaced by the bigger and craftier monkeys and apes; but some prosimians migrated from the African mainland to Madagascar about 50 million years ago, perhaps by floating on vegetation, and thereafter they flourished without the pressure from higher primates or indeed from any significant predators. "They evolved like Darwin's finches," the birds that live on the Galápagos Islands, said Andrea Katz, a research scientist at the primate center. "Each one fills a different niche." Researchers believe the prosimians hold clues to the evolution of social behavior among ancestral primates.

Others are intrigued by the lemurs' reversal of standard sex roles. Among the so-called higher primates, males are often larger than females and thus frequently bully them. By contrast, male and female lemurs are similarly sized, and the female dominates the male, eliciting from him displays of submissive behavior and shooing him away whenever she grows annoyed.

At the Duke facility, Dr. Simons and his co-workers have managed to breed several species of lemur that others had found impossible to rear in captivity, including the golden-crowned sifaka, a slender blond acrobat that leaps from one branch to another in strange sideways arcs. The researchers succeeded by coddling the reluctant primates twenty-four hours a day and supplementing their diet with exotic treats like mango leaves from Florida. "You have to take as much care of them as you would your own children," he said.

Perhaps no challenge will be as great as the one he has undertaken to help the aye-aye. The aye-aye is suffering not only from an ongoing loss of habitat, as are all the lemurs, but also from another problem that makes it especially vulnerable. The people of Madagascar, the Malagasy, either ignore or respect most of their lemurs, calling them "the little men of the forest." The aye-aye is an exception: it is considered an evil omen, a harbinger of death. By one legend, should an aye-aye point its elongated middle finger at you, you are destined to die, swiftly and horribly. To rid themselves of the curse, many Malagasy will kill any aye-aye they see and then place its corpse on a stake at a crossroads, with the hope that a stranger will pass by and absorb the aye-aye's malevolence.

The taboos surrounding the aye-ayes are so pervasive that some think the primate, whose scientific name is *Daubentonia madagascariensis*, gained its common name as a spinoff of the Malagasy expression for "I don't know," suggesting that even to mention the creature is forbidden. While traveling through the countryside in search of aye-ayes, Dr. Simons often heard accounts that the villagers had killed five or more animals just before his arrival. "In the villages they're treated with the same alarm or disgust that people here express when they encounter rattlesnakes," said Dr. Simons. "They ask why on earth would you want to capture those things and take them to another country?"

He said he suspected that one reason the animal is hated is its bizarre appearance. The aye-aye doesn't look like any other primate on the planet, and in fact it was first classified by French researchers in the eighteenth century as a squirrel. Its long fur is a dusky, forbidding shade of black, and in the dark its yellow eyes gleam demonically. The animal also has the dangerous habit of being curious about humans, making it an easy target for those who want to kill it. Dr. Simons said one reason the aye-aye has not been exterminated is that it is nocturnal. Most Malagasy villages lack electricity, so the people generally retire to their homes after sunset, shortly before the aye-ayes begin foraging.

But the animal has its appeal. Its brain is larger and more deeply convoluted than that of any other prosimian, suggesting a somewhat greater intelligence. Its hearing is so keen that it can tap on a tree trunk and detect the hollow regions within, indicating the presence of the beetle grubs it covets. The animal will then rip through the trunk with four chisel-shaped front teeth that, unlike those of other primates, will grow throughout life. And, of course, there is the aye-aye's extraordinary middle finger, a long, thin digit that can bend in every direction, even backward to touch its forearm. The finger is an all-purpose tool for delicately tapping the tree trunks, poking holes in eggs, pumping the liquid out of those eggs, and extracting milk from coconuts.

Given that aye-ayes are night creatures and that Madagascar's long, sodden rainy season discourages most researchers, the animal has scarcely been studied. But Eleanor J. Sterling, who is doing her dissertation on the aye-aye, recently spent eighteen months following the creatures on an uninhabited island off the northeast coast of Madagascar, tagging the primates with radio collars and tracking them from dusk to dawn, her effort illuminated by a headlamp. She learned that the animals, long thought to be solitary, in fact spend a considerable amount of time socializing. They build huge sleeping nests in the forks of trees, and they willingly trade nests from one night to the next, with the animals seeming fairly communistic about their property. Their diet proved richer in fruits and vegetables than anybody had suspected, and they seemed able to breed several times throughout the year, rather than only during a single season, as other lemurs do. She also discovered that aye-ayes adopt a kind of *Kama Sutra* approach to lovemaking. When a female decides she is ready to act, she will hang upside down from a branch, and a male will position himself by entwining his legs around her ankles, himself facing downward, and then grasp her about the chest, with the weight of both supported by the female. The pair will then copulate for an hour or two, much longer than the usual primate session. "In the meantime, a bunch of other males will be climbing up the tree, trying to get him off her and mate with her as well," said Ms. Sterling. "The whole thing is a three-ring circus." The female may eventually mate with more than one partner before her estrus is through. She did not determine how long the gestation period is, although it is likely to be at the upper end of lemur pregnancies, around 140 days. Dr. Simons said he believed that the newborn Blue Devil was conceived during just such gymnastics in the forests of Madagascar in November 1991, only days before the infant's mother, Endora, was captured by the Simons team and taken back to Duke along with three other aye-ayes. There they joined three already at the center.

Dr. Simons has found that, contrary to long-standing claims that the creature is limited to patches of forest along the coast of Madagascar and thus is too rare to risk taking from the wild, the aye-aye also lives in woods farther inland. The primate center is optimistic that another of its females may have recently conceived. Eventually, if the aye-ayes reproduce well in captivity, the primate center may distribute several to zoos around the country. The only zoo in the Western Hemisphere with aye-ayes is in Paris.

It will be more difficult to devise a long-term strategy for the primates on Madagascar. Since the first Indonesian settlers arrived on the island 1,500 years ago, about 85 percent of its spectacular tropical forest has been slashed and burned by humans for wood, farm, and grazing land. The island's thin soil is badly eroded and its nutrients depleted, further threatening the forests that remain; and the human population continues to grow at 2.1 percent a year, one of the fastest rates in the world. Yet scientists say there is an enormous will now to rescue Madagascar, which is plush with thousands of species found nowhere else, including 142 species of frogs, 106 types of birds, 6,000 species of flowering plants, and half the world's chameleons. Recognizing the potential of its wildlife as a source of income through, for example, "ecotourism," the government has opened its doors to researchers, conservation groups, and other international efforts. But whether the wealth of species can be preserved while so many Malagasy remain impoverished, and whether the people can ever learn to view the aye-aye as lovable rather than malicious, remain frighteningly open questions.   [NA, MAY 1992]

FOR PARROTS, INTELLIGENCE HAS ITS DANGERS

IN ancient India, where they appeared in the earliest literature, they were cherished as symbols of love: the *Kama Sutra* stipulated parrot training as one of sixty-four practices men had to master. The Romans taught parrots to speak, festooned them with ivory, kept them in golden cages, and sometimes valued them more highly than slaves. No other bird seems more human, more intelligent, or more affectionate. Take a baby parrot out of the nest and it will not only learn human speech but also, given a chance, become so attached to its keeper as to become a second shadow. Parrots can also be willful and demanding, jealous and contrary. They may screech and yell at anyone who walks into the room, and they can imitate any sound—a dripping faucet or a ringing telephone or the barking of a dog. Yet for all the rich lore on parrots, biologists are only now beginning to penetrate their unexplored world, both in the laboratory and in the wild. They are finding that parrots are even more intelligent than believed, with mental abilities that may equal those of chimpanzees and dolphins.

Researchers are learning that they can deal with abstract concepts, communicate with people, understand questions, and make reasoned replies rather than merely, well, parroting human speech.

But even as some of the parrot's wonders and secrets are yielding to new scrutiny, nearly a quarter of the world's 300 parrot species—and nearly a third of Western Hemisphere species—are at risk of extinction. For some species, including the splendid macaws, the reproductive rate is so low that they are poorly equipped to face what may be the most serious threat ever to their existence. This is partly because humans are destroying the tropical forests where parrots live. The birds mostly dwell in holes they find in trees, and the destruction of the forest increases the already high odds against reproductive success for some species.

Parrots are also victims of the very fascination they hold for humans. In greater demand than ever as pets, they are being trapped by the millions. Many of the birds die in transit. The United States alone imports at least 250,000 parrots a year, according to Traffic U.S.A., the trade-monitoring arm of the World Wildlife Fund in this country, which says that the vast majority of imported parrots come from the wild. The big macaws of South America and the impressive crested cockatoos are particularly prized as status symbols. And the rarer a species gets, the more valuable it becomes and the more avidly it is sought. A number of American conservation groups and representatives of the captive breeding industry, led by the World Wildlife Fund, have proposed national legislation to phase out the importation of exotic wild birds over five years. "Of paramount concern to us are parrots," said Ginette Hemley, the director of Traffic U.S.A. Under the proposed bill, the demand for pets would be filled by birds bred domestically for the purpose. Another group, led by the Defenders of Wildlife, has proposed an immediate ban on imports. Bills embodying each approach are expected to be introduced in Congress. [The bill was passed in 1992.]

There are cockatoos and cockatiels, parrotlets and parakeets, lorys and lorikeets, amazons and macaws. There are caiques and conures, keas and kakapos, lovebirds, budgerigars, and just plain parrots. Whatever the variety, it is especially tempting, despite the danger of being misled, to assign human characteristics to parrots. To begin with, a parrot's foot has opposable toes, two each in front and back, and is the closest birds come to having a hand. With this foot, a parrot can hang on to a branch and eat a seed or nut the way humans eat a sandwich. Many species live about as long as humans. A middle-aged person buying a large parrot as a pet is unlikely to outlive it. Most parrots mate for life, although divorce is common in some parrot societies. Mates go everywhere together and—unlike most other birds, which avoid physical contact except in coition—parrots spend much of their time snuggling up and preening each other. They also like to have their heads tickled. These are among many pieces of lore contained in a recent book that is part of a general surge of interest in parrots. The book, widely praised by experts as an accurate survey, is *Parrots: A Natural History* by Dr. John Sparks, a zoologist who heads the natural history unit of the BBC, and Tony Soper, a writer and filmmaker with the unit.

Parrot parents invest a lot of time in raising their offspring. Like monkeys and apes, young parrots undergo training in family groups, where the wisdom of the elders is transmitted. In some species, fledglings join nursery groups. Like primates, parrots play, some scientists believe. Why else, Dr. Sparks and Mr. Soper ask, does a New Zealand variety of parrot called the kea slide down the roofs of alpine huts on its back?

And there is, of course, parrot speech. In captivity, their mimicry flowers naturally. "No formal lessons are required," write Dr. Sparks and Mr. Soper. They recall that Sparkie, a British budgerigar, got himself into the *Guinness Book of World Records* in the 1950s with a virtuoso performance in which he recited eight four-line nursery rhymes without drawing a breath.

Many scientists have shied away from studying parrots. They are hard to study in the wild because tropical foliage screens their activities, and they can be stubborn and cantankerous laboratory subjects. But now, not least because of the endangered status of so many parrots, renewed interest is stimulating research efforts. In a project that has attracted wide attention, Dr. Irene Pepperberg, an ethologist at the University of Arizona, has been probing the limits of parrot mental ability. "Basically," she said, "we've shown that the parrot is working at the level of the chimpanzee and the dolphin."

Her star subject is a fifteen-year-old African gray parrot named Alex. In a paper published in 1990 by *The Journal of Comparative Psychology*, she described a study in which Alex was trained to recognize and label objects, colors, and shapes, and when questioned, to say names in English. Alex was able to identify the color, shape, or name of an object correctly about 80 percent of the time. In the *pièce de résistance*, he was shown a variety of objects—for instance, a purple model truck, a yellow key, a green piece of wood, a blue piece of rawhide, an orange piece of paper, a gray peg, and a red box. "What object is green?" he was asked. "Wood," he responded.

In another test, Alex was shown a football-shaped piece of wood, a key with a circular head, a triangular piece of felt, a square piece of rawhide, a five-sided piece of paper, a six-sided piece of modeling compound, and a toy truck.

"What object is five-cornered?" the experimenter asked.

"Paper," Alex replied.

Asked forty-eight such questions, he was right 76 percent of the time—100 percent of the time for questions involving shape. Dr. Pepperberg interprets this as statistically significant evidence that Alex understands the questions as well as the abstract concept of category, and that he thinks about the information to come up with an answer. In other tests, Dr. Pepperberg said, the parrot has distinguished between the concepts of bigger and smaller, and among the concepts of biggest, smallest, and "middlest," which is, "actually, a difficult concept for children. This is not just stimulus-response," she said, pointing out that to answer the questions correctly, Alex must understand them and think about the information. She does not go so far as to say that Alex is using language, but she does describe what is going on as communication between bird and human.

"It's very remarkable stuff, and it is a further indication of how exceptional these birds are in terms of their intellect," said Dr. James Serpell, a zoologist who directs the Companion Animal Research Group at the University of Cambridge department of veterinary medicine in England. "I liken parrots to primates," he said. "They are like monkeys: intelligent, highly manipulative. They use objects almost like tools." Other scientists urge caution about the Alex experiments, pointing out that they are based on a close, long-term relationship between experimenter and subject, and that the experiment is not easily amenable to normal controls and replication. Experts note the difficulty of inferring the thought processes of any animal, whether ape, dolphin, or parrot, from its behavior. But, said one bird expert who counsels caution, Dr. Fernando Nottebohm of Rockefeller University: "That bird is doing some things that look awfully clever and thought provoking. It does understand questions and gives what seem to be answers."

Many parrots, scientists say, go off the deep end when they are taken from the wild and placed in captivity. When a parrot is removed from its world and from the tight bond it has formed with its mate, said Dr. Serpell, it is likely to transfer its attachment to a human being. "This is all very well," he said, "but the human being is constantly going away. This is completely unnatural. The parrot would normally never experience that kind of thing." The resulting frustration, he said, leads to abnormalities like repetitive behavior, in which the bird's head weaves back and forth, or in which it shifts constantly from one foot to the other; abnormal grooming, in which the bird plucks out all its feathers; and aggressive behavior. "A lot of them become quite spiteful," said Dr. Serpell. A parrot "might solicit someone to come groom its head and then suddenly reverse itself and bite you," he said.

The wild macaws of Latin America, especially, "make stupid pets," said Dr. Charles A. Munn, a conservation biologist with Wildlife Conservation International, an arm of the New York Zoological Society. "They have tons of neuroses in captivity," said Dr. Munn, who studies wild macaws in the Amazon. "They develop dislikes. They will attach to one owner and hate the other," he said, and become jealous, screeching and yelling, for instance, when a husband and wife sit close together.

Generally, conservationists say, parrots bred in captivity do not display these disturbing quirks. "When they are hand-fed as babies and bond with humans," said Ms. Hemley of Traffic U.S.A., "they do not develop the problems of wild-caught birds." Overwhelmingly, scientists and conservationists urge people to buy only parrots raised in captive breeding programs and advise them to question pet-store owners carefully. "Ask where the parrot was captive-bred," said Dr. Rosemarie Gnam, a parrot expert at the American Museum of Natural History. "You can check it out by calling up the place." If the store owner hesitates, she said, the buyer should be suspicious. In some states, including New York, it is illegal to sell parrots that come from the wild.

Habitat destruction, trapping, and hunting are threatening the existence of seventy-five parrot species around the world and forty species in the Western Hemisphere. Dr. Gnam, who studies the endangered Bahama amazon parrot of the Caribbean, has found that in some years fewer than a third of the eggs hatch successfully. Most are eaten by predators. And Dr. Munn, observing macaws in the Amazon, has found that only 10 to 20 percent of adult macaws attempt to breed in a given year. "These are glacially slow reproductive rates for an animal that's pretty small," he said.

One limitation may be the supply of the holes in trees that parrots require for nests. The macaws seem obsessed with them. "They have a real fixation for cavities," said Dr. Munn. "They can't pass up a good cavity. They're examining things that might be a cavity five years from now." The search for cavities becomes more difficult as deforestation of the tropics proceeds. Another drag on reproductive success is that the first chick that hatches from the macaw's two-egg clutch gets most of the attention and food, and the second chick frequently dies.

Assiduous efforts are required to gather such data. Dr. Munn, for instance, spends long days in a harness high above the floor of the rain forest, observing macaws through telescopes and binoculars as they gather spectacularly on the bank of a river each day to eat clay. They need clay, scientists believe, to neutralize poisons in the seeds they eat. By watching the daily congregation at the "clay lick," Dr. Munn and colleagues have learned to identify individual birds by their facial markings and observe their relationships and social structure over several seasons. They find that young adults stay with their parents in a tight family unit for several years.

As research goes on, scientists and conservationists are pressing ahead with conservation plans. Conservationists hope parrots will serve as charismatic "flagship" species whose powerful appeal can be harnessed to the cause of rain forest preservation. In the Bahamas and elsewhere in the Caribbean, there have been education and advertising programs aimed at promoting parrot protection. A broader strategy involves the promotion of parrots as a valuable tourist attraction. One big clay lick in Peru, for example, is near a lodge that has already been established for purposes of what has come to be called ecotourism. So many macaws fly around the lick, and the sight is so brilliantly colorful, spectacular, and photogenic, said Dr. Munn, that it is "like Disneyland for parrots." Native Indians hunt the macaws for food, said Dr. Munn, and he has been trying to convince them that the birds are worth more alive, as a generator of tourist revenue, than dead. One village headman, he said, has expressed support. "Nothing in the rain forest is worth more than big parrots," Dr. Munn said, "and unfortunately, they are shot and captured in unsustainable ways in most places." [WKS, MAY 1991]

MUSHROOMS IN PERIL
FROM THEIR DEVOTEES

BARRISTER'S wig, candy cap, chicken of the woods, short-stemmed slippery Jack, man on horseback, chanterelle, and matsutake: these are the names of the highly prized edible wild mushrooms that grow in the verdant mountains of the Pacific Northwest. But the valuable mushrooms, like the gold for which prospectors once combed these ancient forests, are in danger of being collected to exhaustion, while the forests themselves are being damaged by ever-increasing troops of mushroom hunters.

While many more Americans have developed a taste for the wild mushrooms in recent years, nearly all of the Northwest's harvest goes to Europe and Japan, where declining forests are failing to provide enough mushrooms to satisfy the large demand.

Under these conditions, a skilled mushroom collector can make $1,000 a day. As the collectors pound the forest floor in search of its bounty, they leave behind mushroom beds picked clean, and sometimes filled instead with trash, provoking concern among conservationists and forest officials. Researchers in both Oregon and Washington in June 1992 began the first long-term studies to determine the impact of this intensive harvesting.

"There are more and more people every year," said Dr. Tom Atzet, area ecologist with the United States Forest Service at Grants Pass, Oregon. "My son came home the other day and said, 'Gee, do you know where any morels are?' and I said, 'Yes, but I'm not going to tell anybody.' He said one of his friends from school went out picking on Saturday and made two hundred dollars. The word is out. When you come right down to it, people can go out there and make some good money without a lot of effort if they know where things are."

Until recently the usual mushroom hunters were children spending a few hours a week to earn pocket money or a local gourmet chef searching for the perfect mushroom. They have now been joined by sizable bands of migrant harvesters, who together with professional buyers have begun changing a quaint hobby into a multimillion-dollar industry.

"There's a little airport just outside of Shelton, Washington," said Ron Post, chairman of the conservation and ecology committee of the Puget Sound Mycological Society. "The forest ranger there estimated to me that millions of dollars worth of chanterelles are picked out of that one area every year. Think about how many acres of forest there are out here. That's just one little site."

Wayne Gammon, special forest products coordinator for the Siskiyou National Forest in Oregon, said: "This thing has turned out to be a bigger job than we ever thought. Mushrooms, Pacific yew, bear grass, cedar boughs. People collect all kinds of things." Some of the plants are used for floral arrangements and others are used as medicinals.

"It's not just the transients," Mr. Gammon said. "People are getting out of work here because of the timber situation and the forest still provides many products for them to supplement whatever small incomes they might have."

Conservationists say they believe there is already evidence of the toll taken by these high-intensity harvests. "Every year I go to areas that were very nice before," Mr. Post said. "And the foliage has been all broken up, the moss gets all turned over, and the area is ruined. You don't have to turn up the moss to get the mushrooms, and with the moss carpet all disturbed, that area may not produce again."

Dr. Mike Amaranthus, a mushroom expert with the Forest Service, said that even though there are millions of acres of forest to harvest, "Recreational and commercial pickers are in conflict and it's going to get worse."

Many of the local people who sell mushrooms on a small scale blame the commercial pickers for the damage to the forests. But the effects of intensive mushroom collecting have not yet been assessed.

Mr. Gammon said commercial pickers who use leaf blowers may not be doing as much harm as believed. "People will rent these leaf blowers and blow the leaves around and off the mushrooms," he said. "Some people thought it was harmful, but our experts say it doesn't seem to be a problem. I think the problem is that some people can't afford them, and they don't want anyone else using them."

Dr. Amaranthus agreed that emotions could run quite strong about mushrooms. "You don't want to come out to your favorite little mushroom-hunting spot and find that commercial pickers have come and gotten everything," he said. "That's a horrible feeling, I'll tell you."

The most lucrative fungi in the Northwest are chanterelles, yellow trumpet-shaped mushrooms with the faint smell of apricot or pumpkin and a peppery taste, and morels, which resemble a cone-shaped sponge with their dark, pitted caps. Most valuable of all is the matsutake, or pine mushroom, a cinnamon-scented delicacy said to be in demand in Japan.

David Arora, author of *Mushrooms Demystified*, which some call the bible of mushroom hunters, said the matsutake was highly prized for its spicy smell. He added: "They pay premium prices in Japan for matsutake that are still really young and look quite phallic. The more phallic they look the more they'll pay."

Dr. Amaranthus said the Japanese believe these mushrooms maintain health and vigor.

All avid mushroom hunters enjoy a chance to wax eloquent about the pleasures of collecting and eating wild mushrooms.

"Garlicky, nutty, apricoty—they have a variety of textures and tastes," Dr. Amaranthus said. "Once you've eaten these wild edible mushrooms you can't go back to grocery store mushrooms. There's just no going back."

Some conservationists say they fear mushroom yields have declined abroad because of overharvesting, and they fear a similar decline in the United States.

"Why should a commercial company be able to bring in a busload of people from outside an area who will spend several days basically stripping the ground of the forest for commercial export when locals won't even see much or any of that money?" Mr. Post said. "Washington State should not be the wild mushroom table for the rest of the world's dining."

Mushrooms like chanterelles and matsutakes play an important role in the forest ecology since they live in a symbiotic, or mutually beneficial, relationship with certain trees. The mushrooms form a sheet on the roots of trees such as the mighty Douglas fir. Their roving filaments deliver nutrients and water to the tree and the mushrooms receive sugars in return. Botanists have found that if a Douglas fir seedling does not quickly form an association with mushrooms, it will die.

Botanists say the relationship must also be vital to the mushrooms since they cannot be found except in association with their host tree. This relationship with huge forest trees is what makes the matsutake and chanterelle so difficult to cultivate.

Finding a Douglas fir does not ensure finding one of the prize mushrooms. "It's a real hit-or-miss type thing," Mr. Gammon said. "Maybe they'll be under madrono or pine or a Doug fir stand. Gold is where you find it."

Other mushrooms have their own special needs. Morels, for instance, prefer disturbed areas, particularly those that have been ravaged by fire. Mr. Arora said European landowners sometimes burned their forests in hopes of a crop of morels.

A mushroom is not a whole plant but just the fruit produced by a fungus. The cues that prompt a fungus to produce mushrooms are not well understood. Mushroom hunters thus have no scientific guide as to where to look. Even experts investigate many promising-looking bumps that hold only humus and leaves.

Loreli Norvell, a graduate student at the University of Washington, says preliminary results of her studies indicate that mushroom picking may actually stimulate mushroom productivity, but she warns that this may just be a short-term effect. Dr. Norvell's study is scheduled to continue for ten years.

Dr. Amaranthus is heading another long-term study of mushroom harvesting in six national forests in Washington and Oregon.

"The mushroom inventory is part of the Pacific Northwest Research Station sustainability experiment," Dr. Amaranthus said. "It's not just looking at fungi, but at sustained forest productivity. We'll be harvesting and looking at how that affects things, abundances and species present of birds, wood fiber, a variety of things." Dr. Amaranthus said the study was scheduled to continue for twenty years.   [CKY, JULY 1992]

HAWAII'S BIRDS AND THE BROWN TREE SNAKE

O N the peaceful tropical isles of Hawaii, military and civilian forces alike are gearing up to fend off a deadly invader. The menace is the brown tree snake, infamous for having wiped out most of Guam's forest bird species. This five-foot-long serpent first descended like a plague on Guam just thirty years ago, but it has bred so fast that there are now as many as 30,000 snakes per square mile in some areas. In Hawaii, the beast has been kept at bay so far. At least that is what Hawaii's officials keep hoping as they intercept the snakes that occasionally drop down from the holds and wheel wells of planes flying into Hawaii from Guam. The snake would be a social menace as well as a threat to Hawaii's already endangered native birds. Its behavior on Guam could well furnish scenes for a horror movie: armies of snakes crawling at night along electrical wires and hanging off fences; parents waking up in the morning to discover the coils of one of these serpents wrapped tight around their baby in a crib, chewing the child's fingers; snakes swallowing puppies, kittens, domesticated rabbits, and chickens wholesale, and, in bathrooms all around the island country, hundreds of snake heads popping out of drainpipes, ready with a painful and slightly venomous bite.

Six brown tree snakes have been discovered in Hawaii so far. All were in airports, having presumably hitchhiked on planes from Guam. By 1991, authorities began to understand how easily the snakes could reach Hawaii when two snakes were found in Oahu on the same day, one on the runways at Hickam Air Force Base and the other at Honolulu International Airport. The snakes like to climb, and they apparently make their way into the planes' cargo bays or wheel wells. Each snake found on an airport runway is a reminder that others may have survived their hard landing and slithered off to take up residence in their new home. "The two in one twenty-four-hour period really freaked everybody out," said Dr. Sheila Laffey of the National Audubon Society's office in Hawaii, "but the one that actually was still alive—that was incredibly disturbing. All it would take would be one female who was already fertilized to start a population here."

Hawaii has no native snakes, so the islands would be wide open to colonization by alien reptiles. Biologists say the invasion of Hawaii by the brown tree snake would be an ecological disaster because the animal would have unsuspecting prey and no native competitors. Dr. Leonard Freed, a biologist at the University of Hawaii who studies the islands' native birds, said, "Something like a snake, which the birds may no longer recognize as a predator, will be especially dangerous. Maybe where they roost they are not protected or it's not hard for the snake to get to. We would expect the birds here to be greatly susceptible to the snake—literally sitting ducks."

Many of Hawaii's unique bird species have become extinct or severely endangered, in part because of imported predators like wild domestic cats and the small Indian mongoose. For many species, the brown tree snake could be the coup de grâce. "This place was a giant aviary at one time," Dr. Freed said. Like so many island fauna, Hawaii's birds evolved in unique ways, producing many species of honeycreepers and unusual birds like the Hawaiian duck and the Hawaiian stilt. Dr. Freed said that the threat posed by the brown tree snake "should be considered a national problem, not just a State of Hawaii problem."

The brown tree snake, native to the Solomon Islands, New Guinea, and to the northern coast of Australia, is thought to have been transported to Guam by United States military traffic from New Guinea. Dr. Thomas H. Fritts, a research biologist with the United States Fish and Wildlife Service and a specialist on the brown tree snake, said there appeared to be no way to eliminate the snake once it has established a foothold. Baited traps are too costly. Dr. Fritts and his colleagues are trying to devise barriers to keep the snakes out of Hawaii and to fence in any snakes that manage to make it to places like Honolulu International Airport, from which their escape would be disastrous. The experimental barriers consist of a wall of plastic netting accompanied by an electric fence.

Everyone agrees that the best way to deal with the snake is to make sure that it never gets a chance to become established in Hawaii. As part of that strategy, planes landing in Hawaii from Guam are being searched, special snake-sniffer dogs are being recruited and trained, and the public is being alerted and educated. The Department of Land and Natural Resources has begun operating Snake Watch and Alert Teams, and former President George Bush signed the Brown Tree Snake Control Act, which calls for eradication of the snake as well as research.

According to Pat McGarey, legislative director for Senator Daniel K. Akaka of Hawaii, recent legislation has made the military responsible for preventing the importation of snakes on air force planes and has charged the Department of Agriculture with keeping civilian traffic snake-free. "There are a lot of cracks through which this problem could fall," Mr. McGarey said.

Mobilizing early to prevent an infestation could save Hawaii from the disaster experienced in Guam, said Dr. Fritts, who works on the snake in Guam. "Everyone—the customs inspector, the guy that does the mowing on the lawn at the Honolulu International Airport—all of those people can help by being alert to the snake and realizing what to do if they see evidence of the infestation," he said. "Every snake counts. Even if we only catch half the number that come in, we decrease the chances of a population getting established."

[CKY, JULY 1992]

THE DECLINE OF SONGBIRDS

T HE steady disappearance of migratory songbirds from North America's woodlands has been widely ascribed to deforestation of their winter habitat in Central America and the Caribbean. But a new study suggests that United States land development may be a much more potent factor in slashing songbird populations. In a twenty-three-year investigation of two species of warblers, Dr. Richard T. Holmes of Dartmouth College, Hanover, New Hampshire, and his colleague and former student, Dr. Thomas W. Sherry of Tulane University in New Orleans, found that deforestation of the birds' winter refuges in Jamaica did not account for the decline. Instead, they report, the warblers' worst losses, occurring in spring and summer, result from the steady encroachments of suburban development on the United States mainland. The findings were reported in a paper published as a chapter in a book called *Ecology and Conservation of Neotropical Migrant Landbirds*.

"In our censuses," Dr. Holmes said, "we found a strong correlation between the breeding success of a warbler population in one season and its overall population the following summer, regardless of how the birds fared in Jamaica during the intervening winter. Loss of winter habitat in Jamaica is a potential problem for the birds, but at present, it doesn't seem to be the major threat." Conservationists generally accepted the results of the study. "Holmes and Sherry have done more work on this than anyone else, and I feel comfortable with their conclusions," said Deanna Dawson, a research biologist of the United States Fish and Wildlife Service at the Patuxent Wildlife Research Center in Maryland.

The scientists routinely counted all birds in their survey area, but focused on two species: the American redstart and the black-throated blue warbler. The two birds were studied and banded at both their summer breeding grounds in the Hubbard Brook Experimental Forest in the White Mountains of New Hampshire and in their winter area on the island of Jamaica. The migrants lead difficult lives, living on average only two or three years, Dr. Holmes said. Despite their problems, the hardier birds, which weigh less than a half ounce each, sometimes survive far longer than their less-experienced flock mates, and the relatively rare older birds produce many more offspring. "There's one male warbler that we banded nine years ago, and he's turned up every year since," Dr. Holmes said. "That means he made eight round trips to Jamaica, a lot of flying for a little fellow."

The spread of humans into former woodlands has two dangerous effects on songbirds, naturalists agree. The first comes because predators accompany human populations. To determine the extent and type of predation on songbird nests, the scientists set up automatic cameras overlooking artificial warbler nests with eggs like those of songbirds. "The eggs were raided constantly by a dozen or so different types of predators," Dr. Holmes said. "They included not only domestic and feral cats, but also raccoons, squirrels, chipmunks, skunks, blue jays, and even black bears, most of them animals that live near human communities, feeding on garbage or handouts."

The second major threat to the species studied, and probably to most other songbirds, is parasitism by cowbirds, small members of the blackbird family, which, like cuckoos, lay eggs in the nests of other species. Cowbird fledglings, larger and more aggressive than their songbird nest mates, demand and get the lion's share of worms and caterpillars brought by harried foster parents. The number of surviving songbird chicks declines drastically. Cowbirds, like cats, congregate near human communities, especially farms. They are attracted by spilled grain and stay to use the free nursery service provided by songbirds. "Studies in Illinois and other Midwestern states have shown that wood thrushes are basically raising nothing but cowbird chicks at this point," Ms. Dawson said. "So far, only about 10 percent of the wood thrush nests in the Washington area have been parasitized by cowbirds. The problem varies regionally."

Loss of habitat is not limited to the felling of trees, Dr. Holmes said. The real problem is the fragmentation of large forests into housing lots that offer predators entry into the habitat. Songbird populations do not suffer equally. "In the area we studied," Dr. Holmes said, "populations of some species increased somewhat and others

remained stable, although over all, populations declined. In general, the birds did better during periods of major caterpillar infestation."
[MWB, NOVEMBER 1991]

GIANT PANDAS SLIDE TOWARD EXTINCTION

I N a quiet enclave in the heart of China's Sichuan Province, two giant pandas ambled playfully among the rocks and bamboo, oblivious to the growing fear that their species could become extinct within decades. Millions of dollars have been spent to preserve panda habitats and save the animals from hunters who kill them for pelts. But the efforts have been stymied by red tape and infighting among government ministries. The result is that the panda is losing its competition with humans. "I'm rather pessimistic about the giant panda," said Yin Lin, a technician who conducts artificial insemination in the panda at the Chengdu Zoo. "There is a very strong trend toward extinction." According to China's official statistics, there are only about 1,000 pandas left in the wild, and another 100 in zoos all over the world. Privately, some experts say the number of pandas in the wild is as low as 700.

Pandas eat bamboo, but their digestion is so poor they must eat practically all day long to get enough nourishment. But in China, where arable land and wood are scarce, both local residents and the government have cut down substantial areas of bamboo forests. Many specialists say the panda's best chances for survival are in the wild, rather than in the zoos, but the wild panda reserves do not necessarily get the funds, and when they do success is limited. "Our hearts are aching with anxiety," said Pan Wenshi, a panda specialist at Beijing University. "We know the panda must rely on man to survive. But man has not yet offered a good way of helping it."

Researchers and officials are often limited in what they can do: they lack funds, they do not have enough decision-making power, or they are overruled by the bureaucracy. Sometimes the panda projects are bogged down by petty jealousies and proud bureaucrats, both

Chinese and foreign experts say. Money and time are often wasted on repetition of effort, and more money does not necessarily mean better results. For example, at the Wolong Reserve, a large panda preservation about ninety miles northwest of Chengdu, officials built a research site with $1 million donated a decade ago by the World Wide Fund for Nature. Experts envisioned a program to breed pandas and put them back in the wild. In the past decade, however, the center has bred only one panda, and it died.

One problem is that China's reserves and zoos do not work together to share specialists, resources, or even good breeding pandas. Specialists at the Chengdu Zoo have not been welcomed at Wolong, and panda experts from Beijing have been turned away, researchers say. Part of the reason is that pandas in the wild are controlled by the Ministry of Forestry, whereas pandas in captivity are managed by the Ministry of Construction. "We do have some contact, but there are some administrative obstacles," said a panda researcher under the Ministry of Construction. "It's a problem. But if we had a leading group overseeing panda work, who would lead it?"

Wolong appears to be opening up to outside researchers, and the Chengdu Zoo sent its first male panda to the center for mating this spring. Academics say that although this is progress, there are still many turf wars and problems. "It's territorial behavior," said Wang Song, a biologist at the Academy of Sciences in Beijing. "The Smithsonian and the American government departments cooperate very well. Under socialism, we should be better but we're not."

China's fourteen panda reserves also face other challenges. They are isolated from one another, and sometimes they have so few pandas that the fertile ones have difficulty finding mates. As a result, there are problems with inbreeding as well as relatively low reproduction rates. The World Wide Fund for Nature has proposed linking the reserves to address these problems, but some experts say this is often not feasible.

Another problem is that even in the reserves, the pandas have two-legged neighbors. Frantic researchers at Qinling Reserve in Shaanxi Province are trying to raise money to relocate the reserve's 2,200 human residents, who have slowly encroached upon the bamboo forest. In Wolong Reserve, new houses have been built for 3,000 residents, but the residents refuse to move unless they are fully compensated for farming income they would lose. Meanwhile, the authorities built a power station to prevent them from further destroying bamboo trees for fuel. "Everything about pandas gets mired in politics, and sometimes it's forgotten that the main purpose is to save the pandas," said George B. Schaller, director for science at Wildlife Conservation International in New York.

Many experts say the panda population has dwindled to between 700 and 900 over the past decade, although Chinese officials have been unwilling to announce the results of a panda census completed in 1988, and the official government estimate remains about 1,000. In any case, some experts say the census faced enormous obstacles and was not very thorough. Some say it is possible there are more than 1,000 pandas. The previous census, in the late 1970s, counted about 2,000 pandas, experts with firsthand knowledge say. But the government announced that the panda population was about 1,000, apparently because it anticipated a decline and did not want to be blamed for it. Some experts believe that the authorities reported a lower number to attract more attention and funds to help the pandas.

Scientists say poaching is the principal reason for the population decline. In Wolong, the panda population dropped by half: from 145 to 72 in the twelve years from 1974 to 1986, according to a recent report by the World Wide Fund for Nature. "Hunting is the most serious immediate problem," said Mr. Schaller. "If poaching isn't checked, the panda will disappear." Pandas have become so prized that the value of a pelt has risen to more than $10,000 to $20,000 in some parts of China, according to various Chinese and foreign reports. The pelts make their way through a long chain of underground dealers before they end up abroad, especially in Taiwan and Japan. China recently decreed the death penalty for poaching and trading in panda pelts, and so far at least four men have been sentenced to death. A recent report in the official *Public Security News* said that in Sichuan alone there have been arrests in about 200 cases of trafficking in panda pelts in the last few years.

The impact of poaching is particularly serious in light of the panda's poor reproductive abilities. A female panda ovulates once a year, and may raise about half a dozen babies in her lifetime if she is lucky. Breeding in zoos has been difficult because not all researchers know how to tell when a panda is ovulating. Even when a panda is born, it frequently dies in the first few weeks or months, either because the mother accidentally crushes it to death, or because it is not fed properly. "In the best of worlds, the panda reproduces at an incredibly slow rate," said Devra G. Kleiman, a zoologist at the National Zoological Park of the Smithsonian Institution in Washington. "That's why the loss of even a single breeding period of a single panda is a real loss."

For this reason, some experts say that among pandas in captivity, all efforts should be concentrated on breeding, rather than putting them up for exhibition. But pandas for exhibition have become an enormously lucrative business for the Chinese zoos or institutions that control them. A Chinese zoo can make more than $500,000 on the loan of a single panda for a few months, and the drive to make money often interferes with panda breeding. Peter Karsten, director of the Calgary Zoo in Canada, has also asserted that Chinese zoos sometimes lend mismatched panda couples—either pairs of the same sex or pairs that are unlikely to breed—to avoid being embarrassed if a foreign zoo is able to arrange a mating that has eluded the animals' home zoo. He also said that China tries to control the supply of pandas outside China, perhaps for commercial reasons. At a broader level, experts complain that there is a fierce competition among institutions that control the pandas, and the result is that zoos and ministries guard, rather than share, pandas as well as knowledge about how to care for them. Thus, after nearly twenty years of panda breeding in China, only twenty-eight pandas have been bred and raised successfully in captivity there, Chinese panda experts say.

Because of the poor track record, some specialists are skeptical about breeding programs and, more broadly, about panda preservation in China. Even Chinese experts have some difficulty in waxing optimistic. "It will take several generations of researchers before we have success," said Hu Jinchu, a panda expert at the University of Nanchong in Sichuan. "This may be 100 to 200 years. But if the government policy is good, the economy is good, the educational level is improved, and we get international cooperation, then maybe there will be hope." [SWD, JUNE 1991]

BATS, VICTIMS OF IGNORANCE
AND SUPERSTITION

BATMAN'S youthful imitators may forever try to terrorize those who refuse them Halloween treats. But real bats are not the aggressive, dirty, or dangerous creatures of lore. They are, in fact, industrious and invaluable assets to people and the planet. And they are succumbing worldwide at a frightening rate to human ignorance, greed, and destruction. In misguided efforts to protect people, crops, and livestock, bats are being poisoned, blasted with dynamite, asphyxiated by burning tires, or entombed alive by the millions in caves and mines where they seek a day's or a winter's rest. Many others are felled by hunters or die when spelunkers disturb their dwellings. "Bats are disappearing at a faster rate than any other group of vertebrates," said Dr. Merlin Tuttle, a real-life "batman" who has spearheaded international efforts to save the versatile and vital animals.

As scientists learn more about bats, they are discovering how vital they are to hundreds of environmentally and economically important plants and trees, including major features of the tropical rain forest, African savanna, and American desert. And the demise of insect-eating bats has permitted a population explosion among insects that pester people and devour crops. Bats, the only mammals that can fly, account for nearly a quarter of all known species of mammals. But 40 percent of bat species are listed as endangered or threatened. Several of the nearly 1,000 species have become extinct within the last two decades, some disappearing before scientists could determine their precise role in the chain of life.

Yet conservation organizations, conscious of the creature's charmless image, are loath to intervene. "When I first approached major conservation organizations ten years ago, they wouldn't touch bats with a ten-foot pole," said the fifty-year-old Dr. Tuttle, who since his high school days has been one of the furry animal's staunchest advocates. "They either didn't understand bats or viewed them as so unpopular as not to be worth the effort." So Dr. Tuttle, then curator of mammals at the Milwaukee Public Museum, took bats literally and figuratively into his own hands. In 1982, he founded Bat Conservation International to sponsor research and educational programs about bats and their vital roles. Four years later, he left his museum job and moved the fledging organization to Austin, Texas, a state that has the most bat species—32 of the nation's 42 kinds of bats—as well as the world's largest remaining bat colony in Bracken Cave in Central Texas, where 20 million Mexican free-tail bats congregate.

Since then, Bat Conservation International has far surpassed its founder's dreams. Having arrived in Austin in 1986 with two employees and a few hundred members, it now boasts 17 full-time staff members and 12,500 members from fifty-five countries. Dr. Tuttle is the subject of a new biography for young people, *Batman: Exploring the World of Bats*, by Laurence Pringle, and his own book, *America's Neighborhood Bats*, is the University of Texas Press's best-selling volume. A 1991 cartoon by W. Miller in *The New Yorker* is further testimony to Dr. Tuttle's mushrooming success: one of a group of bats hanging in a cave says to a roostmate, "We're starting to get media coverage. Pass it on."

As bats decline drastically throughout the world, scientists are scrambling to understand more about their unique biology, their critical ecological roles, and their basic survival needs. At the 21st Annual North American Symposium on Bat Research in Austin in October 1991, some 300 scientists gathered to exchange new findings and suggest ways of rescuing bats from their only serious natural enemy: people. At one time, bats were vulnerable only during their nightly feeding frenzy and only to predators like owls with limited appetites. Now people attack them during the day in caves, trees, and abandoned mines, and under bridges and eaves. Bats are especially vulnerable to mass annihilation because most species congregate in huge groups when not eating.

Chased from most of their traditional roosts in caves, they moved into abandoned mines. Now thousands of mines are being sealed to prevent injury to curious people, and other mines are being reactivated or used for other purposes. In Wisconsin, for example, where 95 percent of the state's bats hibernate in old mines, Dr. Tuttle rescued hundreds of thousands of insect-eating bats by staying the hand of a landowner who was going to fumigate them so he could use the shafts to store cheese. In tropical Central and South America, where the three species of blood-sipping vampire bats do an estimated $50 million worth of damage to livestock, ranchers who cannot tell one bat from another have destroyed millions of fruit-eating and insect-eating bats. Vampire bats, which roost in small groups, are far harder to find than the millions of insect-eaters that gather in caves, where they can be smoked out by burning tires.

The critically important fruit-eating bats, however, have not fared well at human hands. In Southeast Asia, for example, giant fruit-eating bats known as flying foxes are routinely hunted for food and export, commanding as much as twenty dollars apiece from wealthy islanders who consider them a gourmet treat. These huge bats, weighing as much as a pound and with wingspans of up to six feet, are easy targets for shotguns while they hang by the hundreds from treetops. Dr. Tuttle said that one of the Philippines' flying foxes, first discovered by scientists in the 1960s, was extinct by the 1980s.

Some 250 species of bats pollinate or disperse the seeds of hundreds of trees and shrubs, including those that bear economically important products like bananas, avocados, vanilla beans, dates, peaches, figs, cashews, and agaves, the source of tequila. In a single night, one short-tailed fruit bat can disperse as many as 60,000 rain forest seeds. A recent study by Bat Conservation International documented that more than 300 plant species in the Old World tropics alone rely on bats. These plants are the source of more than 450 commercial products, including medicines, timber, ornamentals, fiber and cordage and dyes and tannins, as well as foods and drinks. In Africa, fast-declining flying foxes are the only known seed dispersers for the iroko tree, the source of millions of dollars worth of timber annually. The giant baobab tree, an ecologically critical feature of East African savannas, depends on bats to pollinate its flowers, which open only at night. The fruit bats of West Africa disperse nearly all the seeds of "pioneer plants" that start forests growing again on cleared land.

To Donald W. Thomas, an ecologist at the University of Sherbrooke in Quebec, fruit bats are "the keystone species on many tropical islands," where they are the sole pollinators and seed dispersers of long-lived rain forest trees. In studies on the Ivory Coast, Dr. Thomas showed that when the seeds of tropical fruits pass through the digestive tract of fruit bats, they nearly always germinate, but those seeds that simply fall to the ground from the trees mostly do not. Furthermore, he found by studying bat droppings that the animals dispersed most of the seeds far from the mother tree, which greatly enhanced a seedling's chances of taking hold.

Migrating nectar-eating bats from Mexico were recently shown to be a key to the survival of the giant cactus and agaves that are the distinguishing features of the Sonoran Desert. Dr. Theodore H. Fleming and colleagues from the University of Miami at Coral Gables found that lesser long-nosed bats, a federally listed endangered species, follow "nectar corridors"—a succession of blooming organ-pipe and saguaro cacti—as they head north into Arizona in spring and then follow a reverse succession of blooming agaves when they head south to Mexico in late fall. With each foray into the nectar trough of a desert flower, the long-nosed bat emerges covered with pollen, which is deposited at the bat's next stop. Without these long-nosed bats, which are ideally constructed for their job as pollinators, the giant cactus and agave could die out.

Bats that eat insects find their night's meal by emitting high-frequency sounds and locating targets by the returning echoes. All six species of bats that live in and around New York City are insect-eating "microbats," some of which consume up to 3,000 insects a night. Although all can see, their sonar tells far more than eyes can about a potential meal on the wing in the dark. The high-frequency sounds bats emit and the echoes they process give these voracious hunters detailed information about the movement, distance, speed, trajectory, size, and shape of possible prey. Bat sonar can detect an object as thin as a human hair and only eight-hundredths of an inch long. Dr. Nobuo Suga, a biologist at Washington University in St. Louis, studies electrical impulses generated by individual neurons in the auditory center of the pearl-sized brain of the mustached bat. He has determined that by using pulses with different frequencies the animal derives very precise details about a potential meal. He also found that the bats use harmonics to avoid collisions with other bats while hunting in dense packs.

Dr. Tuttle noted that a half million pounds of insects typically succumb each night to large foraging colonies of insectivorous bats. The million or so Mexican free-tail bats that roost under the Congress Avenue Bridge in downtown Austin eat fourteen tons of insects a night from March to November, said Dr. Tuttle, who convinced the city not to destroy them but instead to turn the bat colony's nightly emergence into a tourist attraction.

Dr. James H. Fullard, a zoologist at the University of Toronto, noted that before bats evolved more than 60 million years ago, moths and other nocturnal insects owned the night sky, flitting about unmolested by predators. The appearance of bats forced them to evolve a novel antibat strategy—a way of hearing the echolocating calls of hunting bats, in effect a radar detector. Moths with this strategic advantage are 40 percent less likely to be eaten, Dr. Fullard said. When they hear a bat speed up its sonar beam, indicating that it has begun its final approach, the moths launch into a wild acrobatic act, looping up, down, and around to evade the less agile bat. If that is not enough, the moths fold their wings and dive to the ground, where the bat is hard put to find them. Other moths emit their own sonar signal, blasting out high-pitched clicks that startle the bat. Still others use an auditory guise to dissuade bats by mimicking a sound produced by a foul-tasting moth.

But some tropical bats are like Stealth fighters, acoustically invisible to moths. They emit echolocation calls "so high-pitched that even the sensitive ears of moths cannot detect them," Dr. Fullard said. Dr. Paul A. Faure, a biologist at Cornell University, has studied these "whispering" bats, which forage among vegetation rather than in the air. By implanting electrodes into the auditory nerves of the moths, he showed that the insects were deaf to the bats' high-pitched emissions. Others hunt without making any noise at all. Dr. Z. M. Fusessery of the University of Wyoming reported that pallid bats are silent hunters. The enormous ears and finely tuned auditory systems of these bats are so sensitive they can hear an insect as it walks and detect the wing flutter of a moth about to take off. Frog-eating bats have evolved yet another strategy, Dr. Tuttle found. They simply tune into the frog's mating call and silently pick off the amorous amphibian.

The extraordinary vulnerability of animals that congregate by the millions in a few well-defined locations demands fast action from those trying to spare the woodsman's ax. Kirk W. Navo of the Colorado Division of Wildlife, who reported that "about 2,000 of the mines in Colorado have already been sealed without any input from wildlife experts," said he and his colleagues have recruited and trained dozens of volunteers to survey mine sites for bat life. Armed with bat detectors that pick up the animals' sonar, the volunteers work night shifts to monitor bat activity before the mines are closed. But with more than 20,000 inactive mines in the state, the volunteers are hard put to keep up with closings.

Two years ago, Dr. Tuttle said, one of the largest remaining bat populations in New Jersey, a hibernating horde of 20,000 little brown bats, was sealed into a rural mine. A member of Bat Conservation International noticed the closing and called headquarters, which got the mine reopened in a few days. The mine and its surroundings have since been made a protected reserve for bats.

"Bat gates," vandal-proof metal grids that allow access to bats but not people, are increasingly being used to protect caves and mines that are major bat roosts and hibernation sites. Dr. Tuttle explained that each time human visitors arouse a hibernating bat, it uses up ten to thirty days' food supply. More than a few arousals a winter can easily result in an entire colony's starving to death before insects reappear in spring.

Dr. Elizabeth D. Pierson, a bat researcher from Berkeley, California, reported the successful relocation of a bat colony by the Homestake Mining Company, which was planning to reactivate an area containing a bat-occupied mine. After the colony emerged at night, the mine shaft was sealed and the colony moved into another mine nearby that was protected by a bat gate.

Finally, Tracey Tarlton of Bat Conservation International has been analyzing bridges to uncover design features that make ideal bat roosts. Instead of killing off bridge-inhabiting bat colonies "because bridge workers are afraid of them," she proposed structural features for bridges and overpasses that could provide safe haven for these valuable animals.   [JEB, OCTOBER 1991]

APPETITE FOR SUSHI THREATENS THE GIANT TUNA

MAN and boy, Bill Camp has been sallying out into the Atlantic for a quarter of a century in one of angling's great quests: the chase for the bluefin tuna, one of the world's most magnificent vertebrates. The bluefin is a fish to which superlatives cling. Growing to 1,500 pounds and fourteen feet, it is the biggest bony fish in the world and quite possibly the strongest. It is certainly one of the fastest, as both sprinter and marathoner. By revving up its warm-blooded metabolism, it can make short dashes of fifty miles an hour. And it can cross 5,000 miles of open sea, migrating across an entire ocean, in fifty days. All in all, marine scientists say, the bluefin is a marvel of evolutionary adaptation.

In the mid-1960s, when Bill Camp was a teenager, fishermen would catch as many of the biggest bluefins, called giants, as they could handle. Old photographs of the big fish, towering over the people who caught them, grace the walls of the shingled watering holes nestled around Montauk Harbor, Long Island. But those catches are gone. "There is no comparison between then and now," said Mr. Camp, the mate on Captain Joe McBride's charter boat, *My Mate.* "The best guys around here are lucky to get eight or nine giants a year. We used to get seven or eight a day."

The bluefin appears to be in serious trouble, at least in the western Atlantic. Environmentalists and some charter-boat operators say it is a victim of money lust. A giant bluefin—defined as weighing 310 pounds or more—can bring $10,000 to $15,000 on the open market in Japan, where its high-fat meat is avidly sought for sashimi and sushi. (Canned tuna is prepared not from the highly prized bluefin but from other tuna species like albacore, yellowfin, skipjack, or bigeye. Yellowfin is the most common source of tuna steaks, increasingly popular in the United States.) As the bluefin's numbers have shrunk, the price has risen, approaching twenty dollars a pound in some years. This has prompted sports anglers to join commercial fishermen in the enthusiastic pursuit of swimming dollars.

Although international fishing quotas were imposed on bluefins a decade ago, scientists charged with monitoring the situation say there are only 10 percent as many giant bluefins in the western Atlantic as in 1970, and the scientists say the decline is continuing. The status of the giants is crucial because only they are mature enough to spawn, and it is the spawners on which the future of the species depends.

In response, the National Audubon Society has taken the highly unusual step of formally proposing that the bluefin be listed as endangered, and that international trade in the species be banned, under an international treaty called the Convention on International Trade in Endangered Species of Wild Fauna and Flora, commonly known as CITES. It is believed to be the first time that a commercial fish has been proposed for the international endangered list. The proposal has touched off a spirited dispute, pitting commercial tuna fishermen against the environmentalists and many sport fishermen and charter operators. The commercial fishermen challenge the scientific basis for the conclusion that giant bluefins continue to decline and assert that, in fact, aerial reconnaissance shows that they have turned the corner and that their numbers off North America are rebounding. They maintain that while stocks of the northern bluefin tuna did decline in the western Atlantic after 1970, the species itself is not endangered worldwide. (A separate species, the southern bluefin, inhabits the South Pacific.)

The United States Fish and Wildlife Service is expected to announce whether it will recommend some sort of further protection for bluefins under the CITES treaty. If it does, the final decision would be up to the signers of the treaty when they meet in Kyoto, Japan. Countries adhering to the treaty, which include most of the world's nations, could decide to ban international trade in bluefins. They could also allow the trade but make it subject to more stringent controls, including measures to track the trade better and hold down violations more effectively.

In mid-September of 1991, when the tuna season should have been at its peak, an informal survey of Montauk Harbor showed that not a single giant had been caught. The largest bluefins taken were immature fish weighing about seventy pounds. The smallest weighed about twenty pounds at most—babies, less than a year old. These were "pathetically tiny" by bluefin standards, said Dr. Carl Safina, the director of marine conservation for the Audubon Society and a veteran tuna fisherman. Marina operators said that an average of less than one giant tuna a day was being taken last week, and that almost none had been caught in the weeks immediately before. When one is taken, it is invariably snapped up by a fish buyer, usually for export to Japan. Trucked from Montauk to Kennedy International Airport and shipped directly to Narita Airport outside Tokyo, it goes on the auction block the next day. The payoff is handsome and immediate, and the very scarcity of the resource tends to keep prices up, making the situation advantageous for commercial fishermen.

Sport fishermen, who often sell their catches to pay their considerable fishing expenses, have transformed the nature of the sport. "The first thing a guest asks is, 'How much are they worth today?' " said Mr. Camp. "People used to come because the fish fought, not because they were worth a lot of money. It was neat then. I hate it now." Dr. Safina tells of being out on the water and listening on the radio as one boat captain admonished another to keep one or two fish and let the rest go "so that there'll be some for tomorrow." The response came back: "Nobody left any buffalo for me." But most times, he said, fishing is so poor, compared with years ago, that no one catches enough bluefins of any size to fill out the federally imposed sportfishing limit of four fish per person per day.

Like other tunas, the bluefin is warm-blooded, its body temperature reaching 85 degrees Fahrenheit. Its circulatory system is designed to both shed and conserve heat, as needed. Its entire makeup is geared toward speed and endurance. And in more ways than one, the bluefins are the mightiest tunas of all. Even a smallish one, says Mr. Camp, remains upright and defiant when brought alongside the boat, its characteristic blue back, golden side-stripe, and silvery belly gleaming, while other tuna species roll on their sides, spent.

Spawning in the Gulf of Mexico, western Atlantic bluefins migrate throughout the North Atlantic. Occasionally, fish caught and tagged have been found to swim from the Bahamas to Norway, from the East Coast of the United States to the Mediterranean, and from Spain to Virginia. Scientists are not sure precisely why they migrate but believe it is because they follow changing food supplies. The bluefin reaches sexual maturity and begins spawning at about eight years old, which is when it enters the giant class. A single female may shed 25 million eggs, only a few of which develop into fish that will survive to maturity. A bluefin's life span is more than twenty years.

For purposes of managing the northern bluefin fishery, the western and eastern Atlantic (including the Mediterranean Sea) are considered separate populations, since the interchange between them is relatively small. Most of the fishing in the western Atlantic occurs off the northeastern United States and eastern Canada. In that area, the population of giant fish was found to have declined to 30,000 in 1990 from 319,000 in 1970, a decline of nearly 90 percent. By 1989, the total bluefin population had declined to 219,000 from more than 1 million in 1970.

The analysis was made by the standing committee on research and statistics of the International Commission for the Conservation of Atlantic Tunas, based in Madrid. The commission is charged with regulating the Atlantic tuna fishery. Its scientific committee, which analyzes data from various member countries, also found in 1990 that the stock of fish under one year old was about as depleted as that of adults. It found, too, that the stock of fish one to five years old had stabilized at about 25 percent of 1970 levels after tighter quotas on the bluefin catch went into effect in 1982, and that the population of fish six to seven years old had rebounded since 1981 to about 50 percent of the 1970 level. The commission has established a ceiling of 2,660 metric tons, some 5,000 to 6,000 individual fish of all sizes, on the annual catch of bluefin from the western Atlantic. The quota is divided among the United States, Canada, and Japan, the three countries whose fishermen operate in the waters. The commission's scientific panel found that in 1989 the total catch was 2,800 metric tons.

The study's finding of a continuing depletion of giant bluefins has been challenged by the East Coast Tuna Association, an organization of commercial tuna fishermen and wholesalers. It says that some of the study's methods were flawed. The part of the study said to be flawed was performed by the Southeast Fisheries Center of the National Marine Fisheries Service in Miami. Dr. Brad Brown, the regional science and research director there, said that the major flaw had been corrected and the study rerun, and that there was no change in the long-range downward trend of the giant bluefins.

The tuna association asserts that its members have been catching an increasing number of "small" giants, those in the range of 310 to 400 pounds, that these fish were spawned in 1982 or 1983, and that they represent the first fruits of the commission's restrictions. They say that this might not be reflected in the commission's study because data on tuna catches, from which population trends are calculated, lag behind the present. Dr. Brown placed the lag at about a year and a half. The commission's assessment "doesn't seem to come close" to reflecting the recovery that commercial fishermen are seeing, said Gerald Abrams, the president and founder of the East Coast Tuna Association.

Roger Hillhouse, who owns an interest in tuna fishing boats operating out of New Bedford, Massachusetts, and who flies a spotter plane looking for fish, says "small" giant bluefins have turned up in abundance off Nova Scotia, where the water is colder. These should migrate southward as the more southerly waters get colder, he said. All parties agree that the study, which is carried out each year, is somewhat inexact and that it could be improved, and the fisheries service and the tuna association have agreed on some ways in which that might be accomplished.

Dr. Safina of the Audubon Society, who is basing his petition to place bluefins on the international endangered list on the commission's study, holds that the study is the best available estimate of what is going on. If the commercial fishermen's group "can convince the scientists that they have overlooked something and the science is revised, we will certainly accept that," said Dr. Safina.

Although parties may argue about the state of the fishery, all agree that it must be preserved. "I'd like to see it regulated while there's something left to regulate and not wait till it goes extinct," said Tommy Edwardes, dockmaster and fish buyer at the Montauk Marine Basin, where many bluefin catches come in. Mr. Edwardes dispatches many of those fish to Tokyo. "I'm not in this for the short haul," he said. "I'd like to be in it for a long time to come."

[WKS, SEPTEMBER 1991]

EXPERTS RACE TO SAVE DWINDLING RHINOS

FOR tens of millions of years, the rhinoceros has rumbled across the world's landscapes. Squat, muscular, thick-legged, and broad-chested, it is the very embodiment of raw animal power. One species, a prehistoric behemoth that stood eighteen feet at the shoulder, ranks as the biggest land mammal ever to live on Earth. And as recently as the last century, millions of rhinos still roamed Asia and Africa. But now, despite strong efforts by conservationists over the last few years, fewer than 11,000 of these powerful animals remain on the planet—the total is down by more than 80 percent in the last two decades—and the number continues to drop. Some scientists fear that none of the five remaining species of rhino is large enough to maintain long-term genetic health. A desperate attempt to reverse the decline is under way, and some experts say the rhino's unfettered days as a creature of the wild may be numbered.

Rhinos are being crowded out of their natural habitats by development and slaughtered for their horns. These trophies fetch thousands of dollars in much of Asia, where they are prized as an ingredient of folk medicines, and in Yemen, where they are made into dagger handles. Consequently, the rhinoceros has reached a point where the only way to rescue it from extinction, say some experts, is to confine it to well-guarded, intensively managed sanctuaries where it can no longer roam over its natural range. Only there, some conservationists argue, can rhino populations be manipulated to preserve both their numbers and the gene pools that will enable them to survive in the long run.

The growing effort to establish these sanctuaries is seen as a last resort now that other attempts to cut the rhino's losses to poachers and habitat destruction have fallen short. The goal is to reintroduce the rhinos to a fully free existence someday. But for now this is considered an uncertain prospect, given escalating human disruption of the landscape.

Is the rhinoceros about to disappear from the wild? "I hope not," said Dr. Oliver Ryder, an expert on the rhino at the Zoological Society of San Diego. "But if we don't take this step, we're going to see the end of the rhino. Full stop." Dr. Ryder, a geneticist at the zoo's Center for the Reproduction of Endangered Species, was the organizer of a conference in San Diego in May 1991 at which scientists and conservationists from around the world gathered to assess the status and future of the rhinoceros.

The outlook is not hopeless. In Asia, vigorous protection measures have enabled the great one-horned, or Indian, rhinoceros to recover slowly from near extinction early in this century to a population of about 2,000 today. Recent studies have found that the gene pool of this species remains healthy, and it is being successfully reintroduced to parts of Nepal from which it had disappeared. Similarly, the white rhinoceros of Africa has been painstakingly brought back from the brink of oblivion. About 4,500 now exist, and it, too, is being reintroduced to its former range.

But poaching and habitat loss continue to chip away at populations of the Indian rhino, according to the World Conservation Union, and a political insurgency in the Indian state of Assam, where most of the Indian rhinos live, has clouded the animal's future. In 1989, insurgents invaded a major sanctuary, killing guards and wresting the sanctuary from government control. "The political instability on the Indian subcontinent doesn't provide a very good long-term prognosis" for the rhinos, said Dr. Thomas Foose, an expert on the breed who heads the captive breeding specialist group of the World Conservation Union. The same is true in Nepal, he said, where a democracy movement confronts the monarchy, and also in South Africa, where much of the white rhino population lives.

Political instability is just one of a number of possible threats, including epidemics and natural disasters, that could wreak havoc on populations that even in the case of the white rhino remain small, Dr. Foose said. A catastrophe of any kind could mean a giant, possibly irreversible, step toward extinction. The other three rhino species, the Javan, the Sumatran, and the African black rhino, are already staring extinction in the face. Scientists place the population of black rhinos at 3,000 to 3,500, down from about 3,800 in 1987; of the Sumatran, or hairy, rhinoceros, at about 700, and of the Javan rhino—the rarest large mammal in the world—at fewer than 60. For these three species "it is the last stand," said Dr. Eric Dinerstein, a rhinoceros specialist at the World Wildlife Fund. Globally, says Dr. Foose, "the general trend is downward; right now it's a very desperate situation." All five species have been declared endangered under an international convention barring trade in rhino horns.

The rhinoceros dates back 60 million years. Starting out as a small, three-toed relative of the early horse and looking much the same, it evolved into hundreds of species and forms. It first appeared in North America and made its way eventually to Asia and Africa. It reached something of a zenith about 35 million years ago with the appearance of the indricotherium, also called the baluchitherium, largest of all mammals. This hornless rhino weighed nearly five times as much as the biggest known elephant and could browse among tree branches twenty-five feet above the ground.

Its modern descendants, the largest of which are about a third as tall as the indricotherium, are second in size only to the elephant among today's land animals. The rhino is solid muscle, and its armored appearance brings to mind the image of a tank; its irresistible charge, the image of a locomotive. It can run as fast as a horse, about thirty-five miles an hour, and like the horse, the rhino is a vegetarian. The distinctive horn of the modern rhino is made up of thousands of tiny strands of keratin, the substance of which human fingernails are composed. Rhinos can grow a second horn if one is lost, and they use the horn to plow up ground while foraging and as a weapon.

They live relatively long lives—about forty years in the case of the African rhinos—which means that any genetic deterioration would take place relatively slowly. That is a conservation plus. But they have relatively few offspring—one every two or three years for the African rhinos, at most—which means that it takes a long time to rebuild populations once they are depleted.

In Asia, the population of Indian rhinos was sharply reduced by sport hunters in the nineteenth century. Overhunting, combined with habitat destruction caused by agricultural expansion, originally brought the Indian, Javan, and Sumatran rhinos low, and in recent years both habitat destruction and poaching have maintained the pressure.

Rhino hunting in Africa, like elephant hunting, was strictly licensed and controlled by colonial administrators, but rhinos were extensively eradicated to make way for human settlement and farms. Estimated conservatively, there were 2 to 3 million black rhinos in Africa at the turn of the century, said Dr. David Western, a Nairobi-based expert on both the rhino and elephant for Wildlife Conservation International, an arm of the New York Zoological Society.

Poaching in search of the valuable horn is the main cause of the black rhino's most recent decline. Twenty years ago, there were an estimated 60,000 to 70,000 black rhinos; as recently as 1980, there were 15,000. Today their numbers are so few, said Dr. Western, that the loss of only 400 to 500 animals a year would more than offset births and continue to drive the population down. Trading in rhino horn has been banned internationally since the 1970s, but it continues nonetheless. Unlike elephant ivory, Dr. Western said, rhino horns are very easy to smuggle, and the market is "extremely diffuse," making it hard to halt the continuing trade.

A worldwide ban on trading in elephant ivory has been in effect since late 1989, and it has been credited with largely shutting off the trade. That is an effective strategy, said Dr. Western, since about 600,000 African elephants remain. But with so few black rhinos, even a trickle of illegally traded horns can have a major impact on their population. The result is that black rhino populations have declined by 98 percent in parts of East Africa in the last fifteen years. Efforts to combat poachers throughout the black rhino's natural range have proved frustrating, said Dr. Ryder, because the available antipoaching forces are spread so thinly over the animals' vast territory.

The emerging new strategy, in both Africa and Asia, is to sequester the rhinos in small defensible sanctuaries. A similar strategy has enabled the North American bison to rebound from a few hundred in the late nineteenth century to an estimated 75,000 today. Black rhinos are being moved into sanctuaries throughout Africa, and there are already signs that where the approach has been tried, it is having an effect.

In Kenya, for instance, about two thirds of the black rhinos are living under intense surveillance in sanctuaries, some of them fenced and some not. As a result, said Dr. Western, the Kenyan population bottomed out at about 400 and is now increasing by about 20 animals a year. Across Africa, he says, "I think we've got a little bit further to go. But the slowdown in the decline is very significant, and I think that within the next five years we should see a turnaround in numbers, provided the sanctuary approach continues to get the attention."

But Dr. Ryder and Dr. Foose say that simply protecting the rhinos in sanctuaries is not enough to ensure long-term health for the five species. "It is a necessary step to stop the decline in numbers, but the populations are really going to have to be managed," said Dr. Ryder. Because the rhino populations are so fragmented and small, he said, human intervention is necessary to maintain their genetic viability over the long term. He and Dr. Foose say it will be necessary for humans periodically to transfer animals from one sanctuary to another for breeding purposes, to make sure that significant deterioration of the rhino gene pool does not take place.

Genetic deterioration can take the form of inbreeding, for instance. Or it might result in a small, sequestered population when a small number of males dominates all the others, blocking the transmission of the other males' genes to future generations. Genetic deterioration poses a separate threat, apart from poaching and habitat loss, to the rhinos' future.

To combat this, a number of scientists advocate transplanting the techniques of captive breeding programs to the sanctuaries, turning them into what Dr. Foose calls mega-zoos. Just as zoos are becoming more like nature, he said, so should the wild sanctuaries become more artificial. This is especially required, Dr. Foose argues, because surveys of each of the five rhino species suggest that none of them is numerous enough to constitute what conservation biologists call a "minimum viable population." Dr. Foose has calculated, for example, that 2,000 rhinos may be required to maintain the gene pool for any one species or subspecies. Since there are at least four subspecies of black rhino, he says, a population of 8,000 may be required.

How long will this kind of management be required? As long as human population growth and development continue to disrupt the ecosystems where rhinos live, some conservationists say. It may still be possible for rhinos sequestered in sanctuaries to live somewhat as they would in nature if humans had never entered the picture. "But as far as being far-ranging and completely unfettered by man," said Dr. Ryder, "that's completely unrealistic at this time."

[WKS, MAY 1991]

RHINO NEAR LAST STAND
IN THE AFRICAN WILD

EXTENSIVE poaching among the largest remaining population of the black rhinoceros in Africa has pushed the species close to extinction in the wild, biologists and game wardens here say. More than half the remaining black rhinoceroses in Africa, members of one of the continent's most endangered species, are in large sanctuaries, protected by fences and guards. Those that are left in the wilderness, mostly here in the dense scrub along the Zambesi Valley in Kariba, Zimbabwe, may not last another two years, a wildlife expert said. "The black rhinoceros is on the brink of collapse in Africa," said the expert, Glen Tathum, the chief warden for operations in the Zimbabwe national parks department. "Two years from now, we'll have them on farms and sanctuaries but not in the wild. And they'll be threatened there."

How many of the bulky, nearsighted black rhinos are left in Africa is uncertain, but it appears to be far fewer than the 3,000 usually mentioned. This is because wildlife officials had said earlier this year that Zimbabwe held nearly 2,000, though only 150 in sanctuaries. Mr. Tathum says the actual number in Zimbabwe was probably between 400 and 1,000. David Pitman, the chairman of the Zambesi Society, a group dedicated to biological diversity in the Zambesi Valley along the Zimbabwe-Zambia border and author of a recent book, *Rhinos: Past, Present—and Future?* comments, "I'd be very surprised if 2,000 black rhinoceros are left on the continent."

The black rhinoceros population, 65,000 in 1976, was slashed to 10,000 in the course of several years by poachers in pursuit of the animal's two skyward-arcing horns. The horn fetches tens of thousands of dollars on the black markets of Asia, where it is reputed to have medicinal powers, particularly in enhancing male sexual potency. In Yemen, the horn—which consists of densely packed hair with keratin, somewhat like a human fingernail—is coveted for ornate dagger handles.

The classification of the rhinoceros as endangered by the Convention on International Trade in Endangered Species in the early 1980s appears to have done little to halt the trade, experts say. Indeed, here in Zimbabwe the poachers appear to be making a last dash for the horn while it is still available. In the last six months, 60 rhinos are known to have been slaughtered. But because of the solitary habits of the black rhino and the density of the bush, no one knows how many more may have been shot. In the Matusadona National Park in northwest Zimbabwe, there were thought to be 150 rhinos in January 1992. In June, only 15 could be found.

In a last-ditch effort to try to save the rhinoceros from the poachers, the Zimbabwean parks department started dehorning some of the animals last year, a procedure pioneered in Namibia three years ago. The idea of dehorning had initially been rejected in Zimbabwe because the rhinoceros uses the horn in mating, in defending itself against other animals, and in browsing. In addition, the horn grows back at about several inches a year, making the dehorned rhino a worthwhile poaching target in a relatively short time, the Namibia experiment has shown.

The operation is not simple, and for a poor country like Zimbabwe, not cheap. A marksman shooting from a helicopter first tranquilizes the rhino. Then workers saw off the two horns and file down the base. That horn, along with two and half tons seized from poachers over the years, is kept under guard in a government storehouse, Zimbabwean officials said. But poachers armed with AK-47 assault rifles are shooting even the dehorned animals. Mr. Tathum said he believed these animals were killed by mistake, although other conservations, like Mr. Pitman, say the slaughter may be out of spite.

Despite the depredations of poachers, Zimbabwe has clung to the idea of keeping rhinos in the wild and resisted following the example of South Africa and Kenya, which have put most of their rhino population in sanctuaries. South Africa says it has about 700 black rhinos, the vast majority in protected areas. Esmund Bradley Martin, a consultant to the World Wildlife Fund and a leading expert on rhinos in

Africa, estimates that there are 410 rhinos in Kenya today and said the low point was 330 in 1986. Zimbabwe itself has moved a few rhinos to sanctuaries and about 50 have been moved out of the country, to zoos and sanctuaries in Texas and Australia for safekeeping in captive breeding programs.

But, Mr. Tathum said, Zimbabwe's preference for rhinoceros in the wild may have become unrealistic. He warned that Zimbabwe may one day share the situation of Zambia, where perhaps 50 black rhinos remain; Zambia's last two white rhinoceroses were killed in the zoo in the town of Livingstone in 1986. "The situation has become so grave that unless we have a very big international effort, it's over," Mr. Tathum said. He favors United Nations pressure on the Zambian government to prosecute poachers and middlemen and perhaps changes in Zimbabwe's extradition rights if the Zambian government won't prosecute them. His antipoaching unit is undermanned and underfinanced in its battle with bush-wise gangs of poachers who walk over the border from Zambia, slaughter the animals, hack off the horn, and return home. The horn is usually flown out of the Zambian capital, Lusaka, to Asia or Europe, Mr. Tathum said. Mr. Pitman said he believed the Zambian poachers were getting more help than usual from Zimbabwean farmers, who were suffering the effects of a drought.

The black rhinoceros once ranged throughout the African sa-vanna, avoiding only the equatorial forests and the most arid desert. Another species, the white rhinoceros, has always kept to southern Africa and a belt north of the equatorial forests in Zaire. Despite their names, both the African species are gray. The name "white" is believed to have arisen from a mistranslation of the Boer word "wijde," or wide, a reference to the broad square lips that contrast to the nar-rower, more pointed lips of the black rhinoceros. Both the black and the white species are very large animals: the black can measure more than four and a half feet at the shoulder and can weigh as much as 3,000 pounds; the white rhinoceros measures about five and a half feet and weighs 5,000 pounds. The white rhinoceros, in contrast to the more solitary black, lives in small groups on the open plains.

The white rhinos are not as threatened as the black because the former were placed in sanctuaries after facing near extinction in the 1920s, said Dr. David Western, a zoologist and head of Wildlife Con-servation International, a division of the New York Zoological Society. The rescue of the white rhinoceros provides a good argument for a similar method to be used with the black species, he added. "There were less than 100 white rhinoceros in the 1920s, all of them in South Africa," Dr. Western said. "Now there are more than 5,000. By the 1950s, for example, they were increasing by 10 percent a year."

Kenya has gingerly started to build back its black rhinoceros population. Twenty years ago, there were 20,000 rhinos in Kenya; it went down to 330 in 1986, and today there are nearly 500. In the late 1950s, there were no rhinos in Nairobi National Park, but after reintroduction in the early 1970s, the population had climbed to 61 and the park was able to provide rhinoceroses to other sanctuaries, Dr. Western said. The big danger in Zimbabwe, Dr. Western said, is that the numbers in the wild will become so small that the chances of a male and female meeting and mating would dwindle. It is also possible, he said, that a few males would continue to impregnate the same females and genetic inbreeding would develop. "If you don't have a high density of animals, you begin to lose genetic viability," Dr. Western said.   [JP, JULY 1992]

TO CONSERVE OR CATALOG
RARE SPECIES

WHEN Edmund Smith saw a nondescript black-and-white bird that he couldn't recognize flying over the hood of his car in central Somalia, he had little idea that he had caught a glimpse of the Bulo Burti boubou, an extremely rare species of shrike previously unknown to Western science. Working with Mr. Smith, a biologist, researchers in Somalia quickly captured the bird, still the only known example of the new species. But when they did, they found themselves in an ethical quandary becoming more and more common among biologists: to kill or not to kill.

Scientists out discovering new species have a long history of dutifully shooting, poisoning, drowning, crushing, or otherwise doing in their finds to preserve them for future reference and study. The team of biologists who discovered the boubou (pronounced BOO-boo) bucked over 200 years of tradition. Instead of preserving their only specimen as skin and skeleton, they kept it captive for a year, then returned it to the wild, hoping it would help propagate its presumably beleaguered species. When the robin-sized bird flew off, it left behind a handful of feathers, some photographs, a few blood samples, and an intense dispute about whether a very rare animal is more valuable dead or alive.

When a species is discovered, biologists normally choose one individual, the "type," as the standard that determines whether any other individual belongs to that species or to another. Because it was the only one they had, biologists chose the boubou as its species type. To systematists, biologists who specialize in discovering, naming, and understanding the evolutionary relationships of species, the idea of letting the boubou type fly off was almost criminal.

The description of the new species was first published last year in *Ibis*, an ornithological journal, and was written about in a recent issue of *Trends in Ecology and Evolution*, a news magazine for scientists. The lone shrike has since engendered strong feelings and harsh words both in letters to journals and in conversations among biologists. While preservation-minded biologists have praised the release of the bird, others, especially museum systematists, call it shortsighted and overly sentimental.

As species after species approaches the brink of extinction, this choice has become more common and more pressing. Many new species are so rare that if biologists collect and kill even a single animal, they fear that they could actually push the species into extinction. But other researchers contend that if scientists do not keep and kill their find, there will be nothing left with which to study the species but the fragmentary information and material that can be gleaned from a quick look at the live animal. Besides, they say, any species so close to extinction is doomed anyway. Dr. Nigel Collar, research fellow at the International Council for Bird Preservation in Cambridge, England, was the conservationist who strongly advised the biologists in Somalia to release the boubou. "I have no concern at all, absolutely no concern at all it was the right thing to do," he said. "It was totally and absolutely the right thing to do. We cannot possibly, as conservationists, advocate the collection and killing of a species right at the edge of extinction. That's not what we're in business for. One obviously feels sorry for some systematists that they don't have as much information as they might want."

But systematists like Dr. Storrs L. Olson, curator of birds at the National Museum of Natural History at the Smithsonian Institution in Washington, reject the notion that taking one bird from a species could be enough to tip the scales from survival to extinction. He called this view pseudoconservation. "It's sentimentality getting in the way of good science," he said. "It's not rational. It's not logical." Most systematists say the release of a bird that defines a new species is a serious mistake. "We have standards," Dr. Olson said. "There's a reason for the standards." And for systematists, unlike conservationists, studying an extinct bird, even a fossil bird, can be just as instructive as studying a living species. Dr. Scott Lanyon, head of the division of birds at the Field Museum of Natural History in Chicago, said that it was time for systematists to take a stand. "If we don't respond to this kind of action, then others will feel that it's all right," he said. "This is a step backwards. There's a misconception out there that the birds are thoroughly known. There are lots of field guides out there based on museum specimens. Now people are asking, 'Since we've got the field guides, why do we need the specimen?' There've even been suggestions that once you've figured out what you want to know from specimens, why not just trash them? There's no way you can know today what you'll need to know about an animal a hundred years from now."

Dr. Richard Banks, a bird systematist with the United States Fish and Wildlife Service, says the trend away from traditional preservation is growing. "There were two or three instances within the last several years of people publishing photographs of birds, describing new subspecies, with nothing to serve as a specimen," he said. "I think that it's bad business, bad science. It's not science at all to describe a species on the basis that they did and without anything to serve as a type specimen."

In the case of the boubou, much is unknown and may remain so. The scientists were not even able to determine whether their bird was male or female. Unfortunately, most of the information biologists want cannot be gleaned from photographs or blood samples. Biologists interested in comparing the bird's bones with fossil skeletons, measuring its gut length, or studying the details of the patterning of its feathers—the list could go on and on—are out of luck.

Even apart from this dispute, this bird has from the start seemed unable to avoid drama. After capturing the boubou, biologists videotaped, photographed, tape-recorded, and took a blood sample from the bird. But the blood sample was lost through an airline baggage mix-up while en route from Somalia to the biologists in Europe who could have analyzed it. Civil war in Somalia forced the caretaker of the lone shrike back to Europe, taking the bird with him to Germany. When it was returned to Somalia more than a year later, the shrike could not go to the place biologists suspected it called home; they left it instead in the Balcad Nature Reserve, safer from the war than the shrubs around the Bulo Burti hospital grounds, where it had been found.

Eventually one of the boubou's genes was analyzed with DNA from feathers that were preserved in alcohol. And more blood for future analysis was taken from the bird and preserved. When the DNA data were analyzed and compared with the segment of DNA from other shrikes, the results confirmed what biologists strongly suspected when they first saw the bird: the Somalian shrike was different enough from the other known shrikes to be considered a new species. The biologists named the bird *Laniarius liberatus* "to emphasize that the bird is described on the basis of a freed individual," they said in the *Ibis* article.

Dr. Lanyon said of the biologists: "I realize that these people see themselves as heroes. But that bird is almost certainly dead now anyway. If that bird is from the area that they captured it in, why would you ever want to put it out somewhere else? The best chance of having it find a mate, especially if it's so rare, is putting it back where you found it. This is supposed to be about species conservation, not individual conservation."

To a population biologist, says Dr. Lanyon, the idea that a casual observer could see the last of a species or even one of the last of a species is unlikely at best. Most species of small birds and mammals are not limited in their numbers by their abilities to reproduce or to find a mate but by the amount of habitat available to them, he said. These animals typically produce too many offspring to be supported by the environment, and removal of one or a few individuals should not affect the fate of these species in the slightest, he said.

Dr. Jared Diamond, a research associate in the bird department at the American Museum of Natural History, said this logic was flawed. "If the thing is in trouble, it's in trouble," he said. "But it would be absurd to say that everything in trouble is doomed." Dr. Diamond said that some species had grown back to strength from very few individuals. "The famous cases that come immediately to mind," he said, "are the Chatham Island black robin, in the New Zealand region, that came back from seven individuals, of which two were females and five were males. There was a breeding program launched, and it's now back up to one hundred. And the Mauritius kestrel, I believe, came back from one or two pairs. No conservationist is willing to give up on a species."

The dispute over whether to kill or to let live extends to other animals as well. It recently flared over an endangered shrew after two specimens were killed and kept. The discoverers had named the shrew *Crocidura desperata*, "to point out the desperate situation of the new species." "The days of shooting everything in sight as a means of identification are long past," said Dr. Charles Walcott, executive director of the Cornell Laboratory of Ornithology. "And if you'd got the last ivory billed woodpecker, you'd feel rather awful about collecting it. I think you're caught between a rock and a hard place, and these situations are only going to get more common."

[CKY, APRIL 1992]

PLIGHT OF THE SEA TURTLE

E VERY spring, the sea turtles begin returning to the beaches of Florida to lay their eggs. It is a treacherous journey. Shrimpers' trawls drown them, lights on ship and shore confuse them, and dredging equipment routinely grinds them up. But a more intractable problem awaits the females lucky enough to make it to shore: in many places, erosion has left them with no place to dig a good nest.

Conservationists, oceanfront communities, and state officials say they want to help the turtles, but they cannot agree on how. Every time someone proposes a remedy, someone else is quick to explain how it will only make things worse. Because the possible solutions involve access to the beach, a crucial part of Florida's lucrative tourism industry, the arguments are bitter. And because all sea turtles in the United States are either endangered or threatened, the stakes are high, particularly for loggerhead sea turtles, since 90 percent of the loggerheads in the Western Hemisphere nest in Florida. No one knows exactly how many loggerheads remain, but over all the number of nesting females is declining, experts say. The controversy centers on beach nourishment, a method of restoring an eroded beach by dredging sand from the ocean floor and pumping it onshore as a slurry. Many famous beaches, including Miami Beach, are maintained this way.

Short of requiring the turtles to bring their own sand, advocates say, renourishment is the only way to save them. But the National Research Council reported in 1991 that beach renourishment could result in "significant reductions in nesting success." The sand on renourished beaches is so tightly compacted that it is difficult for turtles to nest in it, the report said. Further, when the renourished beaches erode, they often form sharp scarps that the 250-pound turtles cannot climb over. Nourishment itself can destroy nests or leave them buried under so much sand that hatchlings never make it to the daylight. So the state has proposed banning renourishment for up to eight months a year to give the turtles time to nest and the eggs time to hatch. The proposal has provoked outrage among those who make their living in replenishment and those who rely on it to maintain their beaches. Dredgers say they will not be able to renourish beaches in the winter months, when it will be allowed. In winter's heavy weather the work is far more dangerous, they say, and so expensive that most projects will never be done, leaving the turtles with less and less beach each year. Dredging and nesting can coexist, they say, if workers survey the beaches closely early each morning in nesting season, follow the trails of the nesting females, retrieve their eggs, and incubate them on protected beaches or in hatcheries.

But conservationists who work with other kinds of turtles say they are not persuaded that hatchery-born turtles can survive and reproduce in the wild. They say it is better to let the turtles take their chances with the beaches that remain. The Florida Shore and Beach Preservation Association attempted to resolve the dispute at a conference in St. Petersburg in February 1992. The scores of government officials, dredgers, coastal engineers, geologists, and biologists who attended could hardly agree on anything, except that fewer and fewer turtles return to nest each year.

In part the problem arises from the strict standards the turtles must meet as they lumber out of the surf in the darkness of a warm spring night and look for a spot to scrape out their nests. Below the high water line, the eggs will be flooded; if the eggs are laid too close to the dunes, raccoons, crabs, ants, and other predators will make a meal of them. "Eroded and eroding beaches present one of the greatest long-term threats to the sea turtles," says Richard H. Spadoni of Coastal Planning and Engineering, a concern in Boca Raton, Florida, who advocates nourishment. On one stretch of beach, he said, nest density rose from 90 per mile to almost 900 per mile after the beach was renourished.

But another speaker at the conference, Dr. Peter C. H. Pritchard, vice president of the Florida Audubon Society, said his research had left him doubtful that renourishment projects would help the turtles, especially if they involved moving turtle eggs. He cited the Kemp's ridley turtle, a species that nests almost exclusively at a small portion of the Gulf Coast of Mexico, about 250 miles south of Brownsville, Texas. In the 1940s, he said, at least 40,000 nesting females could be found on the beach on one day. Today there are probably only 600 females left and conservationists try to retrieve all their eggs for raising in hatcheries.

After almost three decades of this, he said, "the recovery of the species has been negligible." The most likely—and alarming—explanation is that hatcheries are somehow turning out imperfect turtles that cannot compete and reproduce in the wild. But he added, "The effects of hatcheries and renourished beaches on turtles are unknown." He said, for example, that scientists discovered only about ten years ago that the sex of a baby turtle was determined by the temperature of its nest and that small differences could alter the ratio of females to males.

Randall W. Parkinson, a geologist at the Florida Institute of Technology, told the conference that a two-year project monitoring replenished and natural beaches at Sebastian Inlet, Florida, found no appreciable difference in nesting and hatching rates. Either the effects of renourishment were not significant, the study said, or they were not detectable in the time frame of the study. For example, scientists do not know exactly how long sea turtles live in the wild, or when they begin reproducing, so some problems might not immediately appear. "We are so ignorant of sea turtle population dynamics," Dr. Pritchard said. [CD, MARCH 1992]

GIANT CLAMS HELPED TO NEW HOME

THE Australian Navy has stepped in to help the giant clam, an endangered species that has been driven to extinction in waters off many South Pacific islands and heavily fished on the Great Barrier Reef by poachers. Over a three-day period in April 1993, a heavy landing craft, the *Tarakan*, was used to transfer 3,000 clams weighing a total of more than twenty tons from experimental beds off Orpheus Island, where they had been artificially bred by marine biologists, to an undisclosed location on the outer Great Barrier Reef.

John Lucas, a professor of zoology at James Cook University at Townsville, who coordinated the research on the artificial breeding of the giant clam, *Tridacna gigas*, said the operation was believed to be one of the biggest relocations of marine organisms in quantity and weight. Eighteen divers from the *Tarakan* and the Great Barrier Reef Marine Park Authority retrieved clams at high tide from a seabed about 100 yards from the shore of Pioneer Bay and lifted the mollusks, some measuring two feet across and weighing 40 pounds, into dinghies powered by outboards. As each dinghy was loaded with ten to twenty clams, depending on their size, it returned to the *Tarakan*, anchored half a mile away. The bivalves were gently unloaded by hand, placed in two-foot plastic tanks filled with seawater, and then covered with shade cloth to minimize stress.

White buoys marked a rectangular area of about 200 square yards where the divers, wearing thick gloves for protection from coral, collected the clustered clams. One diver, Mike Bugler, a project officer with the park authority, said some of the mollusks were up to seven years old. "The water is clear and ideal for diving, but the bigger and heavier clams can be difficult to grasp on the seabed and then bring to the surface," Mr. Bugler said. With daytime temperatures in Pioneer Bay averaging above 90 degrees, the Navy began lifting the giant clams out of the water about an hour after sunrise to avoid stress to the mollusks during the hottest part of the day, and they were in the tanks aboard the *Tarakan* within thirty minutes of being lifted from the seabed. After three hours, with 2,000 clams resting in more than thirty tanks, the *Tarakan*'s crew erected an aerial spray eight feet above the deck to deliver a fine mist of seawater to an area normally crowded with army tanks, trucks, and military equipment.

Tridacna gigas, prized by poachers for its shell and the high level of protein in the meat of its adductor muscle, is listed by the International Union for Conservation of Nature as an endangered species. To protect the clams and allow them to reproduce undisturbed, the place on the Great Barrier Reef where they were moved was not disclosed, but Lt. Rick Watson of the Navy, who commanded the *Tarakan*, said it was several hours' sailing time from Pioneer Bay. An estimated 12,000 of the artificially bred mollusks remain in the experimental beds off Orpheus Island, fifty miles north of Townsville on the north Queensland coast.

The relocated clams will assist research on population outbreaks of the crown-of-thorns starfish, known for its destructive grazing of reefs. Recent satellite studies of reefs and currents, and other modeling of dispersal of starfish larvae, have indicated possible "source" and "sink" reefs, with currents from the source reefs tending to carry the larvae from released populations to the sink reefs. "The clams are being used to test this by loading some source reefs with these groups of genetically related clams from the same stock," Professor Lucas said. "If the source and sink hypothesis is true, then on the sink reefs we may see increased recruitment of juvenile clams which are shown to be genetically related to the parent stock."

James Cook University is helping the South Pacific island countries of Fiji, Tonga, and Cook Islands to develop their own clam farms. It is supplying one-year-old clams grown at hatcheries on Orpheus Island, and villagers can harvest the clams when they grow to maturity over three to four years. "The first two years are the most difficult, as growth is fairly slow, and the islanders are going to need encouragement during those early years, but a reliable estimate of yield at about five years old is eight tons of clam meat per acre per year," Mr. Lucas said. At four to five years old, about 32,000 giant clams can be farmed in one acre of clear, warm, offshore tidal waters, enabling Pacific Islanders to preserve their clam resources, and at the same time farm the mollusks for a food source.

The project has advanced mariculture methods significantly with the development of a simple technology for large-scale marine culture methods in five phases: spawning, hatchery, nursery, ocean nursery, and growth to maturity. The bivalves are hermaphrodites, containing both male and female sex organs, or gonads, and they usually spawn into the seawater during the summer months, with some spawning up to a billion eggs. "It is one of the most fecund animals in the world, and yet it is never naturally abundant," Mr. Lucas said. "It is a real mystery why *Tridacna gigas* spends so much energy and effort on reproduction and then has so few progeny." The oldest giant clam, weighing more than half a ton, was found on a reef near Townsville, and sectioning of the shell established it at sixty-three years old.

[NB, APRIL 1993]

THE VIOLENT WORLD OF CORAL

D ENSELY abloom with a wealth of life unsurpassed for bizarre beauty, coral reefs seem to exist in a state of dreamy tranquillity. Not so. The reef is in truth a realm of violent struggle and constant disruption. Coral colonies wage unrelenting chemical warfare on each other, their polyps stinging, dissolving, and poisoning each other. Bigger reef creatures savage large chunks of colonies and fill the water with toxins. Sooner or later, an irresistible force like a hurricane or a change in sea level lays waste the whole teeming ecosystem and the corals must rebuild. But rebuild they do, and this resilience is at the heart of a dispute among marine biologists over the contribution of human activity to the stresses on coral ecosystems.

One school of thought holds that corals worldwide are now in serious peril because of human assaults like global warming, overfishing, pollution, and physical destruction of reefs by fishermen and tourists. An opposing school holds that while some reefs are indeed in big trouble, many others remain pristine, and even the damaged ones have adapted in the past to natural forces at least as destructive as human activity.

Any serious threat to corals would be an ecological tragedy. The biological diversity of coral reefs compares with that of tropical forests. Reefs themselves, built from the calcified skeletons of polyps, are the largest structures created by life. The many strange toxins evolved by reef denizens for their biological warfare hold considerable promise as treatments for various human diseases. For all these reasons, there has been a heightening of scientific interest in corals of late, including an outpouring of research on coral ecology and chemistry.

Coral colonies, each composed of innumerable tiny, tentacled polyps, take the forms of trees, shrubs, fans, plates, and huge boulders. The phantasmagoria of shapes creates a habitat for other marine creatures like fish, lobsters, sponges, mollusks, octopuses, and sea anemones. Competition with no quarter given is the rule in this interdependent but mutually hostile world. When polyps in one colony come face to face with another in a constant competition for scarce space, they expand their bodies to engulf their rivals and exude digestive juices that turn the competitors to jelly. As a countermeasure, polyps in the second colony grow "sweeper tentacles" studded with special stinging organelles that "zap the neighbors," says Dr. Judith Lang, a reef ecologist at the Texas Memorial Museum at the University of Texas. Still other polyps enshroud their enemies in a sticky mucus that dissolves the tissues. Combat with toxins is also thought to be a common mode of warfare, though the toxins have proved hard to pin down in actual use.

Coral reefs may be one of the most naturally poisonous environments on earth. One study found that 73 percent of 429 species of exposed invertebrates commonly occurring on Australia's Great Barrier Reef were toxic to fish. Although much remains unknown about how the toxins are used, they have "tremendous potential" as pharmaceuticals, said Dr. Drew Harvell, a coral reef ecologist at Cornell University. For example, Dr. Harvell said, some toxins produced by soft corals "are anti-inflammatory agents, some have potential as being effective against AIDS, and some as anticancer drugs, and that's just one class of organisms."

Because of this great potential, the reefs have recently become prime prospecting grounds. Many potentially useful compounds have been discovered and are now undergoing further testing, said Dr. David J. Newman, a chemist in the National Cancer Institute's Natural Products Branch. The center has been collecting about 1,000 samples of coral-reef organisms a year for the last five years. The prospecting effort is still young; the journey to market for any drug derived from natural sources typically takes five to fifteen years.

In nature, the coral toxins may play an indirect but key role in the reef ecosystems' resilience in the face of disturbance. Dr. Robert

Endean and Dr. Ann Cameron of the University of Queensland in Australia, who have long studied the Great Barrier Reef, postulate that extensive boulderlike coral colonies have been able to exist continuously for hundreds and even thousands of years because they are so successful in using toxins to ward off predators. Because the shape and mass of these long-lived "persister" colonies protect them from the storms that devastate more fragile corals, Dr. Endean theorizes, they form the staunch backbone of the reef ecosystem. They must be protected from destruction by humans at all costs, he warns.

Scientists generally agree that humans are putting serious stress on at least some coral reefs. Sediment from dredging and agricultural runoff, sewage, chemical pollution, dynamiting of reefs by fishermen, damage from boat anchors and scuba divers, shell collecting, mining of reefs for calcium deposits, and overfishing that shatters ecological checks and balances all play a role. "I don't know how to state it in strong enough terms," Dr. Harvell said of the destruction. There has been especially widespread degradation in the Philippines and other Southeast Asian waters. "It's not just that there aren't any fish on these reefs," Dr. Harvell said. "That's bad enough, but there aren't any corals on many. You don't want to panic everybody that the world is falling apart, but some places are."

There is disagreement about the extent of the degradation, about the ability of the reefs to withstand human-induced stress, and about whether some of the damage is caused by humans at all. Some scientists contend that the threat is global. But "very few people have looked at reefs all over the world and have the big picture," said Dr. Richard Grigg of the University of Hawaii, who edits *The Journal of Coral Reefs*. Although it is true that the human impact has been heavy in Southeast Asian and Caribbean waters, he said, reefs in wide areas of the Pacific remain pristine. "There is no one answer," he said. "You have to look at it case by case."

Some threats seem more general, but there is doubt as to whether humans are responsible. In recent years, corals in several parts of the world have turned white and died. Coral polyps are largely nourished by carbon compounds produced by algae in their cells. The algae also give the polyps their brilliant colors. Some scientists testified before Congress that because the algae die when the water gets too warm, human-induced global warming was a likely cause of the bleaching. But many other scientists say that although warmer water does cause coral bleaching, it is too soon to tell whether the oceans are warming as a result of waste industrial gases that trap heat in the atmosphere. The warmer water, they say, could be a natural phenomenon.

Some scientists also say human activity is to blame for widespread damage to corals by a population explosion of the highly predatory crown-of-thorns starfish. The starfish's own natural predators were decimated by overfishing, it is contended. Other scientists, noting that the starfish population is just as out of control on pristine Pacific reefs, argue that natural fluctuations in animal populations are at work.

But since some human-induced damage is indisputable, does it portend disaster? One body of thought, with which Dr. Endean has been associated, sees reef ecosystems as being so delicately adjusted to natural conditions that disturbance by humans could impoverish them indefinitely. An opposing view says that far from being in fine balance, reefs are always recovering from some natural disturbance or other, and that there is little effective difference between natural disruptions and those caused by humans. "Nature can be and often is more perverse than man," Dr. Grigg said.

For example, in 1980 Hurricane Allen smashed vast stretches of treelike staghorn corals in the Caribbean, causing a total collapse of this formerly dominant ecosystem element along the north coast of Jamaica. And at the end of the last ice age, most of the world's corals died when rapidly rising seawaters shut out the sunlight on which their life-giving algae depend. Most of today's reef ecosystems developed after that. The oldest are about 8,000 years old.

The question of coral reefs' hardiness depends on what time scale is considered, said Dr. Jeremy B. C. Jackson, a senior scientist and coral reef ecologist at the Smithsonian Tropical Research Institute in Panama. Corals are among the most ancient of animals. On the longest scale, they have also been among the most fragile; living reefs have disappeared from the planet entirely as part of more general extinctions of life in the remote past. But for the last million years, despite temporary setbacks like the one at the end of the last ice age, they have generally been remarkably stable. On the scale of a human lifetime, Dr. Jackson said, it may look as if "the sky is falling, and in some cases with good reason." That is, he said, if a hotel owner in Grand Cayman or Jamaica suddenly finds that the coral reefs that attract tourists have become trash, things look pretty bad and unstable. From this viewpoint, and that of other people who have much to lose from reef destruction, scientists on all sides of the question say that what humans are doing to the reefs is serious. The longer the stress continues, the longer natural recovery is delayed.

But Dr. Grigg, no adherent of doomsday thinking, posed this question: "How many corals are extinct from either natural or human-induced changes in the last couple of hundred years?" And then he answered: zero. Even so, he said, a new coral-reef doomsday is not unthinkable. Although corals over the last several million years have survived "all manner of catastrophes," including meteor and comet impacts and some twenty ice ages, he recently wrote, this proof of robustness "may hold little consolation" in the face of a vast and rapid expansion of human population. Unless the expansion is reined in, both corals and people themselves could be threatened; and that, he wrote, may be the real truth spoken by the reefs.

[WKS, FEBRUARY 1993]

COASTAL FISHERIES ARE FISHED OUT

FISH are disappearing at an alarming rate in United States coastal waters, and nearly one third of all species have declined in population in the last fifteen years, researchers say. In separate reports in 1991, a Massachusetts agency and two national environmental groups reached the same conclusion about the fish population off the coast: unless the National Marine Fisheries Service imposes stricter conservation measures and fishing regulations, many fish species may decline or be wiped out in the next decade.

"The plundering of our coastal waters has imperiled most fish species," said Amos S. Eno, director of conservation programs for the National Fish and Wildlife Foundation, a nonprofit conservation group in Washington, which recently issued a report on the management policies of the federal agency. From haddock and flounder off Georges Bank in New England to Spanish mackerel off the Gulf of Mexico to striped bass off California, many fish species are threatened by overfishing and an advancing tide of pollutants and urban development on the coastline that have degraded habitats and wetlands, which fish use as spawning and migrating grounds.

The National Marine Fisheries Service, which controls and regulates 2.2 million miles of coastal waters, says it is taking steps to control fish depletion, including tougher restrictions on net sizes and quotas. "The bottom line is that there is a strong recognition that fish depletion has become a dire situation," said Roddy Moscoso, a spokesman for the agency. "The traditional belief that the fisheries are open to anyone with a boat does not work."

Scientists say that a change in the population of any one species of fish, particularly those at the top of the food chain, could have unforeseen effects on marine environments, disrupting ecosystems and affecting birds, marine mammals, and smaller organisms that depend on fish and their habitats to survive. Nearly one fifth of the world's annual fish and shellfish harvests is caught within 200 miles of the United States coastline. Yet only 15 percent of those fish species are yielding stocks near their potential level, according to the report by the National Fish and Wildlife Foundation. At least fourteen species found off coastal waters are in danger of being depleted, including Atlantic salmon, swordfish, Pacific Ocean perch, shad, California halibut, mackerel, cod, haddock, and flounder, the three studies found. In New England, overfishing has devastated so many species that most highly valued fish are being replaced by those of lower value, which are better able to survive, the study by the Massachusetts Offshore Groundfish Task Force found. "The 1990s will definitely be a time of reckoning in the fishing industry," said Brian J. Rothschild, a biologist at the University of Maryland. "Technically, you can stop overfishing as quickly as you can snap your fingers. But nobody is doing it."

All three reports, by the Massachusetts task force, the Center for Marine Conservation, and the National Fish and Wildlife Foundation, recommend that the fisheries service restrict commercial catches to allow fish stocks to recover. It would take five to ten years to recover depleted stocks with little or no fishing, said John P. Wise, author of the report by the Center for Marine Conservation, a nonprofit group based in Washington.

Fish tend to be more resilient than wildlife, and few reach the point of extinction. But biologists say they are increasingly concerned about preserving habitats from pollution, development, and energy projects. Bays, estuaries, and wetlands are among the most imperiled habitats.

The study by the National Fish and Wildlife Foundation found that pesticide contamination has been found in twenty-one of seventy-eight estuaries—the coastal bays, inlets, and rivers where fresh water mixes with shallow salt water to provide a rich environment for marine life and to support most of the nation's commercial catch. In Puget Sound, groundfish like cod, haddock, flounder, and pollack have had an alarming incidence of cancerous liver tumors caused by pollutants. In San Francisco Bay, the population of striped bass has declined 60 to 80 percent because of contamination. In the Albemarle and Pamlico sounds of North Carolina, low levels of dissolved oxygen in the water have suffocated hundreds of thousands of striped bass, crabs, and eels.

Urban development also continues its steady encroachment. The Atlantic salmon, historically a vibrant denizen of wild, free-flowing rivers, had been eliminated from New England, except for Maine; its upstream passage to spawning grounds has been blocked by dams. On the Connecticut River, Atlantic salmon must pass five dams before reaching good spawning grounds, and it is estimated that 40 percent of the fish never make it upstream.

Biologists are also tackling the problem of overfishing. They say that fishermen recognize they are just on the edge of destroying the marine environment or allowing it to survive. In New England, over-fishing has drastically changed the population of fish stocks, the Massachusetts study found. On Georges Bank, highly valued stocks like sole, pollack, yellowtail flounder, and fluke, which composed 65 percent of all fish stocks in the 1960s, now make up only 25 percent of all stocks there. They have been replaced by lower-valued species like spiny dogfish, skate, and shark, said Steven A. Murawski, head of population dynamics for the Northeast Fisheries Center in Woods Hole, Massachusetts, a branch of the National Marine Fisheries Service, and an author of the Massachusetts study. Mr. Murawski said that while fish populations tended to rise and fall in cycles, the current decline had permanently changed the dynamics of Georges Bank. "This isn't fiction, it's physics," he said. "It's uncomfortable for a scientist to be an advocate, but we are looking at the facts of a declining fish population."

Biologists are concerned that too many species are being depleted as factory ships tow large nets across the ocean, sweeping paths clean of all living creatures and leaving long, empty corridors in their wake.

In Alaska, once-abundant pollack populations have dwindled since the fish became popular in fast-food restaurants, where it is processed into fillets. Anne Kinsinger, author of the National Fish and Wildlife Foundation report, said: "There is very little known about fish, how they survive, and the effects on the ecosystems. Environmentalists don't want to touch the idea of fish conservation. People giggle if you talk about saving fish."

The report by the Center for Marine Conservation said that there were no biological or catch data for nearly 30 percent of all fish species, and that more species may be in decline, but that there is little information on them. Officials at the National Marine Fisheries Service blame foreign fleets that raided the fishing grounds before Congress passed the Magnuson Act in 1976, which banned foreign fishing within 200 miles of the coast. But the reports state that the rise in commercial fishing came about because the agency's eight regional councils are dominated by local fishing interests. Industry representatives say they are simply complying with federal rules. "There is much talk about the poor fishermen dying on the vine, but they have brought it on themselves," said Giulio Pontecorvo, an economist at Columbia University who has studied the effect of overfishing on the economy. "It is largely the inability of the National Marine Fisheries Service to get the industry under control."   [ANON., JULY 1991]

SAVING THE MANATEE

A T the flash of a hand signal in the water, Stormy, a 1,200-pound, seven-year-old manatee, swam to place his head in the wire hoop suspended in his tank. Seconds later, a light came on at the end of the tank, signaling that it was time to swim out of the hoop and bump his lips against a paddle suspended to the right of the light. When he responded correctly, his trainer blew a whistle that told him to collect his reward, a monkey biscuit. The behavior Stormy was learning will soon be used to develop a manatee hearing test. Stormy will swim to insert his head in the hoop, and a tone will be sounded in the water. When the light comes on, Stormy will indicate if he heard the tone by swimming to the left paddle if he did and to the right if he did not.

In February 1992, Dr. Edmund Gerstein of Florida Atlantic University began Stormy's training at Lowry Park Zoo in Tampa. When Dr. Gerstein advances to the hearing test, he will be studying Stormy and another manatee, Dundee, to try to find out why nearly every manatee spotted in Florida's waters seems to have collided with a boat. Could it be that manatees cannot hear approaching boats, so they are unable to swim out of harm's way? The research is part of an effort to protect manatees, seallike marine mammals sometimes called sea cows, that grow up to thirteen feet long and weigh up to 3,500 pounds. Although they have been on the endangered species list for nearly two decades, protection programs have been slow to develop. Under a recovery plan for manatees that got under way in 1983, federal and state officials are doing basic research to determine their life history and habitat requirements, and they are taking steps to protect their habitats, reduce mortality, and educate the public. But no one can say for sure whether the plan will work. "We're playing catch-up right now," said Patrick Rose, the administrator of the Office of Protected Species in the Florida Department of Natural Resources.

Scientists say that at least 1,800 West Indian manatees roam the coasts and coastal rivers of Florida and southern Georgia, but, given the difficulty of spotting the animals under murky water, no one is certain how many there are or whether the population is increasing or decreasing. In 1991, at least 174 manatees died in Florida. Fifty-three of those died of injuries caused by boats, according to the Department of Natural Resources, which determines the cause of death in each case. The boat-related deaths set a new record, but just barely. The death toll has been climbing for several years, and scientists are not sure about how long the population can withstand such a high mortality rate. "Right now it's anybody's guess whether the number dying exceeds the number being born," Mr. Rose said. "Regardless of where the population is today, the animal's ability to recover gets more difficult every day. "Some see the manatee as a warm, cuddly issue," he said. But he added, "They are the barometer of how well we are able to protect coastal ecosystems. As the manatees fare, so do systems."

The research on the manatees' hearing was originated by Geoffrey Patton, a senior biologist at Mote Marine Laboratory, a nonprofit research organization in Sarasota. He is collaborating with Dr. Gerstein. "One manatee in Florida has been hit at least twelve times, judging from his scars," Mr. Patton said. "Why don't they learn to avoid boats?" Mr. Patton and Dr. Gerstein say the solution may be to learn to warn the animals of oncoming danger. Once they determine the manatees' hearing range, they will try to find out how well manatees hear in the presence of background noise and whether they can tell the direction of the tone. "If we could determine their hearing ability, it might be possible to modify the sounds that boats make so the animals could locate them and get out of the way," Mr. Patton said. "It could boil down to some simple plastic device on the hull that would vibrate at the right frequency and cue the animal."

A few feet away from Stormy's tank, two wild manatees were recovering from their injuries under the watchful eye of zoo volunteers. One had a collapsed lung that had probably been pierced by a rib broken in a boat collision. The other had been caught in a crab-trap line that had cut off the circulation in his flipper. Both were expected to recover.

The manatees of Florida, which are genetically distinct from a small population of manatees found in the Caribbean and South America, are protected under a state law that dates back to 1893, as well as by the 1972 Marine Mammal Protection Act and the Endangered Species Act of 1973. During the 1970s, however, relatively little was done to help the manatees, primarily because of a lack of money, staff, and commitment from both the Fish and Wildlife Service and the State Department of Natural Resources. Protection efforts increased in the 1980s but were still insufficient, so, at the urging of the Marine Mammal Commission, a federal advisory group, a new recovery plan was written in 1989. In that same year, Florida established the Save the Manatee Trust Fund, which relies on the public to make donations and purchase special manatee license plates to finance the state's program.

One priority of the recovery plan is to determine the manatees' life history and habitat requirements. Since the late 1970s, scientists have conducted aerial surveys to estimate populations at specific locations, for example, near the warm-water outfalls of power plants and the natural hot springs, where the manatees congregate in winter. But those surveys opened "only a very narrow window into their lives," said Dr. Tom O'Shea, director of the Sirenia Project, the manatee research agency of the Fish and Wildlife Service.

The federal agency and the state are now using tracking techniques that allow them to follow an animal continuously for weeks and months. About twenty wild manatees have been fitted with harnesses above their tails; a stiff tether extending from the harness holds an electronic transmitter above the waterline. The electronic signals are picked up by satellite, enabling scientists to find out where these animals congregate and how long they stay there. That information, along with the findings from manatee carcasses and other data, is used to make decisions on which areas are essential to the manatees.

The service is also keeping track of 900 manatees that can be identified by the distinctive scar patterns left from their collisions with boats. Each winter, when the manatees congregate at warm-water sources, biologists identify individuals, take photographs, and try to determine the condition and reproductive status of each animal. The information is used to gauge birth and death rates and migration patterns.

The injured manatees at the Lowry Park Zoo were being cared for under the recovery plan's mandate to rescue and rehabilitate as many injured or diseased manatees as possible. Rescue teams transport injured animals to one of five ocean areas, like the Miami Seaquarium, where marine-mammal veterinarians try to nurse them back to health. "Our goal is to release as many of those animals back into the wild as we can so they can reproduce naturally," said Robert Turner, the manatee-recovery coordinator for the Fish and Wildlife Service. In May 1992, three manatees were released at the Merritt Island National Wildlife Refuge, including a female who had been injured, and her calf, which was born in captivity. Most released manatees are fitted with transmitter harnesses so their progress can be tracked.

Although the survival rate for released manatees is good, Mr. Turner said, orphaned calves and rehabilitated manatees who have spent long periods in captivity may not know where to go or how to get food. "It's like taking a pet and throwing it into the woods," he said. To improve survival rates for such animals, the service plans to build a special pen at the refuge, sort of a halfway house, where manatees that are ready for release can become acquainted with wild manatees across the fence until they are ready to be turned loose.

The most controversial aspect of the manatee program is the attempt to slow boats down near manatee habitats. The Department of Natural Resources has set speed limits for hundreds of miles of waterways in nine counties and plans new speed limits for four more. The regulations, which are imposed after consultations with the counties, require boats to go very slowly in some manatee gathering spots and travel corridors, and they prohibit all human activities in some areas. While manatee advocates endorse the plan, many water skiers and boaters have fought the rules. In Sarasota County, speed zones were adopted in December 1991, and signs were posted in the waterways in July. But even before the signs were posted, the County Commission had decided to review the regulations and consider suggesting changes to the state.

Rick Rawlins, owner of the Highland Park Fish Camp in Volusia County, said the rules adopted there last year would put him out of business because the slow-speed zones lengthened the time it took to reach fishing spots. "The rules would add as much as five to six hours to a day of fishing," Mr. Rawlins said. "My customers are leaving me. Some said they are not going to fish anymore. Others are going to other counties." Mr. Rawlins has formed a group called Citizens for Responsible Boating to fight the regulations. The group filed an administrative appeal with the state; when that was turned down, it filed suit against the Department of Natural Resources, arguing that the economic impact on local businesses had not been fully considered. That suit is pending.

The boating speed limits are not the final step. Each county is also required to develop a comprehensive plan for manatee protection. Each plan must address issues like controls on marina sites and other development, and the plans could include more stringent speed regulations. Despite the increased efforts of recent years, no one is certain that the manatee will thrive in future years. "We'll be able to tell something once the manatee-protection plan starts taking effect," Mr. Turner said. "If we start to see mortality decline, then I have good hope that we can do something. If, after all these efforts, we still see increases in mortality, I really don't know what the next step will be." [CD, AUGUST 1992]

FROM ENDANGERMENT
TO EXTINCTION

A NEW analysis of federal efforts to protect endangered species suggests that rare plants and animals are often listed for protection so late along a slide toward extinction that their populations have already become unnecessarily and perilously small. According to the report, published in the March 1993 issue of the journal *Conservation Biology*, animals often are not designated for protection under the Endangered Species Act until their numbers are so low that extreme and expensive rescue measures, including captive breeding programs, may be their only guarantee for long-term survival. The study showed that most plants are, if anything, even more imperiled by the time they receive formal federal protection.

The statistical study, conducted by three scientists at the Environmental Defense Fund, looked at the 492 species listed as threatened or endangered under the act's provisions between 1985 and 1991. Species are classified as endangered if they are at imminent risk of extinction, and classified as threatened if they are at risk of moving into endangered status. The median numbers of surviving animals listed in both categories were about 1,075 for vertebrates and 999 for invertebrates. The median number of surviving plants was far lower: 120. Research in population biology suggests that as the population of a species drops, and groups become fragmented and isolated from one another, the probability of local extinctions from factors like inbreeding or random disasters like fire and hurricanes can rise sharply. Eventually, a patchwork of local extirpations can mean total extinction.

Dr. Michael Soule, a biologist at the University of California at Santa Cruz, who is a leading theorist on extinction threats facing small populations of animals, noted that population sizes necessary to ensure survival vary widely among species. But he said that the numbers in the new report were disturbing. "We normally think of the low thousands as an absolute minimum for most vertebrates," he said.

Dr. Eric Menges, a plant ecologist at the Archbold Biological Station in Lake Placid, Florida, said the results for plants also were "a surprisingly small number," adding, "At that level, almost any plant would already be extremely vulnerable to extinction. For some plants that are long-lived and hardy and produce a lot of offspring, a few hundred might be enough. But if the median population size of plants at the time of listing is down to one hundred and twenty, you'd have to infer that the listing process is far, far too slow. For most plants, you need to start a recovery action when the population is much larger."

The low population numbers might be a reason that only five species have recovered and been removed from the federal list of threatened and endangered species, as well as a reason many recovery efforts have proved so expensive and difficult, said Dr. David Wilcove, a senior ecologist at the environmental group and chief author of the study. Dr. Wilcove said the low populations pointed to a need to restructure the endangered species program to list species when population numbers were considerably higher, when there was evidence of rapid decline of the species or its habitat. "We're not arguing that every species in some kind of decline be listed," he said. "That would be foolhardy. But we need to get better control of the trajectory for those species that are in serious decline." As an example of how such a process might work, Dr. Wilcove pointed to the case of the Steller sea lion, listed by the federal authorities in 1990 as threatened under emergency provisions of the act after environmentalists warned that they would sue. Even though an estimated 66,000 individuals remained, surveys had shown that in rookeries in one part of Alaska, numbers had plummeted to about 25,000 from 140,000 since 1960.

Dr. Soule agreed that such low numbers suggested that "we need to develop a more sophisticated and graduated system, a kind of early warning system that would kick in long before species are so vulnerable to extinction." The Fish and Wildlife Service endangered species office, however, is already laboring against an immense backlog of species that are candidates for protection. Currently, about 3,600 species of plants and animals appear on such candidates' lists. In fact, some species on such lists have become extinct or virtually extinct while federal authorities deliberated. For instance, by the time one mollusk, the winged maple leaf mussel, was listed as endangered in 1990, 99 percent of its habitat had been lost, and only a single population that was no longer reproducing remained in the St. Croix River on the Minnesota-Wisconsin border.

Similarly, a Puerto Rican plant, the polo de jazmín, was listed in 1991 when only one individual remained, that one damaged by Hurricane Hugo. And several recently listed Hawaiian plant species were added with asterisks beside their names to indicate the rather poignant fact that since no individuals had recently been seen in the wild, the species may have become extinct while waiting to be called endangered.

In 1990 the General Accounting Office calculated that at current levels of financing and staffing, it would take fifty years to decide the status of each of the more than 3,000 candidate species. Presumably, additional species would find their way onto the list in that time. Since then, the Fish and Wildlife Service has approximately doubled its classification rate. And, in December 1992, in settling a lawsuit by several environmental groups, the agency agreed to make decisions about the listing status of all of the roughly 400 species on its top-priority "Candidate I" list within the next four years.

Bob Ruesink, chief for recovery and consultation in the Fish and Wildlife Service's endangered species office, acknowledged that "for many species, protection has been coming too late." But, he added, the agency had taken tentative steps to focus on declining species earlier, including an enhanced "prelisting" program to try to find ways to protect some plants and animals not yet formally listed but clearly at risk. Dr. Wilcove said the numbers in his study pointed toward a need for more money in the endangered species program so the laborious process of analyzing the survival status of species can be accelerated. "Obviously, they need more manpower and more encouragement to list species earlier," he said. Mr. Ruesink said: "I suspect you're going to see more movement in that direction. I think you'll see announcements coming out in the next few weeks that are at least starting to do what these folks are asking for."

In February 1993 Interior Secretary Bruce Babbitt announced his intention to redirect his department's efforts to identify and protect entire ecosystems. Advocates of such an approach believe that biodiversity would be far more effectively protected by protecting key ecosystems before sharp declines of the species within them began.

Dr. Wilcove suggested that his study and Mr. Babbitt's announcement were based on "the same theme." However, he said: "The Endangered Species Act remains the very last safety net before species fall into the abyss of extinction. We're saying that, even with better ecosystem management, we need to raise the level of the safety net for those species that need it."

The report also addressed suggestions from some critics that the Endangered Species Act was being applied too extravagantly, that it focuses too much on protecting not full species, but subspecies and regional populations. Listing an imperiled subspecies or population, even though the species as a whole is not endangered, is sometimes done to protect geographically important and, in most cases, genetically distinct, groups of animals. For example, grizzly bears, although considered threatened as a population in Montana and Idaho, are thriving as a species in Alaska.

Indeed, in the smoldering debate over the status of the northern spotted owl in the Pacific Northwest, critics from the logging industry repeatedly have pointed out that the bird is a subspecies, suggesting that any threat to its survival is obviated by the presence of a genetic cousin, the southern spotted owl, in Southern California and the Southwest. According to the new study, most of the listings, some 80 percent, involved full species, with only 18 percent involving subspecies, and 2 percent regional populations. However, the proportion of listed subspecies was much higher among birds and mammals, which, Dr. Wilcove suggests, may have led to misconceptions. Earlier placement of declining species into the threatened category could introduce more flexibility into the protection process, Dr. Wilcove said. Ultimately, he suggested, that could mean fewer and less rigid constraints on development in at least some habitats, and lower costs. "If we've got 50,000 individuals to work with, losing a few to disturbance or development isn't going to have the same kind of impact as losing the same number from a tiny population," Dr. Wilcove said. "It gives us more options and more flexibility. If we had tackled the spotted owl issue twenty years earlier when there was more old-growth forest, we might have been able to design a much less painful transition toward protecting enough spotted owls to ensure their survival."

[JRL, MARCH 1993]

Courting Disaster

THREATS TO ECOSYSTEMS

No ONE would deliberately turn a wilderness into a wasteland, convert a river into a running sewer, or so load the air with toxic filth that to breathe freely requires refuge in a salt mine. But where individuals may know better, governments often do not. In trying to resolve conflicting interests, governments may choose expedience over common sense.

When the Soviet system collapsed, its political legacy vanished like snow in the desert. Far more enduring was its legacy to the environment. Forty-five years of unbridled industrial pollution have ravaged the face of

Russia and Eastern Europe, poisoning air and land and water on an unimaginable scale. The central planners never had to consider the ecological cost of their five-year plans or bow to the protests of those whose distant fields or villages their grandiose smelters or steel mills destroyed. The East German government was regularly informed of the lethal pollution released by its chemical industry and how to abate it. But the Communist functionaries in East Berlin kept the figures secret, while cynically imposing enormous fines on the industry. "A lot of crimes have been committed in this country, and not only by the secret police," said an East German who held office between the fall of communism and reunification.

The articles in this section recount the devastation that came into view throughout Eastern Europe when the Berlin Wall came down. Communist governments have no monopoly on myopia. In Japan, where government officials do not have a vigorous environmental movement to take into account, ecology often takes second place to development. The ministries in Tokyo still cannot bring themselves to offer generous recompense to the victims of the long-ago Minamata mercury poisoning.

In Mexico, now entering a phase of full-tilt industrial expansion similar to that of Japan thirty years ago, the same compromises have led to similar consequences. Even the capital, Mexico City, is wreathed in a miasma of air so foul and fetid that vigorous exercise is deemed unhealthy and foreign diplomats are advised not to have babies while stationed there.

The worldwide urge for economic growth and better standards of life cannot be resisted. But planners in country after country, from Prague to Beijing, from Moscow to Mexico City, have pursued their goals with little attention to preserving nature's balances, succumbing to the folly that they could pay the piper later.

THE DEATH OF FORESTS
IN EASTERN EUROPE

ACROSS a mountain range where East Germany, Czechoslovakia, and Poland meet lies the bitter fallout from industrial schemes conceived in the Kremlin four decades ago. Barren plateaus stretch for miles, studded with the stumps and skeletons of pine trees. Under the snow lie thousands of acres of poisoned ground, where for centuries thick forests had grown.

This is the heart of Europe, the sick heart of Europe, its people call it. Below these mountains, in a broad belt from Leipzig in East Germany to Cracow in southern Poland and across northern Czechoslovakia, are the bulk of Eastern Europe's heavy industries. A phalanx of power plants stands beside them, spewing smoke heavy with sulfur and soot as they drive steel and chemical works and heat homes.

In the rush to compete with the West, the three countries have stoked these plants with millions of tons of lignite, a geologically younger coal that is dirty, cheap, and abundant here. (Just 10 percent of the coal mined and burned in the United States is lignite.) The hunt for cheap energy has come back to haunt the planners: the brown coal smoke and other noxious emissions have wreaked havoc on buildings, penetrated people's lungs, and poured acid rain over farmlands and forests. As post–Communist Eastern Europe is taking stock of the impact of callous industrial rampage, at least a dozen cities in this grime belt are vying for the title of Europe's most polluted place. "Basically we are seeing an ecological catastrophe," said Frantisek Urban, director of nature conservation in Czechoslovakia's new Ministry of Environment.

While acid rain damage to forests from car and industrial exhausts all over Western Europe has been reported for more than a decade, forestry experts in Prague said no other place had such an extent of forest deaths in Central Europe's industrial belt. They cited a stretch of some 350 miles where more than 300,000 acres of forest had disappeared and surviving trees were so sick their life span would be short. Winds churn the sulfurous air around this "Bermuda Triangle of pollution," as the foresters dubbed it, and carry this over long distances. With prevailing winds blowing east, Czechs blame East Germans for half their pollution and Poles blame both neighbors for as much. Poland's fallout is also felt in Ukraine and in Sweden.

A trip along the crest of the Erz Mountains, at the Czechoslovak border with East Germany, and over the Riesen and Sudeten mountains of southern Poland, illustrated the results of production pressures from Moscow. In village after village, foresters in Poland and Czechoslovakia said they had warned of the widespread deaths of trees for almost twenty years.

A thick brown haze hung over much of north Czechoslovakia, something people described as normal for eight months of the year. It took on the sting of tear gas between Usti and Chomutov on the edge of the vast brown coal basin of northern Bohemia. The basin maintains ten power plants.

In just the last few years, Czechs said that the country had spent a fortune on Soviet desulfurization scrubbers. "We were promised 80 percent efficiency, but they are continuously breaking down," Mr. Urban, in Prague, lamented. "When they work, they clean only 30 percent." Usti, lying black in its own sticky soot, spews carbon monoxide, nitrogen oxide, sulfur, and heavy metals from chemical, glass, and cooking-oil plants. Sulfur in the air here has been reported at twenty times the permissible level. Jaroslav Jirgle, who heads Usti's modest Research Institute for Forestry and Game Management, took a visitor through the region's bedraggled forests. These had been dense woods, known from the chronicles of the Napoleonic wars when Russian, French, and Austrian armies clashed here. Pulling his coat against the winds of March, Mr. Jirgle pointed, mile after mile, to withered beeches, the thinned crowns of silver firs, stunted oaks, brush spruces, and comb spruces looking ragged or nude.

Conifers, exposed all year round, suffer most, said the forester, explaining that the emissions clog the pores of the needles, damage the wax, and interfere with respiration. Trees that survived grew to less than a quarter of their healthy size and died early instead of living a normal eighty to one hundred years.

On top of the Erz Mountains, the undulating tablelands, now covered in snow, bore only stumps and barren stems as though a great fire had raged. Some experimental patches now bore seedlings of sitka spruce, a hardy North American type. "Who knows if they can stand this," said Mr. Jirgle, explaining that down to the south were the plants of Litvinov and ahead lay Dresden and East Germany's industrial basin, which has eighteen coal-fueled power plants.

Beyond the forest death, the pollution has unchained a far more complex range of damage along the Erz, Riesen, and Tatry mountains. Alfred Shima, an agronomist at Usti, said soil in the region was extremely acid, with a pH between 4 and 3, which is a point at which the aluminum trapped in the clay is released. Other specialists said the aluminum was poisoning the groundwater, killing tree and plant roots and filtering into drinking water. With the trees gone, birds of prey have disappeared, triggering a plague of mountain mice. The large mice are chewing up the seedlings.

The harshest side effect, specialists said, is the near-disastrous change in the water budget. In dense forests, the snow used to melt slowly and trickle into creeks and rivers. Now, on the barren sites and in balder forests, it melts with the first sunshine and rushes down in three weeks, causing erosion and flooding in spring and water shortages in the summer.

Experts at a Prague meeting attended by foresters from six East European nations said quantifying the damage was difficult. Forest resources for many years were treated as a state secret, they said. Dead forests have been entered into the records as grasslands, and researchers often depend on the memory of local people. Hungary reported the least damage, with 75 percent of its forests unaffected. In Bulgaria, more than half the forest was still completely healthy. East Germany reported the loss of more than 125,000 acres of woodlands as well as some damage in 35 percent of its forests and severe damage in 20 percent. Acid rain has killed as much forest in Poland as in East Germany, and almost 60 percent of the pine forests are affected. Czechoslovakia, Europe's worst case, reportedly lost more than 80,000 acres and suffers some pollution damage in 44 percent and more serious damage in close to 30 percent. The Czech Academy of Science says the famous forests of North Bohemia are more than 80 percent damaged.

Jerzy Wawrzonizk of the Forest Reserves Institute in Warsaw said Poland and the Central European countries should immediately reduce forest cutting, stop exporting altogether, and plant new species because mixed forests are hardier.

Even if emissions were to stop now, specialists say, it will take years and millions of dollars to rehabilitate the soils and the woodlands. Czechoslovakia has been using helicopters to spray lime on its most acid soils, a technique others criticized as costly and too much of a shock therapy.

"The acidification has built up over twenty-five years," said Karl Panzer of the West German Federal Research Center for Forestry, who has studied damage in the industrial belt. "It will be hard to roll back. Rehabilitation has to start with plants that can survive in poisoned soil, and that is very difficult."

Some experts say it will be so costly to outfit the old power plants and industries with scrubbers that it is worth building new ones. Even the new environment-minded politicians say the emissions are likely to go on for five to ten years until remedies or new and cleaner sources of energy are in place. "At least we can discuss it openly now," said Mr. Urban. "For many years we could not publish that forests were dying. We could only say that some of it was in danger."

[MS, MARCH 1990]

THE FOULING OF THE DANUBE

S WOLLEN and pearly gray, the Danube makes a spectacular turn in Esztergom, pushing into the gentle Hungarian woodlands as it surges south toward Budapest. It is the river at its most seductive: winding through the valleys of Central Europe, where it has inspired poets and composers and generations of painters who still work on its banks today.

But love and splendor have not shielded Europe's grandest waterway from abuse. From its source in Germany's Black Forest, sweeping through a catchment area of 80 million people and eight countries, it runs a gantlet of urban sewage, discharge from factories, and runoff from farms.

Along its 2,000 miles, it is continuously fed by polluted tributaries. Slowly it loses life until, sluggish and befouled, it reaches the Black Sea. Bane of the Balkans? Scientists are just beginning to study the entire length of the Danube's rich and changing ecosystem, its myriad islands, the content of its nutrients, and its dragging movement through the Balkans. Such investigations were severely restricted under Communist rule, and the results were kept secret. "We could never get access to the Soviets' own studies of the lower Danube and the estuary," said Kasimon Salevich, a specialist in Danube water management in Austria.

But self-interest is beginning to stir concern in Moscow for the far-off Danube. The Soviet Academy of Sciences sponsored a conference on the plight of the river, and in 1989 Soviet scientists talked to their Hungarian and Bulgarian counterparts about the need to stop contaminating it. The scientists agreed that an enormous volume of pesticides, fertilizers, detergents, and other chemicals had turned the Danube into one of the main polluters of the Black Sea. They also warned that phosphates and nitrates are causing a record amount of algae blooms in the shallow and land-trapped sea.

Despite the extent of pollution in the Danube, specialists say the waterway seems robust compared with the grid of rivers that drain the northern plains of Eastern Europe and spill into the Baltic Sea. Industries built over the last three decades, they say, have pounded the Elbe, the Oder, the Neisse, and the Vistula to near biological death.

Environmentalists say the poisoning of the Danube and other rivers in Eastern Europe suggests that pressure to fulfill Communist production quotas has been as rapacious to nature as capitalism's urge for profit. The difference, they say, is that pressure groups in the West have forced capitalist industries to start cleaning up. The West, it appears, has now also accepted the task of rescuing the marred waters of formerly Communist countries, whose new governments have neither the capital nor the technology to clean up the mess.

West Germany, which shares the Elbe with East Germany, plans to start work on the lower river and build a sewage-treatment plant at Dresden. Experts in Bonn said the Elbe is in a "dramatic state": in addition to a concoction of lead, copper, zinc, phosphates, and sewage, it carries about twenty-five tons of mercury, more than eight times the load of the polluted Rhine. Although Bonn recently signed several environmental contracts with its neighbors, "they would never discuss the Elbe or give us the information we needed," said Marlene Muhe, an official with the West German Environment Ministry.

Sweden has pledged help to Poland, whose rivers are a major

source of pollution in the Baltic Sea. The Oder and the Neisse begin as pristine streams in the mountains of northern Czechoslovakia. By the time they turn north and become the long-disputed border between Poland and East Germany, they are already laced with discharge from Bohemian and Moravian pulp, steel, glass, and ceramics works.

The Vistula is still a modest stream when it reaches Cracow. Already the color of molasses and heavy with brine, it plods past this city. Poland has turned its main artery into the nation's principal dumping ground.

Upstream from Cracow, Silesian coal mines permeated with salt pour more than 200 million liters of saline discharge into the Vistula each day. Recent studies have shown that this brew has contaminated groundwater and wells. It is also gnawing at the foundations of Cracow and its fine medieval and Renaissance monuments. "The buildings are attacked from above, from the sulfur dioxide in the air, but they are also sucking up the salt and other corrosives from the contaminated groundwater," said Prof. Zdzislaw Malecki, pointing to blisters and damp stains on ancient walls. Professor Malecki, director of the local Institute for Environmental Engineering, is participating in Cracow's restoration. "Every building has become a pollution-absorbing device," he said. "There is even more damage from below than from the top."

As the Vistula pushes north, it collects effluents, chemicals, and sewage from each factory and town along the way. It is now unfit for irrigating land, or even for industrial use, because it kills soil microbes and plants and corrodes pipes and tanks. By the time it reaches Gdansk and the Baltic Sea, "the pollution is just flabbergasting," a Swedish diplomat said. "We are not innocent either, but already 25 percent of the Baltic Sea is dead." Sweden will supply equipment for some water-treatment projects, he said, but cleaning the Vistula will require hundreds of millions of dollars.

In Budapest, the eye is drawn to seven magnificent bridges over the Danube, but hidden pipes are spitting the raw sewage of 2 million inhabitants into the water. Neither Bratislava nor Belgrade nor most other towns along the waterway treat their waste. In Czechoslovakia, Yugoslavia, Romania, and Bulgaria, industries freely spill oil, cellulose, and chemicals into the Danube.

The barrage of pollution, specialists say, is rapidly diminishing the river's capacity to cleanse itself. The contaminants come in small and large doses, some easily absorbed in the great volume of water, others permanently polluting its environment.

The Danube, at the center of Europe, may appear to have no obvious guardian. But tens of thousands of people have become devoted to its protection in recent years. One of their greatest successes came in 1989, when activists halted construction on the giant Nagymaros hydroelectric dam complex.

Behind Dunakiliti, a small village in the area where Austria, Hungary, and Czechoslovakia meet, lies a portion of the large, stalled project. New channels along the Hungarian side of the Danube had been readied to serve the weir and deviation canals. Across the river, on the Czechoslovak side, a new power station was poised to link up with the spillway. Tons of concrete, already poured, and long strips cleared of vegetation have turned these banks into bleak places. But the bulldozers and cranes at Dunakiliti are silent and the workers have gone. "It's been like this since before Christmas," said a lonely guard in 1989.

Environmentalists, citing studies by engineers and biologists, argued that the impact of the complex would be devastating: it would drown fifty islands and miles of forest, disturb the flow in tributaries, and interfere with the sandy layers that clean the drinking water for Budapest. Raising the groundwater level would also damage the foundations of Esztergom, a twelfth-century city that lies downstream. And Hungarians complained that much of the electricity generated would go to Austria as payment for the dams. Members of the Danube Circle, Eastern Europe's first large environmental group, say they fear that the project may still be alive. The three nations involved have already invested millions of dollars and plan new contractual negotiations.

In the meantime, environmental leaders have other pressing concerns. They report that a Czechoslovak nuclear power plant on the Vag, a Danube tributary, is raising the water's temperature and has leaked radioactive material. "There is a lot of unrecorded contamination," said Andras Lukacs, a geophysicist who heads the Foundation for the Protection of the Environment in Budapest. Although most industries in the Danube basin lack adequate filter installations, at least they are there to be seen. But "much of the used oil from vehicles is not collected," Mr. Lukacs said. "Many storage tanks of petrol stations and depots leak. Toxic waste is badly stored. All this gets into the groundwater or into the river. We know that much of Hungary's groundwater is polluted."

Environmentalists in Yugoslavia are demanding that Serbian industries contain their fallout. They have charged that the drinking water in much of Yugoslavia is not safe. In Bulgaria, the environmentally oriented political group Eco-Glasnost has begun a campaign against a caustic-soda plant in Giurgiu, Romania, that contaminates both the Danube and the air. Everyone agrees that cleaning up the river will take years and a fortune that is not available.

As the barges and pleasure boats arrive with spring, defenders of the Danube are planning to step up their more modest campaign among people who find pleasure and rest in the river's beauty. In Austria, environmental groups have begun a drive to outmaneuver developers by buying land along the banks and creating nature reserves. "It is going very well; we already bought two parks," said Gunther Lutschinger, a biologist with the World Wide Fund for Nature, who manages the two reserves. "We are going to raise more funds. We see that many people love the Danube." [MS, MAY 1990]

THE CHOKING OF THE BLACK SEA

For centuries, the Black Sea produced dolphin skins and caviar and fish so plentiful that no one thought such bounty could ever end. But now this ancient highway between Europe and Asia is suffering extensive changes, the proportions of which are only just becoming fully known. All along its 2,500-mile coastline, fishing boats sit in port, idled by the collapse of sturgeon, mackerel, anchovy, and other commercial fisheries. Bathing beaches near Constantsa in Romania and Odessa in Ukraine were closed in 1990 and 1991 because of chemical pollution and the smelly froth of algae blooms. Now scientists warn that this inland sea is rapidly losing its oxygen and the ability to purge itself.

The Black Sea and its unusual biological traits, which are still little understood, have long fascinated scientists. The end of communism permitted specialists from the whole region to meet for the first time at a conference in Varna, Bulgaria, recently and freely debate the Black Sea's problems. But political turmoil in the former Soviet Union held up a new international agreement to stop the marine pollution already banned off other coasts, and ships from many nations still clean out their oil tanks, flush their ballasts, and dump loads of dangerous sludge and toxic waste into the Black Sea. Biologists also worry about the growing tide of human, farm, and industrial discharge pouring in from the four Black Sea countries—Bulgaria, Romania, the Soviet Union, and Turkey. Newly published surveys show that every town, industry, and mine along the shores of the sea uses this land-trapped water as dump and sewer.

More than sixty rivers and streams deliver waste from a catchment area of 160 million people. The four largest are the Danube, the Don, the Dnieper, and the Dniester, and they arrive here after sweeping through a region now recognized as one of the most polluted in the world. Scientists say that every year these rivers carry many tons of toxic materials—oil, lead, phosphorus, nitrates, chromium, cadmium, and others. In spring, when the melting snow washes the land, the river waters from the north, especially the Dnieper, carry radioactive fallout from the 1986 nuclear accident at Chernobyl. "I know of no other inland sea under such pressure," said Stanislav Konovalov, director of the Soviet Institute for Biology of the Southern Seas at Sebastopol. "This is much more degraded than the Baltic."

Biologists like Mr. Konovalov, who have spent much of their lives exploring the Black Sea, say they are shocked and surprised by the collapse of its fisheries and other extraordinary changes in its ecosystems.

At Vinizi, a small community of summer houses and fishermen on the Bulgarian coast, Atanas Stefanov remembers the time when he and his father hunted dolphins and seals to sell the fat and the skins. "Our biggest year, we shot 1,024 dolphins," said Mr. Stefanov, who has been going to sea for fifty-five of his sixty-eight years. "That was 1947. Everybody did it. Of course it's forbidden now."

For much of their lives, these fishermen have caught three-foot-long, caviar-laden sturgeon and loads of fat horse mackerel. "Today we get these little things," Mr. Stefanov lamented, showing a pot full of small scad.

Aboard the Bulgarian research vessel *Akademik*, Hinko Klisarov said that the crew still spots dolphins, but that the other mammals, the seals, have disappeared altogether. And like creatures in a science fiction tale, some jellyfish are getting bigger and bigger. "They are now appearing at thirty pounds or more," he said. Yuvenaly Zaitsev, a Soviet biologist based in Sevastopol, argues that the sturgeon were finished by overfishing. The total catch, he said, dropped from more than 1,000 tons per year in 1950 to less than 10 tons in 1989. Worse than that, he said, of the twenty-six commercial fish species abundant in 1970, only five are left in commercial quantities. Mr. Zaitsev says the proliferation of jellyfish has caused part of the problem because they eat the eggs and the larvae of other fish. A new arrival is a plague of ribbed jellyfish, a recent intruder that is found on the Atlantic coast of North America and probably arrived here in bilge water.

Whatever the cause of the changes, they are far-reaching. Some 2 million people live directly or indirectly off fisheries. On Turkey's 700-mile Black Sea coast, fishermen have been hit hardest, and anchovy fleets are paralyzed at Trebizond, Sinop, Samsun, and other ports. The Ankara government says that between 1987 and 1989, the Turkish Black Sea catch dropped almost 95 percent, from 340,000 tons to less than 15,000 tons, and it has declared a moratorium on anchovy fishing.

"Nobody really knows why all this is happening," said Umit Unluata, an oceanographer at the Turkish Institute of Marine Sciences. "It may be a combination of overfishing, pollution, climate change, and shifts in the food chain."

Geologists say the greatest change in these waters happened some 8,000 years ago, when the Black Sea was still a freshwater lake but the sea level rose and the Mediterranean spilled through the Bosporus. As salt water rushed in, geologists believe, it killed the life adapted to freshwater, and this produced a mass of hydrogen sulfide, which remains trapped in the deep waters beneath the top 100 yards or so of oxygen-bearing water. More than nine tenths of the Black Sea has such high levels of hydrogen sulfide that it is lifeless.

"It's really a geological freak," said David Aubrey, a senior scientist at the Woods Hole Oceanographic Institution in Massachusetts, which organized the first large international Black Sea conference in October 1991 in Varna. "If you put a piece of metal in deep enough, it will come out black. If you turned the Black Sea over, it would smell of rotten eggs." "In this fragile setting," Dr. Aubrey added, "man has now created an environmental catastrophe." The mass of hydrogen sulfide and methane is sealed off by the lid of oxygenated water.

Scientists say that if the sea "turned over" because of an earthquake or a chemical upheaval—something that they call unlikely but possible—the escaping gases could kill people on the shore.

Modern change began thirty years ago with the frantic industrialization along the rivers in Eastern Europe that brought runoffs of toxic chemicals, detergents, and fertilizers to the Black Sea. In addition, Soviet dams and irrigation projects have diverted so much river water that by Soviet estimates the Black Sea is today receiving almost one-fifth less fresh water and becoming more salty. Some scientists believe that the poisonous hydrogen sulfide is welling up, reducing the oxygen layer and thus causing fish kills.

Others blame the detergents and fertilizers. In the estuary of the Danube, a 70-mile-wide wetland of channels, lakes, and swamps, algae blooms have grown wildly in the 1980s. "By the end of the summer, much of the delta is covered in spume," said Mircea Staras, a Romanian biologist. Mr. Staras lives in Tulcia, close to the mouth of the Danube. "When the algae die, everything else is killed," said Mr. Staras, "even the underwater plants. This was an important spawning ground for sturgeon, for carp, for pike. We lost all the big fish."

Radioactive fallout from Chernobyl is being monitored by scientists. Elements like cesium 137 and strontium allow monitors to trace their movements, and hence to see how pollutants behave, how long they stay on the surface, how fast organisms take them up, and how the Black Sea mixes and circulates. "It's an unexpected bonus," said Gennadi Polykarpov, a Soviet monitor. "The fallout is a problem in the Dnieper water because it is used for irrigation, but it is not a health hazard in the Black Sea."

As awareness of the degradation grows, hopes of reversing it are running up against the reality that the Black Sea countries do not have the immediate means or the political will to change their practices. "Even if we stopped all the pollution as if by magic," Mr. Zaitsev said, "it would be impossible to go back to the 1950s. Nature has its own laws."

Cleaning up many areas would cost a fortune. The large and handsome bay at Burgas, Bulgaria, was a popular beach resort until two decades ago, when chemical plants were built on its shores. Today the bay is off-limits to bathers, and water and air here look equally greasy and opaque with contaminants. Farther south, near Chernomoritz, researchers have found hot spots of uranium radiation along the inlets and beaches that they believe was spilled by a nearby mine. Local guesthouse owners, though, have repeatedly taken down signs warning people to keep away due to radioactivity. They say the signs ruined their business.

But the scientists at the Black Sea conference agreed that even if a cleanup is too costly or difficult in the short run, a huge effort should be made to stop the pollution from getting worse. A convention to diminish pollution of the Danube, which is fed with sewage and waste from eight nations, was recently held, although no agreement has yet been signed. A convention to protect the Black Sea has been in the works since 1989. Initially, it was delayed by the Soviet military. Now a new complication is that the Ukraine, Russia, and Georgia, caught up in their own domestic political turmoil, will probably have to debate and sign the agreement separately.

"The two conventions are absolutely essential for any future action," Dr. Aubrey said. "They will help change legislation in the different countries, and they can trigger foreign aid." "A new legal framework will be a quantum leap," said Lawrence Mee of the United Nations Environmental Program. "It made a tremendous difference in cutting back pollution in the Baltic Sea. It showed us that the law can work." [MS, NOVEMBER 1991]

THE POISONING OF BULGARIA

I N this valley under the snowcapped Balkan Mountains, old people remember the time when everyone in Srednogorie, Bulgaria, grew roses, acres of roses, which were pressed into oils for perfume and medicine. They also recall the excitement when the copper plant arrived; this was evidence of progress under Communist rule, they were told, that would bring them new jobs and modern homes. What most people here still do not know is that for much of the last thirty years this enormous and shabby industrial compound on a hillside above the town has been poisoning their land and, in many cases, their bodies with lead and arsenic. Arsenic has been found in alarming quantities as far as twenty-five miles away, but the authorities have kept this secret from the local population. When the plant spilled about 200 tons of arsenic in 1988, contaminating farmland and killing cattle and sheep, the disaster was covered up for nine months.

At the local hospital, doctors speak of a frightening rise in the number of babies born with deformities and of cases of cancer and chronic mouth and lung disease. They say infant mortality here is almost three times the norm for Bulgaria, and they cite an abnormal number of people with high blood pressure and dental problems among the town's 35,000 inhabitants. "When I started here in 1976, there was no cancer," said Dr. Nikolai Ivanov, a hospital surgeon. "Last year we had at least forty-five cases."

But local officials have repeatedly assured workers that tests show nothing abnormal in their blood or in the environment. Doctors complaining to the plant management were promptly denounced as troublemakers by local Communist party bosses. In other parts of polluted Eastern Europe the authorities have started to make an inventory of the disastrous legacy of unrestrained industrial growth and are asking for help in the West. But in Bulgaria the subject is still treated as a state secret.

Environmentalists, who include doctors and engineers, say that even in today's more politically lenient climate they are harassed, followed, or intimidated. Several physicians said that medical reports in state-run factories are routinely hidden or falsified. The arsenic, lead, and copper in the dust of Srednogorie—at least seventy times the permissible level, according to a secret government document—is said to make this town one of Bulgaria's most dangerous. But at least ten other cities are struggling with their own serious pollution problems. Sofia, the capital, once praised for its clear mountain air, lies trapped in frequent haze oozing from two giant steel plants at Pernik and Kremikovsti. The latter alone reportedly dumps 20,000 tons of grime a year on Sofia's center, eight miles away, and siphons off one third of the capital's water. In the northern city of Ruse, a chemical plant just across the border in Romania often makes breathing difficult. But when a "Defend Ruse" committee was formed, some of its members were run out of the Communist party and others lost their jobs. Industries have poisoned the bays of Burgas and Varna on the Black Sea.

The gradual poisoning of Bulgaria is equal in scope to the enormous pollution and environmental disasters now being recognized throughout Eastern Europe. Such a fate was less inevitable for Bulgaria, though, because Stalin originally assigned Bulgaria, with its fertile soils and moderate climate, to be the East bloc's garden, providing grains, fruits, and vegetables to its neighbors. That agricultural vocation began to change in the 1950s as heavy industries came in. In 1989, Bulgaria, which once exported two thirds of its farm produce, was forced to import food. A Communist party report says that almost 60 percent of the land is now "damaged" by excessive use of fertilizers, pesticides, and industrial fallout.

The steel and chemical industries are also increasingly having trouble finding workers. To attract laborers to the steelworks at Kremikovtsi, the government has promised to exempt young men from military service if they will work there five years. From the outside, Srednogorie's copper plant, which employs 1,500 people, looks grimy enough, with its bulky slag heaps and its chimney spewing yellow smoke. Inside, it seems more like a battlefield. The grounds are strewn with rusting metal and discarded machinery. An old sulfur plant has disintegrated into a forest of blistered pipes and tanks. Some workers in a great hall with cauldrons and smelters wear gas masks. Others do not bother to protect themselves.

Twice in 1989, when controls failed, the plant emitted such dangerous toxic clouds that it had to close down, and the children of Srednogorie were evacuated to other towns, said Deltcho Vichev, an engineer of the Ministry of Metallurgy and a plant consultant. But the worst incident came in December 1988, when workers discovered cracks in the retaining walls of a vast reservoir, the dumping ground for the plant's toxic waste. Its mud contains high concentrations of arsenic, lead, and other discards left after copper, silver, and gold have been taken from the ore.

"The government decided secretly to let water out of the reservoir to diminish the pressure on the walls," said one expert familiar with the incident. The highly poisonous sludge was spilled into the Pirdopska River, which feeds the Topolnika River, which is used to irrigate some of Bulgaria's best agricultural land. According to an unpublished government study, 200 tons of arsenic was released, and some lands irrigated with this river water had concentrations of arsenic at 4,000 times the permissible level. Near the village of Poibrene, farmers told researchers that their sheep were aborting and cows "were going mad" and dying.

"The government knew everything but said nothing," an expert, himself a government employee, said. "The whole summer they let people go swimming and fishing in that river." Nine months after the spill, after continuous pressure from experts and from Eco-Glasnost, the Bulgarian environmental movement, the authorities imposed a five-year ban on fishing, swimming, or using irrigation water from the Topolnika. But they have not warned people against eating produce from the area. Experts say at least 150,000 acres of badly contaminated land should be banned for agriculture. The arsenic in the soil around Srednogorie and on the fields downstream is likely to remain there. "It does not decompose," said Mr. Vichev, who joined Eco-Glasnost because "those of us who understand the seriousness of pollution must speak out." [MS, MARCH 1990]

EASTERN EUROPE'S POLLUTED AIR

IN the depths of a salt mine in Poland, men, women, and children lie in bed, bundled in coats and tugging at heavy blankets. In an upside-down world, they have come to this underground clinic to breathe clean and healing air. Aboveground, in more conventional clinics, doctors using portable inhalators administer moist and purified air to children. "Whenever the smog is heavy, the wards fill up," said Dr. Henryk Kowalski, a laryngologist at a regional children's hospital.

Clean air has become a luxury here and in the industrial zones of Central Europe, where poisonous gases and toxic dust roam freely. As the secrets of the Eastern bloc's formerly Communist nations become known, this one may be the saddest. In the years when Soviet-bloc rulers claimed that they were forming "a new Socialist man," they were in many instances condemning this man and his family to severe lung and heart disease, cancer, eye and skin ailments, and, often, sickly children and shorter lives.

In much of Eastern Europe, comprehensive health surveys are not yet available because Communist governments hid or ignored many of the medical statistics. But from East Germany to Bulgaria, physicians, biologists, and other health specialists are now eager to talk. And visiting experts from the United States and Western Europe have said that Central Europe's pollution is more dangerous and widespread than anything they have seen in the Western industrial nations, and that it occurs on a far greater scale than in the developing world, which does not have nearly as much industry. Health specialists throughout the region said that diseases traceable to a poisoned environment were consuming a large portion of public health budgets. Similar problems from pollution affect many parts of the former Soviet Union as well.

A study of new mothers in the industrial region of Katowice and Cracow in southern Poland showed concentrations of lead, mercury, cadmium, and other toxic metals in the placenta of every woman. The study's author, Dr. Josef Niwelinski of the University of Cracow, said more than half of the 1,000 placentas examined were deformed or damaged, "most likely by the high level of carbon monoxide and sulfur dioxide in the air." The findings were all the more worrisome, he said, because "we studied only the most healthy mothers with normal births."

Another group of doctors is studying why in this region so many babies are born prematurely or die in the womb. Its preliminary conclusions are that at least 50 percent of the cases are caused by chemical changes in the mother's blood that leave the child short of oxygen.

In the former East-bloc nations as well as in the Soviet Union, the quality of air, water, and food has deteriorated sharply over the past two decades as heavy industries and vehicles multiplied. To Western experts, the polluting practices seem all the more ruthless because they increased at a time when their dire consequences were already widely known. Experts said the technology to control pollution from antiquated installations was well known and in some Eastern European countries was even produced for export. Yet there are only minimal controls on much of Eastern Europe's industrial emissions, or none at all. Poland's pollution is widely described as the worst. The Polish Academy of Science said a third of the nation's 38 million people live in "areas of ecological disaster." It said conditions were most hazardous in the coal-and-steel belt of Cracow and Silesia.

The Chorzow hospital in the sprawling industrial zone around Katowice, an area of extravagant pollution with more than 1.5 million inhabitants, seems to bear witness to the degradation. Almost across the street from the hospital is a vast steel mill that has left the air dry and scorching. It forms a hellish circle with a power station and a chemical plant. The sting and smog from the plants are unmistakable inside the hospital wards.

Three members of the hospital board, eager to share their grievances with a visitor, cited a litany of ills. They said that there had been a sharp rise in cancer, heart disease, and emphysema, and that too many men were dying in their thirties and forties. Although general statistics for adults were scarce, the board said it was widely accepted that the life expectancy for adults in this region was four years shorter than the average for adults in the rest of the nation. They said public health was degenerating to the level of the postwar years. "We have been telling the authorities about this for twenty years," said Dr. Jan Kern, director of health services. "They always told us they were doing research, that they were putting in new technology. But they cannot fool us. We get the patients."

If the environment is harsh for adults, it is harder on the children. Dr. Bozena Cichos, a pediatrician in the children's hospital at Chorzow, said that in her nine years there she had seen a sharp rise in chronic bronchitis, asthma, pneumonia, meningitis, and rickets. Underweight babies are becoming common, she said, and pregnancies of just thirty-six weeks—three or four weeks shortened—"are so normal now we don't even consider them short. Quite a few of these babies keep coming back," she said.

A new study in the Katowice area said 21 percent of the children up to four years old are sick almost constantly, while 41 percent of the children under six have health problems, including hearing or vision disabilities, anemia, and low weight and height. Some health experts in Eastern Europe say that as the environmental disaster is debated, there is a tendency to attribute all illness to pollution. They note that many adults and children eat unhealthfully, with high-fat or unbalanced diets, and that heavy smoking is common. But even those habits are aggravated by smog, said Dr. Marion Glowacz, an internist.

Although levels of pollution in Eastern Europe vary according to the type of industry, it is clear that wind and water spread the hazardous substances over large areas, and that sulfur from coal burning affects the breathing of millions of people. Unsafe levels of heavy metals in drinking water and on land used for agriculture are widespread. In Silesia, the Polish authorities have banned the growing of vegetables in the widely contaminated soil.

The Czechoslovak Academy of Sciences recently disclosed that 50 percent of the country's drinking water does not meet even its outdated, lenient norms. In Prague, a city plagued by smog, many people complained of permanent headaches, asthma, nausea, and intestinal trouble. And in northern Bohemia, home to many power plants and chemical works, officials said infant mortality was 12 percent higher than in the rest of the country; they said schoolchildren had to be sent to the mountains with their teachers at least one month a year.

"Fifteen years ago we knew our forests were dying, the children were losing immunity, and water stopped being drinkable," said Pavel Seifer, a spokesman for the Czechoslovak Green Party. "But there was a party directive that the media should avoid information about the environment." Mr. Seifer, who at the time was a journalist, added: "We were told we have to fight the efforts of the West. They want to bring us to our knees through ecology."

Several physicians in Hungary and Bulgaria said that warning of the degenerative effects of industry on people's health was frowned upon, perceived as an attack on the system. When Dr. Nikolai Ivanov complained recently about a copper plant in Srednogorie, Bulgaria, that was causing arsenic and lead poisoning among his patients, he was publicly criticized by the local Communist party leader.

Although health officials in eastern Germany are still reluctant to respond to questions about public health, new unofficial reports indicate that in the industrial cities of Leipzig, Halle, Dresden, and Karl-Marx-Stadt, rates of deaths caused by cancer and lung and heart diseases were 15 to 25 percent higher than in Berlin. Even in the mountain towns of northern Czechoslovakia and southern Poland, long famous for their spas, smog has set in and acid rain has killed large stretches of forest.

Dr. Teresa Sregorczyk, a lung specialist in a sanitarium in Karpacz in southern Poland, said that her clinic was still operating effectively but that smog was hampering treatment in the sanitariums of the Jelenia Gora valley nearby. She said she often wonders what will happen to her little patients—220 children at the moment—who already need prolonged treatment for asthma, bronchitis, and tuberculosis. "Most have been exposed to terrible pollution," she said. "I know we are, too, but at least we developed our vital organs under more healthy conditions."

Curing was less orthodox in a nearby uranium mine where about 500 adults were descending for regular breathing sessions. On a recent morning in the salt mine at Wieliczka, near Cracow, adults and children were resting in the dim light, surrounded by gray salt rock. The air 650 feet below the surface felt chilly but moist and exhilarating. Dr. Isabela Wroblewska pronounced it "as good for you as sitting in a strong sea breeze."

Stanislaw Pasierbeck, a factory worker from Zywiec who said his asthma attacks became unbearable five years ago at age forty-nine, seemed accustomed to the alien world as he slipped off his blankets, fixed his miner's lamp, and walked toward the nurse's station. "This is very good air," he said. "It is the only place where I can breathe deeply." [MS, APRIL 1990]

THE BITTER LEGACY OF BITTERFELD

CAKED with coal dust, Bitterfeld has grown used to foul air and to the knowledge that it is slowly being strangled by a huge chemical complex here, the largest in East Germany and one of the biggest in Eastern Europe. Its workers, about 20,000 of them, know the fumes from the complex on the edge of town often make them and their families ill. The farmers have seen the soiling of the rivers and land. And the mess, like most wrongs here, was once attributed simply to years of Communist ineptitude and sloppiness. But recently, senior officials at the complex—which produces basic chemicals, aluminum, pesticides, dyes, plastics, and hundreds of other products—have said the region was poisoned willfully in a scheme to raise money for the state.

In the decade before the Communist regime's overthrow in 1989, the officials said, the authorities extracted hundreds of millions of dollars from the complex through "fines" for dumping all its highly dangerous residues into the nearby creeks and rivers. The assessments were little more than a thinly veiled form of exploitation under the byzantine methods of Communist bookkeeping because, the officials said, whenever plant managers asked for money to build antipollution devices, they were overruled. The charges of the plant officials have gained support from East Germany's new non-Communist government. "The State Planning Commission milked the chemical industry like a cow," said Fritz Cotta, a longtime executive. "They wanted the money. They preferred the funds to spend them on other things." Mr. Cotta, who is now in charge of closing the industry's most polluting branches, added: "We said we needed treatment plants. The fines could have paid four times for those treatment plants."

The assertions of Mr. Cotta and other experts at Bitterfeld suggest that Communist leaders were far more callous and cynical about the health of thousands of workers and their habitat than East Germans knew. While declaring environmental statistics a state secret, Communist officials here had preached concern about the environment or had blamed the West for holding back antipollution technology.

Some environmentalists now contend that the responsible officials should be criminally charged. "A lot of crimes have been committed in this country, and not only by the secret police," said Gerhard Behrend, East Germany's Under Secretary for the Environment. Mr. Behrend, who was a research chemist, said in an interview in East Berlin that he had learned of the "astronomical" and wasteful fines forced on the chemical industries. Efforts to reach former members of the State Planning Commission for a response to the charges were unsuccessful.

The Bitterfeld Chemical Combine, which consists of eighty separate factories supplying the domestic market and other Eastern European countries, generated at least 4 percent of the state's income, said Eberhard Grahn, the official long in charge of developing new technology at the plant. He said the Industry Ministry and the planners in East Berlin were regularly informed of the industries' lethal emissions and of ways to remedy them.

Among the smokestacks, blistered tanks, and rutted roads of Bitterfeld's chemical works, neglect is blatant even to an uninitiated eye. The air stings, and the water in brooks and rivers has turned to syrup. As Mr. Cotta and Mr. Grahn tell it, the Bitterfeld Chemical Combine for years has poured an average of 200,000 cubic meters of untreated waste water a day into creeks and the Mulde River. More than half the waste contained heavy metals like mercury, cadmium, and lead, untreated acids, and other highly toxic compounds. The stew is carried by the Mulde to the Elbe River and then to Hamburg and the North Sea. One study asserts that about 30,000 tons of lead alone have settled on the bottom of the Hamburg harbor, most of it from

East Germany. Officials in West Germany said billions of marks will be needed to clean up the East's industrial zones and the waterways they have polluted.

In the soot-covered town hall of Bitterfeld, meanwhile, the small environmental office is struggling with questions more fundamental than cost. "We need to establish if people can still live here at all, if they can eat the food," said Rainer Fromman, the office chief, who is an agronomist. He said early studies had shown that parts of the industrial belt, studded with villages and small towns with about 120,000 inhabitants, were no longer fit for human habitation. Help that has been promised by Berlin and Bonn has not come, he said, but the West German town of Bielefeld recently sent some expert help. A recent study showed that milk from local cows contained toxic substances exceeding the permissible level by nine times, Mr. Fromman said.

Dust and soil from the center of the village of Greppin, he said, contained dioxins more than one hundred times higher than the level allowed in soil used for food crops. The dioxin level, he said, was well above the level at which under West German law the topsoil must be replaced. Most alarming, he said, was the dust taken from a kindergarten playground in Wolfen. It showed extremely high levels of heavy metals, posing a threat to the children's bone development and vital organs. "We have not published the results because we do not want to drive thousands of people crazy," said Mr. Fromman. "We need to do more tests."

At the headquarters of the chemical complex, managers said thirty-nine of the eighty plants were scheduled to close. In the balance are not only 20,000 jobs, but the region's entire economy, which centers on the dilapidated installations. "Every week, there are one or two explosions, and the leaks are constant," said Mr. Behrend. "At a chlorine and hydrogen plant, there are so many explosions that the workers stay in a bunker." Recently, thirteen plants have been closed for environmental reasons, said Mr. Cotta, who is in charge of closing the worst offenders. Four more have been shut because they are no longer economically viable, he said.

Manfred Steinbaum, a spokesman for the complex, said that as the 4,000 different products of the complex were being scaled down to 3,000, the daily load of poison cast into the environment was being reduced. But even if the complex closes and the people of Bitterfeld move, environmentalists say, it will take years to cure the mangled lands. [MS, SEPTEMBER 1990]

THE URANIUM DUMP AT WISMUT

BARREN and black, the ashen hills of nuclear waste stand like treeless offspring of the wooded mountains that cradle the towns and villages of this German frontier region. They were once shrouded with the secrecy of the Wismut uranium mines, begun in the first fever of Stalin's drive for atomic weaponry and for years the largest supplier of uranium for Moscow's nuclear effort. In early 1991, this vast troubled landscape afforded a sobering dose of the realities united Germany is up against in cleaning up eastern Germany's environment.

The uranium mines that produced these grim hillocks and lakes of polluted sludge are being shut down. The last operating mines, near the hamlet of Schlema, have also closed. The veil of secrecy is lifting, as reports appear about the history of the mines and the diseases of those who toiled there, subjects that were untouchable not long ago. Wismut, the company that ran the mines, is designing a $3.6 billion cleanup program, which the Bonn government will finance, to fill mine shafts and cleanse the mountains and lakes of radioactive waste.

Government medical experts and some local officials contend the problem of the waste piles is mainly cosmetic, not toxic. Mayor Konrad Barth of Schlema, for example, cites government studies that found few points in towns like Aue where radon emissions exceeded acceptable levels. But in Schneeberg, a former silver-mining town, roughly 5 percent of the houses were found to have extraordinarily high radon levels. Nevertheless, government medical experts who examined a father and four children in a house where radon emissions measured 120 times the maximum acceptable level said they found no abnormalities. Still, the experts concede that little is known of the long-term effects of low-level radiation like that spread by the heaps and lakes of waste material, and they urge that the health of local people be carefully monitored. They also acknowledge that potentially greater dangers loom from the presence in the waste piles of other toxic materials, like arsenic.

Thus far, the citizens of towns like Aue (population 30,000) say all the publicity about their environmental woes has done only damage, frightening away potential investors. Worst of all, the mines themselves, like most of the muscle-bound East German industrial economy, are an albatross. The local ore is virtually depleted, the technology outmoded and costly, and Soviet orders for uranium gone. Where 40,000 people toiled as recently as last year, more than half are now unemployed or working shorter hours.

Wismut was flung up by the Soviets after 1945 in a crash project to break America's nuclear monopoly. Until 1954, Soviet officials ran it alone under a shroud of military secrecy, hauling the uranium to the Soviet Union without paying the Germans, as part of reparations payments imposed on East Germany for World War II. The site, where the northern slope of the Erzgebirge climbs toward Czechoslovakia, was chosen for its history as a source of radioactive ores. The Czechoslovak side of the range produced the uranium salts that led the French physicist Henri Becquerel to the discovery of radioactivity in 1896. They built the project big, in the prevailing spirit of Soviet gigantism. With little technical finesse, tens of thousands of workers were assembled, often digging with picks and shovels. From 1946 to the present, officials say, the mines delivered more than 200,000 metric tons of yellow cake, or uranium oxide, to Soviet military and civilian nuclear programs, extracted at great cost from pitchblende, a brownish-black ore that is the principal mineral source of uranium. Now Bonn is seeking agreement to acquire the 50 percent Soviet stake in Wismut. In exchange, Moscow will be released from the liability of cleaning up the environmental mess.

Michael Beleites, a church-affiliated researcher, recalled the primitive conditions of Wismut's birth in a samizdat study he published in 1988, before the fall of communism here, titled, "Pitchblende: East German Uranium Mining and Its Consequences." "The number of uranium miners rose faster than quarters could be built," Mr. Beleites said. "Thus in Johanngeorgenstadt, cots were set up in apartment hallways to afford at least sufficient places to sleep. In such a situation, labor-hygienic conditions played as good as no role. They drilled dry, so that the miners constantly breathed in radioactive dust."

Among the region's people, the consoling memory of a time when things were much worse is decreasingly vivid. Wismut, which was transformed into a Soviet–East German joint venture in 1954 and quickly developed into a state within a state, with its own police, communications, and transport systems, is now struggling for survival. The last of about 400 to 500 Soviet engineers and managers departed in December 1990, and under a scheme drawn up with the help of Western consultants, the huge concern now hopes to market its skills in mining, environmental cleanup, and construction to create jobs for some of its remaining 29,000 employees.

But the harshest legacy is the environmental mess. One problem is the mine shafts, a vast warren of tunnels and cavities that stretch for thousands of miles under the mountainous landscape, some piercing depths of 6,000 feet. "We must remove grease and oils and some toxic materials, and take out steel supports, rail tracks, and old air-conditioning equipment," said Christoph Rudolph, who runs the mining operations in Aue. The empty cavities, like giant rotten teeth, will then be pumped full of cement fillings, he said.

More troubling still are huge mountains of waste and lakes of slush that were waste products of arduous mining and extraction processes. Ores from the Erzgebirge were never rich, Mr. Rudolph explained, yielding about nine pounds of uranium for every ton of ore mined, or about four tenths of 1 percent, compared with 12 percent for some rich Canadian and Australian ores. The waste was dumped in huge heaps that now dot the landscape, and now day by day dilapidated Soviet-built dump trucks haul the material to new sites to flatten the hills, which will then be covered with topsoil and reforested. But the wastes, which contain residues of uranium and radium, emit radon gas. "Not a place for grazing cows or building homes," Mr. Rudolph said.

Other pollutants are equally alarming. Separating the uranium from the waste involved scrubbings with sulfuric acid and caustic solutions that were discarded and collected in vast lake-like basins, whose waters were gradually fed into local rivers and streams. Wismut officials acknowledge that such waters are heavily laced with toxic substances like arsenic, uranium, and radium, and environmental activists regard local rivers like the Zwickauer Mulde and Weisse Elster as radioactively polluted. Officials say they focus on protecting the water table and gradually ridding the landscape of these grim ponds. In his study, Mr. Beleites chronicled reports by miners and their families of frequent cases of lung and testicular cancer, leukemia, and such conditions as hair loss, temporary impotency among men, and fatigue. Local miners called Oberrothenbach, on the shore of a waste basin, "the tired village."

Horst Richter, a geologist who became Wismut's chief executive officer in 1990, conceded that in the early years medical care was deficient. Later, however, the company organized health care services exclusively for its workers that were far above the level enjoyed by most East Germans. Mr. Richter said that about 5,400 cases of lung cancer were recorded in secret medical data the company kept over the years on some 450,000 employees, roughly the same as the national average. More widespread, he acknowledged, were such conditions as silicosis, a lung ailment marked by shortness of breath common among miners, and rheumatic ailments of the joints and back that resulted from measures taken to reduce the threat of contamination by radioactive dust. For one, mining surfaces were constantly wet. Moreover, air-conditioning of the mines meant workers stood continuously in cold air streams. Only now, however, are company medical data being opened for research. "We still don't have independent evaluation," said the Reverend Andreas Krusche, the pastor of Saint Wolfgang's Church in Schneeberg. "Wismut was autarkic. They themselves evaluated the results of their own evaluations."

Now passivity, bewilderment, and pessimism abound. But some say the greatest potential for the region's redevelopment may lie in its very radioactivity. Before World War II, Schlema was Europe's most important radon spa, with a radiological institute and more than 300 boardinghouses catering to thousands of guests who came each year for radioactive treatment. In 1946, after the Russians took over, the spa buildings were torn down and the radiology institute's valuable library hauled to the Soviet Union. Now Mr. Barth has revival plans. A scholarly conference is planned to begin the project. "We have to perform a giant somersault," Mr. Barth said, "out of a valley of death into a valley of hope." [JT, MARCH 1991]

THE CENTRAL EUROPEAN COAL BELT

O N the edge of an open-pit mine in the mountains of Bohemia stands a small cluster of medieval buildings, the last remainder of a town that survives only in the minds of its former inhabitants. The town of Most, Czechoslovakia, was built on a coal field, a good enough reason for officials in Prague to order it knocked down to make way for the giant shovels now dropping chunks of its soil onto the mine's conveyor belt.

Former residents talk of mounds of earth where the theater, the brewery, one of the four churches, and even their own homes once stood. For three decades, nothing has been allowed to stand in the way of Czechoslovakia's hunger for coal. And in this region alone, twenty-eight villages were destroyed and 80,000 people evicted from their homes in the name of five-year energy plans. Bulldozers have turned towns, farms, and woodlands into coarse brown deserts and gaping hollows. The smokestacks of the power plants that turn the coal into electricity now mark a skyline thick with soot. On days when the smog is heaviest, the radio warns people to keep their children indoors.

The scene is repeated throughout the Central European coal belt, from East Germany through northern Czechoslovakia and across southern Poland. Across this basin, the quest for fuel has razed villages and ravaged the land and is making people nauseated and asthmatic with sulfur-loaded air. As the three countries move toward democracy, their new governments are talking of the monumental challenge and costs involved in dealing with this legacy of the Stalinist drive for industrialization at any cost. Yet the cost of cleaning the air and restoring the land is only part of the problem. Even with freely elected governments, the three most industrialized countries of Eastern Europe depend overwhelmingly on coal for jobs and energy.

East Germany, by far the largest coal producer of the three, meets 70 percent of its energy needs with coal, and its open-pit, soft-coal mines tear up the equivalent of 8,000 football fields' worth of land each year. In Poland, which still mines much of its coal underground in Silesia, brown and black coal accounts for 78 percent of the country's fuel and a big portion of its hard currency earnings. In Czechoslovakia, coal covers 60 percent of its energy. In the three countries, close to 200,000 people earn their livings from mining coal, moving it, and transforming it into energy.

The new town of Most, which now has 68,000 people, sits on a hillside overlooking the mine that gradually gobbled up the old city in the late 1960s and early 1970s. In the valley below are a few medieval buildings that were spared. The finest among them, a fourteenth-century Gothic church, was put on giant rollers in 1975 and, in an extraordinary transplant, was moved 1,000 yards. It now stands safe near the edge of the mine. The rest of the buildings were razed and their inhabitants were paid to move into the rows of drab apartment buildings that make up the new town. "Some people were happy to take the money they were offered," recalled Vlastislav Trefny, planning chief of the new city. "But others wanted to stay in the place of their grandparents, to keep their gardens, dogs, and chickens. We had to use force. They budged only after their water and electricity were cut off."

In Mr. Trefny's office in the town hall, coffee was served in a cup with the inscription "Trebusice, 1391–1979." That was one of the razed villages, explained Mr. Trefny, who was born in Kopistry, adding, "Seventy-five hundred people, and also gone." Did it make economic sense, all this moving, knocking down, and rebuilding, just to extract the inefficient, highly polluting brown coal?

"We never knew the cost of a ton of coal," Mr. Trefny replied, pondering on the Communist economy of subsidies and barter. "The system has been so convoluted, it's too difficult to take it apart and see if it makes sense. We only know that open-pit mining is cheaper," he continued. "Underground you get only 40 percent of the coal, on top you get 90 percent, and it's less dangerous. Of course, in an open mine you have total devastation of the land."

The gradual switch to surface mining is ending a mining culture that has gone on here for generations. Over a beer in the Murom, a tavern frequented by miners, Yaroslav Gryner recalled with nostalgia that he was once "a real miner." Now with the shafts closed and the camaraderie of the dark and dangerous world underground gone, he drives a truck in an open-pit mine. It is not men's work, he said, but he is staying because mining salaries are twice as high as those in other industries. The men blame the power station and the new chemical plant just down the road in Litvinov, rather than the strip mine, for "ruining everyone's life," as Vaclav Stirek put it. He had spent half his life underground, he said, "and down there it was never clean. But you came up and you got clean air," he added. "Today, the miner comes up, and he gets even worse air. And so do his children. There is no more way out."

Hanna Vravska, who works in the new town hall, said she cannot get used to the dismal landscape, the housing blocks, the feeling of suffocation. She panics every time parents are warned not to take their children outside because of extreme pollution. "I feel guilty raising my children here," she said. "I hope public pressure will force some changes."

Since the end of Communist rule, changes have been few. The same officials and managers are in charge, although the huge sign on top of the mining office that proclaimed "Glory to the Communist Party" is gone. A new signal of the right to know has appeared in the town hall: a board listing the daily air pollution count. The sulfur dioxide from the power plant and a menu of noxious gases from nearby chemical works, it is said, often exceed levels considered harmful to human health in the West. During temperature inversions, they reportedly exceed such levels by up to ten times.

The plan of the Communist government, demanding 600 megawatts of electricity from Bohemia every five years, no longer exists. But digging and stripping of the soil is expected to go on. The rich fields of Bohemia have already yielded 1.5 billion tons of brown coal, and with reserves of a further 5 billion tons, the officials said, six more villages had been slated for destruction.

When President Vaclav Havel visited Most in 1990, he told the miners that the country would need their coal for many years to come. But the people from the doomed villages, it is said, planned to petition him to save their homes.   [MS, APRIL 1990]

CLEANING UP CRACOW

I N Cracow, this city of rapid political change and some of the foulest air, water, and soil in Poland, a former farmer has moved into a local palace, pledging that the fight against the filth has begun. He is the new mayor of Cracow, Jerzy Rosciszeweski, the first Green Party mayor of any large city in Europe. His election in February 1990 stunned and annoyed the Solidarity movement, which leads the new Polish government.

"It's not me, it's the environment that won," said the mayor, a man of modest manner who was once a breeder of horses and sheep. Just four weeks after being elected to the job by the municipal council, he is still unaccustomed to the limelight, the crush of local supplicants, and the salesmen from America, Europe, and Japan now filing through his waiting rooms. The foreigners are offering the latest industrial filters, scrubbers, and other technology to protect the environment, as well as the newest blueprints for efficient plants. The mayor is not yet buying, but he is listening.

Cracow is one of the fine medieval cities of Europe, yet in the name of industrial growth and social equality it has been turned into a grubby, soiled, and, physicians say, extremely unhealthy place. Sharing the blanket of pollution that drifts over much of southern Poland, the city is further irritated and corroded every day by tons of dust and fumes from its own blast furnaces and power plants, and from the stoves and cars of its citizens. By some accounts, eight tons of dust fall on every square mile each year. "By June, we can cut the dust by 25 percent," said the mayor, perhaps uncommonly optimistic for a man whose task is painfully evident to the city's 750,000 people.

The view from the mayor's windows in Wielopolska Palace was blurred recently by gray and sour air trapped by a temperature inversion in Cracow's poorly ventilated valley. The Vistula River, behind the palace, was running heavy with waste. "Nothing but a sewage canal, unfit for human use," the mayor said. Experts have also told him that in the Old Town, around the sweeping central market, 95 percent of the 4,076 buildings deemed of historical importance were in poor or even alarming condition. There, acidic fallout had eaten so many noses and fingers from statues and blunted so many reliefs from Renaissance facades that Darek Kuzniar, a guide, wondered, "If the air can do this to stone, what is it doing to us?"

The Green Party mayor and his staff have been working late hours and weekends, hoping, they said, to overcome the years of apathy. Offering his strategy for change, the mayor sounded more like a military leader than a man of the farm. "We start with the air," he said, which meant tearing down part of the giant Nowa Huta steel mill on the edge of town, which employs more than 30,000 people. The plant had been a Communist prestige project, aimed at mixing the recalcitrant bourgeoisie and the intelligensia of Cracow with a contingent of workers. But for every ton of steel it produced, Nowa Huta poured twenty pounds of dust and ashes over the social experiment. "Work it out," said the mayor, noting that the mill has been logging five to seven million tons of steel a year.

Cracow would create new jobs with nonpolluting industries, electronics, and tourism, the mayor said. "We have no shortage of offers," he added, with an eye to his waiting room. But a short-term solution for cleaner air, the mayor said, was to switch from the low-grade, inefficient Soviet ore to an energy-saving, better-quality ore, or even pig iron from Brazil. The mayor seemed shocked when told that such pig iron is the bane of the Brazilian Green Party because it is processed with charcoal made from tens of thousands of Amazon region trees. "In that case," he said quickly, "their trees are as important as ours."

Next on the mayor's hit list was the city power plant, which stokes 1.5 million tons of polluting coal a year, twice as much as the steel mill, to produce Cracow's heat and electricity. "I'm an enemy of nuclear power," said the mayor, "but we want to heat the city with a new Canadian nuclear process that does not produce radioactive waste." Clean electricity and heat could also discourage Cracow residents from burning the 600,000 tons of high-sulfur coal they use in their home stoves and heaters.

In fighting pollution, Cracow hopes to borrow from the World Bank and other international lending institutions. Help promised from abroad has not yet arrived, the mayor said. "So far there has been a lot of handshaking and applause."

But what of the $15 million for environmental assistance pledged by the United States government? "A very nice gesture," he said, nodding, "but putting things into perspective, it will have the same impact as if you give a man whose whole family is starving a single roll of bread. The deficit and damage caused by forty-five years of communism is staggering." [MS, MARCH 1990]

THE RUIN OF ROMANIA .

F OR about fifteen miles around, every growing thing in this once gentle valley of Romania looks as if it has been dipped in ink. Trees and bushes are black; the grass is stained. The houses and streets look like the inside of a chimney. Even the sheep on the hillsides are a dingy gray. There are two factories here. One makes black powder used in the manufacture of rubber. The other produces zinc, lead, copper, cadmium, and other nonferrous metals. Together they spew out 30,000 tons of particles and soot each year, leaving Copsa Mica, with about 6,000 people, one of the most polluted places in all of Europe.

The black powder is only the most visible pollutant. For those working in the metals factory, there is the constant stench and taste of sulfuric acid. But the more significant danger comes from the invisible pollution—high levels of lead and an undetermined threat from the stew of toxic compounds in the air. The soot and filth afflicting this quiet region 200 miles northwest of Bucharest are not new to Eastern Europe, just an extreme case. There was little chance to speak out against pollution and environmental health hazards during the long years of Communist control. And unlike the case in the West, where pollution and acid rain pose a similar threat, there is little ecological movement to speak of here.

Romania and other Eastern-bloc nations now hope to clean things up. But the cost of such efforts could place a serious burden on the economies of Central Europe, which are trying with great difficulty to gain a sound footing as communism recedes. In the meantime, the pollution and its fallout grow worse.

Dr. Alexandru Balin, thirty-eight years old, has been working for thirteen years in the occupational health clinic connected to the metals factory at Copsa Mica (pronounced COPE-shah MEE-kah). He has watched as the workers' health deteriorated dramatically. In 1977, there were 70 people diagnosed with excessive or dangerous levels of lead in their bodies; today, there are more than 400. More than half of those working in the metals factory have above-normal levels. Lead poisoning produces various symptoms, of which the most common are nervousness and anemia. The side effects are temporary paralysis, rheumatism-like symptoms, acute abdominal pains, respiratory problems, and rare cases of encephalitis. Long-term effects are unknown, doctors say, because comprehensive studies are lacking and workers disappear from the clinic's charts after retirement at age fifty.

Still, in 1985, Dr. Balin compiled a detailed report on the alarming situation, and he knows that the study landed on the desk of Nicolae Ceausescu, the Romanian leader who was deposed and executed in December 1989. Two things happened as a result. The factory got the money to build a 750-foot tower that now sends the sulfuric emissions wafting in the direction of nearby mountain villages. And Dr. Balin was once again called to the offices of the Securitate, the secret police, which has since been disbanded, and asked why he was making so much trouble.

Before the Romanian revolution in December 1989, Copsa Mica was generally shielded from foreign eyes. The metals factory, considered crucial to the Romanian economy, produced for the domestic market only. In the late 1970s, a Japanese company came to bid on a contract to install filters at the powder factory, but the contract was later withdrawn because it was considered too expensive. "Nobody knew about us," Dr. Balin said. "Now people come, and they say we are the most polluted town in the world."

Cut off from the outside world, Dr. Balin and the other doctors did what they could to keep up with medical science and with the latest theories on treatment for lead poisoning. But they did not need foreign textbooks to know that the best prevention was to reduce exposure. At a similar factory in West Germany, Dr. Balin said, workers are given three years' pay for a maximum of two years' work. "Man is the most idiotic animal," he said. "Horses can stay here only two years. Then they must be sold and sent to the mountains, or else they die."

Ioan Zaharie, who worked at the factory for seventeen years, visited the clinic recently for backaches, a recurring problem. He is the only one in his family to work in Copsa Mica, although the pay here is more than double the national average. "One in the family is enough," said Mr. Zaharie, forty-seven years old, who remembers when flowers still grew in Copsa Mica. But like many who live in the area, Mr. Zaharie sees the dirt as part of life, much like other miseries common to the Ceausescu era.

The health problems that Dr. Balin and his colleagues have chronicled are not just those caused by pollution. Hepatitis B and tuberculosis are common in Copsa Mica; so is alcoholism. Hot water was not available in many apartments until recently, and many older houses have no indoor plumbing. Food supplies were marginally better here than elsewhere, but the difference, Dr. Balin said, was between getting salami eight times a year, or three. "I would say to them, you must eat and not drink," said Dr. Balin. "And they would ask me where to find something to eat. I would say, you must wash more often, and they would say, where to find the soap. When you have money, you have civilization; when you don't, you don't."

Now the Romanians are scrambling to make up for lost time. A new independent trade union visited Bucharest in January 1990 to wring promises of higher pay and more safety equipment from the new government. Last week, half of the metals factory was closed for repairs, and plans call for it to be rebuilt from the ground up. But Dr. Balin, who has accumulated new duties as a member of the town council and an adviser to the union and to local ecologists, said that restoring people's health would be more complicated. "We still don't know how all these compounds react together," he said. "There is no city in the world with all these toxics, and since we can't make tests, we still don't know."

The damage is not restricted to the working population. Dr. Balin quoted one report that showed children in Copsa Mica testing more than 5 percent below average on intelligence tests. In the region, hospitals have reported a striking increase in the number of babies born with malformed hearts: sixteen were reported in 1988, Dr. Balin said, compared with five from 1977 to 1983. Bronchial asthma and other respiratory illnesses are common among children, according to Dr. Ute Deutschlander, the local pediatrician.   [CB, MARCH 1990]

IN THE ARCTIC, A SOVIET
RADIOACTIVE WASTE DUMP

For three decades the nuclear-powered Soviet Navy and icebreaking fleet have dumped much of their radioactive waste in the Arctic, Russian authorities now acknowledge. The dumping, in the shallow waters of the Barents and Kara seas, has potentially serious consequences for the Arctic environment.

At greatest risk for Norway and Russia, two of the world's biggest fish exporters, are the bountiful Arctic fishing grounds. Radioactive contamination in the shallow seas where the marine food chain begins could contaminate the fish population and endanger the industry, officials of both countries said in interviews. Norwegian scientists who have been testing the Barents and Norwegian seas for several years have detected no significant radioactive contamination in the water and in fish. But the director of the nuclear energy safety authority in Oslo said waters near the dumping sites had not been tested, and sunken waste containers a few hundred feet below the surface could pose a serious environmental threat over decades as they begin to leak.

Reports about the dumping practices were first made last fall by a member of the old Soviet Parliament who is a radiation engineer with the state company that operates the icebreaking fleet from the port of Murmansk. The charges became more detailed through the winter as other witnesses stepped forward after the collapse of the Soviet Union. After meetings in May of 1992 between Russian and Norwegian government officials, the Russian environmental authorities told their Norwegian counterparts that the reports were essentially correct and that they would cooperate in what could be a huge and costly international cleanup effort.

The first scientific expedition to map the dumping sites and test for contamination was scheduled to start on July 10, 1992, and included twenty researchers from six countries aboard a Russian ship. "At this stage, we would like to go down to the bottom with diving equipment and really see the waste itself," said Knut Gussgard, Norway's nuclear safety director. "We would like to see whether it is barrels or parts of submarines and reactors, and we would like to take measurements and samples because we are concerned about future contamination from really big sources over ten to a hundred years."

At present, Norwegian authorities say fish testing near Norway's waters has shown radioactive contamination that barely registers and may be attributed to historic contamination from such sources as atmospheric testing and the Chernobyl disaster.

Some of the worst dumping occurred in the 1960s and 1970s, but radioactive wastes were dumped throughout the 1980s. The navy's dumping continued until last year, said Andrei Zolotkov, a radiation safety engineer in the Murmansk Shipping Company, the state enterprise that operates the nuclear-powered icebreakers. He first researched and compiled the dumping allegations while a member of the Soviet Parliament. Other officials suspect that some dumping may still be going on, although in 1976 the Soviet Union signed an international protocol outlawing dumping in shallow seas.

One account of the dumping given to international environmental organizations by Mr. Zolotkov indicates that at least twelve nuclear reactors were disposed of in shallow gulfs off Novaya Zemlya, the large Arctic island that the Soviet Union used as a nuclear test range beginning in the early 1950s. A complete submarine that suffered a major reactor accident is believed to be sunk near the island, along with still-radioactive sections of other submarines.

Mr. Zolotkov said in an interview that three of the reactors from the first nuclear-powered icebreaker, the *Lenin*, were encased in an epoxylike substance and then blasted through the hull of the ship to the bottom of a shallow gulf off southeastern Novaya Zemlya in 1967. The *Lenin* had earlier suffered a serious reactor accident. After its radioactive power plant was purged by the explosions, the ship was towed to port and refitted. About half of the dumped reactors went to the bottom with their highly radioactive nuclear fuel still inside, according to the information collected by Mr. Zolotkov. In addition, thousands of containers of solid radioactive wastes from the *Northern Fleet* and other icebreakers were dumped. In cases where they would not sink, Soviet seamen are said to have cut holes in the "sealed" containers so that they would. In 1984, Mr. Zolotkov said, a container measuring a high level of radioactivity washed ashore on Novaya Zemlya and was dumped again.

Wastewater from naval and civilian reactors was also dumped, by special ships that diluted radioactive liquid with seawater and then discharged it through a pipe that extended below the ships' propellers.

Mr. Zolotkov said he took part in one of these dumping missions in 1974. For five days afterward, the crew found measurable levels of radioactive cesium in seawater samples in the dumping zone, he said, but officials assumed that if other nations detected the radioactivity, they would attribute it to fallout persisting from atmospheric nuclear tests or from other sources. "Those nuclear tests served as a sort of cover for these dumping operations," Mr. Zolotkov said.

The Northern Fleet operates more than 200 nuclear propulsion reactors in its ballistic missile and attack submarines, which are based along the fjords of the Kola Peninsula. Together with surface ships and naval air forces, they represent the largest concentration of former Soviet naval power. Northern Fleet officials declined requests for an interview for this report. This reporter's request to visit the main Severomorsk naval base was granted and then canceled without explanation.

Russian officials do not dispute the dumping accounts and some officials said in interviews in Murmansk that they believed environmental investigations now being planned would bear out the allegations that are based on ships' logs and witnesses. "No one knew the scale of the operations carried out over twenty-five years," Mr. Zolotkov said. "No one tried to survey all of the materials and study the consequences."

The 1972 London convention on ocean dumping outlawed the disposal of high-level wastes at sea and required that nations wishing to dispose of low-level radioactive wastes do so in ocean basins at depths greater than 12,000 feet. Depths in the Barents and Kara seas, where the Soviet dumping has taken place, range from 200 feet to 1,000 feet.

Russia has agreed that any evidence collected in the investigation will be sent to relevant authorities, but officials said there was no remedy other than international pressure to disclose and perhaps clean up the worst sites, some of which may lie in international waters. Ivan I. Menshikov, who is President Boris N. Yeltsin's political representative for the Murmansk region, said in an interview that he applauded Mr. Zolotkov's exposure of the dumping practices. "This is a problem created by the government we had before, and the present leadership must solve this problem," said Mr. Menshikov, a retired army colonel. Where the financial resources will come from is less certain. The cost of cleaning up the waste sites is another expensive and complicated liability that Moscow is ill equipped to cope with as it struggles with drastic economic reforms, inflation, and the general social and political chaos of the post-Soviet transition.

Just downstream from the icy port of Murmansk, dozens of rusting nuclear submarines are moored side by side awaiting decommissioning and the removal of tons of toxic spent nuclear fuel from their reactors. The new commander of the Northern Fleet, Vice Admiral Oleg Yerofeyev, said in a meeting with Russian reporters in Murmansk in mid-April of 1992 that he must scrap ten atomic submarines by 1995. He complained that the cost of cutting up each submarine was on the order of 100 million rubles, roughly $1 million at today's exchange rate.

At the end of April 1992, the Russian managers of the submarine building yard at Sverodvinsk, the largest in the world, opened discussions with Norway's Fridtjof Nansen Research Institute, seeking Western expertise and money for the decommissioning of about fifty nuclear submarines before the end of the decade. Russia seeks to cut the size of the fleet by a third by 1995. "They do not have the resources, and they are facing a major environmental challenge and they do not know how to handle it," said Willy Oestrang, the institute's director.

Some senior officers in the former Soviet military have asserted that the dumping charges are exaggerated and that the waste-handling practices pose no long-term risk to the environment, but this assertion is under challenge by environmental organizations. The military appears to be supporting a proposal to build a permanent radioactive waste repository on Novaya Zemlya using one or more of the shafts built for underground nuclear explosions. But Mr. Zolotkov and some of his allies in the civilian government are trying to ensure that control of any permanent storage site does not rest with the military, which they say was most involved in the illicit dumping. "The consequences of this program reach out into the new century," Mr. Zolotkov said, "and that's why we need a modern nuclear waste facility using experts from abroad and monitored by international organizations." Norway also showed its concern by banning the Russian icebreakers from entering Norwegian ports to take aboard tourists for $20,000 excursions to the North Pole.

Russian civilian officials have expressed concern about the scale of the dumping, which was kept secret within military and government circles while Soviet diplomats maintained publicly that the nation's nuclear-powered fleet conducted no dumping at sea. In an interview in Oslo on April 29, 1992, the Norwegian prime minister, Gro Harlem Brundtland, also expressed concern, saying the dumping represented a "security risk to people and to the natural biology of northern waters."

Norway's defense minister, Johan Jorgen Holst, speaking in an interview in Oslo, referred to the more immediate threat to the region's economy, saying, "If the rumor gets around that Norwegian and Russian fish are contaminated with radioactivity, we aren't going to sell many fish." The United States and many Western European countries import substantial quantities of Norwegian fish, and Russia now depends on fish exports as a critical hard-currency earner.

Practices that would shock Western environmentalists are common in Murmansk. The Soviet nuclear authorities kept tons of spent nuclear reactor fuel in "floating" storage along the busy waterways of Murmansk harbor and within the corporate limits of this city of 450,000 people. The toxic spent fuel remains there for three years while its high level of radioactivity "cools" enough so it can be shipped by railcar to Chelyabinsk in the southern Ural Mountains for reprocessing. "I do not see the need for keeping spent nuclear fuel from all of the icebreakers floating in Murmansk harbor with the risk of fire and collision," Mr. Gussgard of Norway's radiation safety agency said in Oslo. "I don't think it is safe, and I cannot imagine that it would be approved in any Western country." The dumping allegations have received wide coverage in the Russian press, and local political pressure has added to the demand for accountability from the navy and the icebreaker fleet.

Public revulsion over the dumping is running well ahead of the scientific efforts to verify it in detail. A longtime merchant seaman said residents of Murmansk were inclined to believe the rumors that two barges containing radioactive wastes sank while at anchor in the harbor some years ago. Referring to the dumping allegations, Leonid B. Gurevich, the member of the Russian Parliament from Murmansk, said, "I have no doubt about this information, because I know the regime I was brought up in."

Norway has registered small amounts of radioactivity in the Barents Sea for years, but it has attributed this to the fallout from Soviet nuclear tests and from the explosion that released a cloud of radioactive material from the Soviet nuclear power station at Chernobyl in

1986. But virtually no independent testing has taken place in the waters near Novaya Zemlya and in the Kara Sea, which the Soviet Navy regarded as home waters and which remained effectively closed during the cold war years.

The dumping allegations have broken the traditional military grip on this area. In a meeting with Norwegian officials in Moscow in mid-April 1992, Russian officials agreed to assemble the first inventory of radioactive waste sites in Arctic waters and present it to Norwegian officials in May. Then, from July 10 to August 6, scientists from Russia, Norway, and four other countries launched an expedition aboard a Russian research vessel to locate and map dozens of underwater dumping sites. They collected samples of the seabed and marine life to test for radioactive contamination.

[PET, MAY 1992]

MERCURY AT MINAMATA

I T is more than thirty-five years now since the cats in this fishing village along Japan's rugged southern coast began to foam at the mouth, tear at themselves, and, in fits of crazed blindness, throw themselves into the sea. Next came the townspeople. Older residents of Minamata still tell vivid stories of watching their parents and children die excruciating deaths from mercury poisoning.

For years now, Japan has tried to sweep beyond the horrors that made the name Minamata synonymous with industrial disasters. In the official histories of Japan's industrial resurgence after World War II, the story of how the Chisso Corporation dumped tons of mercury into one of Japan's richest fishing grounds was long ago relegated to brief mention. The question of why it took nearly a decade and 1,000 deaths before the government took significant action is almost never discussed. But the negligence, the bitterness, and the country's long-standing unwillingness to come to terms with the surviving victims of Minamata disease have unexpectedly blown back now with a fury on a stunned government here.

More than a half-dozen separate courts have issued a surprising series of decisions virtually ordering government officials to recognize 2,000 more people who say they are victims of Minamata disease and to negotiate compensation for them quickly, before they die. In a highly unusual standoff, the government of Prime Minister Toshiki Kaifu refused to comply—in part, it seems, because negotiation itself would be tantamount to an admission that Tokyo bore significant responsibility for not acting more swiftly to prevent the gruesome deaths. And the settlements would just be a start: an additional 8,000 people who have not taken court action say that they, too, have suffered brain damage, paralysis, or loss of hearing or sight stemming from the Minamata case.

"We talk a lot about how immature the Japanese political system is, how the national government tries to control everything, including the courthouse," said the governor, Morihiro Hosokawa, who as the direct descendant of the feudal lords who once ruled the region holds great sway here in his battles with Tokyo. "But there are few cases that show so clearly how perverse the Japanese system has become. So I decided to tell the prime minister that before you look up at the world's environmental problems, look down at your toes, where the problem is."

Indeed, the environmental disaster that struck Minamata has never really ceased. Though much of the mercury has been dredged from the bay overlooking the Shiranui Sea, the fishing grounds are still dangerously polluted and the fishermen, who numbered heavily among the victims, are gone. Minamata's population has declined by a third, to fewer than 35,000, and most of those who are left are elderly. Young people who flee for the cities after graduating from high school say they go to great lengths to conceal their origins, because elsewhere in Japan Minamata's residents are often regarded as "polluted," even if they do not suffer from Minamata disease. "You simply cannot get a position in a company if people know you are from Minamata," said Tsuginori Hamamoto, a leader of one of the many victims' groups, who is himself confined to a wheelchair because of mercury-tainted fish he ate. "For young people, it is almost impossible to find a marriage partner."

Moreover, Minamata itself is bitterly divided. Mr. Hamamoto and other victims are constantly pressing for memorials and commemorative museums that they say would restore some dignity to the victims; many other residents want all reminders of the disease swept away in hopes that Chisso, whose factory still dominates the town, will invest further here. Years of protests and sometimes even violence have splintered the victims themselves, some supporting Japan's Communist party, which has provided them with legal aid that they could not get from the government, and others arguing that the Communists have cynically used the victims to advance their own candidates.

Minamata's government talks of turning the bay, now being filled in to cover the polluted seabeds, into an environmental park that will draw conferences and tourists. To outsiders, that plan seems almost like a cruel joke in a town that most Japanese go out of their way to avoid. For Tokyo, however, the vexing issue is not tourists but the victims and alleged victims, who after a generation still refuse to drop their claims. Their case hinges on the slowness with which both Chisso and the government reacted to the mounting evidence that mercury poisoning was setting off the convulsions, severe birth defects, paralysis, and loss of speech and hearing that rippled through the town. Though fish that swam close to the plant were seen for years floating belly up, Chisso was not formally identified as the source of the poisonings until 1959, in part because the company, citing trade secrets, refused to cooperate with health investigators. A commission to study the causes was dismissed when it reached an unpopular if obvious set of conclusions.

"The social situation in the town was such that the company could not be told to stop emitting wastewater," said Masazumi Harada, a medical professor at Kumamoto University who has devoted much of his career to studying the case. "And people in Tokyo did not even know where Minamata was." Families refused to report that their relatives were dying from mercury poisoning, for fear it would lead to ostracism and be a cause of shame for generations. The government did little, refusing even to ban fishing in the bay until 1968, after another outbreak of the disease closer to Tokyo forced action.

Today Chisso's giant plant, which dates from the turn of the century, still dominates the town. It has shrunk to a fraction of its size at the time of the disaster, employing only 900 people, who now make much of the world's supply of liquid crystal, the organic material used to form numbers and letters on the flat-panel screens of calculators and laptop computers.

But the company is barely profitable, in large part because of a settlement it reached with several hundred victims and survivors in

1973. That settlement covered the most obvious victims, people like Mr. Hamamoto, whose muscles still visibly tremble, and it nearly bankrupted the company.

Now both the local and national governments, and Chisso itself, are facing court decisions that raise the specter of thousands more compensation cases. Chisso says it simply cannot afford to pay. "We cannot survive without the government's help," said Norio Ishida, the manager of Chisso's legal affairs department.

The courts have effectively dismissed the narrow definition of Minamata victims long used by the government, a definition that embraced only 2,900 people, a third of whom have died. That was a rare act for the Japanese judiciary. "I think everyone in the government assumed they would win, as they usually do," said Governor Hosokawa. "They were shocked when suddenly the courts said otherwise." Takenori Goto, a Tokyo lawyer who has spent most of his career working for the mercury-poisoning victims, said, "The national government's policy is that if the case drags on long enough the plantiffs will die." It is difficult to tell what maladies are caused by mercury poisoning. "These are people who are completely different from the first patients, and the problem is whether they are truly victims of Minamata disease or not," said Akimori Ogawa, an official of the Environmental Protection Agency.

He is speaking of people like Masato Ogata, a fisherman who was six years old at the height of the poisonings, which killed his father in 1959, only two months after he first developed symptoms. The next year government doctors tested Mr. Ogata, and their records, which were kept from the victims for more than twenty-five years, show they found 182 parts per million of mercury in his hair, a dangerously high level. "My limbs and head still feel very numb," he said, "and parts of my body still suffer from spasms and cramps." But his symptoms are nearly impossible to trace directly to mercury poisoning. Mr. Ogata says he has given up fighting for recognition as a Minamata victim, out of frustration.

The government has shown a few signs of giving in. It is talking about some additional medical care for those who claim they are victims, though the amounts would be small. And in Minamata, many people just want the memory to go away, for fear that Chisso, still the town's biggest hope, will be driven into bankruptcy. It is a form of dependency that Professor Harada says has deep roots in Japan. "In

the Edo period, farmers had to offer much rice to the feudal lord,"
he said, referring to the era that ended in 1868. "But not many
peasants complained, because they thought they could not live without
the lord. The same is still true." [DES, JANUARY 1991]

MEXICO CITY'S POLLUTED AIR

WHETHER the weather is cold or hot, one thing is usually certain
in the northern Mexico City suburb of Ecatepec: it snows.
Snow, at least, is the word that residents of Ecatepec use for the fine
white powder that blankets their streets and houses every morning.
And it is a fitting description for what scientists say is a lingering
cloud of wind-borne chemicals that hangs above the working-class
neighborhood, raised from a giant caustic-soda plant beyond the horizon. "It even kills the trees," said Pedro Quesadas Herrera, a forty-
year-old accountant, pointing to lifeless shrubs on the block where he
lives with his wife and four daughters. "There's no way to get away
from it."

Amid the bare concrete houses and flat, rubble-strewn fields of
Ecatepec, many adults and children have developed respiratory problems, and dozens bear large patches of rough, discolored skin on their
faces and arms. The neighborhood air is so foul with sharp, industrial
odors that it burns a visitor's eyes and throat. Yet by Mexico City
standards, Ecatepec's toxic snowfall is just one symptom of a deepen-
ing environmental crisis that has left the Mexican capital with the most
polluted air of any major metropolitan area in the world.

Trapped by unfavorable geography and explosive population
growth, Mexico City has what scientists say is an unequaled collection
of atmospheric poisons. It is overwhelmed by industrial emissions,
smoke, vehicle exhaust, and human waste. Saturated with contaminants, the gray-brown blanket of pollution that covers the Mexico
City valley now routinely exceeds—by as much as four times—the
maximum exposure limits established by the World Health Organization. Infectious diseases like salmonella and hepatitis can be contracted

simply by inhaling bacteria suspended in the air. And doctors say that even mild outdoor exercise, like jogging, has now become a calculated risk.

As pollution problems have worsened, the Mexican government, pushed by Mexico City's mayor, Manuel Camacho Solís, has adopted increasingly stringent measures to force reduction in harmful emissions. Since late 1989, every automobile in the city has been required to remain idle one business day a week. In 1991, the authorities banned traffic in fifty square blocks around the central plaza, the Zócalo, and have begun shutting down dozens of industries for violating pollution laws. Those efforts have been redoubled as environmental concerns have become central to the free trade agreement grouping Mexico, the United States, and Canada. In the fall of 1990, the Mexican government announced a $2.5 billion, four-year plan to rescue the capital's air quality. In March 1991, President Carlos Salinas de Gortari ordered the shutdown of the city's giant state-run oil refinery. Despite such measures, daily concentrations of pollutants like ozone and nitrogen dioxide have continued to rise. In 1990, Mexico City exceeded maximum ozone limits four out of every five days of the year—more than twice the level of Los Angeles.

Until now, renewed economic expansion has canceled out the hard-won gains of mandatory conservation programs, and well-intended decrees have been emasculated by lax or corrupt enforcement. But as Mexico City has labored through the worst season of contaminated air in its history, government officials and environmental groups agree that the struggle against pollution has become a high-stakes battle for the city's survival. "The citizen of Mexico City gets up every morning, and the first thing he confronts is the pollution," said Homero Aridjis of the Group of 100, a group of writers and artists that has taken a leading role in antipollution efforts. "There is a contaminant for every hour, every activity. It has reached the level of an ecological catastrophe."

It takes just a glance from a high-flying aircraft to understand the causes of Mexico City's pollution crisis, which is defined, like the city itself, by a semicircle of volcano peaks that reach as high as 16,900 feet. "It is like a giant cup or bowl that is open only to the north, where the prevailing winds come from," an American scientist said. "So it acts like a catch basin, collecting every fume."

Carpeting the broad Mexico City valley is a seemingly endless sprawl of urban industries and ramshackle neighborhoods that have pushed the valley's population from 5 million to roughly 16 million in the last forty years. That growth has made greater Mexico City the largest metropolitan area in the world, filling the valley with 2.8 million vehicles and tens of thousands of poorly regulated businesses— from cement factories to public baths—that foul the air with furnaces, incinerators, spray paint, solvents, and open-air chemical stockpiles. They release a total of 4.35 million tons of pollutants into the city's atmosphere every year, government statistics say. The effect of those emissions is compounded by the city's high elevation, 7,280 feet above sea level. It reduces by 23 percent the oxygen needed for breathing and effective burning of fuel.

In the vast areas covered by urban squatters, where latrines and sewers are often nonexistent, that dust carries with it tons of dried fecal matter. A confidential United Nations study conducted in 1989 said that about 30 percent of Mexico City residents have no sewerage service, and their solid waste, deposited in open areas, contributes about 600 tons of fecal dust to the city's pollution each day. Even where sewage is channeled into rivers or other means of disposal, it often remains exposed aboveground, where it is carried into the air as gases or microscopic particles.

By the time it crosses north-central Mexico City, one such river, the Río de los Remedios, appears to be less a body of water than a thick, venomous stream of black sludge. On the surface, the foul-smelling river shines with rainbow-colored slicks of oil and industrial discharges. But organic processes from untreated waste cause the river to release bubbles of gas from within, making it appear to boil as it slowly works its way across the city. Once released into the air, scientists say, the chemical and bacterial pollutants are pressed down by early-morning inversions of hot air. Ground winds and local temperature variations then ensure that the pollution becomes an equal-opportunity affliction, choking rich and poor neighborhoods alike.

Trying to calm public fears about rising pollution levels, national officials have repeatedly asserted that there is no proven link between pollution and medical problems in otherwise healthy adults. But years of studies in other polluted cities like Los Angeles and Tokyo have demonstrated the adverse health effects of such individual pollutants as ozone and nitrogen dioxide—everything from skin reactions and eye irritation to weakness, lung disorders, and increased susceptibility to heart attacks. There is even less doubt about the health implications of the microorganisms carried in Mexico City's fecal dust. Among the infectious ones identified in the 1989 United Nations study were salmonella, streptococcus, staphylococcus, shigella, and amoeba.

Having found no government answers to their patients' pollution concerns, doctors at one of Mexico City's leading private medical centers, the American British Cowdray Hospital, have pushed ahead with their own studies of lead and other contaminants and are raising money to construct their own pollution-monitoring station on hospital grounds. Other physicians who deal regularly with large numbers of poor and working-class patients have been more outspoken in their assessment of the city's environmental crisis. Dr. Juan Ortiz Feijoo, director of a state-administered hospital that serves more than 400,000 patients in north-central Mexico City, estimated that his staff has seen a doubling of cases of bronchitis and other respiratory ailments in 1991 alone. Similar increases, he said, have been noted for conjunctivitis and other eye disorders, with the most acute problems among children, the elderly, and patients with preexisting illnesses.

Such statistics have been more than enough to sway many officials of private institutions, particularly those responsible for children. The superintendent of the American School, one of Mexico City's most prestigious preparatory academies, Fred J. Pasquale, explained why parents and teachers decided early in March 1991 to cancel all outdoor sports for the school's 2,300 students. "The question was whether vigorous exercise is beneficial in Mexico City," Mr. Pasquale said. "The conclusion was that it is not." School officials are studying the possibility of building a new sealed recreation area with filtered air for grade-schoolers.

Embassies and corporations have reached similar judgments about the pollution crisis, renting houses outside the capital for their staffs and advising diplomats' families not to have babies while stationed there. While applauding the government's antipollution efforts, the United States pays its diplomats a 10 percent hardship premium for enduring the city's air. Converting medical concerns into free publicity, one small group, the Mexican Ecological Movement, has repeatedly drawn headlines by asserting its intention to install pay-per-breath oxygen booths across the city.

When he took office in December 1988, President Salinas declared the job of cleaning up Mexico City's air to be one of his principal objectives. In twenty-eight months, the government has pushed through dozens of strict measures, including the nationwide introduction of unleaded gasoline, the replacement of more than 3,500 smoke-belching city buses, and the mandatory changeover of at least 94 major industries to low-sulfur fuels.

Those measures, officials say, have already reversed the growth of the two most dangerous pollutants, lead and sulfur dioxide. But peak measurements of harmful particles suspended in the Mexico City air have reached record levels, and other pollutants like carbon monoxide have, after drastic sacrifices, merely been held constant. Even efforts like unleaded gasoline, which still accounts for only 3 percent of all gasoline burned in the city, have yet to prove their worth as long-term solutions. Other gains, like sewer-extension projects, have quickly become a perpetual race against the city's continued growth. Since the restrictions on car use were imposed, more than 275,000 additional cars have been registered in the city, as many as 10 percent of them purchased specifically to avoid the restrictions.

Above all, there is no clear indication that the government has the means or the will to enforce its ambitious pollution standards. In the southeast Mexico City suburb of Iztapaluca, makers of a traditional clay brick known as *tabique* work unmolested fueling the crude, house-sized furnaces that they have used for centuries to bake their wares. A common fuel for the outdoor furnaces, which are designed to produce fierce, sustained heat, is sawdust soaked in fuel oil. But the local preference is for old rubber tires, which are cheaper and generate a powerful, virtually unextinguishable blaze that lasts for days. Both fuels send up billows of acrid black smoke that blanket the neighborhood and are visible for miles. Asked about such flagrant environmental abuse, government officials said that the brick factories are difficult to find or close because they operate clandestinely and move frequently from place to place.

But members of some of the 350 families that jointly operate more than a dozen furnaces in Iztapaluca said they have worked and lived in the same spot for at least thirty years. Their location is readily discovered by following the columns of smoke on the horizon.

Whether and how soon the government can begin to address such glaring problems and improve its enforcement record is unclear. But there is little doubt what the costs of failure will be. "They have to do something," said Silvia Salmerón Rodríguez, a thirty-three-year-old mother who lives in Ecatepec with her seven children. "The air sticks to you, it chokes you, it burns your children. Nobody can live this way for long." [MAU, MAY 1991]

DAMMING THE YANGTZE AND YELLOW RIVERS

Discontented with the way the heavens have arranged its rivers and rainfall, China is embarking on a program to build huge waterworks that could have a colossal impact on the nation's development in the twenty-first century. The new waterworks projects, which are intended to ease the threat from the country's age-old cycle of devastating floods as well as to transfer water hundreds of miles to revitalize dry areas of China, have been under discussion for three decades or more. Collectively they would represent the country's most significant development projects since the Grand Canal was completed in the thirteenth century to transport hundreds of thousands of tons of grain each year to Beijing.

Preliminary approval has already been given to one project, a proposed 730-mile canal that would pump water from China's south, where rainfall is plentiful, to northern areas around Beijing that are running dry. The $10 billion channel is the first of three that are planned for the next century to reinvigorate a broad swath of northern China with southern water. Government officials have warned that Beijing could not remain the nation's capital without a new supply of water to sustain it.

Much more controversial is an $11 billion project called the Three Gorges Dam that is proposed for the Yangtze River, which drains an area inhabited by 380 million Chinese, or 8 percent of the world's population. Supporters note that the project, which would be bigger than any existing hydroelectric station, would sharply reduce the risk of a potentially disastrous flood. But critics point out that the price is immense: 1.1 million people would have to be relocated from a 375-mile-long area that will be flooded, some of China's most beautiful scenery would be marred, and a rare porpoise would be threatened with extinction.

Preparatory work is already under way on the third major project, the Xiaolangdi Dam on the Yellow River. That $2 billion dam will generate electricity, control silting, make irrigation easier, and reduce the risk of a catastrophic flood on a waterway that is known as "China's sorrow" because of its propensity to overrun its banks. Since 602 B.C., the Yellow River has changed course twenty-six times, sometimes by hundreds of miles, each time wreaking immense havoc.

In addition to these projects, China is planning to build more than sixty other substantial hydroelectric projects in the 1990s to fuel industrial growth in the next century. Such efforts to refashion nature would be important in any country, but they are particularly significant in a country like China, whose culture and history are inextricably linked with water. One of China's legendary heroes, a father-of-the-nation figure, is Yu the Great, who 4,200 years ago coordinated flood-control projects along the Yellow River, where Chinese civilization was born.

"Water looms larger here," said Roy D. Morey, the representative in China of the United Nations Development Program, which is assisting China in its many water projects. "Historically, what rivets people's attention is the fact that you either have too much or too little. One is either lamenting the ever-shifting channel of the Yellow River, or you're talking about the arid or semiarid regions of China that have never had enough water."

Floods are a special risk in China because in some places the rivers are actually higher than the surrounding ground. In these areas the water is held in place by dikes, and if a dike is breached, the river spills out and forms a new channel on lower ground. The rivers' elevation is linked to the tremendous amount of silt they carry. A result of soil erosion upriver, silt is suspended in the flowing water and is gradually deposited on the riverbed, raising the level each year. In the case of the Yellow River, the bed has been built up as many as six inches, leading the peasants to raise the dikes correspondingly, and over the centuries the river has risen higher and higher. In the lower reaches of the Yellow River and in part of the middle section of the Yangtze, the water flows as much as thirty feet higher than the surrounding terrain. "People walk under water," goes a folk saying, "and the river flows overhead."

Some scholars argue that despotism was born in water-based cultures like ancient China's because of the need for centralized organization of irrigation and flood control. In any case, there is no doubt that authoritarianism lives on in China, and some believe that that is one of the fundamental problems of all of these projects: they are not subject to the checks of democratic debate. "Information from those opposed to constructing the dams usually doesn't get up" to the leadership, says William Y. B. Chang, an expert on Chinese water issues at the National Science Foundation in Washington. Mr. Chang says he is concerned that the decision-making has been based more on political than scientific reasoning and that the new water projects may not reflect the best value for the money. He notes, for example, that many areas of China are short of water—in rural Shaanxi Province, peasants may have to hike miles to the nearest well—but that the enormous effort to divert water to the north will feed the political and industrial centers of Beijing and Tianjin, where people already are relatively well off.

The project has already received preliminary approval, and the construction is expected to get fully under way within the next few years. The canal will begin at the Yangtze River and pump water up a slight gradient to the Yellow River, and then pass in a tunnel beneath the Yellow River and from there flow downhill to Tianjin and Beijing. There is not enough water in the Yellow River to supply the project, so the canal must start at the Yangtze much farther away. Although pumping the water uphill will use enormous amounts of electricity, which is scarce, the advantage of the route is that the channel is, for the most part, already in place: the Grand Canal, begun in the year 600 by at least 2 million laborers and extended in the thirteenth century. Parts of the Grand Canal are still in use, although others were blocked when the Yellow River shifted channels in 1855.

The impetus behind the project is simply that nature lavishes water on the southern part of the country but is much more stingy in the north. Some 180 million Chinese in the north are short of water and the situation is becoming more desperate. The diversion project will take 11.76 billion cubic yards of water from the Yangtze each year. Most will be used to irrigate farmland along the route, with only 1.3 billion cubic yards reaching Beijing. The project had to be designed to supply substantial benefits to the provinces along the way in order to win their approval. Jiangsu Province, in particular, bargained hard to get a large share of the water in exchange for its participation. Eventually, the government intends to build two additional systems to carry water to the north from the Yangtze, but they will have to wait until the next century.

Over one of the routes, in the center of the country, the water would run downhill, so this system would not require pumping stations, but it is extremely complex technically and would require extensive tunneling through mountains. The other route would involve construction in remote areas on the Tibetan plateau. In this project, water would be pumped uphill from tributaries of the Yangtze to the headwaters of the Yellow River, and in conjunction with the other two routes this plan is expected to encourage development in the poor and parched areas of northwestern and north-central China.

The intensity of the bargaining with the provinces to win approval for the "south waters north" and the Three Gorges Dam projects is reflected in the many compromises made in the plans. "There are few things that tell you as much about the politics of a country as where it builds its dams, because dams create big winners and big losers," said Kenneth G. Lieberthal, a political science professor at the University of Michigan.

For example, as Professor Lieberthal noted, the Three Gorges Dam is to be almost 607 feet high, with a normal water level of 574 feet. That level will create a reservoir that will just reach the city of Chongqing. The Communist party leaders in Chongqing had insisted that the reservoir reach their city, to give them a year-round river port for large vessels. But the leaders rejected a higher dam, even though this would have helped in flood control efforts, because part of the city would have been submerged. The dam would have a hydropower station with a capacity of 17,680 megawatts, making it the largest in the world except for a proposed Russian project that has been put off.

One of the greatest problems with the Three Gorges Dam and other water projects in China is how to deal with the silting. Each year about 520 million tons of silt is carried down the Yangtze past the site of the Three Gorges Dam, and skeptics argue that in a few decades the reservoir will become an unnavigable pool of mud.

Backers of the project have conducted extensive tests, some of them using a half-mile-long laboratory version of the Yangtze, and they insist that siltation would not be a major problem. In the summer, when the river is the muddiest, they plan to lower the reservoir level and flush the silt through, while in the fall, when the river is clearer, they would build the water level.

Government officials seem to be pushing hard for a final go-ahead on the Three Gorges project in March 1992, at a meeting of the National People's Congress. As evidence of the danger, they cite devastating flooding in the summer of 1991 in which 3,000 people were killed and 3.2 million were left homeless, and they emphasize that the sooner work begins on the dam, the less onerous the relocation requirements will be, partly because of the rapidly rising population.

"The sooner Three Gorges starts functioning, the better," said Su Qianqing, an official of the Ministry of Water Resources in Beijing. "It's going to be more difficult for us to solve the problem of relocation if we don't start now."

The Three Gorges Dam has been under discussion since the 1920s and is by far the country's most controversial construction project. In the relatively open environment of the late 1980s, an incipient environmental movement seemed to have defeated the plan for a dam when a Politburo member announced a postponement of further consideration until at least 1995.

But the project seems to have been resuscitated, and in the aftermath of the crackdown in Tiananmen Square in 1989 most environmentalists and critics of the project have been cowed into silence. Dai Qing, a prominent writer who is one of the dam's foremost opponents, was arrested after the crackdown, and Li Rui, a party elder and water specialist who also opposed the project, was placed under tight restrictions. "I still have some hope that the Three Gorges Dam won't go ahead," Ms. Dai said in December 1991, shortly before she was allowed to go to the United States to accept a fellowship at Harvard University. "If we devote so many resources to the Three Gorges, then everything else will have to wait. Education and science spending will slow, and China's backwardness and burden on the world economy will grow."   [NDK, JANUARY 1992]

THE DROWNING OF
THE THREE GORGES

THE bulldozers are scooping out the yellow earth along the Yangtze River in preparation for the world's largest hydroelectric project, a dam that will create a lake 350 miles long, fuel China's industrial revolution, and save millions of people from the constant threat of flooding. Or perhaps the project will simply create the world's most colossal mud pie. Critics say that silting behind the dam may result in a $30 billion bog that would inundate China's finest natural scenery and stand as one of the most monumental and vexing legacies of Chinese communism.

The disagreement is no surprise, for people have been debating the merits of the Three Gorges Dam since the idea was proposed in 1919. But while the debate seems endless, one thing has changed: work on the dam is finally beginning. "The way things look right now, I don't think it can be delayed anymore," said Jiang Xueyuan, the white-haired spokesman for the Three Gorges project office in Yichang, the nearest city to the dam site in central China. Mr. Jiang, like many other engineers who have spent their careers designing the dam, is delighted that the supporters finally seem to have won the battle.

Those whose homes, farmland, and heritage would be flooded are naturally less enthusiastic. Among the 1.2 million people being forced to move to make way for the project is a furniture vendor in Wanxian, a grimy Yangtze River port. "None of us wants to leave, because our lives depend on this port," said the man, who identified himself only as Mr. Gao, between efforts to interest a foreigner in a four-dollar wicker chair. "Officially, everyone has to support it, but no one wants to go. What'll happen to us?"

A five-day journey down the Yangtze, through the area that will be flooded, found not everyone so opposed to the project, with some peasants so poor that they seem happy to move. The more optimistic—or perhaps credulous—believe the government's promises of fertile new farmland, prosperous new factories, fancy new homes, and lucrative new jobs.

The Three Gorges Dam, sometimes described as the most important construction project in China since the Great Wall, was formally approved in 1992. It involves a 607-foot-high dam stretching 1.2 miles along the third of the Yangtze River's three famous gorges. The gorges, which are as famous in China as the Grand Canyon is in the United States, would be partly submerged. The Yangtze in its middle reaches would look more like a lake than a river. The Three Gorges Dam would not be the highest in the world, nor would its reservoir be the biggest. But its hydroelectric output would be 17,680 megawatts, by far the biggest in the world and nearly three times as much as the output of the Grand Coulee Dam, the biggest in the United States.

The project has a special resonance in part because it would transform the Yangtze, the mightiest river in the nation, known in Chinese simply as the Chang Jiang, "the long river." The Yangtze River basin is home to 35 percent of all Chinese, accounting for nearly 8 percent of all humanity. Among them is a hefty sixty-year-old man with a crew cut who sells dog-eared magazines—mostly with covers of big-breasted women looking either sultry or anguished—on a patch of ground along the main street in the town of Wanxian. "We don't want to move," the man said slowly, speaking Mandarin with a thick local peasant accent. "But what can you do? The water's going to come, and then you've got to go." Still, he accepted the government's logic that the project was fundamentally good for China. Although official propaganda is often regarded with skepticism in the cities, the peasants and workers who will have to make way for the dam seem to accept the official line that it is necessary to control flooding and generate electricity. "People can't help but feel a bit unsettled in their hearts," said Guo Qinglu, a sixty-year-old retiree in Wanxian. "Generations have lived here. Their ancestors are buried here. But the dam is a good thing," Mr. Guo added, nodding his head slowly as he stood in a small restaurant. "It'll produce lots of electricity. So while some people here support it and some are against it, most are in favor of the dam."

Apparently only a few hundred people have been evicted so far, although every official seems to have a different estimate. In any case, the bulk of the work in relocating 1.2 million people will not take place until late in this decade. So far the work on the dam is all preparatory. Laborers with heavy equipment are building access roads on each side of the dam site and are beginning construction of a bridge just downstream to facilitate construction. Workers are also digging a new channel to divert a creek. Housing for the workers and engineers is already in place, and work will begin later this year on a cofferdam, to divert the Yangtze slightly so that work can begin on the main dam. Still, the history of the project has had more twists and turns than the Yangtze itself, and the dam could be killed—or, more likely, postponed indefinitely.

Deng Xiaoping, the eighty-eight-year-old senior leader, supports the project, but he is ailing, and a growing number of Chinese are beginning to accept that he may be mortal after all. Several other top party elders who were among the dam's strongest backers—Wang Zhen, Wang Renzhong, and Li Xiannian—have died since the project was approved early in 1992. One of the strongest supporters of the dam among China's younger leaders is Prime Minister Li Peng. But Mr. Li apparently suffered a heart attack in late April 1993, and he has scarcely appeared in public. The state of his health, physical and political, remains uncertain. "If Li Peng remains out of commission, then I don't think the Three Gorges project will go very far," said a Chinese who circulates among some of the leaders.

For now, the official news media are talking about plans to accelerate the project. It was supposed to take eighteen years to complete, but the leaders are now talking about seventeen years or fewer. Progress reports on the dam are regular front-page news in China, partly because of the historical intimacy here between society and water. Few Chinese can name many ancient emperors, but everybody knows of the Great Yu, the ancient hero who conquered a flood and then built the dikes and water projects that nurtured Chinese civilization. It is difficult to separate myth from history in those ancient times, about 2200 B.C., but some experts believe that Yu, who later founded China's first dynasty, was a real individual. If so, he is one of the first people in human history, outside ancient Egypt, who are known by name.

In the United States, presidents may hope to be remembered for a foreign policy doctrine or a social program. But in China, the best chance for an emperor, past or present, to be remembered is with a huge water project. And that, say critics of the Three Gorges project, is the problem. "It's a political project," said Dai Qing, a Chinese writer and environmentalist, as she nibbled on a salad, studiously ignoring a state security agent eavesdropping from the next table. Ms. Dai, who was imprisoned after the 1989 Tiananmen crackdown and lost her job, has emerged as the leading opponent of the Three Gorges project. Critics like Ms. Dai say that the push to build the dam has less to do with the need for electricity than the desire for a grand monument, which, they contend, is likely to turn into a white elephant. Gigantic projects have often served a political role in China, as a national show-and-tell that can unite people in pride, just as construction of the Aswan Dam did in Egypt and the drive to put a man in space did in the United States.

The main argument in favor of the dam is not the need for electricity, because it would be cheaper and simpler to build several smaller hydroelectric dams; rather, the primary argument is flood control. The Yangtze River, like the Yellow River, has gradually filled in much of its channel through silting. Over the centuries, people responded by building dikes on either side, and when silt raised the bottom of the channel, they raised the dikes even higher. As a result, in some places the Yangtze is known as a "hanging" river because it is higher than the towns on each side. Only the dikes keep the water in place, protecting the millions of people living on lower ground.

One of China's worst nightmares is a devastating flood like the one of 1870, the worst in the last thousand years. If the dikes burst unexpectedly in the middle of the night, hundreds of thousands of people could die. "If we don't build this dam, then who will take responsibility for the flooding?" asked Cui Zhihao, a senior engineer at the Three Gorges head office in the city of Wuhan. "A single flood would cause far more damage and dislocation than the Three Gorges Dam." Proponents of the dam say that the existing Jinjiang dike can withstand only a ten-year flood, meaning the worst that can typically be expected in a decade. But it may be in their interest to exaggerate the risk, so as to make the construction of the dam seem more urgent. The engineers grumblingly acknowledge that no recent flood has burst the Jinjiang dike, not even the 1954 flood, which is believed to be a one-hundred-year flood, meaning the worst that can be expected in a typical century. When pressed, some engineers say that the Jinjiang dike can withstand at least a twenty-year flood, or a forty-year flood if several catchment areas are deliberately flooded to ease the pressure.

The major technical debate over the dam is the question of silting. The Yangtze sometimes resembles soup more than water, and it carries 523 million tons of sediment each year. Critics charge that the dam will cause the water to slow down and drop silt on the bottom of the reservoir, gradually turning the lake into an unnavigable mud puddle. Government engineers say they have licked the silting problem. They say that tests show that the lake will be navigable for as long as the dam lasts.

For all such technical complexities, the major reason why the project might still be postponed is easy to understand: cost. While official estimates are $10 billion or less, inflation and cost overruns could make that much higher. The Gezhouba Dam, built in the 1970s and 1980s a bit farther downstream on the Yangtze, ended up costing more than three times the initial projection. At a time when the government has a budget deficit and the economy is already overheated, some economic officials apparently think it is mistake to tackle another huge construction project.

Some Western environmental groups are urging the World Bank not to finance the dam, but China believes that in any case it can attract foreign lenders and investors to help pay for the project. And supporters still express confidence that they will see the Three Gorges Dam built in their lifetimes. "This has been discussed and debated for decades," said Luo Shixiao, a fifty-six-year-old engineer who helps run the Three Gorges project office in Chongqing. "There've been lots of different opinions, lots of research, lots of discussions. But the consensus is that building the dam is better than not building it, and that building it earlier is better than building it later." Mr. Luo paused and offered a fleeting and slightly triumphant smile: "I'm confident that construction will go ahead quite smoothly." [NDK, JUNE 1993]

THE FALKLANDS UNDER THREAT

T HE extremities of the earth can be a naturalist's paradise. And this barren grouping of islands in the South Atlantic, 800 miles north of Antarctica and 300 miles east of Argentina, is such a place. Consider the population: 2 million penguins, up to 2 million albatrosses, millions of petrels, 40,000 seals, as well as some of the rarest birds in the world, including the upland goose, the flightless steamer duck, and the mischievous striated caracara, a falcon that one Nantucket sealer in the early 1900s described as forever pilfering "caps, mittens, stockings, powder horns, knives, steels, tin pots, in fact everything which their great strength is equal to." Indeed, the bird life is so abundant in some parts of the Falkland Islands that the islands' government issues a map carefully detailing areas for pilots of small planes to avoid. But the presence of man and sheep over the last 150 years has slowly pushed the vast population of wildlife here to the islands' own extremities. Species of birds once common on the two main islands are now found only on some of the Falklands' outermost islands and islets. And even on several of the offshore islands, the struggle between the demand for bigger flocks of sheep, currently around 750,000 head, and the natural ecological balance continues.

The Falklands' one and only conservationist notes these trends with concern. "We've messed up the main islands, and some of the offshore islands have been hit pretty hard," said the naturalist, Ian J. Strange, who has been studying and documenting wildlife here for thirty-one years. "These islands are very small, and just a few sheep can create a big disaster."

The islands are not idyllic for human life (currently 2,100 people inhabit the Falklands) but they seem to be for bird life. And a brief review gives the impression that the Falklands could be one of the greatest concentrations of bird life available for study. The main reason is an extremely large food supply created by ocean currents. As the cold waters of the southern Antarctic Ocean move around Cape Horn toward this outermost British colony, they split into two different currents, one moving to the south of the islands and one to the north. As the currents reach the islands, underwater ridges reduce the normal depths and create strong tidal actions and upwellings, creating a natural funnel for huge amounts of food, especially krill and squid. These immense reserves of food have helped sustain vast colonies of birds.

Mr. Strange, who is self-employed and supports himself by selling wildlife illustrations, has documented islands where tens of thousands of rockhopper penguins and black-browed albatrosses nest intermingled within an area half the size of a football field. A principal reason why wildlife has been pushed to the outer islands, Mr. Strange notes, is the almost total destruction of the native tussock grass that was once the dominant vegetation. This grass, which grows twelve feet high at times, is unique as a shelter for bird life, such as wrens, thrushes, short-eared owls, vultures, and the striated caracara. Once sheep farming was introduced, the grass's disappearance was inevitable. Now tussock, and much of the bird life, can be found only in places where there are few or no sheep, like the outer islands.

New threats to wildlife have developed from the economic prosperity that followed the unsuccessful 1982 invasion by Argentina, which claims sovereignty over the Falklands. Hundreds of boats a year now ply the waters harvesting the vast reserves of squid around the islands, an industry that since 1988 has brought in as much as $50 million a year. Mr. Strange said that on one isolated island he has studied, near the center of squid fishing, the rockhopper population has fallen by one third over the last three years. "Some serious thing happened to that colony, and the only thing I can say is that it must be related to the reduction in the availability of squid in the area," he said. Sea lions have also suffered. There were up to 630,000 in 1930s, but Mr. Strange found only 63,000 in a survey in 1960, and a mere 8,000 in 1990. "I knew they were still on the decline, but when I found out what really was happening I was shocked to the core," he said. Yet he has no clue as to the cause.

All these developments have moved Mr. Strange to mount a campaign to protect as many islands as possible from further commercial development. Starting in 1962, he began prodding the Falklands Legislative Council to designate specific islands as nature reserves and has since won such status for fifty islands. But the council's acts are not irrevocable, and future governments could revoke them and permit development. So Mr. Strange has also urged islanders to buy individual islands and create irrevocable trusts that preserve them as wildlife sanctuaries. In 1971, along with a partner, he bought New Island, one of the westernmost islands of the Falklands, and set up a wildlife preserve to study the colony of 3,000 fur seals, 10,000 albatrosses, 100,000 rockhopper penguins, 10,000 gentou penguins, and an unknown number of burrowing petrels called thin-billed prions. The island has one of the largest-known breeding colonies in the world.

But since then he has struggled to raise even a fraction of the $1.2 million needed to set up an endowment. Such actions have not all gone unopposed. Although he has lived on the Falklands for more than three decades, he says he still feels like an outsider among the native islanders, who, he says, are suspicious of his efforts to create wildlife preserves.

One issue he has faced several times is whether to make public the whereabouts of islands he has discovered that are so pristine that the birds have no fear of humans. In these places he has been able to walk among the wildlife and have birds hop on his boots and caracaras steal lunch from his hands.

Several years ago, in what he calls one of the biggest mistakes of his life, he published accounts of his trips to the most southern of the Falkland islands, Beauchene. Lying a hundred miles south of the East Island, Beauchene was so remote that until he first stepped on it in 1963, he believes, no human had been there for at least forty years, and perhaps never. There, the dense colonies of albatross and penguins were breathtaking. Tens of thousands of petrels and prions crowded the islands at night after spending the day gliding over the ocean. He also found the largest concentration of striated caracaras. It was here that he was able to do his most extensive work on the caracara and study the ecosystem of the tussock grass.

But once word began to leak out about the location of the island and its uniqueness, others wanted to visit. And he began arguing that such places should be left alone, even by scientists, except for very infrequent visits.

So far he has won only half of the battle. Visitors can go, but only with the permission of the Falklands government, and no one has won a permit for over a year. Still, he said he was concerned that the decision-making mechanism was not more structured. "If you try to count the number of really pristine areas left in the world, they are very, very few," Mr. Strange said. "They should be left entirely alone and used as yardsticks."

Mr. Strange argues that such places, where the wildlife has never seen a human, should be studied only once every four or five years, and then only by aerial observation. If scientists must enter such islands, he says, they should not be allowed to stay for more than a few hours at a time.

The battle over Beauchene left an indelible mark on the fifty-five-year-old naturalist, and he plans to carry several other secrets about the Falklands to the grave with him, in an effort to protect the islands' wildlife from man's intrusion. He says he knows of three other sites on the islands, similar to Beauchene, where nature is pristine and man is virtually a stranger. And he will not disclose the locations.

Also, whereas most naturalists say there are five types of penguins that nest on the islands—the rockhopper, the gentou, the Magellanic, the macaroni, and the king penguin—Mr. Strange says he has discovered a sixth. Somewhere among the Falklands' 200 islands and 150 islets is a colony of royal penguins, its location known only to Mr. Strange. "It's an issue of simply protecting these penguins from the intrusion of man, and I think that's important," he said. "The environment here is very, very fragile. It's really little more than a small garden. A horse gets in and he can trample it to death in a very short time. It's not like a large continent, where there is a buffer effect."   [NCN, JULY 1991]

THE SPOILING OF PATAGONIA

THE isolated coastline here, in Punta Delgada, Argentina, seventy feet below high bluffs, gives every appearance of being a wildlife paradise. This is the season the elephant seals come up on the beach to give birth and to mate. Bull elephant seals with harems of forty to one hundred females loll in the sun and are cooled by the wind, emitting satisfied noises somewhere between a burp and a deep gargle. Snowy sheathbills, known as the Arctic dove, peck at fossilized oyster shells that are more than 13 million years old. A visitor is greeted with a casual over-the-shoulder glance. All seems in balance.

But recently both man and nature have been hard on the wildlife and ecology of Patagonia, which stretches from the Colorado River 250 miles north of here and continues some 900 miles south into Tierra del Fuego. For nature's part, in August 1991 the Hudson Volcano in the Chilean Andes dumped two cubic miles of ash on a large part of the Patagonia plains, threatening to turn the already arid terrain into a desert and certainly killing close to a million sheep and vast numbers of wildlife.

And while man's deeds have been less spectacular, their gravity is setting off alarms among the few scientists who study this region. In September 1991, a mysterious oil spill off the coast northeast of the Valdes Peninsula coated tens of thousands of Magellanic penguins with crude oil as they migrated from the southern waters of Brazil to their nesting grounds in Punta Tombo and beaches farther south. Scientists say at least 16,000, and possibly twice that number, were killed. A stroll along the beaches here almost a month after the penguins started to arrive with oil found a dead bird partly buried in the sands perhaps every fifty feet.

An indiscriminate hunting policy has decimated the populations of the Patagonian rhea, a relative of the ostrich; the guanaco, a relative of the Andean llama; and the Magellanic fox. According to scientists who have studied the volcano, the ash will further diminish their numbers. Plastic pollution generated by the major cities spreads out miles beyond their borders. A drive through the garbage dump of Puerto Madryn, for example, finds that the ever-present winds of Patagonia have scattered plastic bags, bottles, and other material for miles around. Finally, for years the Argentine government based in Buenos Aires has been discussing the possibility of creating a nuclear waste dump near Gastre, an isolated town deep in the heart of Patagonia some 240 miles west of here. Though no decision has been made, the province of Chubut could become one of the major centers of nuclear waste on the continent.

"I'd say that Patagonia is in the middle stage of destruction," said Dr. Claudio Campagne, a thirty-six-year-old Argentine scientist, as he walked among the elephant seals, marking them for identification. "It's not as bad as parts of Africa where the wildlife has been destroyed and is not as complex as the rain forest to restore. We can still do a lot without having to spend an outrageous amount of money." Dr. Campagne, a member of the Patagonia Nature Foundation, a conservation group, and an associate of the New York Zoological Society who left a practice in medicine to become a conservationist, was one of the first to note that in early September 1991 thousands of Magellanic penguins were coming ashore full of oil. The Patagonia Nature Foundation notified the national press, and within days student volunteers from the University of Patagonia in Rawson were coming to help wash the penguins and the public was sending detergents and towels.

Scientists concluded that sometime in late August, a tanker carrying crude oil either had a spill at sea or was washing out its oily ballast, just at the time when the penguins were migrating south. They say no spill was ever reported. After being coated with oil, the penguins, on their way to Punta Tombo 200 miles south, hobbled to these shores and died. Just as many affected penguins arrived at Punta Tombo and died there. By walking hundreds of miles of beachfront and counting the dead penguins, scientists with the Patagonia Foundation came up with the number of 16,000. But they say many more could have died at sea. If this had been an isolated event, environmentalists might not be as concerned, but they say penguins arrive here coated with oil every year. In 1991, they said, the number was perhaps ten times the norm. The survival of the colony is not at stake since the population of Magellanic penguins on the southern coast of Argentina exceeds 1 million birds.

Guillermo Harris, the president of the Patagonia Nature Foundation, warns that while the wildlife on the Patagonia coast seems abundant, that is really not the case. The coastal section is similar to the interior plains, where the relatively few varieties of mammals, birds, and plant life signify a delicate ecosystem that exists in an area of wind and very little rain. "What you see along the coast are large colonies of birds and sea mammals, and as such they are very vulnerable to large-scale disasters," said Mr. Harris. "Any pressure that affects a colony is going to affect a large number of individuals."

To the south at Punta Tombo, which has one of the largest colonies of penguins in the world, with more than 500,000 nesting birds, the scene is both breathtaking and pitiful. Arriving penguins come waddling out of the water; before them are acres and acres of nesting birds standing outside their burrows. But before they can find their nest of last year, they must pass dead penguins covered with oil lying on the beach. One heavily oiled penguin arrived gaunt and seeming confused. A worker quickly picked up the bird and took him to the cleaning area, where some 300 others have been washed and were shivering in the cold wind because all the oil had been taken from their feathers. Workers say that despite the washing attempts, these birds are almost certain to die. Since penguins nest for life, hundreds of birds are wailing alone on their nests, apparently calling out for their mates.

Dr. Dee Boersma, a professor of zoology and environmental studies at the University of Washington in Seattle, has been studying the penguins in Punta Tombo for nine years. "This is like the Galápagos Islands," she said, as she walked among hundreds of nests, measuring the distance between them. "They are tame and accessible to people. They don't run away. The difference is that you can drive here in a car. You don't have to take a long boat trip." Dr. Boersma says she particularly fears the presence of the fishing boats. Not only do the penguins get caught in nets and die, but more important, the fishing industry is taking valuable food from the birds.

The waters off Argentina in recent years have been found to be rich in illex squid, the type preferred in Japan, Hong Kong, and Korea. But that has brought hundreds of boats to an area that once was considered an isolated fishing spot and threatens to significantly reduce food critical to the wildlife here. "Five years ago, I think in a season I saw three fishing boats off the coast here," she said. "Now, in the last two weeks alone we have seen ten boats." The stories of overfishing and illegal fishing abound. Some scientists say they have heard from sailors that many of the captains regularly dump unneeded diesel fuel into the water so their boat can hold more fish.

Professor Boersma proposes that an eighteen-mile marine reserve be created to ensure that coastal animals have ample food supplies. Her associate, Gene Fowler, notes that 75 percent of the chicks that are born die of starvation already. Dr. Campagne has applied to the World Bank and the United Nations for a grant to set up a coastal management plan. But help from the government has been limited. Mr. Harris noted that one sign of government's inability to deal with the threat to Patagonia was that so far little has been found out about the source of the oil spill despite the national attention given to it. He says only three companies—Exxon, Shell, and the state oil company, Yacimientos Petroliferos Fiscales, known as YPF—have oil tankers that ply the waters. "It shouldn't be that hard to find out," he said. "But after this much time, I wonder whether we will ever get an answer." [NCN, DECEMBER 1991]

THE WORLDWIDE REACH OF TRASH

PULLING up in a motorboat to a remote island in the Pacific, a British zoologist was astonished to find that its beaches were strewn with garbage washed up from the ocean.

The island, Ducie Atoll, is arguably one of the most remote islands in the world. It is 293 miles away from the nearest inhabited island, Pitcairn, and more than 3,000 miles northeast of New Zealand.

As the scientist, Dr. Tim Benton, approached the island, he related, his jaw dropped open in surprise. "The island was absolutely covered with junk that would be perfectly at home in a city landfill, not on a very isolated beach," he said.

Along a 1.5-mile stretch of the beach, he counted 953 pieces of garbage, including 6 light bulbs, 171 bottles, a tinned meat pie, 113 buoys, half an airplane, 25 shoes, and a plastic foot mat from a car.

Fewer than thirty passing yachts stop on the island each year; Dr. Benton said he believed most of the junk came from ships throwing their garbage overboard. He added that if so much garbage can be found on Ducie, "it makes you wonder just how much more junk is out there floating on the water."

An international convention governs garbage thrown overboard from ships. The United States Coast Guard said it prohibits the disposal of any form of plastic in the ocean and regulates other materials according to how quickly they sink and their distance from shore. A Coast Guard lawyer said the convention is difficult to enforce.

Dr. Benton, who teaches at Cambridge University, was part of an expedition to study plant and animal life on islands in the Pacific. But both at Ducie and at Henderson Island, 200 miles to the west, he was struck by the amount of garbage on the beaches. He reported his findings in a letter in the July 1991 issue of *Nature*.

One of the bottles on Ducie contained a message, he said. It was dated and read, "If you find this message, please send a message to"— but the rest was obliterated. "Which was very sad," he added.

[ANON., JULY 1991]

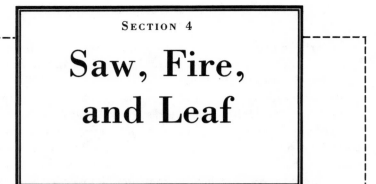

Saw, Fire, and Leaf

THE USE AND ABUSE OF TROPICAL AND TEMPERATE FORESTS

BRAZIL'S TROPICAL forests hold a unique patrimony of plants and animals. Its military rulers during the 1980s believed that as a matter of national security the Amazon jungle should be settled. Abetted by short-sighted foreign lenders like the World Bank, the Brazilian government cut vast highways through the virgin wilderness and offered subsidies and tax breaks to landless settlers to clear the forest and raise cattle.

The settlers pushed out both the Indian peoples, who had lived in harmony with the forest for centuries, and the rubber tappers, who had learned to exploit the forest's wealth without destroying it. The settlers, with their crops and cattle, did just the opposite to the forest. Tropical forests, despite their exuberant growth, do not rise from fertile agricultural land. The richness of the tropical ecosystem lies in recycling nutrients between the thick mat of roots below and the closed forest canopy above. When the trees are cut, the system fails.

The army of settlers sawed down or burned the trees, found the soil so poor it would support only a couple of years' crops, and moved on to clear more forest. Behind this invading army, the barren soil mixed with rain. Where once stood forests vibrant with life, the generals' policies created acre upon acre of unpassable mud. "I am too old to understand the white man," said a Kayapo shaman as he contemplated the vast stretches of empty, blackened land near Redencão, Brazil, where his ancestors once lived.

The tropical forests are rich with fruit and medicines. They can even be cultivated, by those who understand their ways. The articles that follow chronicle the abuse of the great forests of South America and the ways in which they might be exploited without destruction. The section then turns to the temperate forests of the United States, which face different problems but a similar lack of foresight.

Whereas the Brazilian government subsidized cattle ranchers to destroy the forest, in the United States the Forest Service subsidizes timber companies to cut trees that otherwise would be unprofitable. The magnificent old-growth forests of the Pacific Northwest have been extensively destroyed, often by the cheap and ruinously ugly practice of clear-cutting. Prodded by suits from environmental groups and their use of the spotted owl issue, the Forest Service is slowly groping its way toward a policy of treating trees as living things, not just standing timber.

A SPECIAL PATCH OF
BRAZILIAN FOREST

Botanists studying a surviving patch of the dwindling Atlantic rain forest in Brazil have recorded the highest-known tree diversity in the world. Packed into a two-and-one-half-acre plot, 450 different tree species were identified by an American-Brazilian team led by Dr. W. Wayt Thomas, a researcher for the New York Botanical Garden. The discovery, announced in March 1993, displaces a previous density record of 300 species for a similar plot set in 1986 by researchers studying the mountain flanks of the Andes in Peru that descend into the Amazon rain forest. By contrast, a similar plot in a New England forest generally contains only 10 species. "We were very, very surprised at the high diversity we encountered," Dr. Thomas said of the site, located 900 miles north of Rio de Janeiro, in Bahia State.

By contrast, South America's better-known rain forest, the Amazon, has an average density of tree species about half that recorded at the Atlantic forest. "The Atlantic forest is much more diverse than the Amazon forest," said Dr. Andre M. de Carvalho, a Brazilian botanist from Bahia who worked on the cataloging project. The diversity and primitive nature of several species found in patches of Atlantic forest indicate that more than 500,000 years ago the Atlantic forest supplied many tree species to the Amazon, Dr. de Carvalho said.

Although the Atlantic rain forest is one of the world's most biologically diverse ecosystems, it is also one of the most threatened. According to the World Wildlife Fund, the world's two most endangered tropical ecosystems are the Atlantic rain forest in Brazil and the rain forest of Madagascar, an island off the coast of East Africa. In recent decades, Brazilians' demand for farm and ranch land has radically slashed the Atlantic forest.

Today about 9 percent remains from a forest that at the beginning of this century stretched 2,500 miles down the Atlantic coast of Brazil, covering 425,000 square miles. In North American terms, a forest the size of Texas and California has dwindled to an area the size of Maine.

Brazil's oldest area of European colonization, the coastal region once blanketed by the Atlantic rain forest is now home to 70 percent of Brazil's population of 155 million people. "Conservation of the Atlantic forest is fundamental," said Dr. de Carvalho, who is curator of a herbarium at the Cocoa Research Center in Itabuna, Bahia. "There is need to protect watersheds. Water erosion has caused silting of rivers, and many are no longer navigable." In addition to guaranteeing drinking water supplies for Brazil's growing coastal population, there are scientific arguments for preserving the Atlantic forest. "Many plants are unknown medicinally," said Dr. Thomas, who is an associate curator of the botanical garden's Institute of Systematic Botany. "There are timber species that are untapped."

Scientific knowledge of the Atlantic forest is so skimpy that the botanists expect that a full cataloging of the Bahia plot will turn up forty new tree species. Several factors may have induced the high tree diversity found in Bahia, said Dr. Thomas, whose research is financed by the the John D. and Catherine T. MacArthur Foundation. Located only one and a half miles from an Atlantic beach, trees at the study site had canopies that peaked at eighty feet, lower than the one-hundred-foot average found in the Amazon. The lower canopy and a hilly terrain appear to allow for a high density of small trees. When conducting tree surveys in the Amazon and in the Andes, botanists normally count trees that have diameters of four inches or more at chest height. In Bahia, the botanists lowered the minimum diameter to two inches in order to take into account the profusion of small trees. "At four inches, we found 270 different species," said Dr. Thomas. "At two inches, the level of diversity explodes. It goes way off the charts." Although different standards were used, Dr. Thomas said that Amazon and Andean tree densities do not approach the level he found at the Atlantic forest site.

The team counted 2,556 total trees in the study area and 450 species in 61 families. The three most common families represented were Myrtaceae, which includes eucalyptus and guava; Sapotaceae, which includes chicle, and Euphorbiaceae, which includes poinsettias and rubber. In the Myrtaceae family, 92 species were identified; in the Sapotaceae family, 55 species; and in the Euphorbiaceae family, 41 species.

This year, the American-Brazilian team plans to study how the diverse species interact in such close quarters. But a nagging question remains: will the study plot be there when they return? The Bahia plot is part of a privately owned 2,500-acre forest. The site, like most of the remaining Atlantic forest, survived only because it is hilly and unsuited for conventional agriculture. But recently the owners said they were interested in selling.

"What is happening in southern Bahia is terrifying; it has one of the highest rates of deforestation on the Atlantic coast," said João Paulo Capobianco, superintendent of Fundacão SOS Mata Atlántica. Dedicated to conserving the forest, this private group is mapping deforestation through aerial surveys. Mr. Capobianco said that illegal deforestation in southern Bahia was so rampant that his group planned to ask Brazil's secretary of the environment, Jorge Coutinho, to order an immediate moratorium on forest cutting in the area.

[JB, MARCH 1993]

CLEARING THE FOREST WITH FIRE

THE fires that raged around the frontier town of Redencão, Brazil, for three months in 1988 have once more pushed back the jungle and turned forests into black and sapless land. But the mood of Redencão is anything but mournful. The farmers who set the fires in this part of the eastern Amazon have opened up new space for cattle grazing and, in the process, have increased the value of their property. The fires here and across the Amazon basin have caused alarm among environmentalists in Brazil and abroad as evidence has grown of their enormous size and their voluminous emissions of carbon dioxide, which has contributed to the greenhouse effect.

But in many new towns, it is the link between deforestation and development that makes the yearly rituals of destruction so difficult to prevent. Redencão, which was just an airstrip in the bush and some shacks ten years ago, today has 100,000 people. First the gold diggers came, then the road builders, and then the lumbermen. They were followed by cattle ranchers, who in this region get generous government subsidies. "Everybody around here sets fires because flames can do what the hand cannot," said Bolival Alves, a tinder merchant. "It is easier and cheaper. Only the valuable wood is pulled out." Forest trees are piled high in the local timber yards here where saws scream their way through huge mahogany trunks. Giant Brazil nut trees are not spared, even though this tree is protected and the law forbids cutting it. Workers at a large yard said that, once cut into planks, the Brazil nut tree is shipped under a different name. "The yard makes up false documents," a truck owner confirmed. "I never had any trouble with that."

While for a number of years international concern has grown about waste and destruction in the Amazon rain forest, for the first time it has become a national political issue in Brazil. The press has drawn attention to the man-made fires and forced debates in Brazil's National Security Council. In late September 1988 the head of the government Environmental Agency resigned to protest the absence of an environmental policy. Brazilian scientists who began a new program to monitor fires via satellite are still compounding damage. They reported that in 1987, 77,000 square miles of land burned, close to 40 percent of it virgin rain forest. They said that in 1988, in the last three months of the dry season, fires were worse. "We are still recording an average of 5,000 fires a day," said Marcos Pereira, one of the scientists. "The rains are very late. Last year by the middle of September, the burning had dropped off."

Other reasons for the enormousness of the fires offer insights into the methods by which the frontiersmen are conquering Brazil's vast hinterlands. Foresters have asserted that landowners rushed to clear forests before the country's new constitution went into effect in early October 1988, because new articles bring greater legal protection for the environment. Speculators regularly destroy forest to increase the resale value of their land, according to the foresters, or they clear it as a device to assert their ownership over land for which they have no legal documents. Conversations with landowners in this region also give the strong impression that congressional debate on land redistribution has scared many owners. Fearing that "unused" lands will be expropriated, landowners and speculators admit that they clear the land to demonstrate their intention to use it and thus protect themselves. Under Brazilian law, which favors homesteaders, felling trees is considered a form of "improvement" and therefore use of the land.

From the air, much of the region near Redencão and wide swaths across the south of Pará State appear to have undergone such "improvements." Vast dents have been carved into what was a solid forest cover less than fifteen years ago. A thick haze from the fires recently sat over the town and the outlying ranches like a brown umbrella. "I never saw so many fires and such big fires as this year," said Hamilton Lopez, a bush pilot who has flown for more than fifteen years in this region. He was swearing as he dipped and swerved his Cherokee Pathfinder and searched for a landing strip hidden somewhere below the polluted air. To the north, he said, he had seen a ranch on the road to Xinguara burn 15,000 acres. "It took almost a week," he said, "and another like it was burning near Maraba."

Farther north, Pará, Brazil's second-largest state, still has large stretches of virgin jungle. But according to the new satellite survey, Pará, along with the states of Mato Grosso and Rondônia farther west, are the areas most rapidly suffering deforestation. Huge new projects in south Pará include a large dam and the world's largest iron ore mine. Environmentalists have protested plans for twenty iron smelters that will use wood in the form of charcoal as their main source of energy. According to the government, 14 percent of Pará, or about 180,000 square kilometers, was deforested between 1975 and 1986. In the hundred years before that, settlers had cut 18,000 square kilometers.

Around Redencão, the vast stretches of empty, blackened land have baffled the Indians who have inhabited this region since long before the white conquerors from Portugal landed five centuries ago. "What a waste, what a waste," said Beptopup, an aging medicine man of the Kayapo Indians, expressing his grief on a recent visit to old Indian sites. Those lands north of Redencão had now turned into a parched landscape with charred stumps in place of trees. "I am too old to understand the white man," said Beptopup, staring at smoke and ashes. He said he would have to tell everyone in his village that "the place of our grandfathers is gone."

In Redencão, logging and cattle prevail as the local business. "The soil is no good, too acid for planting," said Agenor Brito, a new ranch owner. "You can improve it, but the markets are too far in any case." But for all the growth here, the lumbermen are beginning to feel the pinch of a harvest that is running out. Three years ago, Redencão had almost sixty sawmills. But half of them have left because the area is running out of mahogany and other hardwood trees. Brazil's Forestry Agency recently made its own nationwide assessment. In the

Amazon, it said, only 5 percent of the trees reach the market. Ninety-five percent are either burned or left to rot.   [MS, AUGUST 1988]

AMAZONIA AFLAME

F OR many in the Amazon, fire is the only tool for transforming forest into farm or pasture. The flames hurl tons of fumes and particles into the sky; at night, roaring and red, the forest looks to be at war. Now, Brazilian and American scientists in a recent satellite monitoring program are for the first time pinpointing and measuring the effects of the fires. The destruction by burning of forest here in the Amazon basin of Brazil is so vast, the scientists say, that it may account for at least one tenth of the global man-made output of carbon dioxide, which is believed to be causing a warming of the earth through the greenhouse effect. Burning of fossil fuels accounts for most of the carbon dioxide released worldwide.

Environmentalists have long warned of the destruction that is increasing with each new dry season, and witnesses every year report more cemeteries of trees. The scientists' findings show that in 1987 the burnings ruined more forest cover than previously thought and proved to be major polluters of the earth's atmosphere. In 1987, Brazilian scientists estimate, fires just in Brazil's part of the Amazon basin covered 77,000 square miles, an area one and a half times the size of New York State. Of these, at least 30,000 square miles were newly felled virgin forest, the researchers said. The remainder, they added, involved regrown forest on previously cleared land, savannas, and fields. The pioneering studies, which include the most comprehensive estimates yet of the emissions from the Amazon fires, also found that pollution from the burnings traveled thousands of miles. This has raised questions about a possible link between the gigantic emissions from the fires in the South American tropics and the damage to the earth's protective ozone shield over Antarctica.

Alberto Setzer, coordinator of the satellite data at the Space Research Center in the south Brazilian city of São Jose dos Campos, said smoke clouds from the Amazon fires often rose to 12,000 feet. Their gases and particles were then lifted up higher into jet streams and blown south across the South Atlantic, close to Antarctica. Many scientists now believe that several of these gases, including methane and nitrogen oxides, are among the reactive gases that can directly or indirectly deplete ozone, Dr. Setzer said. "There is no proof yet that the material is interacting with the ozone shield, which is much higher in the stratosphere," said Dr. Setzer. "But we know the material gets to the Antarctic region, and we know that storms can pump it upward. We do not know yet how high it reaches. Several people are working on this."

American scientists who took part in the mission over Antarctica by the National Aeronautics and Space Administration (NASA) in October 1988 said they had not searched for or found evidence of compounds from the Amazon. But NASA researchers are now searching for such traces by satellite. But even without the ozone question, Dr. Setzer said, the "tremendous" emissions coming off the Amazon pose serious problems. "They are large enough to cause significant changes in the chemical balance of the atmosphere and influence the global weather," he said.

In the case of carbon dioxide, for example, the forest destruction is doubly harmful, Dr. Setzer and other researchers noted. The dwindling forest cover becomes less efficient in absorbing and removing this "greenhouse gas," while the fires add new, huge volumes of it. A report prepared by the study group at the Space Research Center estimated that the fires in Brazil in 1987 produced carbon dioxide containing more than 500 million tons of carbon. The fires also produced 44 million tons of carbon monoxide, more than 6 million tons of particles, almost 5 million tons of methane, 2.5 million tons of ozone, and more than 1 million tons of nitrogen oxides and other substances that can circulate globally and influence radiation and climate. "There is enough to compare it to the outburst of a very large volcano," Dr. Setzer said.

The study results on deforestation and emissions from the fires so far cover only the Brazilian two thirds of the Amazon rain forest. Still more of the pollutants are produced by fires in parts of the Amazon basin outside Brazil. "Our findings in general agree with those of Brazil," said Compton Tucker, a physicist who is part of a group studying deforestation and emissions at the Goddard Space Flight Center at Greenbelt, Maryland. The NASA group, he said, is now also analyzing satellite data of other countries of the Amazon basin, including Bolivia and Peru, where burnings have increased. "This phenomenon has been greatly underestimated, and until 1987 no one has ever tried to study this systematically," Dr. Tucker said. "The satellite data are also there for other areas. There are no technical constraints. They just have not been processed yet."

The effects of the fires are felt clearly on the ground in areas where the pace of destruction is greatest, including the state of Pará, in the eastern Amazon, and farther west in northern Mato Grosso and Rondônia. Here new roads have opened, and cattle and soybean farmers are felling huge areas. Newly analyzed data for the state of Rondônia, for example, show that in 1984, when paving was completed on a highway financed by the Inter-American Development Bank, deforestation jumped from 6,500 square miles and reached 10,500 square miles in 1985. By late 1987 it had affected 14,600 square miles, or 17 percent of the state surface.

In August and September in past years, when the thick haze over the region worsened, fires have forced airports to close down, caused boat accidents on the rivers, and brought a rise in respiratory diseases. Early in August of 1988, the annual drama of fire came to the fore as burning spread from a farm in Mato Grosso and set ablaze a national park, the Parques das Emas. The 335,000-acre park, which consists of easily flammable savanna, rich in animal life, has only four wardens, who were unable to maintain the fire corridor. The blaze lasted five days and, according to the forestry service, destroyed 65 percent of the park.

As forestry experts explain it, spontaneous fires are rare in the moist rain forest. Rather, workers first cut the trees, leave them to dry, and finally set fire to them during the dry season. Usually only the felled part is dry enough to burn, and fires remain confined to the intended areas. In the absence of transport or roads, the timber cannot be sold, and burning is the easiest way to clear the land.

In the computer room at the Space Research Center here, researchers capture and analyze the satellite images every day. Marcos Pereira, one of the analysts, explained that the satellite registers the fires as points of intense heat. These appear as dots on the screen and permit researchers to pinpoint their location. Often, the ominous dots form a belt showing the boundary between the virgin forest and the settled areas. "It is very striking how the fires follow the roads," an American researcher said. On the worst day of 1987, September 9, the satellite detected 7,603 fires. Dr. Setzer said that between June and October 1987, covering the whole dry season, the satellite registered more than 350,000 fires. Because burnings may last between twenty-four and forty-eight hours, many fires may have been registered more than once, Dr. Setzer said. Therefore, he added, his group is using a conservative estimate of 170,000 fires for 1987.

As part of the new program, researchers send their findings every day to the National Forestry Service in Brasília. Shocked by the 1987 data, the service has said it will open a nationwide campaign and levy large fines for the burnings. Virtually all the fires are conducted illegally, without the required permits. But the service, which guards the largest forest on earth, has fewer than 900 wardens for a region larger than Europe. "We would need 15,000 to 20,000 guards to be effective," said Carlos Marx Carneiro, a director of the service.

[MS, OCTOBER 1988]

RUBBER TAPPERS AND THE RAIN FOREST

VALERIO da Silva slit an ancient tree trunk with his knife and quickly hooked a cup into the bark to catch the white latex oozing out. "A man who makes poor cuts gets a terrible name," he said. "To damage a tree is as bad as killing a pregnant animal or not paying your debts."

The rubber tappers of Xapuri, Brazil, who once helped advance the industrial revolution of more than a century ago are still collecting latex deep inside the Amazon rain forest. There is no longer much demand for their natural rubber, but environmentalists see these forest people as bearers of a message ever more pressing in a world where nature is widely abused. As the race for development and quick profits consumes vast swaths of Amazon forest, forestry experts and economists argue that the estimated 300,000 people who live off collecting wild rubber, nuts, resin, and other forest produce have demonstrated that exploiting yet preserving the rain forest can go hand in hand and even be profitable.

The killing in December 1988 of Francisco Mendes, leader of the tappers, at first had seemed to fracture their movement and its battle against land speculators and cattle ranchers. But now the tappers seem even more determined to gain reserves for extraction only. Their opponents, the landowners, have used more anonymous death threats to intimidate them. "How can we stop now," Maria da Silva said, scurrying about the small family farm in the heart of the forest and hanging some deer meat to dry in the sun. If it weren't for Francisco Mendes, she added, "all this forest would have been destroyed." A union meeting was coming up and Mr. Mendes's brother, José, and other tappers were visiting the Silvas in their forest clearing, a three-hour walk from the mud road to Xapuri (pronounced shah-poo-REE). Unlike the tappers farther west who continued laboring under the old system—like serfs forever in debt to landowners for taxes and goods—these were independent people working a forest that their parents or grandparents had divided up. They now defended these lands on the basis of the squatter rights recognized by Brazilian law.

Soon the conversation turned to battles still awaiting their movement. With their great knowledge of the terrain and the advantage of surprise, they seem to operate more like an unarmed guerrilla movement than a peasant union. Pedro Rocha, one of the visitors, was recalling the fight for the reserve of Santa Fe that began one day as the tappers saw workers measuring the land on behalf of a man who claimed to be its owner. "They were getting ready to cut," said Mr. Rocha, "so we had to mobilize fast. Five of us left at sunset. We went through the whole forest to warn everyone."

The next morning, he said, "we were sixty-four men, seven women and a lot of children, and we stood in front of the men with the chain saws and we talked with them." The forest dwellers were arrested. But months later, after a court battle, Santa Fe was declared an extractive reserve. Of the forty-five or so blockades, Mr. Rocha thought, the movement had managed to stop the chain saws and the bulldozers about fifteen times.

Other nearby lands, now stripped and sprinkled with cattle, represented battles lost. An estimated 10,000 tapper families have been driven off the land into the towns since 1970, when large companies and private speculators first moved into this part of the western Amazon. Even the majestic growth around the Silva farm had come close to being destroyed when a company claiming ownership threatened to sell it and break it up into farming plots. But this land, known as

São Luis do Remanso, was declared a reserve in June 1988, after long pressure on the government from Mr. Mendes.

Valerio da Silva now works his own four trails that wind past the wild rubber trees—more than 1,000 of them—naturally scattered and amid dozens of other species. He collects the latex, smokes it, and lets it coagulate into blocks. Sometimes he works at night with a kerosene light, like a miner's lamp stuck on his head. The lamp, he says, helps to scare off most animals, except snakes. Adults and children seem to have the ease of shoppers in a supermarket as they move around the jungle. "Have a drink," José Mendes said as he climbed on some fallen trees and reached for a vine overhead. He slashed it and let the water pour out. The nasty sting of an ant was soon soothed with a piece of bark.

Valerio da Silva pointed to leaves that could numb a toothache and a tree whose resin could seal a skin wound or an ulcer. Most families, the tappers said, collected wild honey and had access to soursop, cashew, banana, and jackfruit trees. Men hunted, women grew beans, corn, and manioc. Moreover, they explained, from January to March, rubber tappers collect brazil nuts, which account for almost half of their income.

Stephan Schwartzman, an American environmentalist who has made extensive studies of rubber tappers' lives, has said that with a visible income of close to $1,000 per year, supplemented by planting and hunting, tappers often earn almost twice the minimum salary on which many paid workers in Brazil must survive. The government of Acre State has now conceded four "extractive reserves" to the tappers. Both the World Bank and the Inter-American Development Bank, whose road projects have caused forest destruction in this region, are now looking at ways to promote more reserves and form cooperatives to commercialize forest produce. "It is the best alternative for the fragile soil in the Amazon," said Raphael Negrete, a bank official. "It beats disastrous cattle and colonization schemes." Amid such support, the rubber tappers of the Xapuri region are thankful but wary. "We have some very powerful enemies," said Mr. Rocha. "The ranchers want empty land. We want more forest reserves. It still rains death threats in Xapuri."

[MS, APRIL 1989]

THE VALUE OF STANDING TREES

Providing evidence that environmentalists and Brazilian officials say could slow the pace of large-scale clearing of tropical forests, a team of scientists has found that rain forests are worth more if left standing than if cut for timber or cattle grazing. The study, reported in the July 1989 issue of the journal *Nature*, showed that revenues generated by harvesting edible fruits, rubber, oils, and cocoa from 2.5 acres of tropical rain forest are nearly two times greater than the return on timber or the value of the land if used for grazing cattle. Until now, environmentalists, in calling for a slowdown of deforestation in South America and other regions, have relied primarily on ecological arguments, mainly that clearing of forests releases carbon dioxide into the atmosphere, adding to the level of gases that contribute to global warming.

More than 28 million acres of forest and other woodlands are lost annually around the world, and at the current rate of deforestation it is projected that several countries, including El Salvador, Costa Rica, Nigeria, and the Ivory Coast, will have destroyed all their forests in thirty years. "The study indicates that deforestation is a bad investment," said Charles M. Peters of the Institute of Economic Botany at the New York Botanical Garden, who headed the three-year study. "People who have wanted to save the forest using environmental arguments have not been very persuasive because many of these nations have a large debt," he said. "But these findings offer a very powerful argument for forest conservation." Brazilian Embassy officials in Washington said that although the study was being reviewed by scientists, the Brazilian government "does not find the information surprising. Along with other reports like this and with work being done by our government, the study is likely to have an impact," said Vera Machado, counselor for environmental issues in the Brazilian Embassy. "We expect that the deforestation will be decreasing."

South American governments, along with timber companies, miners, and cattle ranchers, have been criticized by environmentalists, who contend that they have pursued large-scale clearing of forests to create farmland or sell timber without regard for the environmental impact. Brazil, for example, offered economic incentives to private entrepreneurs from 1965 to 1983 to invest in cattle ranching, a policy environmentalists say promoted the destruction of thousands of acres of woodlands.

Amazon forests are regarded as among the richest and most diverse in the world and the source of hundreds of varieties of edible fruits and oils, as well as virtually untapped medicinal products, which are lost forever when the forest is cut. The clearing of tropical forests also contributes to the warming of the atmosphere, and ultimately to the greenhouse effect, because the giant trees contain large amounts of carbon that are released when they rot or burn.

In addition, the destruction of forests in many countries has led to several disasters, says Worldwatch Institute, an environmental research group in Washington. Rainfall runoff, accelerated by deforestation, has triggered widespead flooding in Bangladesh, India, the Sudan, Thailand, and elsewhere.

The 1989 study showed that twelve products, primarily edible fruits and latex, found in about 2.5 acres of forest at the village of Mishana, in northeastern Peru near the Brazilian border, are worth $6,330 if sold in local markets over fifty years, with the cost of harvesting deducted from the market price. The study also showed that the same land if used as a timber plantation would produce $3,184 over the same period, and that if converted to cattle pastures, it would be worth $2,960.

Dr. Peters said people who live in the region harvest and sell all of the products that were detailed in the study, and for many it is their main source of income. The study was also based on the work of Alwyn H. Gentry of the Missouri Botanical Garden and Robert O. Mendelsohn of Yale University.

Some researchers, while agreeing that the study provides important new data, said the value of edible fruits and other produce arrived at by Dr. Peters's group might be artificially inflated due to market conditions. If the forests were managed and large quantities of produce were gathered and sold, the market price could drop significantly, said Susana Hecht, who specializes in economic and environmental development of the Amazon at the University of Southern California in Los Angeles.

Although scientists have believed for many years that the harvest produced in certain regions of tropical rain forests is economically valuable, the study provides the first detailed accounting. "The problem is that we have never been able to quantify those benefits to convince these nations' ministers of this," said Raymond Rowe, a forestry adviser at the International Bank for Reconstruction and Development. Scientists and economists also said that as soil in regions of cleared forest has become fragile after short periods of use, farming has not produced the levels of economic success originally expected. "It appears that keeping it as managed forests has greater economic value," said Lester B. Lave, an economist and environmental expert at Carnegie Mellon University in Pittsburgh. "Brazil has a rapidly growing population and must look to the forest to provide them with a place of employment," he said. "Instead of cutting it and using it for farmland, they now might consider developing it as managed forests." [ANON., JULY 1989]

THE FOREST PHARMACY

S CIENTISTS have developed evidence that harvesting locally used medicinal plants from tropical forests could be more lucrative than clearing the land for farming or growing timber. Such evidence could help convince policymakers that forests should be preserved, as well as show local people who rely on the forest for income, and are tempted to clear it, that they have a stake in its preservation, said the researchers, Dr. Michael Balick, director of the Institute of Economic Botany at the New York Botanical Garden, and Dr. Robert O. Mendelsohn, associate professor of forest policy at Yale University. Dr. Balick and Dr. Mendelsohn's findings, based on research in Belize, were published in the journal *Conservation Biology* in 1992. Preliminary results of the study were reported in January 1992 by researchers who attended a symposium on tropical forest resources at Rockefeller University.

With the help of a local herb gatherer, Dr. Balick collected from two plots of mature, secondary growth hardwood forest all the medicinal plants that could be sold to local herb pharmacists and healers. The plants are commonly used in the treatment of ailments like rheumatism, indigestion, colds, and diarrhea. The first plot, seven tenths of an acre of thirty-year-old forest in a low-lying valley, yielded 86.4 kilograms (about 190 pounds) of five different species. The second plot, six tenths of an acre of fifty-year-old forest in the foothills of the Maya Mountains, produced 358.4 kilograms (about 790 pounds) of four species. At local market rates, accounting for labor costs, the plant materials from the two plots are worth $564 and $3,054, respectively.

Dr. Balick and Dr. Mendelsohn then calculated the value of the plant material in each plot assuming it could be harvested on a sustainable basis. Theoretically, an herb gatherer who owns thirty acres of forest that takes thirty years to mature could harvest one acre each year. Each section would then have thirty years to regenerate before it was reharvested. The current value of medicinal plants on the two study plots, given such a sustainable harvest, they found, is $294 and $1,346 per acre.

When compared to other land uses, medicinal harvesting appears to be one of the most valuable uses of the land. Other scientists have found that clearing rain forest for agriculture is worth $137 per acre in Brazil and $117 per acre in Guatemala. Even the most successful pine plantation in the tropics is expected to yield only $1,289 per acre. Dr. Balick and Dr. Mendelsohn warned that the land value they found in Belize could not be assumed to hold for other areas.

This type of local marketing might work if it is carefully controlled, said Dr. David Ehrenfeld, a professor of biology at Rutgers University, who is editor of *Conservation Biology*. "But any natural system that is coupled to the world market is not likely to fare very well," he said. "Many of the people who are now selling products of the rain forest are not very knowledgeable about the ecology of the forest, and this is a great danger."

Conservationists often argue that tropical forests should be preserved because they may contain undiscovered medicinal plants that would be worth billions of dollars if developed into drugs. Dr. Balick does not discount such notions. But that abstract argument for preservation, which might not pay off for another decade, is of little interest to the farmer who needs to feed his family, he said. "We wanted to identify what is valuable to the small farmer today, because he decides whether to cut his piece of the forest to feed his family or to use it in another way to derive income," Dr. Balick said. "For the first time we are not talking about medicinal benefits that are years in the future. We are talking about benefits that people are realizing today."

The World Health Organization estimates that as much as 80 percent of the world's population relies at least in part on traditional medicine for primary health care. The next step, Dr. Balick said, is to work with farmers to develop nondestructive harvesting methods that would not require entire parcels of land to be cleared.

Hugh Iltis, a professor of botany at the University of Wisconsin, said he had mixed feelings about the study. "It could be done in the secondary growth forest or the buffer zones around the preserves," he said. "But it should not be done in the preserve itself. If it is a good business, people will eventually try to plant pure populations of what they are selling, and you would end up with a drug garden."

[CD, APRIL 1992]

MANAGING FORESTS THE INDIAN WAY

O VER thousands of years, scientists have discovered, ancient inhabitants of the Amazon and their present-day descendants have evolved a sophisticated blend of agricultural and forestry techniques to shape and reshape the region's vast forests, savannas, and river valleys to their needs. In an earlier form, the scientists say, the system enabled the ancient Amazonians to build a civilization whose size, power, and achievements far outshone the conventional picture of the ancients as small, primitive tribes living on the edge of existence. And they say that in its present form, the system has enabled the descendants to prosper, without disrupting the ecology of the tropical forests, in a way that eludes many settlers who follow more modern practices.

Even while the scientists strive to learn more about this remarkable system of resource management, they and others are starting to search for ways in which it might be applied to help head off the destruction of the Amazon forests. And at a time when expanding populations and growing poverty are overwhelming third world economies, they believe, the system could enable millions of poor peasants to make a good, secure living based on self-renewing resources.

Beyond that, the scientists say, the techniques can be used to tap the tropical forests—while leaving them basically intact—for a broad range of export products that under ideal circumstances could bring billions of dollars into the debt-ridden economies of the Amazonian countries. The potential export products include foods, medicines, natural fertilizers, pesticides, body-care products, and fragrances. A study in 1989 by American experts on the Amazon forests calculated that these products would be more profitable than the widespread logging and cattle ranching that today are largely blamed for progressive destruction of the forest.

There is "a whole range of possibilities that could be carried out based on what ancient people did for thousands of years," said Anna C. Roosevelt, an anthropologist and archeologist at the American Museum of Natural History, who has investigated the ways of the Amazonian ancients in depth. Dr. Roosevelt, a great-grandaughter of Theodore Roosevelt and winner of a MacArthur Foundation award, was the co-organizer of a symposium on the past, present, and future of the Amazon at the annual meeting of the American Association for the Advancement of Science in late February 1990 in New Orleans.

The practices of present-day Amazonian natives offer "thousands of ways of making the living forest more valuable than the destroyed forest," said Darrell A. Posey, an American anthropologist who works for the Goeldi Museum in Belém, Brazil, and who has lived with the natives in the forest and observed their agricultural and forestry techniques closely. In one such technique, for instance, Amazonian Indians have learned to manage agricultural plots so that over a period of years they evolve in preplanned phases from cleared farmland back into thick forest. The plots move through stages in which conventional crops predominate at first, but then wild species of useful plants and trees are encouraged to encroach gradually. These are tapped for a variety of uses, including medicine, insecticides, and pesticides. Eventually the forest reclaims a given plot. Meanwhile, other plots are in varying phases. The result is that the forest continually renews itself even while sustaining its exploiters.

Some agencies concerned with development in the third world have begun exploring the feasibility of applying the techniques of traditional cultures more widely. "I think it's time we started looking for some new ways of doing business," said Thurman Grove, a Cornell

University ecologist who has been detached for two years to help the United States Agency for International Development find ways to adapt the traditional techniques to modern use. "Mother Nature has a lot of tricks," he said, and "old cultures have already run a lot of the experiments." The challenge, Dr. Grove said, is to learn how to augment the natural systems so that they can be made productive enough to sustain a large population without, as was true in ancient times, relying so much on labor-intensive methods. "That's a field where I think we are in a very nascent state," he said.

Scientists who have studied the present-day application of these techniques and skills are finding that they provide a more reliable and sustainable living over the long term than can be achieved by neighbors who rely on modern cash-cropping. The system evolved through millennia of practical experimentation in response to changing conditions. In archeological investigations that over the last ten to fifteen years have challenged a number of conventional beliefs about both the Amazon forest and its inhabitants, Dr. Roosevelt and others have traced the origins of the natives' manipulation of the Amazonian environment back thousands of years.

The conventional beliefs have held that the ancient native populations were small, scattered, primitive, and sickly, and that the forest itself was mostly virgin and undisturbed and was poorly suited to sustainable agriculture. But at their peak in the centuries around the birth of Christ, according to archeological evidence that is still unfolding, the ancient Amazonians forged a civilization of agricultural chiefdoms that lasted 2,000 years—a vast, powerful rural economy that some scientists believe sustained millions of people.

Many of them lived in settlements of up to 4,000 people, built atop huge earthen mounds to keep them away from floods. The mounds were linked by causeways, and other causeways led to fields where corn, the staple crop, was grown. The natives of this era carried out their agriculture in the forest, in reclaimed swamps, and on alluvial plains along the rivers. It sustained them well enough, said Dr. Roosevelt, to produce a populace that, on the basis of the archeological study of skeletons, was on the average tall and healthy.

There have been people in the Amazon forest about as long as the forest itself has existed, or since the end of the Pleistocene, 10,000 years ago, and they have exploited it intensively, said Dr. Roosevelt. But their manner of exploitation has allowed the forests to regenerate so completely, she said, that they have fooled some into thinking they are virgin. This is so even though at their peak, the ancient Amazonians greatly outnumbered their modern descendants. "What people did in ancient times may be ecologically sensible," said Dr. Roosevelt. "At least we know the forest survived."

With the arrival of Europeans in the 1500s, a new chapter opened. The Spanish established new economies on the floodplains, and cattle ranching emerged as a major economic activity that survives to this day. This was the forerunner of today's industrial-age exploitation of the forest. Driven by economic pressures, millions of acres of Amazon forest have been exploited for timber or burned and converted to cropland that, under presently employed methods of cultivation, plays out after two or three years and then sustains no one.

The Spanish conquest also brought disease that wiped out most of Amazonia's native population, with 85 percent of the people in some localities dying out within the first year of contact. Many of the survivors fled to the interior, where, in response to new conditions, their peculiar blend of present-day agricultural and forest management evolved from the ancient ways. In one application of this approach to what scientists call agroforestry, the Kayapo tribe of Brazil, studied by Dr. Posey, operates as follows:

A circular field is prepared by felling several large trees at key junctures so that their crowns fall on the periphery of the circle. This also brings down smaller trees that have been weakened by notching. They, along with the leafy crowns of the big trees, also fall on the perimeter, providing nutrients for the highest-consuming plants, which are to be concentrated around the edges.

Yams, potatoes, manioc, and other tubers are planted between the fallen tree trunks. On a windless day just before the year's first rain, the dead, felled trees are burned under carefully controlled conditions. The rains wash the fresh ashes into the soil, where the tubers' root systems are already established.

In this new field, crops are planted in concentric rings radiating out from the center: sweet potatoes and yams in the middle, mixed corn and rice next, then manioc, then more yams. The outer zone contains papaya, banana, pineapple, mango, cotton, and beans. In an older field in its later stages, the corn and rice have disappeared, the potato-yam zone has been expanded, and manioc continues. The forest begins to encroach on the field. Gradually, fruit trees, palms, and medicinal herbs move into the field. Eventually, the forest recovers the field entirely. Each phase of reforestation has its own inventory of useful plants and animals.

Other fields in both Peru and Brazil follow much the same pattern, with varying mixtures of crops, according to scientists from the New York Botanical Garden's Institute of Economic Botany, who have studied the practice extensively. The institute is in the forefront of study about such matters. For a given plot to go from first cultivation back to forest takes ten to fifteen years, said Wil De Jong, an international fellow at the institute, who has taken part in field studies in the Amazon. "Then it's continued for a longer time as forest," he said, "maybe fifty or sixty years." During some stages of cultivation, he said, the plots propagate a number of forest species. "People are preserving their resources by actually multiplying them," he said.

Among the Kayapo, said Dr. Posey, an "enormously wide range" of plants are brought from vast areas of forest and replanted on small plots of three acres or less. Most have multiple uses as, for example, natural fertilizers and pesticides, insect repellants, building materials, medicines, and food. "These islands are sort of supermarkets concentrated in specific places," Dr. Posey said. In creating the islands, he said, the Indians actively reshape the environment, transplanting forest species to the savanna in a sort of "mix-and-match" kind of ecological management. One demonstration of the effectiveness of the native way of farming as compared with modern ways has been documented by Jane L. Collins, an anthropologist at the State University of New York at Binghamton. Working in the Peruvian Amazon, she compared the performance of natives who pursued the old ways with the modern, cash-crop pursuits of migrants who had moved into the local region from elsewhere in the country.

In the modern application, she found, cash-cropping tends to force farmers who pursue it "to be hooked up to the markets differently" from the practitioners of native agroforestry. That is, the cash-croppers, relying on one crop and on debt financing to produce it—as is commonly the case in many parts of the world—tend to "be more dependent on cash, so they need to get more out of the land over the short term."

The natives, on the other hand, tend to produce for their own use to a greater extent and to be less reliant on the market. Although they do sell some of their crop, they have a more stable, long-term source of sustenance. "The migrants don't have the agroforestry management skills," said Dr. Collins, "and often there are lots of incentives to go other ways." For instance, she said, the government provides loans for cattle ranching, which encourages farmers to clear-cut land for pastures. "If push comes to shove," she said, "they can sell the cleared land and move on." Their one-crop practices are also more destructive to the soil, she said: "That's why it gets worn out."

Pharmaceutical companies have long exploited the medicinal properties of plants discovered from native cultures, said Dr. Posey, and the potential for broadening that exploitation into other areas is considerable.

In a study reported in 1991 in the British journal *Nature*, Charles M. Peters of the Institute of Economic Botany, Alwyn H. Gentry of the Missouri Botanical Garden, and Robert O. Mendelsohn of Yale University calculated that the long-term economic value of products taken from the living forest, excluding field crops that might be grown there, is about double that of the timber that might be harvested from it and the cattle that might be raised on cleared land.

Already, as awareness grows, Dr. Posey and many others are worrying about what might happen to the native peoples if the outside world begins tapping their intimate, detailed knowledge of the Amazonian environment in earnest. Will they expropriate the expertise, denying compensation to those who have developed it? That would be "nothing more than another form of neocolonialism," said Dr. Posey, who recently, in a sign of the times, attended an international conference on "intellectual property rights" in York, England. The traditional systems of resource management and the knowledge that undergirds them, he says, "are rare and priceless resources."

[WKS, APRIL 1990]

THE LENGA FOREST OF TIERRA DEL FUEGO

O N this sweeping island of tundra, mountain, and wind, a developing country is in the throes of deciding whether the offer of more than $65 million in foreign investment is worth risking the disappearance of one of the world's most unusual rain forests. Tierra del Fuego, the island off Chile that Magellan first saw when it was ablaze with fires set by the native Indians, has vast and dense stands of lenga trees, a very slow-growing hardwood that covers more than a quarter of a million acres. But the push for foreign investment and economic growth is about to infringe on the isolation of the 10,000-year-old forest. Beginning in the mid-1980s, the government of Gen. Augusto Pinochet began selling off large tracts of the lenga forests to local investors for as little as fifty cents an acre.

Now, a joint venture, Cetec-Sel Chile, Ltd., managed by a Canadian concern based in Vancouver, British Columbia, is proposing to buy nearly the entire forest and exploit it. Officials of Cetec Engineering, Ltd., the Canadian concern, say the partnership plans to invest up to $65 million in Tierra del Fuego and produce finished lumber for the North American and European furniture markets and wood chips for Japan. But the proposal has caused widespread concern from local residents here and in Punta Arenas, the local government seat across the Straits of Magellan. Chilean government officials are concerned both about their ability to control and monitor commercial development of the forest and about just how much of a financial windfall the government is giving the foreign investors.

"We don't want a desert in fifty years," said Juan Morano, a deputy to the regional governor. "They say they will preserve the forest. But if you look at other rain forests such as in the Amazon, Malaysia, and Africa, once companies get in and start cutting they leave nothing."

The lenga forests are fragile. And once the ecological balance is disrupted, scientists say, the forest can quickly die back, giving way to pampas and peat bogs. "If you clear-cut and ship up everything, you're going to lose the forest," said Leonardo Guzmán, director of the Patagonia Institute of the University of Magellanes in Punta Arenas. "That's why you need a careful program of removing just the number of trees that leave the forest intact and give smaller trees a chance to grow."

To understand their concern, scientists say, the biological balance of Tierra del Fuego must be understood. Unlike most other land areas of the world, such as North America and Europe, that are more than 100 million years old, scientists say Tierra del Fuego was one of the last land masses to break off from Antarctica and have its glaciers disappear. Scientists say the land and the lenga trees are no more than

10,000 years old. That means that the soil on the island is both thin—from less than one inch to nearly four inches—and sorely lacking in nutrients. As it developed, the lenga tree formed very dense woods with intertwined top branches, in part to conserve the relatively small amount of rainfall in this region of the island and also to protect itself against the powerful winds that blow almost constantly during the spring and summer and regularly reach one hundred miles an hour. Moreover, with the combination of a cold climate, little water, and high winds, the lenga are very slow growing, often needing seventy to one hundred years to reach maturity.

What concerns scientists is that while the trees slowly regenerate, the high winds can cause extensive erosion, and once a forest is cleared the soil disappears too quickly to permit regeneration. In 1990, for example, a small sawmill operator near here began thinning a stand of lenga trees on his land. But because of the poor soil, the lenga have very shallow root systems, seldom deeper than eighteen inches. The thinning reduced protection against the wind just enough so that when a major storm swept down on the forest in November of that year, it toppled most of the remaining trees. Those that remained were toppled by falling trees. Visitors on a hike through the area, as Andean condors glided overhead and the local guanaco, a relative of the llama, complained about the newcomers, found acres of once dense woods of stately trees that now looked like a battlefield of fallen soldiers.

Stephen Mitten, president of Cetec Engineering, said his company planned to be as careful as it can with the forest. In a telephone interview, he said studies have shown that as much as 90 percent of the forest can be cut down and still provide enough protection from the winds to permit regrowth. But his company is planning on cutting no more than 70 percent, he said. "We are committed to rejuvenating these forests, that is why we are buying them outright" rather than simply buying the timber, Mr. Mitten said. He added that the forests were filled with mature trees that were slowly dying and that development would make way for younger trees.

Chilean dependence on a continual influx of funds from abroad seems to make it all but inevitable that the forests will be worked. Officials have calculated that as much as $4 billion in foreign investment will flow into the country just for the development of forest sector alone over the next six years. Government officials thus say that they are concerned about repercussions abroad and on its economy if this government reneges on contracts signed by the Pinochet government.

Still, they say, they are closely studying the economics of the transaction proposed by Cetec-Sel. One issue is the price of the forest land. In the 1980s, the government sold the land for 50¢ to $1.50 an acre, and government officials now say the company is offering to pay as much as $2.50 an acre. Yet Mr. Morano says that in an effort to buy up small parcels of lenga forests from individual landowners, the company is paying as much as $25 an acre. Mr. Morano also said he was concerned that the local official who oversaw the initial selling of the forest during the Pinochet regime was now representing Cetec-Sel here in its attempts to buy the remaining land.

Edmundo Pisano, a professor of biology at the Patagonia Institute, says he believes the forests can be safely exploited. Others, who have not opposed the project, are still not sure of the outcome. "Look at this abundance," said Alberto Rosas, standing on Cerro Petro, a mountain that overlooks the eastern limits of the lenga forest. Mr. Rosas, now thirty-eight years old, came to Tierra del Fuego when he was eighteen and began working in a sawmill near here. "The only trouble is the people think there is so much abundance that one day they will turn around and it's all disappeared."

[NCN, JULY 1991]

REGENERATING A RAIN FOREST

FROM a forty-five-foot-high observation tower, the American ecologist surveyed a landscape that is increasingly common in eastern Amazonia: white Nelore cows dotting fields of African *colonião* grass that stretched to a distant horizon of rain forest. "Once the forest is beaten down for the pasture, is it gone forever?" asked Daniel C. Nepstad, the ecologist. "That is the conventional wisdom in the United States and Europe." Swiveling, gingerly because of the swaying tower, Dr. Nepstad answered his own question by pointing to a pasture that was abandoned ten years ago. What once was a field was lost under a tangle of vines, woody bushes, and saplings twenty-five feet tall. "This is the future," said Dr. Nepstad, who recently earned his doctorate from Yale University's School of Forestry and Environmental Studies for research here on regeneration of the Amazon rain forest. "It will be missing a whole lot of animal and tree species, but it will be a forest."

Since 1984, an American-financed research team has been investigating human impact on the forest, and researchers feel that their findings will give advance warning of future trends as Brazil's penetration of its vast Amazon wilderness expands and takes new forms in the 1990s. The researchers have discovered that selective logging of the forest is surprisingly destructive, that conditions for vast devastating fires exist, and that regeneration of land used as pasture depends on how heavily it has been used.

Situated three degrees south of the Equator and sprawling over 10,422 square miles, Paragominas was chosen largely because it was considered a "mature" Amazon frontier municipality. The first ranches were cleared from the rolling hills and valleys here in 1964, the year a two-lane highway was pushed through. "It's an old frontier, and you can pick out the patterns," said Christopher Uhl, a plant ecologist from Pennsylvania State University who started the project with funds from the National Geographic Society.

One significant and surprisingly destructive pattern in the Amazon's future will be selective logging, Dr. Uhl warned. Increasing steadily in recent years, wood harvests from the Amazon region now account for about half of Brazil's total, up from 14 percent in 1976. The number of commonly marketed species has jumped from 6 in the 1950s to about 140 today. In Paragominas municipality the number of sawmills has jumped to 300 now from 1 in 1970.

At the current rate of expansion, much of the Amazon forest could be selectively logged by the middle of the next century, Dr. Uhl calculates. In a study of two forest tracts here, only 2 percent of the trees were harvested, according to research by Dr. Uhl and a Brazilian plant ecologist, Ima Celia Guimaraes Vieira. But this selective logging left a destructive trail: 26 percent of trees with trunks greater than four inches in diameter were killed or damaged. Twelve percent lost their crowns in felling, 11 percent were uprooted by bulldozers, and 3 percent had their bark scarred. Cutting 2 percent of the trees also caused the canopy cover to be roughly cut in half, from 80 percent to 43 percent. Such a "gapped" forest is vulnerable to further destruction by wind, vines, and fire.

Virgin tropical forest rarely burns in the Amazon because of its high humidity. But compared with virgin forest, selectively logged forest in Paragominas is 25 percent drier and 33 percent hotter, and has three times as much combustible material, largely dead branches, vines, and saplings. "Six days without rain is enough for the combustible materials to be ready for burning," Dr. Uhl and his colleagues wrote in the August issue of *Ciencia Hoje*, the monthly publication of the Brazilian Society for the Progress of Science.

Ranchers and farmers here and in the rest of the Amazon routinely use fire to clear weeds and tree sprouts from pastures near logged forests. Similar conditions created a mammoth fire in Indonesia in 1982 and 1983 that burned 14,300 square miles of tropical rain forest, destroying an estimated $5.5 billion in hardwood. Studying rainfall patterns with a grant from the World Wildlife Fund, Dr. Uhl and his colleagues concluded, "The data show that conditions already exist for fires of great size in eastern and southern Amazonia."

Tropical forest damage during selective logging can be cut in half if loggers plan the trails used to gain access to the trees to minimize damage. But research here found that loggers have little economic interest in using costly and time-consuming techniques. The loggers do not own the land they forest, and they are under pressure to cut as much wood as quickly as possible. The dry season lasts six months. Faced with the end of government loans and tax credits, and the steady degradation of pasture, many ranchers are selling logging rights to their forest reserves in order to finance bulldozing, replanting, and fertilizing of their pastureland. Given the emerging fire threat from reckless logging practices, Dr. Uhl said, the Brazilian Institute of Environment and Renewable Natural Resources should start a campaign to promote less wasteful logging techniques and then enforce them.

Turning to another future development, Dr. Nepstad has studied the eastern Amazon's emerging "post-pasture ecology." "Most of the land originally cleared for pasture will not be used for pasture—it was only valuable with government subsidies," said Dr. Nepstad, a staff scientist with the Woods Hole Research Center of Massachusetts, which helps finance the research here. As much as 25 million acres of the Amazon was cleared for pasture in the last two decades. But lacking in soil nutrients, much of the land loses its utility for grazing cattle after four to eight years. In recent years, ranchers and small farmers have abandoned as much as 15 million acres of cleared land. "At least 50 percent of the land cleared for pasture will be let go," Dr. Nepstad predicted as he walked by chest-high underbrush covering an abandoned pasture. "The perception in the United States and Europe is that deforestation is a terminal event."

Instead, Dr. Nepstad discovered, forest regeneration depends on the amount of tree roots in pasture soil, the level of old forest seeds in pasture soil, the spreading by birds and bats of seeds from neighboring old forests, and the survival rates for seedlings in the face of drought, cutter ants, and root competition with field species. "There are a series of overlaid sieves that strain out all but a few species," the ecologist said of his work, conducted with National Science Foundation grants. "The cut forest is often gone forever, but clearly something comes up."

Research here has confirmed a popular perception: the lighter the land use, the faster the rain forest regeneration. Fields that had only one year's use as pasture regained after eight years of abandonment about one third, or 80 tons, of the original forest vegetation. These plots supported twenty-one to twenty-five tree species. More common to Paragominas is moderate use, grazing for six to eight years, and weeding with machetes and by fire. Eight years after abandonment, these study plots had regained about 10 percent of forest vegetation, with sixteen to nineteen species taking root.

Given current abandonment rates, Dr. Nepstad believes that a major issue in the Amazon in the 1990s will be, "What do you do with 10 million acres of regrowth forest?" Answering his own question again, the biologist turned to one experiment, a test field planted with seedlings of thirty varieties of fruit and nut trees. Among the undergrowth of the abandoned pasture were seedlings of several internationally known trees: Brazil nut, mango, mahogany and cashew, and seedlings of local Amazon fruit trees—sapota, genipapo, cupuacu, and urucu. "One man with a machete tends 500 plants a week," he said of the seedlings, which on the average would yield a commercial value in four years. "You can restore agricultural production to these lands at a low cost." [JB, OCTOBER 1990]

A FOREST REFUGE IN PARAGUAY

SINCE 1989, when a military coup ended the thirty-five-year dictatorship of Alfredo Stroessner, there has been a democratic awakening in Paraguay, and interest in safeguarding the country's natural resources has blossomed. A major focus of this attention is Mbaracayu, a 225-square-mile extension of Brazil's Atlantic forest system. It is one of the last great tracts of privately owned subtropical forest in South America. "Mbaracayu is unique because physically there is no larger piece of land that is virtually undisturbed," said Alan Randall, Paraguayan program director for the Nature Conservancy, one participant in a coalition of governmental and private entities seeking to protect the larger of Mbaracayu's two parcels on Paraguay's eastern border with Brazil. Alwyn H. Gentry, senior curator of the Missouri Botanical Gardens, called Mbaracayu "one of the most important remaining examples of 'Alto Parana,' a high-forest type unusually rich in endemic species, found there and nowhere else."

Mbaracayu is not formally part of the Atlantic forest, which once ranged thousands of miles along Brazil's coast and which the International Conservation Union in Switzerland considers one of the two most endangered rain forests in the world, along with a jungle in Madagascar. It is, however, a vital haven for numerous Atlantic forest species that have disappeared from the forest proper. "It is the last refuge for many species," said Mr. Randall. "It is a bird sanctuary and is particularly rich in fruits and nuts which provide subsistence for the local Indian population."

The two parcels of land that make up the Mbaracayu property, one of 143,000 acres, another of 27,000, have been owned since 1979 by the International Finance Corporation, an arm of the World Bank that gained title because of the bankruptcy of a timber company. Although the properties, which are about fifty miles apart, have been maintained and their borders protected, the land is threatened by poachers, landless peasants, and those wishing to develop the land. The Moisés Bertoni Foundation, a Paraguayan conservation group started in Asunción in 1988, has forged an unusual preservation alliance. It involves the World Bank, the Nature Conservancy, the United States Agency for International Development (AID), the government of Paraguay, and AES Barbers Point, a private American company that is financing a survey of Mbaracayu property to determine the amount of carbon that will be sequestered by preserving the existing forest. The company is a wholly owned subsidiary of Applied Energy Services of Arlington, Virginia.

In a precedent for the World Bank, the International Finance Corporation (IFC) is selling a property below market value to a conservation organization. After the Paraguayan government rejected a debt-for-nature swap, the IFC asked $8 million for the larger Mbaracayu tract, but it has agreed to sell it to the Nature Conservancy for $2 million. The first grant of $500,000 from AID's Regional Global Climate Change Fund has been pledged to the conservancy to establish Mbaracayu as a nature reserve. The Nature Conservancy will purchase the property on behalf of the foundation. As part of the agreement, the Paraguayan government has agreed to buy the smaller tract with the intention of establishing agrarian reform settlements. The price is still being negotiated.

Because the Mbaracayu forest is far from Paraguay's navigable rivers, it was protected from European colonists. Spanish traders looking for the leaves of a locally grown tea, yerba maté, first entered the forest in the sixteenth century. In the seventeenth and eighteenth centuries, Brazilian slave traders also foraged the forests of Mbaracayu, but its isolation continued to provide a sanctuary for local Indians, the Ache. Today the Ache live in two villages adjacent to Mbaracayu but still use the forest as their traditional hunting grounds. Plans to preserve the wildlife and plant communities of the forest also include programs to allow the 1,000 remaining Ache to hunt and gather there and to help them make the transition to agriculture and animal husbandry. "It is so quiet here, you feel like you are king of the world," said Raúl Gauto, executive director of the Bertoni Foundation, leading visitors on a trail under the forest canopy. He explained that Mbaracayu means yellow macaw in Guarani, the second official language of Paraguay.

The Mbaracayu property holds a range of habitats. Fifteen percent is low transition forest (up to 49 feet tall), 80 percent is high, dense forest (up to 131 feet, depending on the depth of the soil), and 5 percent is natural grasslands, wetlands, rivers, and caves of ecological, biological, and archeological significance. Initial surveys have identified nineteen natural plant communities and a variety of threatened and endemic species. Tapirs, howler monkeys, peccary, giant armadillo, jaguar, and bush dogs are among the endangered mammals found in the area. Rare birds, such as the king vulture, bare-faced curassow, black-fronted piping guan, bare-throated bellbird, and large macaw have been spotted. "The importance of Mbaracayu is not only to maintain this last undisturbed pocket of temperate, subtropical rain forest," said Mr. Gauto, "but it will also set a precedent for preservation that can then be replicated in other parts of the country."

[EHB, MAY 1991]

REGENERATING A TEMPERATE FOREST

TRADITIONAL forestry practices have long been based on the idea that once a patch of forest is stripped of its trees, it will eventually return to its original condition. But a study of southern Appalachian forests that were cut as long as eighty-seven years ago has found that some forest ecosystems may never fully recover. Even if plants and animals do recolonize the area, it certainly will not recover before the next round of logging, said Dr. David Cameron Duffy, the author of the study.

Areas that are considered old-growth, or primary, forests because they have not been disturbed by logging make up less than 1 percent of Eastern forests, and the study shows that "it is absolutely critical that we preserve the remainder of this museum," Dr. Duffy said. For one thing, allowing the forests to be stripped means that important plant species may be lost forever. "A lot of the species in these forests have a reputation in folk medicine," said Dr. Duffy, who was at the University of Georgia Institute of Ecology when he conducted the study. "There could be another yew tree sitting there unknown." The yew, long regarded as a "trash tree" in the Pacific Northwest, is now being investigated for its ability to treat some forms of cancer.

Environmentalists said the study, reported in the journal *Conserva-*

tion Biology, supported their contention that current Forest Service management practices were insufficient to protect the few remaining old-growth stands and maintain biological diversity in the southern Appalachian forests.

Allen Gibbs, a spokesman for the Forest Service in Washington, said it was "too early to draw any conclusions," about the study's impact on management practices in national forests. Forest Service managers and scientists in the southern Appalachian forest said that they had some reservations about the conclusions of the study, but noted that logging practices in some national forests were already undergoing a philosophical change to address such issues.

In the study, Dr. Duffy, now a researcher at the Lyme Disease Research Project on Shelter Island, Long Island, and Albert J. Meier, a graduate student at the University of Georgia, examined the abundance and variety of the understory flowering plants that carpet the floors of cove hardwood forests in springtime. Those forests, found in moist, nutrient-rich, low-lying coves, are known to be some of the most biologically diverse ecosystems in North America. Common understory plants in the cove hardwood ecosystem include trillium, geranium, blue cohosh, and anemone.

Dr. Duffy and Mr. Meier selected nine stands of cove hardwood forests in the mountains of North Carolina, Tennessee, and Georgia that are considered primary forests. They compared the understory plants found in several sample plots on those sites with plants found in similar forests that were stripped of their trees, or clear-cut, forty-five to eighty-seven years earlier. The sites that were clear-cut, and are in the process of naturally regenerating themselves, are known as secondary forests. They found that in the secondary forest sites, understory flowering plants were only one-third as abundant as in the primary forests. The number of plant species found in the secondary forests, a measure of the biological diversity supported by an area, was about one-half that found in the primary forests. Moreover, said Dr. Duffy, there seemed to be no increase in the diversity or abundance of plants in the secondary sites that had had more time to recover, suggesting that there was no trend toward recovery with increasing age.

Dr. Duffy suggested several possible explanations for the failure of the secondary sites to recover. The rate of recovery may depend on the type of disturbance, or the understory may not flourish until trees die and provide nutrients. Or, he said, possible changes in climate conditions over the centuries may make it impossible for the forests to return to their original state. Whatever the reasons for the lack of recovery, Dr. Duffy wrote, the results "strongly suggest that recovery requires at least several centuries, longer than the present logging cycles of 40 to 150 years."

The understory plants are not the only species to be affected by clear-cut timber harvesting. Research by Dr. James W. Petranka, a professor of biology at the University of North Carolina at Asheville, found that salamanders in the southern Appalachian forests may require a hundred years or longer to return to normal population levels after clear-cutting operations. "The Duffy study punches a hole in the argument that you can have a clear-cut and then in a hundred years everything will be back the way it was before," said Dan Boone, a forest ecologist at the Wilderness Society in Washington. "It shows that if you clear-cut the forest you may irrevocably change its ability to support species."

The Wilderness Society is contesting the Forest Service's proposed long-term management plans for national forests in the southern Appalachian region, which typically call for clear-cutting in old-growth and secondary forests. No one knows exactly how much old-growth forests exist in the southern Appalachian region because no complete inventories have been done and there are no standard guidelines for defining such an area. In a lawsuit filed this spring, the society charged that the plan for the Cherokee National Forest in Tennessee calls for excessive logging on the cove hardwood forests and fails to protect biological diversity, as is required by the National Forests Management Act of 1976. The Forest Service denies most of the allegations.

In the Nantahala and Pisgah national forests in western North Carolina, where the conservationists have repeatedly criticized the management plans, Forest Service managers said they had revised their plans so they would rely less on clear-cutting and better protect the biological diversity of the forest, in accordance with a new Forest Service policy of "ecosystem management." "We are trying to reach beyond the traditional ways of managing the forest, given the national mood to move away from clear-cutting," said Bjorn Dahl, supervisor of the four national forests in North Carolina. "This plan is the first one in the country that tries to measure and evaluate biodiversity." Conservationists agreed that the new plan was a step in the right direction, but said that it still failed to protect old-growth forests.

Forest Service researchers and cooperating university scientists are now involved in several studies that address biodiversity in the southern Appalachians, said Dr. David Loftis, a research forest ecologist at the Forest Service's Southeastern Forest Experiment Station. In the Jefferson National Forest in Virginia, he said, scientists are establishing study plots that will be used to examine the effects of various logging methods on current levels of biodiversity. In the Nantahala and Pisgah national forests, researchers are compiling an inventory of areas that might qualify as old growth, and are seeking to define the ecological characteristics of old-growth forests. "The Duffy study is perhaps breaking new ground in this area," said Dr. Loftis. "But there were some problems with the methodology that raised doubts about whether the conclusions are really definitive." Dr. Loftis said he was concerned that the size of the sample plots examined by Dr. Duffy might have been too small to yield a true measure of plant diversity. He is planning to do a similar study next year, and is now trying to determine the minimum plot size needed.

Dr. Don McLeod, a plant ecologist and professor of biology at Mars Hill College in North Carolina, who is conducting some of the biodiversity studies for the Forest Service, also expressed some reservations about Dr. Duffy's conclusions, but called the research pioneering work. "I'm not convinced that those forests will never recover from clear-cutting, but it is certainly a possibility," Dr. McLeod said. "If there is a chance we are going to lose species, we ought to change our cutting practices and we certainly ought to leave some areas alone." [CD, SEPTEMBER 1992]

THE FOREST'S CYCLE

I F you don't believe there's life after death, look closer some spring day at a dead tree lying on the forest floor. Chances are, if it has been there for a while, it is teeming with more life now, after death, than when it was standing erect lifting its leafy arms to pray. Though it lacks the spring finery that inspires poets and lovers, a leafless tree is often more valuable to its forest dead than alive, say ecologists working in the old-growth forests of the Pacific Northwest. This fact, they say, has been largely ignored by wood-hungry forest managers in most of the United States and Europe, where overzealous harvesting of "dead wood" has depleted forests and rendered them highly susceptible to environmental stresses like acid rain. "Rotten wood was once considered just a fire hazard, a waste, an impediment to travel," remarked Dr. Michael Amaranthus, a soil scientist with the United States Forest Service in Grants Pass, Oregon. "More and more we are seeing it as an essential part of the forest system, crucial to its long-term productivity. It provides a reservoir of moisture and nutrients and a variety of habitats and food resources for a wide diversity of organisms. Our understanding of the importance of dead wood has increased a lot in the last ten years."

When nature cries "timber," countless unseen denizens of the forest rush to take up lodging in the fallen tree. Dead trees serve as warehouses and even factories for essential nutrients that enrich the soil and foster new growth. They store carbon, thus curbing atmospheric carbon dioxide and the pace of global warming. They hold volumes of water that sustain growing trees in droughts. And they serve as nurseries for new plant life, providing cozy niches where seeds can gain a firm roothold and outgrow other seedlings struggling to capture the light that penetrates where the tree once stood. The trunk of a dead tree is consumed by a varied succession of microbes, plants, and animals, which help to replenish the soil as they break down the wood. A result, say the two forest ecologists, Chris Maser and James M. Trappe, is "an accumulation of life and nutrients that is greater than the sum of its original parts."

"In a forest where the trees are repeatedly cut and removed, the soil becomes depleted, the structures deteriorate, and the forest loses its resilience for coping with stress," said Dr. Trappe, a forest mycologist at Oregon State University in Corvallis. This has already happened in Germany, where the forests are being severely damaged by air pollution and acid rain, Dr. Trappe said in an interview. "And Germany is the country whose concept of intensive forest management served as a model for our own," he noted.

Fallen trees help to preserve the forest by stemming the erosion of soil from wooded slopes and diverting streams that in straight courses might gouge out soil. In fresh waterways, fallen trees trap nutrient-rich sediments and create pools where fish can spawn and fry develop. Beyond the forest, dead trees help stabilize beaches and create habitats for wildlife in estuaries and salt marshes. Logs that reach the open sea serve as a major source of carbon and other foodstuffs for marine life. "Unfortunately, very little of this is now happening because the oceans are being deprived of this resource," said Mr. Maser, an author and consultant living in Las Vegas, Nevada. "We are beginning to starve the oceans as well as the soil because we are not reinvesting the biological capital nature provides into the forest, ocean, air, or land." "The function of dead trees in the ecosystem has rarely received the consideration that it deserves," says Dr. Jerry F. Franklin, an ecosystem analyst at the University of Washington's College of Forest Resources in Seattle. "At the time a tree dies, it has only partially fulfilled its potential ecological function. In its dead form, a tree continues to play numerous roles as it influences surrounding organisms. The woody structure may remain for centuries and influence habitat conditions for millennia." So, these forest scientists urge, woodsman, woodsman, spare thine ax for fallen as well as standing trees. Think twice before hacking up and carting off those logs dead in name only and dooming them to a brief and limited life as firewood.

As scientists with the United States Forest Service in Corvallis in the 1980s, Mr. Maser and Dr. Trappe produced a technical review, "The Seen and Unseen World of the Fallen Tree," that could easily become Exhibit A in the ongoing case to preserve forests. Their publication, number PNW-164, is available from the Superintendent of Documents, U.S. Government Printing Office, Washington, D.C. 20402. Using the unmanaged 450-year-old forests of Douglas fir in the Pacific Northwest, Mr. Maser and Dr. Trappe demonstrated that dead wood was far more than mere waste or a fire hazard to be removed as quickly as possible. Rather, they showed that dead trees were very much a part of the living forest.

Once a tree falls, it passes through five distinct phases of decay, they wrote. At each stage, the tree supports new life for which it is the sole or principal habitat.

At stage 1 are newly fallen trees with intact bark, a condition soon to be changed as bark and wood-boring beetles tunnel through. These brazen beetles blithely disregard the chemical and mechanical defenses of the conifer's bark that discourage most insect predators. The first beetles create channels for their successors. The beetles also carry in fungi and bacteria that provide food and essential nitrogen for future invaders.

At stage 2, trees still retain bark but as the beetles feast away, the nutritious growing layer of inner bark and the nearby phloem, which transported sugars, become spongy. These tissues are likely to be eaten in a few years. Next in line is the sapwood, which in the living tree housed the water-carrying structures called xylem.

By stage 3 the bark sloughs off. Roots from sprouting seeds now invade the sapwood, and the trunk begins to break into large, solid pieces. In a fallen Douglas fir, the sapwood succumbs to insects and fungi in ten to twenty years, Dr. Trappe said, although the bark of this tree "probably hangs around for centuries."

At stage 4 the heartwood, composed of the dead xylem that forms the bulk of the tree trunk, is all that remains. It now breaks apart into soft blocks as roots invade this dense, highly resistant, and not very nutritious wood. This is the stage, the longest in the decay process, that hosts the most diverse array of wildlife, including mites, centipedes, and snails, as well as salamanders, shrews, and voles.

Finally, in stage 5, the tree is no more than a soft, powdery mass. Ashes to ashes, dust to dust, soil to soil.

Stocked with nutrients, a fallen tree supports more life than when it was alive. Invading fungi ooze out enzymes that liberate the tree's nitrogen for use by other organisms. More nitrogen is provided by bacteria that extract it from the air. The tiny organisms that inhabit the log fertilize it with their excrement. Leaf litter and rainwater laden with nutrients and lichens from the forest canopy fall on the dead tree, adding further enrichment.

Carpenter ants are most active in stage 2. Their catholic diet includes butterflies and the honeydew of aphids. Nesting in fallen logs, they carry nutrients into the tree from the outside. Termites take over late in stage 2, importing in their wood-chomping bodies both protozoa that digest cellulose and bacteria that capture atmospheric nitrogen. By the time a termite colony is ready to move on, it has created a labyrinth of passageways in the tree that can be used by other animals and by the roots of invading plants.

As logs reach stage 3, they begin to become ready for occupation by a wide range of animals. As Mr. Maser and Dr. Trappe wrote about the trees when they reach stage 4: "Various mites, insects, slugs, and snails feed on the higher plants that become established on the rotten wood. These plants also provide cover for the animals, as do the lichens, mosses, and liverworts that colonize fallen trees."

In this microenvironment, mites thrive on the dead plant and animal matter that accumulates on fallen trees. The skeletons of dead mites, in turn, serve as incubators for fungal spores, and the fungi provide sustenance for other invading plants and animals. The folding-door spider is among the many arthropods that thrive in these conditions. It constructs a silky tube in one of the many cracks in the outer layer of a fallen tree that has reached stage 3 or 4 of its decay. The outer edges of the tube are pulled inward to form a slitted cover and the spider waits on the inside for the arrival of suitable prey, which are abundant in the decaying wood.

Among the ecologically important denizens of fallen Douglas fir is the California red-backed vole. The rodent eats mostly fungi and lichens but has a particular passion for truffles, Mr. Maser has shown. The vole then disperses the spores of the truffle, inoculating decaying trees with this valued foodstuff. This benefits other truffle-eaters, including the squirrels and mice that are the principal foodstuffs of the spotted owl and other carnivores. "The spotted owl debate is not a case of owls versus people," Dr. Trappe said. "It's a question of whether we want the diversity of organisms that the natural forest provides, or in its place a monoculture in which many organisms will disappear, not just the spotted owl."

If Dr. Mark E. Harmon, a forest ecologist at Oregon State University, has his way, dead trees as well as living forests will become valued as critical elements in containing global warming. When a tree is cut and processed into paper or a fallen tree turned into firewood, carbon dioxide is ultimately released into the atmosphere. "But a dead tree left on the forest floor holds on to its carbon for decades, even centuries," he explained. Dr. Harmon is directing a project whose lofty time horizon rivals that of the earth-made plaque sent aboard the spacecraft *Pioneer 10* to Jupiter and beyond. More than 500 logs of four different species have been placed throughout the H. J. Andrews Experimental Forest outside Eugene, and their patterns of decomposition are to be studied over the 200 years they will take to decay. Biologists will monitor the insects and microorganisms that colonize the logs, the small plants and large trees that become established on them, and the birds, reptiles, and mammals that use them as dwellings and food sources.

In a parallel experiment on two sides of the Cascades, 800 large trees were felled in 1987 and 1988 and placed in streams. Dr. James Sedell, an aquatic biologist at Oregon State University, said the project had already restored habitats for juvenile coho salmon and steelhead trout. "When a large log falls in a stream, the current scours out a pool around it and other wood gets trapped to form a debris jam," Dr. Sedell said. Fish then go into the pool, which serves as a safe harbor during winter floods and a secure habitat in summer droughts, he explained. The next step is to see if more fish leave the stream and grow up in the sea. "I'm optimistic," the biologist remarked. "Worldwide there's been much more interest in the role of wood in rivers and streams. The Forest Service and several states have begun to recognize that on forested land they need to allow big fallen logs to remain in streams to protect the fish resources."

Now, he and other scientists say, the question on land and water is: How much dead wood must be kept to bring back the many habitats needed to sustain the diversity of life on earth? [JEB, MARCH 1992]

FOREST SOIL HEAVES WITH MICROSCOPIC LIFE

ENVIRONMENTALISTS have focused great attention on spotted owls and ancient trees in the forest of the Pacific Northwest. But a small cadre of researchers who have been studying insects and other invertebrates of the forest soil now say that the old-growth forest has been hiding underfoot perhaps its most astonishing biological secret. Detailed studies of arthropods, including insects, spiders, mites, and centipedes in the soil of the old-growth forest suggest that the soil under the region's forest floor is the site of some of the most explosive biological diversity found on earth. Some experts believe that these temperate forests harbor a diversity of species that approaches the much-touted biological diversity of tropical rain forests.

As part of one of the most detailed analyses of arthropod diversity ever conducted, scientists now estimate that about 8,000 distinct species inhabit a single study site in an Oregon old-growth forest, most of them in the soil. The findings are "especially surprising because we think of that kind of diversity as being related to the tropics, not the temperate forests," said Melody Allen, executive director of the Xerces

Society, an invertebrate conservation group. But scientists say that those numbers are far less significant than still-sketchy hints of the role insects and other arthropods apparently play in the temperate forest ecosystem. "We've come to suspect that these invertebrates of the forest soil are probably the most critical factor in determining the long-term productivity of the forest," said Dr. Andrew Moldenke, an entomologist at Oregon State University in Corvallis.

In tropical rain forests, twigs, fallen leaves, and dead organisms are decomposed rapidly by bacteria and fungi that thrive in the warm, wet ecosystem. But in the temperate forests of the Pacific Northwest, arthropods appear to be linchpins in the decomposition process. Billions of extremely tiny insects, mites, "microspiders," and other invertebrates serve as biological recycling engines that reduce tons of organic litter and debris, from logs to bits of moss that fall to the forest floor, into finer and finer bits. Bacteria and fungi living in the digestive tracts of the arthropods and in the soil then progressively reprocess the finely crushed, once-living tissue into basic nutrient chemicals to feed roots and, hence, the aboveground ecosystem. New techniques for solidifying and examining soil samples offer great promise in increasing understanding of the rich ecosystems in the forest soil. Researchers caution that they still know "almost nothing," about precisely how all the thousands of arthropods interact and survive.

Taxonomists working in the region have been able to identify about 3,400 arthropod species at a single research site, the H. J. Andrews Experimental Forest in Oregon, a sort of living forest laboratory operated by the United States Forest Service. Many of those species have never before been named and described. In comparison, the count of all species of reptiles, birds, and mammals combined at the site is 143. Yet, according to Dr. John Lattin, director of the Systematic Entomology Laboratory at Oregon State University, the number of species cataloged so far probably represents less than half of the estimated species present on just the Andrews Forest site.

Simply to describe and name the yet-unnamed species will take years, in part because of the sheer numbers of arthropods in even a small area, according to Dr. Lattin. Most of the soil arthropods are exceedingly small, as tiny as one or two one-hundredths of an inch long. That is as small as or smaller than the period at the end of this sentence. And surveys have shown that the soil under a single square yard of forest can hold as many as 200,000 mites from a single suborder of mites, the oribatids, not to mention tens of thousands of other mites, beetles, centipedes, pseudoscorpions, springtails, "microspiders," and other creatures.

Dr. Moldenke and his students have in recent years begun studying soil and arthropod ecosystems using a technique called thin-section microscopy, originally developed by oil-exploration geologists. That approach has revealed that the very structure of temperate forest soils, and hence much of their biological and chemical activity, is determined by the dietary habits of the soil arthropods. Thin-section microscopy is accomplished by insinuating epoxy into a carefully removed core of soil, in a pressure chamber. Once the epoxy hardens, the now rocklike soil sample can be sliced into exceedingly thin wafers and polished smooth for examination under a microscope.

The technique preserves the soil, with its parts in place, from larger bits of partly decayed plant matter to microscopic soil particles. On one such slide, Dr. Moldenke showed a visitor the image of what was clearly a needle from a coniferous tree, partly decayed, but still mostly intact. Magnified, however, the small needle in the soil turn out to be an assemblage of thousands of infinitesimal fecal pellets arranged in almost precisely the shape of the needle. Not long after a bit of vegetation falls, millipedes descend on it, grinding it up. Chewed-up bits of vegetation pass through the insects' digestive tracts in a matter of seconds and are redeposited virtually in place as a pellet. A closer microscopic look at each pellet reveals that each is nothing more than chopped-up bits of plant cells, reassembled into a sort of jigsaw puzzle of plant matter. These tiny clumps of cell tissue will, in turn, be eaten by other arthropods. Deeper in the soil, the jigsawlike cell tissues become progressively less recognizable, as successive waves of "microshredder" arthropods crush and partly digest these fecal pellets, like a series of minute millstones grinding food down to finer and finer bits.

Cell tissue cannot dissolve in water. Yet for a living ecosystem to perpetuate itself, nutrient chemicals that are locked into insoluble organic molecules in tissues of dead organisms must somehow be made soluble to be taken up by the roots of plants. Each arthopod extracts only the whisper of nutrition from food that was once living cell matter. But in the process, each arthropod exposes more surface area to decomposer bacteria. The bacteria, in turn, biochemically process a trace more cell matter on the pellet's surface into soluble compounds, making more nutrition available to the next arthropod until, eventually, insoluble cell matter becomes soluble nutrients. In the old-growth forest, the process is sometimes excruciatingly slow. Soil organisms are just now completing the decomposition of some giant trees that crashed to earth about the time Columbus sighted land. Precisely how all these biological and chemical interactions occur, and which of the thousands of species' survival is key to the survival of others, are matters that remain poorly understood. "We've reached the point where we know just a little bit more about the fauna of the forest soil at the end of the twentieth century than was known at the beginning of the nineteenth," Dr. Moldenke said.

Researchers still don't know why there are so many invertebrate species in the forest soil in the first place. "There are still a lot of questions about why there's so much diversity," said Dr. Lattin. "But the fact that they are out there in such great numbers suggests that they play a very, very important role in the ecosystem." Dr. Moldenke agreed. "I don't know what the implications of all that diversity are," he said. "Neither does anybody else. And that's the scary part. I guess what concerns us is that the kinds of aboveground ecosystems that most ecologists have studied in the past [are] a very small part of what's really out there. When you have an awful lot of species, it means almost by definition a great number of processes: thousands of different functions taking place. If we instead continue to manage forests on the basis that the ecosystem is much more simple than it really is, we may be setting ourselves up for a big surprise, and it may not be a nice surprise."

One potential practical benefit of all that diversity lies on the research horizon: the arthropod communities may be able to serve as an exquisitely tuned gauge of changes in the forest ecosystem. In 1988, Dr. Moldenke began plugging data about the tens of thousands of arthropods collected from dozens of sites into a computer for statistical analysis. The results were so surprisingly consistent that he worried that the computer had been misprogrammed. Computer analysis proved that by analyzing the thousands of arthropods in a tin can full of soil from a site, a researcher could predict with accuracy the condition of the site itself. "As a result of knowing that pattern, anyone could take a sample in the Andrews Forest, find out what time of year it was taken, whether it came from a north or south slope, what the moisture content of the soil was," Dr. Moldenke said. "In some areas, it could tell you what kind of tree was nearby and how far away."

As a simplified example, he says, an abundance of tiny mites called Eulohmannia, which are "bright orange-yellow and look like a gasoline truck," indicate that a site is relatively dry and in a young forest. On the other hand, an abundance of Eremaeus mites, which "look like turtles with a pattern of red dots," indicates a moist site in old-growth forest. By analyzing such characteristics among thousands of arthropod data points, a researcher may be able to monitor changes at a site brought on by, say, global warming or herbicide use. "A tree doesn't tell you too much about what's happening," said Dr. Moldenke. "If you want to monitor change in the environment, the worst thing to look at is an organism that's centuries old. But the arthropod community allows you to look at what's happened over a different time frame, as little as a few months. And you can only do that because you have all that diversity."   [JRL, JULY 1991]

A BETTER WAY THAN
CLEAR-CUTTING

CITING mounting evidence that conventional logging could be causing far more harm to forests than once believed, a group of scientists in the Pacific Northwest has proposed a redesigned approach to logging and forest management that they've dubbed the New Forestry. The scientists are calling for foresters, particularly those responsible for managing woodlands in the public domain, to move away from "clear-cuts" that denude logging sites of all trees and leave the forest fragmented in a checkerboard patchwork. Instead, they say, loggers should be required to leave more living trees and natural debris on logging sites to help regenerate the forest. But these sites could be much larger than the current clear-cuts, and they could be cut in a way that preserves larger intact blocks of mature forest.

Although the new approach has been discussed in detail only since 1989, federal foresters are already embracing the techniques in two highly productive national forests in Oregon. In 1990, the Bush administration sent Congress a Forest Service policy statement suggesting that the techniques could become widespread in national forests. The administration's letter with the policy said the outlook might require that even less lumber be produced in areas where logging could not be accomplished without environmental peril. The Forest Service policy says "partial cutting will increase, and clear-cutting will be used less" in national forests.

In part, the approach is seen by some Forest Service officials and politicians as a possible compromise in the conflict between environmentalists and the timber industry over protection for old forests in the Pacific Northwest. But industry officials and environmentalists are both wary of the new approach and are giving it mixed reviews.

These ancient rain-soaked forests, which include some of the largest firs, spruces, and hemlocks in the world, also hold billions of board-feet of high-quality lumber, and loggers have long expected to have access to much of it. But in recent years, environmentalists have pressed for protection of the northern spotted owl, a rare species that is dependent on the old forests. Protection for the owl under federal laws like the Endangered Species Act would presumably also result in the preservation of large expanses of old forests and their ecosystems, which include several other rare species.

In April 1990, the conclusions of a special scientific committee created by Congress to provide a definitive answer on the owl's habitat needs rocked the timber industry. The panel said that to assure protection of the bird, 80 to 100 large blocks of forest, up to 60,000 acres each, would have to be preserved. Economic analysis has suggested that such a level of forest protection could lead to the loss of some 10,000 jobs in Oregon and Washington. The Fish and Wildlife Service is widely expected by various interested experts to rule that the owl will be classified as a "threatened" species, a designation one step below endangered under federal law and requiring stringent protection. This is expected to give further momentum to efforts that would protect both the owl and the old forests.

"New Forestry may resolve the clear-cut versus lock-up dilemma," said Representative Jolene Unsoeld, Democrat of Washington. Ms. Unsoeld has drafted a bill that would require trials of the new logging techniques in three of the areas preserved for owls partly to test whether a sensitive species can coexist with the new approach to logging.

Whether the New Forestry offers much hope to ease conflict is unclear. For the timber industry, there seems little doubt that its output of logs per acre would be reduced. "We don't need a New

Forestry," said Ralph Saperstein, vice president of the Western Forest Industries Association. "There's no crisis in our woods and no reason to be rushing in and making changes when we don't have any problems replanting and regenerating a forest."

Environmentalists, on the other hand, believe they are on the verge of a major victory in preserving old forests over the spotted owl issue and fear that the New Forestry could be a step backward. "The New Forestry is no substitute for protecting old growth," said David Wilcove, an ecologist with the Wilderness Society. The new approach grew out of two decades of studies in the Forest Service's Andrews Experimental Forest, east of Eugene, Oregon. In general, it is based on the growing knowledge of how forest ecosystems evolved over millions of years and how they recover from disturbances like fires; it is a response to calls for forestry that mimics the natural patterns of destruction. "Most forests are driven by disturbances," said David Perry, professor of ecology and forestry at Oregon State University. "So the idea of disturbing a forest to take out commodities is not necessarily a contradiction in terms of maintaining a natural forest." Fred Swanson, a Forest Service senior scientist who directs ecosystem research in the Andrews Forest, said a "pivotal change in the history of forestry" is taking place. "It used to be that we were managing the forests as tree farms," he said. "Now we're trying to manage the forest like an ecosystem."

Dr. Perry said the key to the new technique was that in fires and other disturbances, certain remnant plants typically survive, and these serve as "threads of continuity" that "provide the basis for the recovery of the forest." The remnants include a scattering of large live trees, various trees that are dead but still standing, and a wealth of logs and other debris on the forest floor. These biological legacies, as Dr. Perry and his colleagues call them, provide the shade or nutrition needed by seedlings, greatly help control erosion, or provide habitat for animals that are important ecological links in forest regeneration.

The researchers say loggers should be required to mimic such a disturbance as they cut, leaving behind as many as one fifth of the largest trees as well as many usable logs from the forest floor. Such ideas contradict much of the philosophy of conventional forestry. Especially in the coniferous forests of the West, typical logging involves clear-cuts, which denude large tracts. The cuts are often followed by controlled burns and applications of herbicides to groom a site for economically valuable tree species like Douglas firs, planted in cornfieldlike expanses. The philosophy of such forestry holds that mature natural forests, with their diversity of ages and types of trees and other plants, are far less efficient producers of lumber than carefully tended stands limited to productive species. Clear-cuts in such monoculture forests of similar-sized trees also make mechanized logging easier.

But the research on old forests in the Pacific Northwest has suggested that conventional logging and regrowth may deny regenerating woodlands several long-term ecological benefits. Among them, said Jerry Franklin, Bloedel Professor of Ecosystem Studies at the University of Washington and formerly chief plant ecologist for the Forest Service, include better pest and fire resistance, less soil erosion, and more effective processing of nutrients. But some critics contend that there is virtually nothing new in the New Forestry. "As a theory, there's really nothing radically new here," says Mark Rae, executive director of the American Forest Resources Alliance, an industry trade group.

Mr. Rae and others point out that debate raged as long ago as the 1930s in the Forest Service over whether woodlands in the Pacific Northwest should be thoroughly clear-cut and replanted or larger landscapes should be subjected to selection-cutting, in which only a few trees are removed each year.

The New Forestry differs from selection-cutting. It is essentially a modified clear-cut, in which more trees are removed than in selection-cutting but over a smaller area, which is then abandoned and left to regenerate.

The New Forestry proponents are not advocating selection-cutting, and while some environmentalists favor the technique, loggers generally object to its high cost. Selection-cutting can also create environmental problems, said Dr. Franklin, because it requires more road maintenance and more intrusion of loggers into the forest. While early foresters believed that clear-cutting did imitate fires and natural disturbances, the New Foresters say their research has shown otherwise. "The old view was that whole stands were wiped out," said Dr. Perry. "One-hundred-thousand-acre holocaustic fires came along and destroyed everything in their path. But as we've looked at forest history, we've found that everything wasn't being wiped out when disturbances swept through." Such disturbances may remove many of the trees, he added, but they nevertheless leave behind a complex surviving web of plants and animals. Besides the shade and animal habitat provided by standing trees, both dead and alive, the huge water-laden logs on the forest floor help control erosion and flooding and pump tons of nutrients into soil as they decay, sometimes over as long as five centuries.

To mimic a natural disturbance, the New Forestry theorists say, loggers should leave untouched 20 to 70 percent of the living trees of various species, including huge specimens that could otherwise yield enough lumber to build an average house, as well as downed logs and standing dead trees.

Dr. Franklin, who refers to such a New Forestry site as a "sloppy clear-cut," acknowledges that it might actually appear worse than a conventional clear-cut. Still, biologically, he says, "a little chaos can be a wonderful thing."

Barry Flamm, chief forester for the Wilderness Society, cautions that such a consideration could prove an obstacle for the New Forestry. "Esthetically, this could be pretty unappealing, at least until the forest started to regenerate," he said. "Even with some of the biological merits, that could be a problem on public lands."

Although Dr. Franklin says that leaving 20 percent of the mature trees might be a typical number, Harold Salwasser, a senior researcher at the Forest Service, says that on some sensitive sites, "it might mean going in with a helicopter and taking out only a few trees and not going back for decades." The New Forestry proponents have suggested that in western national forests, where clear-cuts of about forty acres now commonly checkerboard the landscape, cuts should actually be of hundreds of acres. That, in theory, would leave larger, but less fragmented, expanses of forest intact. Emerging ecological theories suggest that many species need larger blocks of deep forest interior habitat than was once believed. Already, supervisors of both the Siskiyou National Forest in southern Oregon and the Willamette National Forest just to the north, the most productive of all the nation's public forests, are experimenting with the techniques.

Officials at the Weyerhaeuser Corporation say that although the company's extensive private holdings of timber in Washington and Oregon include only a tiny fraction of true old-growth forests, they have begun to consider applying some of the techniques to younger, regenerated forests. But Jim Rochelle, manager of environmental forestry research, said the company was approaching the New Forestry cautiously. "We think it's worth experimenting with, but we don't think we should apply it on a broad scale before we know more about it," he said. Many environmentalists and officials of the timber industry have expressed even greater skepticism. "The theory is already being used by people who want to cut as few trees as possible on as few acres as possible, when the theory's central tenet is that you should be able to cut at least a few trees on lands where we haven't been able to cut before," said Mr. Ray of the American Forest Resources Alliance. "As things stand, it looks to us like it's going to become a novel excuse to cut fewer trees."

James Montieth, director of the Oregon Natural Resources Council, an environmental group, takes a contrary view. "New Forestry would be great if it were coupled with a reduction of the cut so we reach a place that's really sustainable," he said. "But there are some in the timber industry who want to keep cutting at a high level and who might think New Forestry is the answer: you just cut in a different way. We're concerned that it not become a placebo for the real problem, which is, we're just cutting too fast in the national forests."

[JRL, JUNE 1990]

A PLAN FOR AMERICA'S FORESTS

IN the time since the Forest Service adopted what it calls "a more ecologically sound approach" to managing the national forests in June of 1992, debate has flourished over whether the policy amounts to a major philosophical shift, a barely modified form of business as usual, or something in between. The agency has given few specific instructions to foresters about how to accomplish the new goals, and Forest Service officials acknowledge that in many ways any application of the concept, much of which is based on relatively new discoveries and theories, will amount to an experiment.

In announcing the new policy on June 4, 1992, Dale Robertson, the Forest Service's chief, emphasized that clear-cutting would be curtailed in national forests. But he outlined a far more ambitious proposal in a memorandum to his staff, ordering that an experimental program called "New Perspectives," tested in the preceding three years in a few forests, become more standard practice systemwide. He dubbed the plan "ecosystem management." Under the plan, logging would continue on much of the 191 million acres of national forests, but it would be managed according to new theories about how to make replanted forests more like natural ecosystems and less like tree farms.

"If all you want us to do is manage the forests intensively for wood, we can do that," said Dr. Harold Salwasser, who has directed the New Perspectives program. "But this policy says that the amount of timber that can be harvested has to be in balance with the desired ecology for the forest." But the lack of specifics from Mr. Robertson allowed different groups to interpret the policy differently.

"Questions are being raised about whether this is a lot of rhetoric allowing business as usual or a major sea change," said Dr. Gerry Gray, vice president for resource policy for Americans Forests, a conservation group. "We tend to think that, given the new information coming from science, the agency really is going to move toward an ecological management approach." Others are more skeptical. Some environmentalists said they believed that the announcement would lead to few real changes, and industry representatives expressed concern that it could lead to sharp logging reductions in national forests.

Many of the concepts involved in the new proposal came from the work of a team of university and Forest Service scientists working at the H. J. Andrews Experimental Forest in Oregon during the last two decades. By the mid-1980s, the Andrews team had concluded that wholesale clear-cutting, followed by plantings of farmlike "crops" of a single species was a poor replication of natural cycles in which forests regenerate themselves. In particular, the researchers found that fires and other disturbances in old-growth stands virtually always left behind some standing trees, as well as tons of fallen timber.

From that and other work, including analysis of the ecological patterns of recovery on the slopes of Mount St. Helens after its explosive volcanic eruption, the researchers concluded that such left-behind elements were "biological legacies" that helped new forest regenerate in a host of previously unsuspected ways. For instance, any remaining large, old trees on a burned site will provide habitat for huge numbers of predatory insects, which in turn suppress insects that might otherwise defoliate newly sprouted trees.

Biologists worldwide, meanwhile, were reassessing the role that the shape and size of habitats have on the species within them, particularly noting that if a larger landscape is fragmented into an archipelago of small islandlike parcels, species could suffer previously unsuspected

extinction pressures. That happens because isolated populations in-
breed, or because predators normally restricted to forest edges suddenly have access to interior habitats.

In the Willamette National Forest in Oregon, foresters have designed a logging plan for the 19,000-acre watershed of Augusta Creek
that Forest Service officials say could be a portent of things to come
under "ecological management." "In the past," said John Cissel of the
Forest Service, "we probably would have taken a standard approach"
to logging the site. That approach, he said, would have meant cutting
and replanting perhaps 1 to 2 percent of the forest each year in a
continual rotation, without much regard to the ecology of specific
sites. Instead, foresters plan to try to mimic the historical fire patterns
in the region, with logging rotations of 200 or 300 years. To arrive at
the pattern, scientists looked for evidence of fire-scarring, which can
be determined by looking for aberrations in trees' growth rings. "We
found that on wetter, cooler north-facing basins, fires have been infrequent but intense and large when they do occur," Mr. Cissel said.
Thus logging in those areas will be infrequent but aggressive. In drier,
hotter, south-facing areas, he said, the fires have been "low intensity,
burning mostly along the ground and then once in a while flaring up
into the canopy and wiping out a pocket of trees." Logging in such
areas will therefore be more frequent but confined to small pockets.

In Michigan, the Forest Service has approved a plan to allow
173,000 acres in the Huron and Manistee national forests to return
to old growth. The forests were completely logged over near the turn
of the century and are just now maturing. In 1986, the Forest Service
agreed in principle to protect that much land in response to a protest
against its logging plans by environmentalists. But where in the past
the agency might have sequestered parcels of land randomly, avoiding
those most accessible and desirable to loggers, it instead studied the
forests' ecosystems and designed a network of reserves, often connected by corridors of habitat along riverbanks. The procedure may
be a sign of how landscapes will be managed in other forests in the
future, said Dr. Drew Barton, a visiting scholar in the biology department at the University of Michigan and a consultant to the Sierra Club
who worked on the design. The result, he said, should be a more
ecologically sound network of old-growth reserves while logging occurs elsewhere in the forests.

The approach, in all its variations, has its skeptics. Jeff DuBonis,
director of the Association of Forest Service Employees for Environ-

mental Ethics, a group often sharply critical of agency actions involving old-growth forests, called the announcement "smoke and mirrors." He suggested that the memorandum, although brief, listed so many exceptions to the clear-cutting ban that the directive was meaningless. Jeff Olson, director of the Bolle Center for Ecosystem Management for the Wilderness Society in Washington, agreed. "On the one hand, it's an important development that they're talking about ecosystem management at all," he said. "I applaud their rhetoric. But we would have hoped to have seen some teeth in the directive." Con Shallau, chief economist for the American Forest Resources Alliance, an industry trade group, suggested that logging costs could soar. Depending on how the directive is interpreted, it could halve timber supply from national forests, he said.

Among forestry scientists, Dr. William Atkinson, professor of forestry at Oregon State University, has been perhaps the most outspoken critic of some of the new approaches. He said his main objection was that too many of the new concepts were likely to be applied without experimentation on a smaller scale first. "Instead of scientific forestry, we're going to have politically correct silvaculture," he said.

Forest Service officials agree that they are experimenting as they go. "We're still fairly early along the learning curve, and we don't really have any cookbook methods for ecosystem management," said Mr. Cissel. "But forestry has always been a process of learning by doing and continually adapting our practices. Ecosystems are incredibly complex, and if you feel you have to know everything and how it works before you try to change something you sense isn't working, you'll never be able to do anything at all." It remains to be seen if the agency can apply the philosophy broadly, given a long history of political pressure from members of Congress from timber-dependent districts to maintain high logging levels. Mr. Robertson suggested in his announcement that after an initial dip of about 10 percent in timber yields, current high yields could be restored under the new program by cutting more selectively over a larger area. But many environmentalists insist that current levels are not sustainable under any logging approach. And some highly placed agency staff acknowledge that for at least some forests, improved ecological management could mean logging reductions.   [JRL, JUNE 1992]

Disturbing the Atmosphere

OZONE LAYER DEPLETION AND CLIMATE WARMING

THE ATMOSPHERE is so vast it might seem immune from human activities. This is not the case. Two principal concerns of environmentalists, and the subjects of this section, are global warming and the ozone layer shield.

Global warming refers to the possibility that waste gases in the atmosphere will lead to greater retention of the sun's heat, which otherwise would be beamed out again into space. Even a slight retention of extra heat, over time, could lead to a warming of the global climate, with serious consequences for agriculture, sea level, and the future distribution of humans and other species.

The principal gas of concern is carbon dioxide, the most copious combustion product when wood, oil, or coal is burned. Steadily accumulating in the atmosphere since the industrial revolution, the transparent gas admits sunlight but traps the resulting heat from returning to space.

Because carbon dioxide and other gases have indeed built up in the atmosphere over the last century, the global temperature should have risen. But has it? The climate has such wide natural swings that it is very hard to see the small warming effect that is predicted. The problem of how to recognize the greenhouse signal is critically important.

If warming is real, however, action to avert it should begin well in advance of the warming signal. Climatologists therefore rely heavily on what they call "models," or computer simulations of the real climate. Though the models are getting better, they are far from exact. The major questions about the degree and timing of climate warming remain uncertain and will probably take many more years to resolve.

Once upon a time the coolant fluid that kept refrigerators cool was ammonia, a troublesome and toxic chemical. Then came the invention of chlorofluorocarbons, or CFCs, a benign family of compounds so stable and inert that they harmed no one.

Unfortunately the CFCs proved to be so stable that they resisted even nature's best cleanser, sunlight. Wafting their way to the top of the atmosphere, a journey that can take some fifteen years, the chemicals are at last broken down, liberating chlorine.

The high atmosphere is very rarefied, and the doses of chlorine that gathered there soon began to have a thoroughly destabilizing influence on ozone, the chemical formed from the action of sunlight on oxygen. Though ozone is a serious pollutant at ground level, in the high atmosphere it screens out part of the ultraviolet radiation from the sun. Since light of this frequency can damage both proteins and DNA, the ozone plays the role of a vital protective shield.

Though governments and industry were at first reluctant to acknowledge the threat, most have eventually done so and production of CFCs is being stopped or phased out. What remains to be seen is how much damage will occur from the rents already made in the ozone shield and from the future assaults of the vast tonnages of CFCs that are still contained in millions of refrigerators, auto air conditioners, and other equipment throughout the world.

A RUNAWAY PHASE
IF WARMING STARTS

A GLOBAL warming caused by industrial and automotive emissions of heat-trapping carbon dioxide could well build on itself and produce even more warming, some scientists argue. The warming, they say, would stimulate the release of more carbon dioxide from natural storage places like forests, grasslands, and wetlands. The case has not been proved, but the issue has been raised by a provocative study that shows that when the production of carbon dioxide by fossil-fuel burning is discounted, global temperature and naturally occurring concentrations of atmospheric carbon dioxide rose and fell in tandem on many time scales between 1958 and 1988—with changes in temperature generally preceding changes in levels of carbon dioxide by a matter of months.

While the findings do not definitively establish that rises in temperature cause rises in atmospheric carbon dioxide, they do suggest it and are "very tantalizing," said Dr. Michael Oppenheimer, a senior scientist at the Environmental Defense Fund in New York and an author of the report, which appeared in the British journal *Nature*. If warming does stimulate the release of more carbon dioxide, he said, it means that the global warming already observed in the last decade, no matter what its cause, could in itself stimulate further warming in the years ahead, even if humans stopped pouring carbon dioxide into the atmosphere now. Carbon dioxide and other heat-trapping gases hold heat inside the atmosphere much as panes of glass hold it inside a greenhouse. And if the industrial and automotive emissions continue, Dr. Oppenheimer said, it could mean that the warming will be even greater in the long run.

Scientists say that the average surface temperature of the globe in 1990, at nearly 60 degrees Fahrenheit, was the highest since record keeping began in the late nineteenth century, and that seven of the warmest years since 1880 have occurred since 1980. But climatologists say it is too early to know whether carbon dioxide and other heat-trapping gases emitted as a result of human activity caused the warming or whether it resulted from natural factors.

The new study was conducted by Dr. Oppenheimer, Dr. R. M. Fujita and Dr. S. R. Gaffing of the Environmental Defense Fund, and Dr. J. B. Marston of Cornell University. It is "the latest bit of evidence" pointing toward the possibility that warming produces more warming by stimulating the release of carbon dioxide from natural sources, said Dr. George M. Woodwell, director of the Woods Hole Research Center in Woods Hole, Massachusetts, one of the first to advance the idea.

Dr. Woodwell maintains that by feeding on itself, the warming could continue indefinitely unless steps are taken to slow or stop it. But he, too, said that the idea of a feedback effect between warming and the release of naturally produced carbon dioxide was unproved, and called it "one of the great uncertainties about the warming of the earth."

Other scientists expressed skepticism about the proposition suggested by the latest study. "I think it's misleading to say the temperature is the primary cause of the increase in carbon dioxide," said Dr. C. D. Keeling of the Scripps Institution of Oceanography in La Jolla, California, who has also analyzed the relationship between temperature and carbon dioxide. Dr. Keeling said that natural factors besides temperature probably influence carbon dioxide levels. These include changes in rainfall and in the upwelling of carbon from deep within the sea, each of which is a product of the natural dynamics of the climate system. It merely happens, he suggested, that "temperature shows a rise somewhat ahead of the increase in carbon dioxide."

Dr. Keeling has analyzed the relationship in which temperature fluctuations precede carbon dioxide fluctuations over the course of the El Niño cycle. In that cycle, incompletely understood natural factors cause sea surface temperatures in the eastern equatorial Pacific to warm every two to six years, touching off worldwide changes in weather. Dr. Keeling argues that these meteorological changes could be responsible for the fluctuations in carbon dioxide. Other scientists say that although the temporary atmospheric warming produced by El Niño is comparable to that expected to result from human-induced global warming, the amount of carbon dioxide produced in El Niño years is trivial.

But, said Dr. Oppenheimer, "we've shown that there's a lot more at work here than El Niño," since the latest study shows that changes in carbon dioxide follow temperature changes over many time scales, from one year to thirty. In this, the findings generally confirm a 1990 study by Cynthia Kuo, Craig Lindberg, and David J. Thomson of AT&T Bell Labs in Murray Hill, New Jersey.

The most recent study goes beyond the 1990 report to speculate that changes in carbon dioxide may follow changes in temperature over even longer time scales. These longer periods are the ones in which any global warming brought about by human emissions of heat-trapping gases would take place, since the effect of the gases is felt only over decades. By analyzing temperature and chemical records preserved in ancient ice over the last 160,000 years, climatologists have also found a correlation between carbon dioxide and tempera-ture over millennial time scales. But because these measurements are less precise than measurements of modern-day temperature, they do not allow scientists to say with confidence whether changes in warming precede changes in carbon dioxide or vice versa. Dr. Oppenheimer and others have argued in the past that the ancient correlation pro-vides evidence that rises in carbon dioxide have caused temperatures to rise.

That would still be true over long time scales, he said, "because it takes a long time for the greenhouse effect to take hold." Moreover, he said, cause and effect could change over time, as various forces are brought into play at different times and at different rates. "Over a shorter time scale," Dr. Oppenheimer said, "it is pretty clear that temperature precedes carbon dioxide. The reason for that is that the greenhouse effect doesn't get going over these short time scales. Over longer time scales, it does."

Scientists say that statistical correlations of the kind that underlie the recent studies are weak indicators unless there is also a plausible mechanism to explain the supposed relationship between temperature and carbon dioxide. Dr. Woodwell and others have identified a num-ber of such possible mechanisms, all of them related to natural move-ments of carbon dioxide in and out of the atmosphere. Under natural conditions, billions of tons of carbon move between the atmosphere, on the one hand, and the oceans, forests, grasslands, wetlands, and soils, on the other. Only a small fraction of this carbon is in the atmosphere at any one time, in the form of carbon dioxide. This, along with methane, is what traps enough heat from the sun to make life possible, scientists say.

Additional carbon dioxide from the burning of fossil fuels is not the only way in which atmospheric concentrations can grow. Dr. Woodwell says that a warmer atmosphere would cause photosynthesis in plants to increase, using up some carbon dioxide. But the amount used would be small, he said, compared with the carbon dioxide that plants would pour back into the atmosphere as a result of increased respiration, the process in which energy is burned. The result would be a net increase in atmospheric carbon dioxide. More carbon dioxide would also be released as warmer temperatures speeded the decay of organic matter, he said, and more methane would be released as frozen bogs in the north began to thaw. How all of this would actually affect the course of future warming "cannot be determined until our inadvertent global warming experiment is well under way," Dr. Oppenheimer said.   [WKS, FEBRUARY 1991]

MAYBE THE GLOBE HAS
A THERMOSTAT

DOES the earth's climate regulate itself, enabling global temperatures to stay within certain broad limits? The question fascinates scientists, especially at a time of concern and contention about global warming, and now climatologists have produced evidence that clouds act as a natural thermostat that keeps the temperature of the oceans' surface from rising above a certain point. Although the evidence comes primarily from the tropical Pacific Ocean, climate experts say it suggests that the earth's closely coupled ocean-atmosphere system could act as a more general thermostat to prevent any warming of the global climate from spiraling out of control.

The evidence raises the tantalizing possibility that a natural regulatory mechanism could set a ceiling on the global warming that scientists say will result from emissions of heat-trapping gases like carbon dioxide. At present rates of emission, they calculate, atmospheric concentrations of these greenhouse gases will double by the middle of the twenty-first century, eventually raising the average surface temperature of the earth by 2 to 9 degrees Fahrenheit. They say that a warming in the upper end of that range would have catastrophic results for the world's climate.

It is not yet known whether the effects of the predicted warming would be mitigated by the thermostatic effect that scientists say they have now demonstrated. But the new findings may rule out the direst scenarios about the greenhouse effect, in which global warming would escalate until it ultimately made the earth inhospitable to life. Scientists and environmentalists who fear this possibility point out that this is precisely what happened on Venus.

"I cannot see how the planet can have a runaway greenhouse effect" given the new findings, said Dr. Veerabhadran Ramanathan, a climatologist at the Scripps Institution of Oceanography in La Jolla, California. With a colleague, Dr. William Collins, he presented the evidence for the thermostatic mechanism in the British journal *Nature*. Even so, said Dr. Ramanathan, global warming could still cause vast climatic disruptions. This, he said, is because the thermostatic mechanism, if it operated globally, would probably lead to a radical change in the large-scale circulation of huge rivers of air, like the jet streams, that create and define regional climates. These climates could be transformed in ways yet unfathomed. Moreover, he said, the temperatures of most of the world's oceans, unlike those in the tropics, are so far below the limit imposed by the thermostat that most of the earth's surface could warm significantly before the thermostat kicked in globally.

The new evidence for a climatic thermostat comes from an analysis of data on changes in temperature and sunlight gathered by satellites and ships. Dr. Ramanathan and Dr. Collins studied the behavior of the ocean-atmosphere system over the eastern and central Pacific at the equator in 1987 when El Niño occurred. In this periodic event, naturally occurring changes in ocean currents caused the equatorial sea surface to warm by 5 to 7 degrees. For Dr. Ramanathan and Dr. Collins, it provided a natural experiment in which to look at the relationship between temperature and clouds as the climate actually changes.

They found that as the sea surface grew warmer, water vapor increased substantially in the air. Water vapor is the most powerful greenhouse gas—it amplifies the effects of other causes of heating, including both carbon dioxide and sunlight—and in this case it produced what Dr. Ramanathan calls a "supergreenhouse effect."

At the same time, huge, tall thunderclouds formed. As they

reached freezing altitudes, the tops of the clouds turned into monstrous, flat "anvils" of cirrus clouds made of ice crystals. Together, at their maximum extent, the cirrus clouds covered nearly 4 million square miles of the earth's surface. Normally, cirrus clouds help trap heat in the atmosphere. But the thicker they become, the more sunlight they reflect. Eventually, said Dr. Ramanathan, "the cirrus becomes so thick and so highly reflective that it shuts off the sunlight reaching the ocean." This was more than enough to counterbalance the warming below, the scientists say, and the net effect was to prevent the sea surface from warming further. Once the cooling begins, they found, the tall thunderclouds and the cirrus dissipate, and the process starts again.

The ceiling beyond which the ocean warms no further, Dr. Ramanathan and Dr. Collins say, appears to be about 90 degrees Fahrenheit on a monthly average. The ceiling might be pushed upward by 2 or 3 degrees, Dr. Ramanathan said, by an unexpectedly large buildup of atmospheric carbon dioxide concentrations. But for that to happen, he said, the concentrations would have to increase tenfold rather than merely double. The thermostatic process also appears to take place in the tropical Atlantic and Indian oceans, the scientists say, although the El Niño experiment is in some ways considered the best test of the thermostat hypothesis.

"It's a very simple effect, but no one had demonstrated it effectively until now," said Dr. Andrew J. Heymsfield, an atmospheric physicist at the National Center for Atmospheric Research in Boulder, Colorado, who wrote a commentary for *Nature* on the new research. In an interview, he called the study "first rate" and said he thought its conclusions were correct for the tropical Pacific. He also called the results "provocative" in suggesting the possibility of a climatic thermostat that might affect human-induced global warming. But, he said, "it's not at all straightforward." It is not clear, for instance, whether heat produced by global warming at the surface of the continents could be transported to the tropical oceans, where the thermostatic effect might offset it. The tropical oceans, with their enormous amounts of heat energy, drive the planet's climate, and in doing so they create huge, circulating wind currents that transport heat from one part of the earth to another.

Another uncertainty, Dr. Heymsfield said, has to do with the source of the warming in the Ramanathan-Collins study and the source of the human-induced global warming that scientists predict. In the former, the source is sunlight and surface sea currents. In the latter, it is heat-trapping atmospheric gases.

Dr. Ramanathan and Dr. Collins add their own caveats. They say their findings constitute experimental evidence of an important feedback arrangement in the climate system. But there are many others about which little is known, and Dr. Ramanathan says that any number of climatic factors could upset the workings of the mechanism on a global scale.

The findings do suggest, he said, that greenhouse warming, if it is large enough, could cause the much cooler oceans outside the tropics to warm to the maximum, establishing a more or less uniform oceanic temperature throughout the world. This in itself would have profound effects on the world's climate, he said, since it is the differences in temperature among the oceans that largely sets in motion the planetary winds that create and shape regional climate. With these differences eliminated, regional climates could be expected to change profoundly and disruptively. This may be the most significant aspect of the Ramanathan-Collins paper, said Dr. William A. Nierenberg, a geophysicist who is director emeritus of the Scripps Institution and who has expressed doubt that global warming will be as severe as some scientists have predicted. A number of feedbacks might act to limit global warming, he said. "In fact," he said, "the average global temperature change could be almost zero" because of the many feedback mechanisms. But the operation of the mechanisms could nevertheless impose a "severe" price in terms of the regional climate changes they would cause.

Some scientists say the Ramanathan-Collins findings could lead to better predictions about the extent of the expected global warming. The predictions rest largely on computerized mathematical models of the climate system that all scientists agree are crude and flawed. One of the major flaws has to do with the effect of clouds. Already, the findings cast doubt on some features of the models. For instance, Dr. Ramanathan said, some models predict that if atmospheric carbon dioxide concentrations are doubled, the surface temperature of the western Pacific will rise to about 93 degrees, well above the ceiling that he and Dr. Collins believe they have discerned. "If our hypothesis is valid," Dr. Ramanathan said, "that's not possible." [WKS, MAY 1991]

NORTHWARD MIGRATIONS IN A
WARMER WORLD

T HE woodland deer mouse, with its long tail, big ears, and pow-
der-white belly, once was so common in the cold forests of northern Michigan that trapping it for study was hardly more difficult than
collecting moths and mosquitoes. Sometime in the last twenty to forty
years, though, the deer mouse all but vanished from the woods here,
its range retreating north to Michigan's upper peninsula, thirty miles
away.

By itself, the deer mouse's disappearance would not have caused
much of a stir along the shores of Douglas Lake, where the University
of Michigan has maintained a 10,000-acre biological field station for
most of the century. But a team of Michigan researchers has documented other striking changes in the geographic distribution of a
dozen other plants and animals in this region. Ferns, fish, and mammals common to the southern mixed hardwood forests of the Middle
West and East are moving into northern Michigan, some of them at
a pace of ten miles annually. Meanwhile, small mammals, trees, and
orchid plants of the north that once were plentiful at the southern
edge of their range in Michigan are rapidly slipping back into Canada,
their major range.

Because the research center has been collecting data for most of
this century, the scientists believe the findings reflect long-term climate
change, not just recent warm years that might or might not be due to
global warming. Although they concede that their work does not
prove the case, their study is the first formal scientific research in the
United States to determine whether documented changes in species'
ranges are being caused by man-made climatic change.

"It's clear there is enough circumstantial evidence now that many
scientists believe the causes of these range changes deserve an immediate and intensive investigation to determine whether they are related
to global warming," said Dr. James A. Teeri, director of the Michigan
Biological Station, who is coordinating the research team. "The real

challenge is to separate possible global warming causes from other changes in land use due to human activities."

Measuring changes in the geographical distribution of plants and animals is often an inexact scientific business. The ranges of organisms are fluid; plants and animals aggressively take ground when conditions are sweet and withdraw in the face of fire, disease, drought, and other threats. To link such changes with global warming makes the issue even more murky. There has clearly been a warming trend in the last decade. What is at issue is the cause; it may be greenhouse gases, but scientists say it is too soon to tell. Scientists in the United States and other nations have hypothesized that the warming trend is a result of industrial and agricultural gases, chiefly carbon dioxide, methane, and chlorofluorocarbons, trapping infrared energy from the earth's surface and causing the heating.

Since 1870, the average temperature of the planet has risen 1.6 degrees Fahrenheit or about 1 degree Centigrade, and if a more rapid rate of increase noted over the last two decades continues, the average temperature could climb as much as 8 degrees by the end of the twenty-first century, some scientists say. British and American scientists in 1991 said that 1990 was the warmest year recorded since people began measuring the planet's surface temperature. Of the ten warmest years recorded, all have occurred since 1973.

It is not yet known whether the warming trend is a long-term result of natural variability or a result of increased emissions of heat-trapping gases. Recent studies have sought to answer the question by looking at changes in natural processes. Scientists have found that the snow mantle covering the Northern Hemisphere is shrinking, that the sea ice near Greenland is thinning, and that the Alaskan snow melted about two weeks earlier in the 1980s than it did in the 1940s.

A study by Canadian scientists showed that the average annual temperature in a region of northwestern Ontario climbed more than 3.5 degrees Fahrenheit from the late 1960s to the mid-1980s, causing more droughts and fires and making lakes shallower and more prone to contamination. In August 1991, scientists from the National Aeronautics and Space Administration and the United States Geological Survey said the ice cap in the Arctic Sea had shrunk 2 percent from 1978 to 1987.

But if projections of a long-term, man-made warming trend are accurate, scientists would expect to observe its results also among plants, animals, and ecological systems that are affected by minute shifts in natural conditions, especially in the colder climates of the Northern Hemisphere. This is a difficult endeavor when working with living plants and animals. Previously, ecologists have noted that the Virginia opossum is rapidly moving from its native range well into New England and northern Michigan. Armadillos, red cardinals, mockingbirds, and several species of rats and mice also are moving north. But at the same time several northern species are moving south. The least weasel, for instance, is expanding out of Nebraska and into Kansas and Missouri.

"Given the incredible difficulty meteorologists have had convincing people there is a global warming trend, it's going to be even more difficult to convince other scientists that the trend has had significant effects on land-animal distribution," said James H. Brown, professor of biology at the University of New Mexico in Albuquerque. "The problem is these changes are dynamic anyway. Even if you demonstrate a species has moved, how can you demonstrate it was caused by climate change rather than some other variable?"

The research under way in Michigan appears to be the first in the United States to test the hypothesis that global climate change is affecting biological systems and to apply rigorous methods to the work. The field station there is an especially useful laboratory for such work. For more than eighty years, biologists have collected a wealth of specimens and data describing the life cycles of an ecosystem that has been largely untouched since the virgin forest was clear-cut at the turn of the century.

The field station also sits at the convergence of two great biological regions: the northern boreal forest of spruce, hemlock, sugar maple, and birch; and the southern mixed hardwood forest of white pine, beech, aspen, and red maple. A persistent change in temperature, the single most important factor in establishing the boundaries of the two great forests, would be expected to affect most dramatically the creatures living at the southern and northern edges of their ranges.

By comparing the current distribution of plants and animals against those documented by previous scientists, researchers here have gained surprisingly accurate measurements of new ranges, like the new, skimpier range of the red-backed vole. A distant cousin of the woodland deer mouse, the vole is dainty enough to stand in a tablespoon, quick enough to catch darting insects, and hardy enough to survive icy winters. Now it is gone from the field station, for the second time this century.

After Michigan's white pine forests were cut in the late nineteenth century, the vole retreated to Canada. As the forest grew back and trees matured in the 1920s, the vole proliferated again in the lower peninsula. The evidence of this is contained in the university's collections at the field station and in Ann Arbor: every specimen, and there are hundreds, has an accompanying data card documenting the date and location where it was trapped, and the statistics indicate that from 1920 to 1940, the vole was plentiful and thus popular for study. So was the woodland deer mouse. Philip Myers, a biologist and associate curator at the University of Michigan's Museum of Zoology and a member of the university's research team, was the first to notice the disappearance of the red-backed vole and the mouse. In 1985, he began laying traps at the field station in the same places as his predecessors. Since then he has caught one vole and no deer mice. "Both of these creatures are common to the northern forests and you'd expect that the habitat is better now, since the forests are ninety years old, than it was fifty or sixty years ago," said Dr. Myers. "But something is interfering, and one explanation is that the habitat is changing because of global warming."

Another member of the team, Dr. Gerald R. Smith, a curator of fish in the Museum of Zoology, is mapping the movement of southern-climate fish into Michigan. The orange-spotted sunfish is common in small streams and ponds from the Gulf of Mexico to Ohio. It had never been seen in Michigan until the late 1950s and early 1960s. The sunfish is now as far north as the Saline River just south of Ann Arbor, said Dr. Smith, and is moving quite rapidly because winters have been milder. Two northern fish that were once common in Michigan no longer are. The finescale dace, a minnow that thrives in cold water, was first described in the nineteenth century by Edward Drinker Cope, a renowned naturalist, as existing as far south as a lake in southeastern Michigan. The dace is extinct farther south than Saginaw in central Michigan, one hundred miles northwest of where it was first situated. The grayling, a sport fish that is a relative of the trout, was common on Michigan's northern peninsula as far south as the Au Sable River near the town of Grayling, and its range expanded north to the Arctic. Graylings have been extinct from Michigan for fifty years, said Dr. Smith. "There are other explanations for what we've found," he said. "The forests were cut here, and that causes siltation in streams. Agricultural plowing and chemical use may be a factor. The grayling was a sport fish and people caught them by the hundreds. But I would argue that can't be the explanation. The finescale dace retracted its range at the same time as the grayling and nobody was fishing for it. Rising temperature keeps coming back as an explanation."

Plants, too, appear to be responding to warming conditions. The ebony spleenwort, a species of fern common throughout the South and the East, was rarely seen in Michigan and only in the southernmost portion until the middle part of the century. In the 1960s, botanists began to find colonies as far north as the Upper Peninsula. Now it is common throughout Michigan and has a consistent range limit 300 miles north of where it used to be in the 1950s. Dr. Anton A. Reznicek, a botanist and associate curator of the university's plant collection, has also found striking changes in the range of the calypso orchid, a native northern flower not commonly found in boreal forests. In Michigan, the orchid was found in cedar swamps and cedar forests as far south as central Michigan. The university's field station here, more than one hundred miles north, is now at the plant's southern limit.

[KS, AUGUST 1991]

SOME COUNTRIES WOULD LIKE IT HOT

I N a finding fraught with sensitive political implications, some scientists say that if global warming takes its expected course, some parts of the world could come out winners, while many others reap disaster. A few regions, mainly in colder climes, may well benefit, according to computer models of climate change. The computer models merely simulate global climate change and are still being refined. They are therefore a rough guide to what may happen to various regions as the world warms, not an exact forecast. For many other regions, including North America, the computer models predict both pluses and minuses whose overall balance cannot yet be assessed. But for developing countries, scientists say, the general picture is negative: most are more vulnerable to climate change and less able to adapt to it than are the industrialized nations of the cooler latitudes.

The question of whether some countries might gain from global warming has been bubbling just beneath the surface of discussions about climate change. Some politicians and environmentalists have been reluctant to confront the issue for fear it might disrupt efforts to forge an international agreement to head off global warming from gases being produced by human activity. Others, including some scientists, assert that although there might be some temporary winners, there will be none over the long run, especially if global warming is severe and if it occurs as rapidly as scientists predict. Not least, they say, the natural ecosystems that undergird human life everywhere would not be able to adjust fast enough to escape catastrophe.

The winners-losers issue is becoming more prominent, even as delegates met recently at Chantilly, Virginia, in the first of several sessions to negotiate a treaty limiting the emission of "greenhouse" gases, which trap the sun's heat in the atmosphere. Scientists predict that these gases will heat the earth's surface by 2 to 5 degrees Fahrenheit over the next century unless checked.

Some experts note that if any countries gain from global warming, they will probably be the ones that now emit most greenhouse gases, primarily carbon dioxide, methane, and chlorofluorocarbons. "In the long run, there are good reasons to believe that those who are responsible are the winners," said Dr. Klaus Meyer-Abich, a physicist and philosopher at Germany's Science Center of Rhine-Westphalia and at the University of Essen. He has served as an expert adviser on climate change to the German parliament and has extensively studied the question of climatic winners and losers.

Whether industrialized countries enjoy absolute gains or not, they stand to increase their already huge overall economic advantage over the third world. Countries that see themselves as undoubted losers include small island nations that fear a major rise in sea level and more frequent and severe tropical storms, both of which are expected to result from global warming. These nations have formed the Alliance of Small Island States to press their case for stringent controls on greenhouse gas emissions. They are preparing to demand that the industrialized countries cut their own emissions and also help the island nations adapt to climate change, said Naresh Singh of Castries, St. Lucia, the executive director of the Caribbean Environmental Health Institute, an umbrella organization for sixteen English-speaking Caribbean countries. Mr. Singh was a delegate to the Chantilly meeting.

If the level of the oceans rises by more than two feet by the year

2100, as climate experts predict, low-lying nations like the Maldives and some Pacific islands could be inundated. Other places at high risk include Bangladesh, Thailand, Indonesia, Egypt, coastal China, Louisiana, and the southern coast of the North Sea, according to a recent assessment by the Intergovernmental Panel on Climate Change, a body set up by the United Nations to advise the treaty negotiators and their governments.

Additional populations vulnerable to global warming "are populations in semiarid grasslands and the urban poor in squatter settlements, slums, and shantytowns, especially in megacities," says a report by the Intergovernmental Panel on Climate Change. People living in third world slums are judged more vulnerable because their existence, already precarious, could be made even more so by disrupted food supplies.

Developing countries are also considered vulnerable because they are more dependent on agriculture, forests, and other natural resources for economic health, said Dr. Dennis Tirpak, director of the Environmental Protection Agency's global climate change division and member of the American negotiating team at Chantilly. Global warming is expected to intensify drought in wide areas and also to cause severe damage to forests and grasslands. Many third world populations already live on the margins of subsistence and lack the resources to cope with climatic disruption.

Apart from these broad outlines, the effects of warming appear mixed and quite complicated. "In some places the climate will get better and in some it will get worse," said Dr. Michael H. Glantz of the National Center for Atmospheric Research in Boulder, Colorado. But beyond that, he said, much remains unknown. Dr. Tirpak explained: "It's not a case where you can simply pick a date and have one set of countries that will win forevermore and another that will lose. It is not a very easy thing to characterize."

The Intergovernmental Panel on Climate Change, nevertheless, has tentatively identified potential gainers and losers. The identification is based on results of mathematical simulations of how the earth's climate would behave under global warming, and is therefore uncertain. "We should not take these studies literally, as a prognosis that every detail will just come as it is written now," Dr. Meyer-Abich said. But he said the general pattern "will not be changed very much" as more is learned.

The relative advantages and disadvantages are perhaps most tellingly reflected in the effects of warming on agriculture. This will occur in forms like shifting rainfall patterns, drier soil, increased evaporation of surface water, increased loss of water by crops, and reduced snowpacks in the mountains, resulting in lessened runoff in the spring. Warming would also bring more rainfall to some areas and more warmth and longer growing seasons to regions that are now too cool for maximum agricultural production.

The following examples of possible gains and losses are not all-inclusive, but suggest the variety and range of changes expected: Northern Europe would become a winner, according to the Intergovernmental Panel's analysis. Northern Scandinavia "stands to gain more from global warming than perhaps any other region of the world" because it would become warmer and wetter, the panel's report said. The grasslands that feed Iceland's sheep would become more than twice as productive as they are now.

Yields of grass and potatoes would increase in much of Ireland, Britain, the Low Countries, and Denmark. A temperature increase of more than 2 degrees would improve the agricultural potential of much of the European part of the former Soviet Union. But substantial decreases in productivity could occur in Southern Europe. A warming of 2 to 7 degrees would enable cultivated areas to creep 500 feet to 2,000 feet closer to the summit of the Alps. Northern Japan, including Hokkaido and the northern part of Honshu, would enjoy increased yields of rice, corn, and soybeans. By contrast, drier soils would disrupt food production in regions like Northwest and West Africa, the horn of Africa, southern Africa, western Saudi Arabia, Southeast Asia, Mexico, Central America, and parts of eastern Brazil.

For North America, the overall climate picture is mixed. Large parts of the northern United States and Canada would enjoy a pleasanter climate and attract more inhabitants, Dr. Meyer-Abich wrote in a recent review. In Europe, too, he said, these "privileged regions" would be extended farther to the north. Agricultural production in the United States would also shift northward, according to a study by the Environmental Protection Agency, with Minnesota, Wisconsin, and northern Michigan being gainers. But 10 to 50 percent of all agricultural acreage in the South might have to be abandoned. Production would probably decrease in the Corn Belt. Drier soil would cut yields of spring wheat in Canada, although there would be a small increase near the northern limit of current production. Yields of corn, barley, soybeans, and hay would decline in all of Canada but northern Ontario.

A rise in sea level could inundate coastal wetlands, damaging or destroying spawning grounds that sustain commercial fisheries. Beachfront communities would have to invest billions of dollars in coastal protection, and some settled areas on the coast would probably be inundated. Northern cities would be spared considerable expense in heating costs, snow removal, and road maintenance. But air-conditioning bills would soar in the South and ski resorts could be in deep trouble.

In one sense, national borders are the wrong framework in which to consider global climate change. "Looking at it on the nation-state level may not be appropriate," said Dan McGraw, a professor of international environmental law at the University of Colorado. "If significant climate change occurs, it's going to be a lot of individuals in the world who are disadvantaged. At one level, it doesn't matter so much which country they're in." But when it comes to negotiating the treaties to moderate climate change, it is nations that do the negotiating. On that level, Mr. McGraw said, he has detected a reluctance to discuss winners and losers. "Some folks feel that any discussion of the question will tend to polarize the possible participants in any sort of international solution," he said. The fear, he said, may be that "as countries start focusing on whether they are likely to be a winner or loser, that will influence whether they cooperate."

Temporary advantage aside, all nations are interdependent in the long run, note observers like William Nitze, a former State Department official who coordinated government policy on global warming until September of 1990. If the third world suffers, the industrialized countries suffer as well, he said, noting: "Developing countries are a tremendous market for us. We have a large stake in their long-term future prosperity."

Vice President Al Gore, who favors strong action to combat global warming, contends that talk of winners and losers "is just another cop-out that people use for not dealing with this threat." He cited the prospect of waves of "environmental refugees," fleeing ravaged third world economies or low-lying areas and causing "enormous destabilizing pressures" for industrialized countries. Indeed, the number of refugees could amount to 100 million, said Dr. Michael Oppenheimer, a senior scientist and expert on global warming at the Environmental

Defense Fund in New York, a research and advocacy group. The pressure they may bring on the rest of the world "is enough in itself to make people who think they're going to be winners take notice and reassess," he said.

He concedes that if the world warms by only a degree or two over the next century, then "without question, some people could be labeled winners." But with an 8-degree warming, the upper limit predicted by some computer simulations, "the world would be so different at those higher levels that it is very difficult to argue that any significant number of people will find it beneficial."

[WKS, FEBRUARY 1991]

GLOBAL WARMING: HOW TO RECOGNIZE THE DANGER SIGNS

A N ever-lengthening string of extraordinarily warm years has renewed fears of the greenhouse effect—the trapping of the sun's heat by gases that a rapidly industrializing world is pouring into the atmosphere. Most scientists are far from ready to announce that greenhouse warming has arrived, since the warming recorded in the decade since 1981 could also be part of a natural climatic change. Instead, they are struggling to answer a crucial question: how can a greenhouse warming of the climate be recognized and distinguished from natural warming? They are focusing their detective efforts on various subtle changes that a greenhouse warming would be expected to induce. These signs are known collectively as the greenhouse "fingerprint." The task, climatologists say, is by no means as easy and straightforward as it might seem.

They know that certain gases, chiefly carbon dioxide, chlorofluorocarbons, and methane, admit the sun's energy but block heat from escaping back to space. They know that the gases are steadily building up, largely through the burning of fossil fuels. And they know that the average surface temperature of the earth has indeed been rising for the last decade. In 1990, at a shade under 60 degrees Fahrenheit, it was the highest since global measurements began in the late nineteenth century. But as provocative as all this evidence is, the scientists believe, it in no way establishes a cause-and-effect relationship between the greenhouse gases and the recent rise in the average global temperature. The rise is consistent with greenhouse warming, they say, but not enough to prove a connection.

If the greenhouse effect is indeed warming the planet, as scientists predict it will, this will ultimately become so obvious that "a kid on the street can tell what's going on," said Dr. Tim P. Barnett, a climatologist at the Scripps Institution of Oceanography in La Jolla, California. It will become obvious, scientists say, because the rate of warming is expected to outstrip that of any climatic change in the last 10,000 years.

But the greenhouse "signal," if in fact it is there now, is still so small on a global scale that it is obscured by the "noise" of the many other factors that influence climate. These other factors, the climatologists say, could well be the cause of the overall global warming observed in the last decade. Or, equally possibly, they could have produced an overall cooling that partly offset an even larger greenhouse warming than the rise in average global temperature might suggest.

To help resolve these uncertainties, the climatologists are trying to develop a diagnostic set of features that would indicate a greenhouse-caused warming. No single climatic feature can be relied on as the proof of greenhouse-induced warming. "You want to look for it in a number of places so you don't get tricked by one," said Dr. Barnett, a leader in the effort to develop a reliable detection strategy. Scientists have identified a number of promising candidates to be included in the greenhouse fingerprint. Among the leading ones are these:

- *Global temperature patterns.* In greenhouse warming, scientists believe, the continents would warm more than the oceans. Subarctic latitudes are expected to warm more than tropical latitudes in the Northern Hemisphere, but not in the Southern Hemisphere. The lower part of the atmosphere, or troposphere, would become warmer while the stratosphere would become cooler.
- *Sea surface temperatures.* They are expected to rise fairly uniformly with greenhouse warming, while naturally occurring changes vary more from one part of the globe to another.
- *Water vapor in the atmosphere.* The vapor would not only increase with the warming but, in a classic feedback effect, would also inten-

sify the warming by amplifying the effect of the greenhouse gases. Moisture content would be expected to increase more in the tropics than in higher latitudes like the temperate and subarctic zones.

- *Changes in seasonality.* Greenhouse warming is expected to be more evident in winter than in summer, particularly at high latitudes.
- From computer simulations of the earth's climate, scientists believe these indicators of the greenhouse signal are so distinguished from natural, internal fluctuations of the climatic system as to be characteristic of greenhouse warming. One example of the natural fluctuations is the phenomenon of El Niño, in which periodic changes in sea surface temperatures in the tropical Pacific Ocean affect global temperature and rainfall patterns.

On a geological time scale, the earth has undergone periods of substantial natural warming. Between 5,000 and 6,000 years ago, scientists believe, temperatures in various parts of the world were about 2 to 5 degrees warmer than benchmark levels in the late nineteenth century. By comparison, the average global temperature has increased by about half a degree to one degree in the last century. There were other warm periods about 125,000 years ago, when parts of the globe were 3.5 to 14 degrees warmer than the benchmark temperatures, and 3.3 million to 4.3 million years ago, when they were 3.5 to 35 degrees warmer, depending on location and season.

These warm periods were presumably caused by natural factors originating outside the ocean-atmosphere climate system. These include changes in solar radiation, changes in the earth's position relative to the sun, naturally occurring increases in greenhouse gases, and changes in relationships between the land and the ocean. These latter changes, brought about by the movement of the earth's crustal plates, are thought to have altered patterns of ocean circulation that play a critical role in shaping climate. A modern cause of nongreenhouse climate change may be pollutants, apart from greenhouse gases, that humans are throwing into the atmosphere. Many of these can affect temperature, moisture, and atmospheric functioning, complicating efforts to detect greenhouse warming. "We've put a lot of junk in the atmosphere" in addition to greenhouse gases, said Dr. Barnett, "and it seems to be pretty well dispersed. What would that do to the climate?" he asked. "I don't think that's been computed, but it could have a large-scale effect."

For example, climatologists say, fine pollution particles emitted by industry cause clouds to form, and these can have warming or cooling effects, depending on the types of clouds and their location. These effects are uneven from one part of the globe to another, further complicating matters. Another source of distortion, said Dr. James E. Hansen, a climatologist at the Goddard Institute of Space Studies in New York, is the depletion of the earth's ozone layer because of the release of chlorofluorocarbons into the atmosphere, a change that causes cooling at some levels of the atmosphere in northern regions of the globe. This may affect the expected temperature difference between latitudes and even between land and ocean, for instance, obscuring the greenhouse signal. "As soon as you start looking at these kinds of details, you're in trouble," Dr. Hansen said, adding that detecting greenhouse warming depends on observing all the competing external influences on climate.

Climatologists say the effort to rule out all the greenhouse effect's possible competitors as causes of global warming is slowed and frustrated by a lack of observational data in many key areas and by the state of the art of climatic science. "Whenever you try to do this quickly, you run up against our ignorance and the quality of the data," said Dr. Michael E. Schlesinger, a climatologist at the University of Illinois at Urbana-Champaign, who has worked closely with Dr. Barnett.

An especially significant indicator of greenhouse warming would be any increase in atmospheric water vapor. It is "the first thing you'd expect," said Dr. Veerabhadran Ramanathan of the University of California at San Diego, who has studied the matter extensively. In greenhouse warming, more water would change into vapor. This vapor is critical to greenhouse warming because it would amplify by five times the relatively small initial warming impulse provided by carbon dioxide and other greenhouse gases. "You should clearly be seeing that in the observations," said Dr. Ramanathan. "If that's not there, you'd know it's not greenhouse. If it is there, the case would be compelling that it is greenhouse." But "we don't have the answer to that question," he said, "because we don't have the observational records." Satellite observations provided such data from 1984 to 1989, but the satellite has stopped working. No measurements have been made since then, although the Department of Energy plans to establish a series of ground-based observation stations that could fill the gap. New satellites are also expected to help fill it later in the decade, and Dr. Hansen and others are pressing for an earlier date.

In this and some other areas, scientists say, existing records are too short to discern either trends in natural variability or signs of greenhouse warming. The best and most complete climatic observations are those of surface temperature. Scientists trying to develop a reliable fingerprint are comparing observed temperature patterns in these records with those expected to result from greenhouse-induced warming.

Climatologists at the Max Planck Institute in Hamburg, Germany, and at the University of East Anglia in Britain, for example, have analyzed the globally observed pattern of surface temperatures and are measuring it against model predictions. Developing reliable signs of the greenhouse model depends heavily on improving the computer models of the atmosphere that predict greenhouse-induced changes. The models are continually being refined, but are still imperfect representations of the real world. "Some things, the models don't simulate so well," Dr. Barnett said. "Other things, they seem to simulate quite well." He said scientists would first have to "isolate the best model and the best of the observations" before they were set to do their detecting.

Some climatologists think that refining the models is more important at this point than the accumulation of data. "I don't think more data is going to reduce uncertainties in the next few years," said Dr. Phil Jones, a climatologist at the University of East Anglia. The short-term answer, he said, "is going to be in improvement of the models and better agreement between models."

For the next few years, the public and policymakers will have to rely on all these efforts to tell them what is happening. "We'd better find out as soon as we can," Dr. Hansen said. If action to reduce emissions of greenhouse gases is delayed, "either the climate changes are going to be larger and the impacts on people are going to be greater, or we will have to make more painful and expensive efforts," he said, adding, "The earlier we know, the easier it is to minimize the impacts or to adapt to them."

A reliable fingerprint could also make it easier not only to detect the human-induced greenhouse effect but also to measure its future magnitude with some assurance. Since the ocean absorbs and holds much of the heat before ultimately releasing it back into the atmosphere, there is a lag of up to several decades between the emission of greenhouse gases into the air and their full effect on climate.

Given all the obstacles, when can answers be expected? Some scientists say in a decade or so, but Dr. Barnett says nobody has really made a good estimate. "Some of my colleagues say detection is premature because the models aren't good enough," he said. "Others say, 'Detection is a red herring—let's do something about the greenhouse effect right now because the consequences are so bad.' I think we're going to be forced in the next five or ten years to take what we have and make some decision."   [WKS, JANUARY 1991]

MEASURING THE TEMPERATURE
OF A WARMER CLIMATE

SCIENTISTS may be zeroing in on a tighter estimate of just how much the earth's climate stands to be warmed by industrial waste gases that trap the sun's heat. Such estimates are usually made by computers programmed to simulate the world's climate. These computer models, however impressive, are no better than the assumptions fed into them. Now comes a substantial independent check on the models: an analysis of how the earth's climate responded to changes in atmospheric heat-trapping carbon dioxide and other influences in the distant past, based on geological and geophysical evidence.

The new analysis suggests that if the atmospheric carbon dioxide doubles from its present level, the average global climate will become about 4 degrees Fahrenheit warmer. Some previous estimates predicted temperatures much higher or much lower than this. Recent refinements of computer models show similar results; taken together, the new assessments point toward a warming range of 4 to 6 degrees. If no action to restrain carbon dioxide emissions is taken, say the authors of the study, the earth's temperature will soar over the next century to perhaps the highest levels in a million years. This would probably alter the earth's climate with disruptive and possibly catastrophic consequences for both human society and natural ecosystems.

Climate assessments like these are no mere academic exercise but an essential guide to the nations of the world in deciding whether to take stronger action under the global warming treaty signed in 1992 in Rio de Janeiro. The Clinton administration is expected to favor stronger controls on burning oil and coal, which produce carbon dioxide, than its predecessor.

Assuming moderate world population and economic growth, the amount of carbon dioxide in the atmosphere is expected to double by the end of the next century if no further action to reduce emissions is taken. The latest scientific study, reported in the British journal *Nature*, appears to bolster the case for emission reductions. It uses climatic data from two periods in the past, one 20,000 years ago, in the depths of the last ice age, and the other in the mid-Cretaceous period 100 million years ago, when the temperature was 18 degrees warmer than now. From study of these two exceptional periods, the authors have produced one of the first independent tests of computer predictions that until now have been virtually the only basis for assessing future warming. Those predictions, which say that doubled carbon dioxide concentrations would cause a warming of 3 to 8 degrees, have been the scientific basis of international policy until now. The wide range results from uncertainties about the climate system built into the models. Other analyses have suggested that the warming could be as little as 1 degree or as much as 9 degrees. The average global surface temperature is now a little less than 60 degrees. According to various estimates, this is 5 to 9 degrees warmer than in the last ice age.

In the latest study, Dr. Martin I. Hoffert of New York University and Dr. Curt Covey of Lawrence Livermore National Laboratory in California analyzed data, largely developed from geological studies, on how the climate of the two ancient epochs changed in response to various influences. These forces, each of which leaves some measurable change in the geological record, include solar radiation and heat-trapping gases like carbon dioxide, which are produced naturally as well as by human industry. The analysis let the researchers calculate a pivotal property, the sensitivity or extent of response by the climate to each of these "forcing" factors. They found, for instance, that the earth's climate during the mid-Cretaceous was sensitive to carbon dioxide such that a doubling of the atmospheric content of the gas would raise the average global temperature by 4.5 degrees. The sensitivity of the ice-age climate 20,000 years ago was similar: a doubling of carbon dioxide would have produced a rise of 3.6 degrees. Combining the two results, Dr. Hoffert and Dr. Covey calculate that the climate's basic sensitivity to carbon dioxide is such that a doubling of the gas leads to a global warming of about 4 degrees, give or take 1.6 degrees.

The finding "adds to the weight of evidence" favoring the findings of a panel set up by the United Nations to advise signatories to the climate treaty, Dr. Eric J. Barron, an earth scientist at Pennsylvania State University, wrote in a commentary in *Nature*. The United Nations group, called the Intergovernmental Panel on Climate Change, said in 1992 that its "best estimate" of the warming produced by a doubling of atmospheric carbon dioxide was 4.5 degrees.

Some critics of the conventional wisdom on global warming have pointed out that the earth has not warmed up over the last century by nearly as much as the computer models say it should as a result of increasing carbon dioxide. Other climatologists argue that industrial processes also exert a cooling effect by depleting the stratospheric ozone layer and emitting airborne aerosols that reflect sunlight, and that this partly masks the larger warming effect. If emissions were curbed, the climatologists say, the cooling effect of aerosols would dissipate quickly; but carbon dioxide would remain in the atmosphere for decades. Two climatologists at the University of East Anglia, Dr. Tom Wigley and Dr. Sarah Raper, have now calculated the extent of the postulated cooling effect. They find that without it, climate over the last century would have warmed by 6 degrees, much as the computer models have predicted.

In their new analysis, Dr. Hoffert and Dr. Covey examined a number of reconstructions of the ice-age and mid-Cretaceous climates and calculated the strength of all the factors that both warm the climate and cool it. By combining these factors, or "forcings," they arrived at a net warming effect expressed in watts per square meter. Then they examined the corresponding global temperatures of the two periods as revealed, for example, in changing isotopes of oxygen and carbon in ocean sediments. From this information they calculated the change in both temperature and forcings between then and today; and from that, the climate's sensitivity as expressed by the temperature change resulting from doubled carbon dioxide. In a similar exercise some time ago, Dr. James E. Hansen and colleagues at the NASA Goddard Institute for Space Studies in New York also examined climate data from the last ice age and found that a doubling of carbon dioxide would produce a warming of about 5.4 degrees.

The Hoffert-Covey study takes the analysis a big step further: by analyzing both a colder and a warmer climate than today's, it suggests a general level of climate sensitivity that applies universally, in all eras including today's. Dr. Hansen, who has been outspoken in asserting that human-induced global warming is under way, characterizes the kind of paleoclimatic analysis performed by Dr. Hoffert and Dr. Covey as "extremely valid; the best method we have for estimating climate sensitivity."

The weakness of the Hoffert-Covey calculation, a number of climatologists say, is that it introduces uncertainties of its own. Some of the data are "very, very shaky," said Dr. Syukuro Manabe, a climate expert at the National Oceanographic and Atmospheric Administration's Geophysical Fluid Dynamics Laboratory at Princeton University. But Dr. Barron pointed out that the uncertainties have been factored into the Hoffert-Covey analysis and are reflected in the margin of error. And Dr. Manabe, despite his reservations, said of the Hoffert-Covey study: "I feel very comfortable with their conclusions; I think it is encouraging" in helping to produce a more precise assessment.

The beauty of the Hoffert-Covey analysis of ancient climates, as its proponents see it, is that it gets around the key unknown that makes the computer models' predictions so uncertain: climate modelers do not yet know enough about the net effect on the earth's heat balance of clouds, which both trap and reflect warming radiation depending on circumstances, altitude, and the type of cloud. Although carbon dioxide is known to trap heat, the heat sets off an extremely complex network of interactions within the climate system, some of which amplify the heating and some of which lessen it. Climatologists have been trying to include all these interactions in the computer models, but the role played by clouds, especially, has eluded them. The Hoffert-Covey analysis implicitly includes the effect not only of clouds but of all the interactions, since the actual temperatures measured in those ancient periods would be the net result of the clouds and other feedbacks.

Dr. Hoffert and Dr. Covey assert, and Dr. Barron agrees, that the analysis puts to rest claims that a doubling of carbon dioxide would produce a relatively negligible warming of 1 or 2 degrees. That, said Dr. Barron, is "fairly clear; that point in the study is pretty robust." The basic reason, says Dr. Hoffert, is that a climate whose responses are that sluggish would never have been able to produce the temperature extremes of both the ice age and the mid-Cretaceous.

There is no guarantee that the carbon dioxide buildup in the atmosphere would halt once it had doubled, and some analyses indicate that this benchmark will be exceeded late in the next century if the present rate of carbon dioxide emissions continues. Using estimates of future "business as usual" carbon dioxide emissions made by the United Nations panel, Dr. Hoffert and Dr. Covey calculate that if their findings on climate sensitivity are right, the global climate would warm by 5.4 to 7.2 degrees by the year 2100. "Such a warming," they wrote, "is unprecedented in the past million years."

All agree that there is a long way to go before truly precise and confident predictions about global warming can be made. Quite apart from the question of narrowing down the climate's general sensitivity to carbon dioxide emissions, there is the even more difficult and complex matter of how the change will be distributed from one region to another and what it will do, in practical terms, to the climate system. The latest findings, says Dr. Hansen, "imply that you would have a significant shift of climate zones with a doubling of carbon dioxide, but the details of that impact is something we're trying to understand."   [WKS, DECEMBER 1992]

DAMAGE TO AMERICA'S
OZONE SHIELD

THE ozone layer, which protects living things from the sun's harmful ultraviolet rays, has been depleted in many areas of the globe, and at the latitudes of the United States the loss is proceeding more than twice as fast as scientists had expected, the Environmental Protection Agency announced in 1991. The agency said the declines measured in the late fall, winter, and early spring of that year amounted to 4.5 to 5 percent in the last decade. The weakened ozone shield lets in more ultraviolet light, a cause of skin cancer. According to agency calculations based on the new ozone findings, over the next fifty years about 12 million Americans will develop skin cancer, and more than 200,000 of them will die. These would be in addition to the more than 8,000 deaths a year now caused by skin cancer. Under previous assumptions, 500,000 added cancer cases and 9,300 fatalities were forecast from ozone depletion.

The 1991 data announced showed that ozone depletion extended farther south than had been thought, reaching the southernmost parts of the country, and that it lasted longer, starting in late fall and extending in some cases into May, said Dr. Michael Kurylo, the director of the space agency's upper atmosphere research program. The analysis was conducted by Dr. Richard Stolarsky, an atmospheric scientist at the Goddard Space Flight Center in Greenbelt, Maryland. His research was supported by Dr. Kurylo's office.

The findings make necessary a reappraisal of both United States and international policy on the control of the ozone-destroying chemicals, chiefly chlorofluorocarbons. These chemicals are used as the fluid that transfers heat in refrigerators and air conditioners. They have many other industrial uses, including as solvents and propellants in aerosol cans. Most of the world's nations vowed in June 1990 to halt production of the chemicals by the end of the century, in the case of developed countries, and by the year 2010 in the case of developing nations.

Michael Deland, chairman of the Bush White House's Council on Environmental Quality, said that neither he nor other concerned officials had reviewed the findings as of this writing. But he said they "would not come as a great surprise," since measurement techniques are becoming more accurate, and he added, "I think that before we undertake a major overhaul of United States or worldwide policies, we need to very carefully scrutinize this and other reports to evaluate the accuracy in a deliberative and comprehensive scientific way."

The environmental agency's announcement was based on the agency's analysis of ozone measurements made by an instrument called the total ozone mapping spectrometer, aboard a satellite operated by the National Aeronautics and Space Administration. The data had been circulating in the scientific community for some time, but specialists at the environmental agency only recently completed their analysis. Earlier, less extensive ground-based measurements had suggested that ozone over the United States had been depleted in the wintertime by about 2 percent from 1969 to 1986.

The new satellite measurements refer to what is called "column ozone," the amount of ozone over any given spot on the earth. According to the satellite measurements, ozone losses over the last decade occurred at the same rate throughout the Northern Hemisphere temperate zone, which includes North America, Europe, the Soviet Union, and most of Asia. The world has responded in increasingly strong terms to the ozone threat. In 1987, fifty-seven nations met in Montreal and adopted a treaty calling for a 50 percent reduction in the production of chlorofluorocarbons, or CFCs, and other ozone-depleting chemicals. At that time, no depletion of ozone had been observed over the United States, said Eileen Claussen, an environmental agency specialist on ozone.

By the June 1990 London conference, measurements of ultraviolet rays from preliminary satellite surveys and ground stations indicated a 1.5 percent decrease in high-level ozone over the United States. The 1991 measurements, unlike the preliminary satellite readings, were taken over more than eleven years, thereby making it possible to account for, and filter out of the analysis, changes in ultraviolet radiation caused by the solar cycle. The measurements began in 1978 and ran until mid-1990.

Losses were progressively worse toward the pole. At the latitude of Hudson Bay and Sweden, the ozone losses exceeded 8 percent over the decade. Measurements from aircraft in 1989 placed the column ozone loss near the North Pole at about an additional 6 percent. There were no significant losses over the tropics. In the Southern Hemisphere, the picture is complicated by the huge ozone "hole" discovered over Antarctica in the mid-1980s. Inside the hole, column ozone has been depleted by as much as 50 percent in some winters since the mid-1980s. Elsewhere in the hemisphere, losses averaged roughly an additional 2 percentage points more than in the Northern Hemisphere, and the period of depletion lasted longer, Dr. Kurylo said. No average global loss was calculated on the basis of the satellite data.

Scientists estimate that for every 1 percent decline in the high-altitude ozone shield, 2 percent more ultraviolet radiation reaches the earth's surface. Besides skin cancer, the harmful ultraviolet radiation can cause eye cataracts. Scientists say it also can affect the human immune system adversely; that it harms the ability of phytoplankton, tiny plants at the basis of the oceanic food chain, to reproduce, and that it can damage some crops and wild plants.   [WKS, APRIL 1991]

OZONE LAYER: PROSPECTS FOR RECOVERY

How much worse will ozone depletion get? The most important industrial chemicals that chew up the ozone layer are known as chlorofluorocarbons, or CFCs. Used ubiquitously as solvents and to transfer heat in air conditioners and refrigerators, the CFCs take years to waft up from ground level to the height of the ozone layer. Although many years of CFCs are thus in the pipeline, the end of the steady increase in destructive chemicals that reach the high atmosphere may be in sight. Concentrations in the atmosphere will continue to grow until the end of the century, reaching a peak 12 to 30 percent above present levels, scientists say, and then start to subside. Once fewer CFCs reach the ozone layer, the shield should start to recover, regaining full strength after a century or so.

This forecast assumes that the world's industrialized nations will stand behind the pledge they made at a meeting in London in June 1990 to halt the production of CFCs and other related chemicals, like halons, methyl chloride, and carbon tetrachloride. Industrialized countries vowed to eliminate production of these chemicals by the end of the century, and developing countries by 2010. The pledges were made after less stringent deadlines, adopted in Montreal in 1987, were later found inadequate to meet the threat.

It is uncertain how much more damage to the ozone layer will result before the new controls take effect. "We really don't know," said Eileen Claussen, an ozone specialist at the Environmental Protection Agency, which issued a report early in April 1991. Previous attempts to forecast ozone depletion, based on mathematical models, were proved so inaccurate by events that "basically, we have thrown out the models," Ms. Claussen said. Despite the uncertainty, or perhaps because of it, health authorities are reemphasizing the need for protection from the sun. "There's no question that the ozone problem is really a problem that's not going to go away," said Dr. Clark Heath, chief epidemiologist for the American Cancer Society. "One should

take sun exposure seriously, particularly in the middle of the day."
Ultraviolet radiation of a particular frequency, called UV-B, causes
skin cancer and eye cataracts and impairs the human immune system
as well. Biologists fear that higher fluxes of UV-B would also at some
point damage plants, crops, and the phytoplankton in the ocean that
are the basis of ocean food chains. Dr. Heath advised people to avoid
the sun in the middle of the day and to wear hats, don a sunscreen
lotion and protective clothing such as long sleeves when they are
exposed to the sun's rays. He said it was unclear at what point the
ozone-depletion issue would become severe enough for the cancer
society to develop more detailed suggestions.

Some pioneering countries have undertaken concerted public cam-
paigns to get people to adopt good sun habits. In New Zealand, where
ozone-depleted air from the wintertime ozone "hole" over Antarctica
has been detected, the public campaign is aimed at getting people to
abandon the ideal of a suntanned body. Children there are encouraged to wear cotton sun hats with protective visors and protective flaps
in back. And they are urged, for instance, to sit under a tree when
eating lunch in the playground. Television advertisements and posters
extol the virtues of covering up.

Although scientists are uncertain about the future severity of ozone
depletion, they have come to a confident consensus on the essential
scientific nature of the threat. Largely because of this consensus, there
was no factional argument within the Bush administration on either
the science of ozone depletion or the need to halt the production of
the destructive chemicals. By contrast, the infinitely more complex,
uncertain, and expensive proposition of dealing with the threat of
global warming has caused considerable divisions in Washington.

Molecules of ozone-destroying chemicals, when released, spend
most of their time—up to one hundred years in the case of CFCs—
below the stratosphere, said Dr. F. Sherwood Rowland of the University of California at Irvine who, along with Dr. Mario Molina, first
reported that they destroy ozone. When a molecule reaches the stratosphere, he said, "it gets zapped by ultraviolet radiation, and chlorine
is released, and that atom eats up 100,000 molecules of ozone." Eventually, it degrades, and that ends the process. Ozone is constantly
being created naturally, but this natural replenishment is incapable of
keeping up with the destruction of ozone by the chlorine. Since ozone
blocks the penetration of UV-B to the earth, the chlorine weakens the
shield. Dr. Rowland says concentrations of another ozone-destroying

chemical, methyl chloride, have remained constant, and it is believed a natural constituent of the atmosphere. Including methyl chloride, he said, atmospheric concentrations of the destructive chemicals have increased to 4 parts per billion in 1991 from .8 part per billion, or just above natural levels, in 1950. He forecasts an additional rise of .5 part per billion by around the turn of the century, followed by a steady decline, if the 1990 controls pledged in London take effect as planned. That would be an increase of 12.5 percent. The Environmental Protection Agency forecasts a similar trend, generally speaking.   [WKS, APRIL 1991]

ANTARCTICA: COPING WITH ULTRAVIOLET

DESPITE growing anxiety about the "ozone hole" that has begun appearing each year in the stratosphere above Antarctica, inhabitants of the white continent seem to be taking the resulting seasonal blasts of solar ultraviolet radiation in stride—the wildlife, by producing protective pigments, and the humans, by wearing dark glasses, heavy clothing, and sun-blocking lotions. But while scientists say the dangers of exposure to intense ultraviolet, or UV, are at present under control, the hazard is expected to increase sharply in the coming years, and experts have begun the most comprehensive environmental monitoring study of its kind to keep track of it.

Dangerously intense solar radiation is not new to our planet. The risk posed by ultraviolet radiation from the sun has become serious many times during the long history of life on earth, as the protective ozone layer has thinned out or disappeared altogether. Atmospheric ozone, a compound consisting of three oxygen atoms, is created primarily by the exposure of oxygen to intense ultraviolet radiation from the sun. But it can be destroyed by a variety of chemical processes; some occur naturally, whereas others are fueled by chemicals let into the atmosphere by people. Nature has met the challenge posed by the unreliability of the ozone layer by evolving a variety of protective sun-blocking compounds. But many scientists believe that the protection of the ozone layer may be diminishing so rapidly that many species will fail to adapt quickly enough to survive. The vegetable plankton at the base of Antarctica's food chain, as well as many of the organisms that feed on it, have developed a wide range of special pigments that absorb ultraviolet radiation and prevent it from damaging the cellular mechanisms essential to life. At least one major chemical company is investigating the use of natural sun-blocking compounds as the basis of new protective lotions for human beings.

But coping with ultraviolet radiation is likely to be increasingly difficult for wildlife and people in the coming years, scientists believe. The threat created by ultraviolet penetration of the infamous annual ozone hole, as well as the overall depletion of the global shield of stratospheric ozone, is certain to worsen, they agree. Almost every year since its first major appearance in 1986, the Antarctic ozone hole has become more severe during the several weeks it persists, and the episode in October 1991 was the worst since records have been kept. The holes are regions in which chlorine atoms or compounds interact in complicated ways with ozone, destroying it. Nearly all of this chlorine, scientists believe, results from decomposition of chlorofluorocarbons, called CFCs, released into the atmosphere by various human activities and products.

Most nations of the world have agreed to phase out the manufacture and use of CFCs by the end of the century, although some of the proposed substitutes also tend to destroy stratospheric ozone. CFCs are used as refrigerants in air conditioners and refrigerators, as thermal insulators, as foaming agents in plastics, and as cleaning solvents. The Antarcticans themselves—Chilean and Argentine families who live in Antarctica for years at a time—have become wary, though not fearful. These families are settled in Antarctica by the Chilean and Argentine governments, mainly to support the rival territorial claims of the two countries to a large sector of the continent. "In summer, my husband and I don't let any of our three children out the door without their sunglasses," said Laurette Brahm Gilabert, one of the women living at a Chilean Air Force base on King George Island. "In winter, of course, even when they're outdoors for a barbecue or football game or snowball fight, the sun never rises, so there's no danger. In summer, it's still cold enough that we all bundle up, so there's very little skin exposed to the sun."

Scientists and doctors discount stories circulating in rural Chile that sheep, rabbits, and other animals have been blinded by solar radiation leaking through the damaged ozone layer, although such rumors are widely believed by laymen. In any case, clinical studies have found evidence of a link between excessive exposure to ultraviolet radiation and cataracts. Chileans take this evidence seriously; throughout the country during the Southern Hemisphere summer, most Chileans seem to have taken to wearing sunglasses. Dr. Jaime Abarca of Punta Arenas, the only dermatologist practicing in southern Chile, says there has been no increase in Chile or Antarctica in the rate of skin cancer caused by solar radiation since the ozone hole appeared. "This is not surprising," he said, "because we would not expect to see any effect in less than ten or twenty years. But we have every reason to worry about the possibility of a future epidemic of skin cancer."

Medical experts are not particularly worried that ultraviolet radiation will harm the Antarcticans themselves or the thousands of tourists who come to Antarctica by ship each year or who stay for a few days at the Villa las Estrellas Hotel at Chile's Marsh Base. "As the depletion of the ozone layer spreads to lower latitudes," Dr. Abarca said, "the real danger is for sunbathers at such beach resorts as Chile's Viña del Mar, where people go on exposing their skin, even in the face of dangerous radiation." But many scientists worry about the potential vulnerability of many Antarctic plants and animals to changing environmental conditions, including the increase in ultraviolet radiation. To explore these vulnerabilities and to establish benchmarks against which the collective health of wildlife colonies can be measured, American scientists at Palmer Station in Antarctica have embarked on a six-year "long-term environmental research" program financed mostly by the National Science Foundation.

Although the results of this study will not be directly applicable to terrestrial environments where major human food crops may be at risk from ultraviolet exposure, marine experiments in Antarctica may at least reveal fruitful directions for future terrestrial research. Among the principal scientists involved are Dr. Langdon Quetin, a marine biologist, and his wife, Dr. Robin Ross, an oceanographer, both of the University of California at Santa Barbara. Among their special interests are krill—the shrimplike herbivores that are the main food of Antarctic seabirds, mammals, and many fish. Two other key investigators, also from the University of California at Santa Barbara, are Dr. Raymond C. Smith, a former high-energy physicist who is an expert in remote-sensing underwater instruments, and Dr. Barbara Prezelin, who evaluates the effects of underwater currents and temperature gradients on the flow of nutrients and the prosperity of colonies of algae and higher organisms.

The increase in ultraviolet radiation has produced a dilemma for marine organisms, Dr. Prezelin says. On the one hand, algae must be near enough the ocean's surface to obtain the solar energy needed for photosynthesis, in which carbon dioxide and water are converted into carbohydrates. But on the other, the closer an organism is to the surface, the more intense is the potentially dangerous ultraviolet radiation to which it is exposed. Ultraviolet-B, the most dangerous kind, has been found to have biological effects on organisms as deep as one hundred feet below the surface. Among the animals at risk are krill. According to Dr. Ross, when krill lay their eggs, the eggs sink to great depths, where they develop in darkness into larvae. But eventually the larvae must rise to the surface to feed on phytoplankton, and at that stage they are vulnerable to ultraviolet. "It may be," Dr. Ross said, "that if levels of ultraviolet begin to exceed certain amounts, we will begin to see major declines in the breeding success of krill and many other organisms. One of our present objects is to determine just where the danger point may be."

Another principal member of the Palmer Station team, Dr. Deneb Karentz of the University of California at San Francisco, has devoted much of her career to the study of colored compounds called "microsporine-like amino acids." Of fifty-seven species of Antarctic organisms, including invertebrates, fish, and algae that Dr. Karentz and her colleagues have studied, some 90 percent contained microsporine-like amino acid pigments, all of them believed to offer protection against ultraviolet radiation. These pigments come in many colors—green, blue-green, red, and brown among them—lending color to plankton, sea urchins, and countless other organisms. The pigments are produced by such plant organisms as algae, and when the algae are eaten by herbivores, notably krill, the krill incorporate the pigments in their own pigment-bearing structures or chromatophores. These, Dr. Karentz said, have proved to serve much the same biological function as that of the melanin pigments in human skin created by tanning: they absorb ultraviolet radiation, preventing it from damaging DNA and other substances essential to life. Dr. Karentz and her colleagues have found convincing evidence that increased ultraviolet exposure stimulates marine organisms to produce more microsporine-like amino acid pigments, thereby strengthening their own defenses. More of these chemicals, for instance, are found in the exposed upper parts of barrier reefs than in less exposed parts. "The big question is this," she said. "At what point will phytoplankton and other organisms no longer be able to cope with increasing ultraviolet? We know that there must be such a point. We're not yet seeing any collapse of the ecosystem, but we know some organisms are being affected, and any effect is environmentally unacceptable."

Another member of the Palmer Station group, Dr. Walter C. Dunlap of the Australian Institute of Marine Science, said he believed that natural ultraviolet-absorbing pigments derived from coral reef organisms could be put to use in new commercial products. The Australian branch of the British chemical giant Imperial Chemical Industries has already contended that pigments derived from coral organisms may "revolutionize" the effectiveness of suntan products and the durability of automotive paints. "Life probably originated in an environment saturated by ultraviolet radiation," Dr. Ross said, "and nature has always found ways to adapt. The trouble is that UV exposure caused by human contamination of the upper atmosphere may be increasing faster now than was normally the case in past episodes. Just how much UV-induced stress can organisms withstand without suffering great harm? We hope Antarctica will soon answer such fundamental questions." [MWB, JANUARY 1992]

Diapers to Lawn Mowers

CATASTROPHES AVERTED, SUBTLER ISSUES REMAIN

As COUNTRIES develop economically, they are more willing to pay for a cleaner environment and to abandon the destructive practices of their early growth phase. Over the last quarter century the United States has spent billions of dollars in cleaning up its air, earth, and water. Its environmental problems are not by any means solved, but at least the worst may be over.

Aside from the threat of global warming, the issues that remain mostly concern more secondary problems, like where to site garbage dumps and whether disposable diapers are a menace to the environment.

The automobile has been forced into cleaner habits by the strictures of the Clean Air Act and requirements for greater fuel efficiency. Yet the increasing number of cars on the road means that cleaner exhaust emissions are offset by the larger size of the national fleet. Hence the continuing need to find alternative fuels, less polluting than gasoline.

As the auto's tailpipe contributes less, other sources of pollution become more prominent. Even the mowers that crop suburban lawns have attracted the attention of those who measure the cleanliness of city air.

Some older problems remain. Farmers have not yet been weaned from their addiction to pesticides in massive doses. Nuclear waste is still piling up at civilian power plants, with so little agreement on long-term storage that nuclear chemists are searching for quicker fixes.

Protection of the environment is a task without obvious end; when one menace is averted others emerge in its stead.

LAWN MOWER WARS

To most people, it is a lawn mower, but to the Environmental Protection Agency it is an "uncontrolled mobile source" that becomes part of the suburban swarm adding measurably to smog on a summer's day. And the time has come, the agency says, to clean it up, along with weed eaters, leaf blowers, chain saws, and a lot of other off-road gas-powered machinery. A lawn mower can easily spew as much smog-causing hydrocarbon into the air in an hour as a modern car, experts on pollution say, even though the car has thirty times as much horsepower. Chain saws are worse: the California Air Resources Board says a chain saw operated for two hours emits as many hydrocarbons as a new car driven 3,000 miles. That is because modern cars have microprocessors that can precisely control an engine's mix of fuel and air; injectors to break the fuel into droplets of optimal size, and catalytic converters to catch anything that passes through the engine unburned. Lawn mowers and other outdoor machines have none of these. In fact, they have all the pollution-control equipment of a '57 Chevy—without a muffler.

William K. Reilly, the administrator of the Environmental Protection Agency (EPA), and an organization of electric utilities, announced in August 1992 the start of a program to clean up America's lawn mowers. The effort on lawn mowers will be part of a plan that will eventually cover all kinds of engines, small and large, used off the highway. That would include construction equipment, farm tractors, and even the service vehicles on airport aprons.

Nine utilities around the country will each give away one hundred newly designed battery-powered mowers, taking their customers' old gasoline models in trade and asking them to test the new mowers in the field—or, more precisely, on the lawn—and report back on their performance. Meanwhile, the EPA will haul the old mowers into its labs to study their emissions, in preparation for issuing new air-quality regulations similar to the rules now in place for cars and trucks. In its new get-tough approach, the EPA plans to make an example of the lawn mower. "We joke around and call it the last frontier for mobile sources," said Gay McGregor, an air pollution specialist in the EPA's mobile-source laboratory in Ann Arbor, Michigan.

The lawn mower engine industry, after initial resistance, is acknowledging the mighty little machine's role in air pollution. At the Outdoor Power Equipment Institute, formerly the Lawn Mower Institute, Dennis C. Dix, the executive director, conceded, "We certainly could do better." His industry, which never worried much about exhaust, is being forced by California to abide by new regulations that take effect in 1994 and 1999 and may be extended to other states as well. Ann McClure, the executive vice president of the Professional Lawn Care Association of America, said: "There's an irony in this. Turf actually helps to cleanse the air, taking what emissions there are in the air, removing them, and replacing them with oxygen." At Caterpillar, Inc., in Peoria, Illinois, a big maker of the type of agricultural and heavy construction equipment that is likely to be regulated soon, Rita L. Castle said that the trend was "not unexpected." She added, "They've gone after most of the large emissions sources, and off-road vehicles certainly deserve a close look."

At the Toro Company, Karl C. Kaukis, the director of marketing for the Lawn Boy line, said lawn mowers could be cleaned up, but consumers would find them more costly. He added that he hoped for "a commonsense approach." Specifically, he said, he hoped that the cleanup would not extend to snow blowers, of which Toro is a major producer. "The utilization is so low, and the summer utilization is zero," he said. Smog is a summer hazard, though carbon monoxide, which small engines also emit, is a particular problem in some cities in winter.

Nobody is certain how many lawn mowers are in use or what their emission levels are after a few years without being tuned up, but an EPA study in 1991 suggested that in areas that are already in violation of smog rules, nearly 20 percent of volatile organic compounds and nearly 30 percent of nitrogen oxides come from "nonroad sources." Mixed with sunlight, those two chemicals make smog. The population of nonroad sources varies now from place to place; in the metropolitan New York area, for example, outboard motors on pleasure boats are numerous, but in Colorado they are not.

Most manufacturers will try to lower emissions from gasoline engines by redesigning the combustion chambers, in many cases switching to overhead valves instead of side valves, a change made by the auto industry forty years ago. They also plan to make engines that run on a leaner fuel-air mixture.

California has adopted rules to begin in 1994 for improvements that the state says can be achieved with existing technology, and stricter rules for 1999 that will require new approaches. Meeting the 1999 standards may mean installing catalytic converters. That development would not delight the makers and users of gasoline-powered mowers, because the superhot converters could set fire to grass clippings. It should pose "an interesting packaging problem," said Thomas Bingham, a product engineer at the American Honda Motor Company.

The dirtiest of the outdoor machines are those that burn a mixture of gasoline and lubricating oil and run on a rich fuel-air ratio, like chain saws and weed eaters. Producing such engines is easier for the manufacturer, and their lack of fuel economy is not a concern; it is the rare customer who asks if the chain saw gets six trees to the gallon or seven. Moreover, chain saws, mowers, and the like have always escaped notice because they are outnumbered by cars. But collectively these and other outdoor engines are a big source of pollutants. The California Air Resources Board estimated that in its state, the annual hydrocarbon emissions of such devices equaled the output of 3.5 million 1991-model cars, each driving 16,000 miles.

One reason for the lawn mower problem is that cars must, by law, be maintained and periodically inspected for their emission levels, but lawn mowers, typically, need not. "What is tuning?" said A. Joseph Vandenberg, director of technical services at the Edison Electric Institute, in a reaction that pollution-control officials fear is typical of lawn mower owners. Mr. Vandenberg is helping to organize the swap program. "I've got a spark plug I've left in it for twelve years," Mr. Vandenberg said.

"As long as the thing cranks, you run it. If it doesn't, go out and buy a new one."

One result of the new focus on lawn mowers is that before the much-ballyhooed zero-pollution electric car makes it into the typical suburban garage, the rechargeable electric mower may arrive there first.

The new electric mowers being distributed in the test program, made by Black & Decker, will be able to mow about a quarter of an acre without recharging. A full charge takes twenty hours; an 80 percent charge four hours. The mower, which will sell for about $500, will use about $0.06 worth of electricity per charge. Producing that electricity will result in some air pollution, but studies show that power plant smokestacks are cleaner than auto tailpipes, per unit of energy, and far, far cleaner than lawn mower exhaust. Disposing of dead batteries also poses a pollution problem, but, again, a lesser one.

This is not the debut of a new concept in mowing. Mr. Kaukis said Lawn Boy sold battery-powered mowers a decade ago but found consumer interest very low. The company still sells plug-in mowers that require a heavy-duty, and very long, extension cord. The electric mowers to be distributed to consumers for testing are being provided by Baltimore Gas and Electric, Boston Edison, Indianapolis Power and Light, the New England Electric System, New York State Electric and Gas, Oklahoma Gas and Electric, Potomac Electric Power, Southern California Edison, and Tampa Electric.

The utilities are still deciding how to choose who will receive the new mowers, though they will be seeking a representative cross section of old mowers. The consumers chosen for the test group will get to keep the electric mowers, in exchange for donating their gas-powered machines to science. Switching to electric mowers would eliminate several other categories of pollution, advocates say. For example, the EPA estimates that about 7.5 percent of the contribution to hydrocarbon emissions of lawn and garden equipment comes from spilling gasoline while refueling.

Mark P. Mills, an energy consultant, estimates that the United States has 18 million walk-behind lawn mowers, and that if all of them were converted to electricity, oil consumption would fall 2.2 million barrels a year. Consumption of coal and natural gas to run power plants would rise somewhat, but total energy use would still decline because the electric system is more efficient than a small internal combustion engine, he said. Converting all of this equipment is doubtful, however, since, for one thing, not all lawns are less than a quarter acre, and not everyone will want to prolong the job of mowing the lawn by stopping to recharge the mower. Others, on the other hand, may seize the opportunity for such a respite.   [MLW, AUGUST 1992]

CLEANING UP AFTER THE AUTO

"Love affair" isn't strong enough; the automobile is part of the American identity. And, because of the smog-causing gases it emits, more and more it looks like the Mr. Hyde part.

In fairness, it might be said that Mr. Hyde has already made passable efforts to be a good citizen. The auto manufacturers, often under duress, have managed to produce cars that give off vastly less carbon monoxide, nitrous oxide, and hydrocarbons—three ingredients of smog—than the models of the 1960s. Scared by enthusiastic talk of alternative fuels like methanol and natural gas, the auto makers are pressing oil companies to make cleaner gasoline. But air quality in major American cities has nevertheless continued to worsen. In the 1986 to 1988 period, 101 metropolitan areas did not meet the standard on ground-level ozone pollution, up from 64 that were not complying in the 1985 to 1987 period. Weather was a factor, but most of the problem is caused by cars.

One reason is that the Hydes of the world, not to mention the Smiths and the Joneses, are victims of circumstances seemingly beyond their control or anyone else's. While manufacturers were making cleaner cars, the number of cars and the number of miles they were driven increased enormously. Statisticians try to make the astronomical numbers more comprehensible by expressing them in terms of trips to the moon. Thus, in 1970, vehicle miles traveled in the United States came to about 2 million round trips to the moon. Now cars do about 3 million round trips annually. That is even worse than it looks at first glance. As total mileage rises, emissions can rise even more steeply, because more of those miles are covered in stop-and-go traffic. Trends cut both ways: as the years go by, dirty cars from the precontrol days are replaced with clean new ones, but then the effectiveness of even the new models declines as the cars get older.

Americans are driving more miles than ever because of cheap gasoline, population growth, and longer commutes that are often a consequence of housing costs. They also like to shop, visit, and just plain drive; only about 35 percent of car miles are driven to get to work or as part of work, according to one government survey. The result of all that driving, though, is not necessarily greater convenience but ever-denser traffic, ever-longer delays, and ever-sicklier air. Yet rather than giving up their cars, Americans have responded by transforming their rolling prisons into cocoons of comfort. The gear includes multispeaker stereos, orthopedically correct seats, car phones, air conditioners, heavy soundproofing, even laptop computers and fax machines. These days it's hard to find a car without FM stereo. All these comforts help motorists routinely endure a virtually unbearable environment, even as their idling engines make that environment worse by the minute. Automobiles impose other costs, too, like the environmental damage that is caused by spills from all the oil tankers needed to feed American refineries and the payments to foreigners for 8 million barrels of oil, about 40 million fill-ups, every day.

Technology can ameliorate some of these problems through better fuel economy and cleaner tailpipes, but just treading water is a challenge. For a while rising gasoline mileage helped, but recent statistics from the Environmental Protection Agency run the other way. Moreover, in 1970, people outnumbered cars by 2.5 to 1, but the cars reproduced faster. By 1988, there were just 1.7 people per car. The only limit seems to be that once there is one car for each driver, increases in the car population cannot increase pollution or gas consumption unless the cars learn to drive themselves.

The projection is for more of the same. At the Northeast States for Coordinated Air Use Management, a coalition comprising New Jersey, New York, and the New England states, which in 1989 required the oil companies to produce less-polluting gasoline, Allan C. Van Arsdale, a staff analyst, said that in the next ten to fifteen years, vehicle miles traveled will jump an additional 25 to 40 percent. Some experts say that center-city congestion is not much worse than it used to be. But wide-open roads of suburban counties are getting as bad as city streets. And although there have been some improvements, like one-way streets and staggered timing of traffic signals, these are mostly one-time refinements; future efficiency gains will be harder to find. At some point, simple congestion would seem to put limits on auto growth, but it is not clear where that limit is. "Twenty years ago, if someone had told me that the average speed driving across Manhattan would be allowed to get down to 1.5 miles per hour, I would have said, no, it'll never happen," said Michael Oppenheimer, a senior scientist at the Environmental Defense Fund, an environmental group. "But you don't know what people will stand for."

And car manufacturers have found new ways to help them deal with their frustration. Christopher W. Cedergren, an analyst at J. D. Power and Associates, a Los Angeles consulting firm that measures customer satisfaction with cars, said the next item on the list of standard comforts is compact disc players, which will be in a majority of cars by the end of the decade.

Another accessory that is part of the solution is also part of the problem: the air conditioner. In 1970, 40 percent of cars had them; now 90 percent do, said Mr. Cedergren. That piece of equipment is a synergistic nightmare for environmentalists. Air conditioners do not just encourage people to drive; they also eat gas and are notorious leakers of a chlorofluorocarbon that is particularly dangerous to the atmosphere, encouraging the greenhouse effect and depleting stratospheric ozone. While the ozone above 30,000 feet is being depleted, it is being created at ground level by the interaction of sunlight and auto emissions. Unfortunately, ground-level ozone does not replenish the ozone at high altitude. It instead turns into the smog that causes lung and nasal irritation and, scientists believe, may cause long-term lung damage. It is also damaging to plants and trees.

All of this for a convenience that is becoming a home away from home. The most recent study, conducted by the Census Bureau in 1983, found that 30.1 percent of all miles traveled were logged getting to or from work, 13.4 percent were for shopping, and 15.5 percent were for other personal business. Going to social and recreational activities accounted for 13.3 percent, education, religious, and civic activities for 4.1 percent, and visiting friends and relatives for 13.6 percent. Leisure driving came to just 1 percent and vacations to 2.1 percent.

The energy consumption is vast. Moreover, the private car is not efficient. Mr. Oppenheimer and a coauthor, Robert H. Boyle, point out in a book called *Dead Heat: The Race Against the Greenhouse Effect* that only about one seventh of the energy in gasoline moves the car forward. The rest goes out the tailpipe or the radiator.

But if Americans are doing more driving, it is not irrational from the driver's point of view, because the price of gasoline has gone down. According to the Department of Energy, on an inflation-adjusted basis, the price of gasoline at the end of 1989 was just below what it was in 1973 and 42 percent below its peak price, which was in 1980.

The roads are already built, the car is in the driveway, and the additional cost of driving to a restaurant forty miles away is too small to stop anyone. "We have built a society that is dependent on personal mobility, and we are envied all over the world for that," said Michael R. Deland, the chairman of the Council on Environmental Quality under the Bush administration and formerly regional administrator in Boston for the Environmental Protection Agency (EPA). That mobility, he said, "is consistent with our most cherished national values of independence. I don't think we're going to change that in the near future."

But Mr. Deland believes, with most other experts, that the United States will have to cut its dependence on cars. As Kenneth T. Jackson, a Columbia University historian, put it in *The Crabgrass Frontier*, "The United States is not only the world's first suburban nation, but it will also be its last." The earth cannot sustain many more economies like this one, he said.

If the American mass transit system is 140 million cars and 200 million people to drive them, what is the alternative? One is public transportation, which usually means the bus. But, as the director of the EPA Office of Mobile Sources, Dick Wilson, acknowledged: "It's difficult to tell people they ought to leave the car home when they see the smoking diesel bus. We have to clean buses up so we can promote them with a straighter face." At the coalition of Northeastern states, Mr. Van Arsdale agreed that "to get out of this rut, we're going to have to provide a good alternative to the motor vehicle." But an effective public transit system requires concentrations of population, whereas each year since World War II has seen more dispersal. People travel from dispersed homes to dispersed workplaces, to shopping malls, restaurants, theaters, and schools. To make matters worse, the route maps would not be like simple lines or grids, but like a bowl of spaghetti.

Until World War II, said Dr. Jackson of Columbia, land near transportation lines was valuable and land far away was not. Now, he said, the South Bronx, crossed by subway and train lines, is in ruins, whereas virgin land reachable by car over the George Washington Bridge in New Jersey is being converted to prime housing. "Let's reverse what's been going on for the last sixty years," he said. A start, he said, would be a gasoline tax and an end to private transportation's public subsidies, a category into which he puts everything from road building to snow plowing to police protection of the highways.

Los Angeles is one city that is making preliminary moves to reduce the demand for travel. The South Coast Air Quality Management District and other government units there have drafted a plan that calls for using zoning to intersperse housing with employment centers. It is a long-term solution that even proponents say will be difficult to bring about. Cleaner-burning gasoline and possibly some alternate fuels seem likely to come sooner. But what else can be done to tie the web of modern life together without the automobile? "There's not too much on the horizon right now," said Mr. Van Arsdale, "other than, 'Beam me up, Scotty!' "   [MLW, MARCH 1990]

ALTERNATIVES TO OIL

IN the last ten years, scientists and engineers have taken long strides toward the day when alternative energy sources can compete with oil from the Middle East, and some of the more promising alternatives are on the verge of practicality. But a drastic cut in funds for energy research over the past decade has slowed progress in many areas. And even if the research effort is accelerated now, experts say, the energy system that has grown up around petroleum is so vast, so pervasive, and so entrenched that it will be years and in most cases decades before the alternatives replace oil on a large scale.

It is clear, say the experts, that the biggest and most important gains in the struggle to wean the country from petroleum are to be made in transportation, which accounts for nearly two thirds of all oil consumed in the United States. If alternative fuels and technologies could somehow magically displace gasoline today, they would eliminate at one stroke most of the need for imported oil.

Now, stimulated in the last few years mostly by environmental concerns, scientists and engineers have brought to the brink of fruition, or close to it, a number of alternative ways to power motor vehicles. Many of them are based on resources that are renewable rather than depletable and that emit less pollution than gasoline. Scientists working with advanced enzymatic techniques are steadily

improving the process by which wood is converted to ethanol, a form
of alcohol fuel. By making the process more efficient, they have reduced the cost of wood-derived ethanol to the equivalent of about
$2.15 for a gallon of gasoline, from $5 in 1980, and they expect to
reduce it to about $1.15 by the end of this decade. American gasoline
prices have been around that level in the last few years and are now
higher. The use of wood and other vegetation opens up a potentially
vast source of renewable raw materials, or feedstocks, and researchers
are developing ways to produce the wood more efficiently.

Commercially produced methanol, another form of alcohol fuel,
is already as cheap as or cheaper than gasoline. Recent analyses by
the Environmental Protection Agency (EPA) have found that it now
costs $0.90 to $1.10 to buy methanol that will propel a car as far as a
gallon of gasoline. And as part of an attempt to capitalize on this
economic fact, the agency's emission-control-technology laboratory in
Ann Arbor, Michigan, expects to begin testing the first prototype of
an engine especially designed for methanol.

American automobile manufacturers, meanwhile, have built engines designed especially for ethanol-fueled autos and installed them
extensively in Brazilian cars. Within the last five years automakers
here and abroad have also brought to technological maturity flexible-
fuel engines that burn methanol, ethanol, and gasoline interchange-
ably, or any mixture of the three. The blending makes it possible for
the alcohol fuels to replace gasoline gradually, with a minimum of
disruption in the supply system. As part of its stringent new policy
against air pollution, California is to serve as a preproduction testing
ground for the cars.

By the end of the century, electric vehicles may also be making a
dent in urban transportation. All three major American auto companies have been working on new electric vans and cars. As part of a
demonstration project, General Motors, for example, plans to begin
production of the first sixty modern electric vehicles produced in this
country.

The years and decades ahead are likely to see a vigorous competitive struggle among these fuels and technologies, as well as com-
pressed natural gas, which is being sold experimentally as an auto fuel
in the United States. The potential of these alternatives as an antidote
to dependence on imported petroleum is clear: foreign oil and petroleum products contributed 15.3 quadrillion BTUs, or "quads," to

the nation's energy consumption in 1989; the burning of gasoline, measured then at 13.74 quads, can be said to have soaked up most of the imports.

The extent to which alternatives could displace oil in energy sectors besides transportation is less clear, some experts say. "In theory," alternatives based on renewable resources "could be directed to the replacement of oil in all sectors," said Dr. Thomas D. Bath of the Solar Energy Research Institute, a government-supported national laboratory in Golden, Colorado. But it would take more money and time to direct alternative resources to specific oil targets in industry, businesses, and homes than in transportation, he said.

The gains would probably be incremental and piecemeal—gradually replacing oil heat in homes with solar heat, natural gas, or electricity, for example; or displacing some of the remaining oil in the generation of electricity with renewable alternatives like solar energy or wind power, or with nuclear power. But oil now accounts for only 5 percent of electricity generation, leaving relatively less room for improvement in that sector. Some oil, moreover, is used as feedstocks in the production of petrochemicals and asphalt and is not energy related.

Although some of the alternatives not based on fossil fuels may soon challenge both the technology and the economics of oil, experts say, none is likely to supplant oil in a widespread fashion for some time. "You are very quickly struck by the fact that none of them are ready at all to compete at large scale with fossil fuels," said Dr. William Fulkerson, an associate director of the Oak Ridge National Laboratory who oversees the lab's programs in advanced energy systems and who directed a study of the subject in 1989.

Federal funds for research on energy supplies declined to about $1.5 billion in 1990 from about $5 billion in 1980, in constant 1990 dollars, according to a study by Dr. John P. Holdren, professor of energy and resources at the University of California at Berkeley. "We've allowed our programs for research and development on these new options to deteriorate drastically," he said. "We are just not making the progress that would have been possible if we'd maintained those 1980 levels." Without an increase in research funds, according to a study published in March 1990 by five national laboratories, energy derived from renewable sources would probably grow to 15 percent of the total by 2030. The study included a wide range of renewable energy sources, including, for instance, solar energy, wind power, and fuels made from wood and other types of vegetation, or biomass.

If federal expenditures for research, development, and demonstration projects were doubled, to about $3 billion a year over the next twenty years, the study calculated, renewable energy's share of total energy use could more than triple, from 8 percent in 1988 to 28 percent by the year 2030. It found that under these conditions of accelerated research, the use of transportation fuels made from wood and other vegetation would grow the fastest, accounting for eight quads a year by 2030.

"That seems like an awful lot of time," said Dr. Bath, who headed the study and whose laboratory participated in it. "But what most people don't have a good feel for is how big the energy system is, how much capital is sunk into it. It's 5 percent of gross national product, and changes in anything that big take a lot of time." Because of this, he said, years are required for a new technology or fuel to spread through the system on a large scale, even though it works well and its cost competes with existing energy sources.

The process might be speeded up, experts say, if the price of oil rose high enough and remained there over the long term, either because of market workings or tax policies. But energy experts say that suppliers are not inclined to convert to alternatives more quickly unless they are convinced that oil will be permanently more expensive. Temporary price shocks brought about by Middle Eastern crises are not enough, they say. "Prudent people aren't going to go out and spend some fraction of a trillion dollars based on a dictator grabbing control and manipulating things," said Dr. Robert L. Hirsch, the manager of research at ARCO Oil and Gas Company in Plano, Texas, who was formerly assistant administrator of the Energy Research and Development Administration, the predecessor of the Department of Energy.

Generally speaking, experts say, fossil-fuel alternatives to imported oil are not likely to compete on a broad scale as transportation fuels any sooner than renewables. The fossil-fuel alternatives include, chiefly, natural gas and petroleum derived from coal and oil shale. Synfuels, as these latter have been called, were the object of an intensive federally sponsored research and development program undertaken after the 1979 oil-price shock but abandoned later as prices of crude oil plummeted. For the most part, their use also emits more air pollution than other alternatives, and some energy experts believe their emergence is unlikely in the foreseeable future.

Natural gas may play at least an interim role. Until wood and other vegetation can be more fully developed as feedstocks, for instance, it seems likely to provide the main feedstock for methanol. And coal may not be completely ruled out. Methanol's proponents say that advanced conversion techniques coupled with more efficient engines would make it possible to derive methanol from coal. They say it would emit 80 percent less carbon dioxide than gasoline, reducing an emission that many scientists fear will cause the earth's climate to warm.

In the 1980s, the electric power industry largely weaned itself from oil, but did so mostly through increased reliance on coal, one of the most polluting of fossil fuels. From 1978 to 1988, according to federal figures, oil's share of electricity production dropped to 5.5 percent from 16.5 percent, while coal's share rose to 60 percent from 44 percent. With nuclear energy on hold and fusion power decades away, the industry is now straining to reduce coal's share by expanding renewable sources of energy, like wind and solar power, and to develop clean-coal technologies. Some experts say it would be a mistake for the transportation industry, in switching to alternatives to oil, to go the same route.

As transportation fuels, methanol and ethanol share an advantage in that they can each be produced from a variety of feedstocks—for example, natural gas, garbage, and even sludge for methanol; grain for ethanol; wood for both. Neither alcohol fuel emits as much pollution as gasoline when burned. Both ethanol and methanol can also be used in existing cars if some engine modifications are made, but experts say that new engines are necessary to make the alcohol fuels fully competitive. "We are not suggesting retrofitting," said Charles L. Gray, Jr., the director of the EPA's Ann Arbor laboratory, where the prototype of the new methanol engine is about to be tested. Both alcohol fuels pack less energy per gallon than gasoline, and the new engines are designed to help compensate for this.

"We would probably say methanol is the fuel to beat," said Mr. Gray. This is largely because the enlistment of natural gas as a ready feedstock has already made methanol economically competitive. But pipeline capacity makes natural gas in the United States vulnerable to sudden shortages in times of extraordinary demand, and much of the gas envisioned as methanol feedstocks would probably come from Canada, Mexico, and the former Soviet Union. Moreover, the burning of methanol has been criticized as emitting twice as much formaldehyde gas, a possible carcinogen, as does the burning of gasoline. Mr. Gray says this can be readily controlled, and that methanol emits far fewer other carcinogens than gasoline.

In the United States, ethanol has so far been produced from corn and is sold as an additive that, when combined with gasoline, produces gasohol. It receives substantial federal subsidies, however, and some experts say that ethanol production would be limited by the size of the corn crop. Scientists are therefore looking toward ethanol derived from wood and other vegetation. At the Solar Energy Research Institute, scientists are using a variety of enzymes to break down the cellulose components of wood more efficiently, producing higher yields of ethanol that in turn bring down its cost per unit of feedstock. "If ethanol from cellulose can be commercialized," said Mr. Gray, the proponent of methanol, "it will be very competitive with methanol."

If either ethanol or methanol were to rely heavily on wood as a feedstock, some scientists say, it could put heavy pressure on forests and other stands of vegetation and could create conflicts in land use. Anticipating this, scientists at the Oak Ridge laboratory are working with universities and forestry companies to improve the per-acre productivity of trees by growing and harvesting them, much like crops, on a cycle of six to eight years. Since the growing trees would absorb carbon dioxide, they would offset the carbon dioxide emitted by the burning of ethanol or methanol.

"If you ran the system right," said Dr. Fulkerson, "there would be no net addition of carbon dioxide to the atmosphere." Electric vehicles, of course, emit no pollutants at all—except for those emitted by the electric power plants that recharge the vehicles' batteries—and their development by auto companies is proceeding apace. "I think that by 2000, the impact of electric vehicles should begin to be felt," said Larry O'Connell, the manager of the transportation program at the Electric Power Research Institute, who has been working with auto companies in developing electric cars and vans.

For the most part, their range is still limited by battery technology. General Motors' new van that went into limited, preliminary production in September 1990, for instance, has a range of 60 miles when half laden, said Mr. O'Connell. Its conventional lead-acid battery can be charged overnight; if it is charged when the van is idle throughout the day, it has achieved 175 miles in a day. Its top speed is about 50 miles an hour, half laden. The van is envisioned as an around-town delivery vehicle, and will be tested first as part of electric utilities' vehicle fleets. The Chrysler Corporation is working on a minivan with a nickel-iron battery that represents the next advance. Its range with an overnight charge is between 110 and 120 miles and its speed is about 70 miles an hour—about the same as a gasoline version of the minivan with a 2.2-liter engine. Cars are also being developed that use electricity for city driving but switch to gasoline for longer trips, but all of the electric vehicles are perhaps two decades away, at a minimum, from any large-scale impact since it takes years for existing vehicles to be replaced.

In the farther future, perhaps, are hydrogen-fueled vehicles. Auto companies have experimented with them off and on for years. "It's quite a clean energy system, but the cost has always been regarded as too high," says Dr. Joan Ogden, a research physicist at the Center for Energy and Environmental Studies at Princeton University, who has long studied the problem. The cost could come down close to the range of gasoline, she said, if photovoltaic technology could be harnessed to the production of hydrogen, cutting its cost. A number of European companies are working in that direction, she said, but practical application will not come until some time in the next century.

In the end, given the slow rate at which any of the alternatives are likely to be adopted, many of the scientists and engineers who work with them urge a time-tested interim strategy for reducing dependence on oil: conservation and increased efficiency in the use of petroleum.   [WKS, AUGUST 1990]

THE POLITICS OF GARBAGE

Garbage, garbage, everywhere: images of overflowing landfills, homeless garbage scows, and polluted wells have been widely interpreted as nature's way of telling us to slow down. "The devastation wrought by economic production is closely related to the amount of materials consumed," warns John E. Young, an environmental researcher at the Worldwatch Institute in Washington. But to many solid-waste specialists, the garbage crisis says more about the limits of public management and traditional regulation than the limits of nature or the decadence of the throwaway society. In their view, piecemeal approaches like banning styrofoam cups may be easy options for legislators but, in fact, divert attention from the underlying political issues, besides being of questionable benefit to the environment.

William Rathje, the head of the University of Arizona's research project on garbage, notes that technology has in some ways actually eased the municipal disposal problem since the turn of the century. Home furnaces no longer generate an average of 1,200 pounds of coal ash each winter; cities need no longer clean up after the hundreds of thousands of horses that died each year on the job. Given proper financial incentives, experts argue, households would voluntarily reduce the tonnage of nonhazardous waste left by the curb; the rest could be recycled, buried, or burned with reasonable safety and at bearable cost. But they say it makes no more sense for the White House (or the statehouse) to micromanage these choices than, say, to decide how many minivans should be offered for sale in Dallas next month or how many of them should be painted red. The key to a rational garbage policy is to ensure that the prices people are charged for disposal services reflect the true social costs of getting rid of the stuff.

Until the late 1970s, notes Peter Menell, an economist and legal scholar at the University of California at Berkeley, most solid waste was carted to the wrong side of the tracks and dumped in pits. The biggest garbage worry most householders faced was preventing four-footed scavengers from tipping over the can. But public alarm over air and water quality has changed all that. Some neglected landfills were found to be leaking hazardous chemicals into groundwater and shut down. More significant, communities have blocked efforts to replace landfills as space was depleted; in 1989 the Environmental Protection Agency estimated that one third of the remaining capacity would be gone by 1994.

In New Jersey, the state with the most pressing garbage disposal problem, the environmentally driven landfill shortage has been exacerbated by economic regulation. To stop what was described as price gouging by organized crime, the state decided to regulate waste hauling and disposal as a public utility. And according to Paul Kleindorfer, an economist at the Wharton School of the University of Pennsylvania, zealous opposition to passing costs through to consumers effectively ended investment in landfills. In 1972 there were 331 landfills operating statewide. By March 1988 the number had fallen to 13, with just 2 more waiting for permission to open. Half of New Jersey's municipal solid waste must now be exported to Pennsylvania and Ohio.

Pressed to find alternatives to landfills, which absorbed 83 percent of all municipal solid waste in 1989, many states have looked hard at incinerators. Burning is attractive because it reduces by as much as 90 percent the volume of waste that must eventually be buried. And the heat can be used to make electricity; plastics, the symbol of packaging overkill, actually generate as much energy as fuel oil. Like landfill, however, burning raises issues of environmental safety and industrial nuisance; according to a 1990 survey by the National Solid Wastes Management Association, 37 percent of Americans would object to a waste-to-energy plant in their community. What is more, incineration is hardly cheap: Mr. Menell concludes that it is competitive in cost only in the landfill-scarce Northeast.

"Source reduction is to garbage what preventive medicine is to health," William Rathje wrote in the *Atlantic Monthly* in December 1989. And technology, driven by purely economic considerations, sometimes delivers just what the doctor ordered. For example, according to Harry E. Teasley, Jr., the president of Coca-Cola Foods, a Coke can weighed 2.5 ounces in 1961. Thirty years later, thanks to competition from aluminum and new ways of forming steel, it weighs half an ounce. But prohibiting bulky products or types of packaging is invariably problematic. People rarely appreciate, and can rarely measure, the overall impact of such products on the environment. An analysis in the February 1991 issue of *Science* magazine by Martin B. Hocking, a chemist at the University of Victoria in British Columbia, compared paper hot-drink cups with cups made from polystyrene foam. Foam takes up more space in landfills. On the other hand, the manufacture of the paper cup consumes 36 times as much electricity and generates 580 times as much wastewater. Once buried, the plastic is there to stay—by conventional wisdom, a serious drawback. But as paper degrades underground it releases methane, a potent "greenhouse gas" that is warming the atmosphere.

Or consider the diaper dilemma. The National Association of Diaper Services concluded that paper diapers made up a full 2 percent of the nation's garbage stream and were loading landfills with potentially dangerous organic waste. Threatened with local bans and boycotts of its paper diapers, the Procter & Gamble Company struck back. The manufacturer's consulting firm, Arthur D. Little, Inc., concluded that disposables do indeed generate ninety times as much post-use solid waste. But reusable cloth diapers consume three times as much nonrenewable energy and generate ten times as much water pollutants. Lynn Scarlett, vice president of research at the Reason Foundation, a research organization in Santa Monica, California, suggests more complications. The pulp used to make disposable diapers, she notes, comes from trees grown for the purpose. The fewer disposable diapers consumed, the smaller the desired commercial inventory of immature trees, and the smaller the acreage of forests supported by private enterprise. Then there is the question of water: where groundwater is easily contaminated, landfill leakage can be a big problem. But in the desert of Southern California, Ms. Scarlett notes, room to bury disposable diapers is not as scarce as the water needed to wash the reusable kind.

Recycling offers an equally popular, and far more promising, way of coping with household garbage. About 13 percent of municipal waste was recycled in 1988 and, in theory, the sky's the limit: techniques for recycling aluminum, glass, steel, paper, rubber, dead leaves, grass clippings, and most plastics, which collectively make up more than 80 percent of the municipal garbage stream, are ready to go. But few analysts believe that anything close to this fraction of solid waste will (or should be) recycled in the foreseeable future.

One potentially important form of recycling, large-scale commercial composting of the yard waste that makes up a fifth of all household solid waste, faces the same problem of finding politically acceptable sites as incinerators or landfills. Many other materials, including glass, steel, and paper, are now successfully recycled in modest quantities. But there would be serious problems in finding buyers for a lot more. If supplies grew rapidly, the prices of recycled materials would likely collapse, and with them the existing network of commercial recyclers. Mr. Rathje notes that New Jersey's mandatory recycling law drove the price of newsprint from $40 a ton to the point where communities were forced to pay to have it hauled away.

According to the National Solid Wastes Management Association, thirty-eight states are now trying to jump-start recycling with government procurement preferences for products containing recycled material; seventeen offer private tax incentives to the same end. And many states (including New York and Connecticut) are leaning on newspaper publishers to use recycled newsprint. Wisconsin requires that plastic containers consist of at least 10 percent recycled plastic. But hardly anyone is counting on the overnight development of the markets or collection mechanisms to support extensive recycling. The Environmental Protection Agency has set a short-term goal of 25 percent recycling. Allen Moore, president of the waste management group, a trade association, thinks even this target will prove extraordinarily difficult to hit.

How, then, can America cope with the garbage mountain? One key is making it easier to build facilities for burying, burning, and recycling. Streamlining the process apparently would not put the public health at greater risk. Although buried waste must be monitored indefinitely for leakage, "environmental scientists believe they now know enough to design and locate safe landfills," writes Mr. Rathje. A 1990 technical report commissioned by the United States Conference of Mayors draws a similar (if stuffier) conclusion for burning: "The technology exists to control the incineration of municipal solid waste in such a way as to confidently ensure that potentially harmful constituents are not expected to pose risks to humans and/or the environment."

But disposal facilities certainly are nuisances that nobody is eager to live near. Howard Kunreuther, the director of the Wharton School's Center for Risk and Decision Processes, offers some practical suggestions for making locally undesirable land uses more palatable.

One is to nail down the safety question: issuance of the Environmental Protection Agency's long-promised guidelines for landfill construction would make a difference. State officials might then be required to monitor private facilities and shut them down if they did not meet the federal standard.

Another is to soften opposition by compensating communities and property owners. Wes-Con, Inc., for example, sweetened a proposed landfill in Idaho with free garbage disposal and support for the 4-H Club. Champion International protects the resale value of homes within two miles of its industrial landfills.

Breaking the not-in-my-backyard syndrome will pay bigger dividends if disposal companies retain the flexibility to build for customers from other states. John Turner, general council of the National Solid Wastes Management Association, notes that the Supreme Court has turned back every state effort to limit interstate shipments of nonhazardous waste as an interference with interstate commerce. But Congress clearly does have the authority to impede commerce in garbage; in 1991, the Senate passed a bill granting each state the right to limit garbage imports if it was prepared to show that it would not need to export garbage. That would be a hard test to meet: most states both import and export solid waste, often relying on regional facilities to meet local needs. Only New York and New Jersey regularly solve their disposal problems by shipping waste out of state.

Yet another threat to the construction of new disposal facilities, Mr. Kleindorfer of the Wharton School argues, is price regulation. New Jersey's decision to treat waste disposal as a regulated public utility is particularly sobering when contrasted with the experience of neighboring Pennsylvania. Pennsylvania does not regulate the deals communities make with private landfill and incinerator operators. But the market apparently does: Mr. Kleindorfer believes that Pennsylvania's "tipping fees," which are below the national average, are very effectively limited by competition between disposal facilities. Nonetheless, Mr. Kleindorfer notes, incentives to invest the $65 million to $100 million needed to open a modern one hundred-acre landfill remain adequate: In 1988 there were thirty-one pending applications to open landfills, compared with just two in New Jersey, where average disposal rates are the highest in the country.

The other side of the garbage equation is demand. Like any other service, economists argue, the amount of waste disposal consumers choose to buy varies with the price. And since most consumers' total outlays are unaffected by the amount of garbage they create, they have no incentive to limit the amount left by the curb. Indeed, as the University of California's Mr. Menell points out, "because disposal is free, consumers favor products with more packaging so as to reduce the risk of breakage or increase convenience." One way to right the imbalance would be to tax products according to the postconsumption cleanup cost. That might add, say, a nickel to the cost of laundry detergent in a plastic bottle and a penny to detergent packed in a cardboard box. Consumers would have an incentive to use less wasteful packaging, and manufacturers would have an incentive to adopt waste-efficient designs.

The catch is that disposal costs are very hard to pin down; those who toss their beer cans by the road generate far greater cleanup costs than those who bring them to the neighborhood recycling center. Moreover, disposal costs vary greatly from community to community according to the local price of landfill, incineration, and recycling. Perhaps the more practical alternative, suggests Diana Gale, the head of Seattle's waste utility, is to charge householders according to the amount they put out. Seattle in 1991 charged $13.50 a month for a one-can weekly pickup, plus $9 per additional can. Yard waste separated for composting cost $2 a month, while paper, glass, and metal separated for recycling were hauled away free.

In the first year that per-can charges were imposed, the total tonnage buried fell by 22 percent. Voluntary recycling rose from an impressive 24 percent of waste—Seattle was already environmentally conscious—to an astounding 36 percent. Perkasie, Pennsylvania, a distant suburb of Philadelphia with a population of 6,000, has had even greater success by mixing volume charges ($1.50 for a forty-pound bag) with free, mandatory recycling. In 1988, the first year of operation, the flow to landfill fell by half and the town's garbage bill fell by a third.

Gale notes that in the handful of cities where most people live in apartment complexes, it would be difficult to hold individuals responsible for their actions. But nationwide, designing the financial punishment to fit the waste disposal crime could make a big difference.

[PP, FEBRUARY 1991]

FORESTS THAT LIVE IN CITIES

IN the middle of the Bronx, buffeted and poisoned by the worst environmental insults that urban America can dish out, stands one of the last remnants of the lush forest that once covered New York City: forty acres of hardwoods and hemlocks contained within the public grounds of the New York Botanical Garden. If any patch of old-growth woodlands were going to sicken and succumb to urban stress, this would be it. But ecologists, who have belatedly begun to study urban and suburban ecosystems, have found, to their surprise, that naturally occurring city forests—there are 6,000 acres of them in New York City alone—are adapting in unsuspected ways and appear healthier than might be expected. In fact, they say, the woodlands of the inner cities seem to be performing ecological functions as efficiently as do forests in the more salubrious suburbs, and may even be retaining more of their original character.

Nitrogen emitted by the clanking, fuel-burning metropolis appears to be acting as a fertilizer, spurring soil microbes to break down plant litter more rapidly. The scientists believe this is enriching the trees' diet and boosting their growth. At the same time, because the urban woodlands are islands in a sea of concrete, they may be better protected than the suburbs from invasion by the many exotic species of trees and plants introduced from other countries over past decades. These have especially changed the composition of suburban woodlands.

But the city forest has not remained pristine. Researchers have found evidence of major historical changes in the forty acres of old growth in the Botanical Garden. Human disturbance has caused the big hemlocks and oaks that once dominated the forest to decline in numbers, allowing smaller, more opportunistic species of native trees, like black birch, black cherry, and red maple, to luxuriate and spread.

Nor is there room for complacency about the urban woodlands' long-term health. Assaulted by acid rain, ozone, toxic metals, arson, and other abuse at human hands, the trees are dying at more than twice the natural rate. And the same fertilization processes that now enrich the urban forests could kill them in time, some ecologists speculate. But for now, "they are still alive and still perpetuating themselves; we should give them a hand of applause," said Dr. Mark J. McDonnell, an ecologist at the Botanical Garden's Institute of Ecosystem Studies at Millbrook, New York. He is one of a handful of scientists who have lately begun looking into urban ecology. Urban forests seem "fairly tough and adaptable," he said. "They don't seem to be limping along like an unhealthy person. They're cranking away." Dr. McDonnell reported on the early findings of a long-term study of the Botanical Garden forest at a recent symposium on Northeastern forests at the Bronx institution.

In the past, many ecologists have considered urban and suburban ecosystems as somehow unnatural and therefore not fit subjects of study. Scientists "avoided systems where people lived or that were manipulated by humans," said Dr. Steward T. A. Pickett, another ecologist at the Botanical Garden who also spoke at the symposium. The reason, he said, is that ecology was dominated by a world view in which humans and nature are separate. In this view, nature exists in a harmonious balance that humans disturb. But an emerging new paradigm sees humans as an integral part of nature, and nature itself as being not in balance but in continual flux. Humans, in the new paradigm, are just one of many forces contributing to the flux.

Because of adherence to the traditional view, says Dr. McDonnell, "we know more about the tops of mountains than we know about the forests in New York City." Now, as the new paradigm begins to take hold, that is starting to change, and the larger forest ecosystems scattered about New York and other cities—as distinguished from street trees—are only now beginning to yield some of their ecological secrets.

Actually, the present-day environmental stresses and strains visited on the forests of the Northeast, the most urbanized part of North America, are only the latest in a long series of large-scale disruptions caused by humans and other natural forces. The other forces include storms, fires, and hurricanes, and, 20,000 to 10,000 years ago, the movement of great ice sheets that first destroyed the forests and then withdrew to allow them to reassemble. Perhaps as far back as 9,000 years ago, Native Americans were revamping the forests on a significant scale. The Indians would set fire to the forest in spring and fall to make it more passable and hunting easier, Dr. William A. Niering, an ecologist at Connecticut College, told the recent symposium. The result was large stretches of "open, parklike forest." To create agricultural fields and other clearings, European settlers and their descendants stripped 50 to 70 percent of some Northeastern areas of all their trees. Over many decades, they converted much of the region from a forest ecosystem to an "agroecosystem." These highly disrupted ecosystems began to revert to second-growth forest as early as the 1850s, as settlers moved West and abandoned their farms. Many varieties of exotic plants were introduced from abroad, both accidentally and by design, and they frequently escaped into the wild, where they are still changing the composition and character of the woodlands.

More recently, modern development has fragmented the recovering forests, reducing their capacity to support wildlife. Fragmentation increases the area of "edge" forest, the part of the woods next to a cleared space, where more sunlight comes into play and the mixture of tree and plant species changes. The edge becomes inhospitable to animal species that live in the interior of the forest. As one indication of how prevalent fragmentation has become, Dr. McDonnell cited a study showing that 71 percent of the forest in the rural New Jersey highlands consists of patches smaller than fifty acres. Humans, in short, have created a semicultural, seminatural landscape that is continually changing and evolving, said Dr. McDonnell. The task for urban ecologists, he said, is to try to find out where this landscape is heading.

As one part of the effort, he and his colleagues have studied forests along an eighty-seven-mile corridor extending northeastward from the Bronx into Dutchess County, New York, and Litchfield County, Connecticut. In early results, they have documented a gradual increase in environmental pollution and ecological damage as one moves toward the city. Near the end of that gradient is the Botanical Garden's forest. The forest has never been cut. But otherwise, it has been exposed to the full force of urban environmental stress, making it an ideal laboratory in which to study the effects of that stress. Among the stresses are deposits of acid, apparently from acid rain, and of heavy metals like lead, nickel, and copper, and disruption of the forest by arson, trampling, and vandalism. The researchers have found that the soils of the forest, for reasons they do not yet know, tend to repel water. Over the decades, people have used the forest as a campground and have even washed their clothes in the Bronx River and hung them to dry in the forest. Fires are still frequently set.

The researchers have also discovered that 2.5 to 5 percent of trees in urban areas die every year, compared with a little less than 1 percent for rural areas. Between 1935 and 1975, they found, a combination of human-induced stresses and natural events like storms caused the death of 60 to 70 percent of the very large hemlocks and oaks that dominated the forest canopy. They have been largely replaced by the birch-cherry-maple forest that has now become dominant.

"I don't think that's bad," said Dr. McDonnell. "I think it's terrific, because the forest is regenerating itself with native trees. In the past, I think we've written off a lot of urban and suburban forests as artificial systems, barely functioning, requiring a lot of management just to survive. But our findings suggest they have compensated," he added, "that the ecosystem has adapted. It has surprised us in its resilience."

One reason may be "this soup of nitrogen," as Dr. McDonnell calls it, that has descended on the forest. He speculates that it is produced by the combustion of fossil fuels by automobiles, trucks, power plants, and other industrial sources. The excess nitrogen, he believes, has caused a speedup in the process by which dead leaves and other plant litter decompose into food useful to the trees. This extra nourishment may be what is enabling the forest to remain viable, he said. But extra nourishment may also mean that the trees will not be required to put out as many of the fine roots they use to obtain nutrients and water. If a severe drought should come, this could threaten the trees' existence. "This might be more detrimental to the trees than acid rain in the long run," he said. "Down the road, it might do them in." As a result of this heretofore unsuspected threat, he said, "it is possible that we could wake up in five years and find them dead—not because of obviously toxic pollutants but because we overfertilized them."

[WKS, DECEMBER 1991]

ALIEN INVADERS IN AMERICAN PLANT LIFE

FAMED in song, legend, and movie, the tumbleweed is the plant that best evokes the old American West. And any image of small-town and suburban life in the United States is incomplete without dandelions, clover, and crabgrass. But the tumbleweed, as John Wayne might have been horrified to discover, is a foreign immigrant known to botanists as the Russian thistle. Dandelions, clover, and crabgrass are also naturalized aliens. All four are among some 3,000 plant species from other parts of the world growing wild in North America, just as native American species have colonized other countries.

Humans have been rearranging the planet's flora for centuries, as botanical explorers brought home exotic species and travelers accidentally transferred seeds. The mixing has become so pervasive, botanists and ecologists say, that few of the many plant habitats disturbed by humans remain wholly native. The few exceptions, some say, exist under the protection of *Homo sapiens*, who has now become the universal gardener. Many introductions of new plant species are entirely benign. But some botanists fear that the worldwide transfer of plant species is reaching a point at which it threatens the earth's biological diversity. The problem, they say, is that the weeds of the global garden are getting out of hand. By disrupting natural ecosystems, humans destroy the habitats of some native plants and create openings for a relatively few opportunistic species of exotic grasses, shrubs, and trees to establish themselves. Certain of these weedy species, restrained by predators or pathogens in their natural habitat, can run riot when introduced into new habitats that lack these control factors. They then spread so rapidly as to crowd out many native species. The growth of world trade and air travel has vastly enhanced the spread of plants and seeds, increasing the chance of creating new weeds in unintended places.

When these interlopers choke out native species, ecologists see a danger signal. An ecosystem with only a few species may be destabilized or wiped out if disease or other natural threats attack one species. "Biodiversity is the tool with which you play the game of promoting global stability," said Dr. Peter Raven, director of the Missouri Botanical Garden in St. Louis. "But it also consists of the organisms that give wonder and beauty and joy to the world and that provide the context in which we evolved." What may be emerging, experts like Dr. Raven fear, is a weedier, more homogenized, less stable plant world—and a poorer, less interesting one.

Two recent books explore aspects of the global rearrangement of flora. In *A Reunion of Trees*, Stephen A. Spongberg of the Arnold Arboretum at Harvard recounts the deliberate efforts of scientists, horticulturalists, and others to introduce exotic plants into North America and Europe over the past five centuries. These include popular additions to America like the Norway maple but also intruders like the Japanese honeysuckle, a "pernicious weed" that has invaded thousands of acres of woodland from New Jersey southward, and kudzu, the Japanese import so prevalent below the Mason-Dixon line that it is called the plant that ate the South.

A second book, *Manual of the Flowering Plants of Hawaii*, catalogs the drastic transformation that humans have wrought in the wild flora of Hawaii over the last 1,500 years. The authors, Warren L. Wagner of the Smithsonian Institution, Derral R. Herbst of the United States Fish and Wildlife Service, and S. H. Sohmer of the Bishop Museum in Honolulu, list 861 foreign plants that now grow wild in Hawaii, nearly ten times as many as a century ago. Other scientists say the exotics now dominate Hawaii's lowland areas. At the same time, some 200 native species have become extinct. And although islands are especially vulnerable, some ecologists say, Hawaii's experience may signal an impoverishment of species that awaits the rest of the globe.

Wherever humans have migrated, they have introduced plants.

The Norway maple, Dr. Spongberg notes, was imported in the eighteenth century by William Hamilton, a Pennsylvania landowner, to decorate his estate. Today it lines countless streets in the northeastern United States, despite the tendency of both its seedlings and its deep shade to interfere with the growth of other plants. It has escaped to grow wild along some rivers from the Ohio to the Connecticut, where its brilliant yellow autumn leaves set off the reds and oranges of native upland trees. Hamilton is also credited with importing the hardy mimosa, or silk tree, from Europe, where it was introduced, probably from the Middle East, by André Michaux, gardener to King Louis XVI of France. The mimosa is now widely naturalized from Washington, D.C., southward. Hamilton also bears responsibility for introducing the misleadingly named tree of heaven, or ailanthus, of China. This plant is one of the most persistent American weeds, hardy enough to flourish in the cracks of urban sidewalks. Other immigrants include the Japanese honeysuckle, sent from Japan in 1862 by George Rogers Hall, an American physician turned plant fancier. Kudzu was one of many plants exported to North America in the late nineteenth century by Thomas Hogg, an American consul in Japan.

Plants were imported for their beauty, for scientific study, and for sale. Exotic grasses were imported because they could withstand grazing better than native species, and today they have taken over large areas of the American West. Some exotics hitchhiked in shipments of agricultural seed, others in the ballast dumped by visiting ships, still others in the guts of livestock. Seeds of European plants have been found baked into the bricks from which the Spanish built their early missions in California.

Many of the most familiar and seemingly most American plants are in fact immigrants:

- Dandelions, from which wine was made, brought by early settlers
- Wild onion and crabgrass, the scourge of modern lawns, from Europe
- Timothy, the most important hay grass in the United States
- The salt-spray rose, long familiar on Cape Cod and Martha's Vineyard and in Maine
- Ryegrass, day lilies, plaintain, cocklebur, chickweed, the ox-eye daisy, Queen Anne's lace, chicory, and white and red clover, all from Europe
- The eucalyptus tree, from Australia

It is at least a two-way street. There are no barriers in Japan to the import of American black-eyed Susans, which were brought in for cultivation and escaped; now the flower is common along streams in Japan, said Dr. David Bouffard, a Harvard University botanist. Goldenrod, he said, has become naturalized in Japan and also in Europe, where hybridized goldenrods sold as cut flowers "have escaped all over the place." The American box elder, or ash-leafed maple, is established in the wild all over China and Japan, he said. And the American black locust tree has spread from a patch of the southern Appalachians to colonize much of the United States, China, and Japan.

Not many places on earth remain untouched by human transfers of plants, scientists say. The darkest depths of both tropical and temperate rain forests, as well as harsh subarctic and glacial ecosystems, are major exceptions. In the United States, said Dr. Spongberg, "you can go from the most remote national park to the Grand Canyon and there are non-native species growing everywhere." Some of the more remote places may retain their essential character, he said, "but if you look on the side of the road, you're likely to see a foreign weed." At a minimum, ecologists say, plants introduced by humans are changing the character of native ecosystems. At worst, they are crowding out or obliterating native plants. Islands offer the most extreme examples. Eighty percent of Madagascar, for instance, is occupied by "weedy pasture species from Africa," said Dr. Raven.

In Hawaii, humans decimated native plant habitats and then, in an effort to reestablish the islands' plant cover, imported thousands of exotic species.

First came the Polynesians, who starting 1,500 years ago brought thirty to forty plant species, says Dr. Peter M. Vitousek, an ecologist at Stanford University. Settlers from Europe stepped up the rate of transformation by bringing in cattle, sheep, and goats. The animals ate trees, broke up forests, and greatly reduced the abundance of native grasses. Widespread soil erosion followed, and around 1900 Hawaiians searched the world for plants that could both hold the soil and withstand grazing. They not only imported and planted grasses, they also created huge plantations of exotic trees. One tree, imported from the Canary Islands, is the myrica. Invading the national park on the big island of Hawaii, the myrica covered 1,500 wilderness acres there in 1977 and has now spread over 30,000 acres. "It is displacing the native forest, dominated by the ohia tree and native shrubs," said

Dr. Vitousek. "At the most extreme, nothing is growing with it and nothing is coming in underneath it."

The myrica is also changing the nature of the ecosystem in ways that favor the establishment of exotic plants. The trees absorb unusually large amounts of nitrogen that find their way into the volcanic soils and make them more favorable for colonization. Because of such influences, the exotics have overwhelmed the Hawaiian lowlands. Combined with habitat disruption caused by humans, they have led to the extinction of at least 200 species of native Hawaiian plants. The exchange of plants "is a net loss," said Dr. Vitousek, because the extinct species were found nowhere else.

Ecologists worry that the destruction of native flora in the lowlands of Hawaii may be repeated elsewhere. In the continental United States, the kudzu, the tree of heaven, and the Japanese honeysuckle are not the only threats to ecosystem integrity. The casuarina tree is displacing native beachfront vegetation in Florida and sharpening the slope of the beach by changing the root mats that hold it in place. The purple loosestrife, a tall, spindly plant with hundreds of magenta flowers, is crowding out native marsh grasses in the Northeast. The buckthorn, a large Eurasian shrub with blackish, berrylike fruit, completely takes over low, wet woods in many parts of the Eastern United States, choking out other vegetation. And the Asian bittersweet not only crowds out its native counterpart, it also climbs trees and blots out sunlight so effectively that the trees eventually die.

Of the 18,000 species of plants in the forty-eight contiguous states, Dr. Raven estimates, about 2,000 are seriously threatened and about 400 are in danger of disappearing in the next ten years, mostly because of habitat disruption and competition from foreign invaders. About 2,700 non-native species are growing in the wilds of the forty-eight states, but their ecological impact is greater than their numbers suggest. "The area covered by those species can be enormous," Dr. Raven said. The grass species, in particular, can dominate thousands of square miles.

The more humans disturb and open up natural ecosystems, Dr. Raven said, "the more you enhance the chance for getting very widespread weedy species around the world very rapidly." He went on: "The most hopeful scenarios have the global population stabilizing at two to three times its present size about one hundred years from now. This is the most destructive period of time we've ever undergone." Given a respite, some native ecosystems might reassert themselves in time, especially if humans help them along. But even so, scientists worry that so many plant species will have been lost by then that genetic variety will have been seriously depleted. In any case, the establishment of exotic plant species in many habitats throughout the planet is now a fact of nature. The philosophic concept of nature as a wilderness untouched by human hand is becoming harder and harder to realize in practice. "We're managing it all," said Dr. Raven. "If something is relatively unspoiled, it's because we manage it as relatively unspoiled. The best thing to do, in my book, is to accept the responsibility and get on with it and do the best job we can."

[WKS, DECEMBER 1990]

TREATING NUCLEAR WASTE
WITH ALCHEMY

RENAISSANCE alchemists sought in vain for a way to transmute base metals into gold, but modern nuclear alchemists believe they have hit upon an even more valuable discovery: a means of transmuting America's deadly mountain of long-lived radioactive waste into substances that lose their radioactive sting relatively quickly. New transmutation processes under study at a half dozen major American laboratories, and at institutions in the Soviet Union, Japan, France, and Britain, can treat waste that would otherwise remain dangerously radioactive for up to 10 million years. The waste, which is piling up in temporary storage sites while plans are made for permanent disposal, would be bombarded by nuclear particles and changed into substances that would be relatively safe in 300 years.

The plants that would carry out transmutation and processing of radioactive waste in the United States would be costly; experts said in interviews that it would cost $10 billion to $20 billion to create the kind of nuclear reprocessing capacity in the United States that several countries, notably France, have already built. Reprocessing is also mired in debate; some experts argue that high-level nuclear waste should be processed before deep permanent burial, whereas others maintain that such schemes create new problems, including the proliferation of plutonium that might be stolen by nuclear terrorists, and would merely delay the inevitable and urgent permanent burial.

Some nuclear officials argue that talk of transmutation will further delay permanent disposal. By raising the hope that transmutation might eliminate the need for permanent underground storage, political and legal moves to block the use of waste sites in New Mexico and Nevada gain support, thereby stalling action by the Department of Energy to bury the waste. But scientific experts are in striking agreement that in principle, at least, transmutation will work. They disagree as to how best to carry it out, whether by using a new type of "Integral Fast Reactor" developed at Argonne National Laboratory in Illinois, or powerful particle accelerators.

Transmutation requires a particle accelerator, a reactor, or both, to bombard nuclear waste with neutrons. This forces the long-lived radioactive atoms to undergo fission, thereby producing the lighter atomic variants known as isotopes that rapidly decay to relatively harmless materials. At various stages in the process, chemical processing is used to separate components of the waste—recovering some valuable materials and plutonium reactor fuel, sending dangerous substances back for further processing, and passing on the relatively safe remainder for permanent burial.

Radioactive waste from nuclear reactors that have produced electricity and nuclear explosives since the 1940s continues to accumulate in temporary storage sites that many experts regard as menaces. Some 30 percent of this spent reactor fuel was produced by weapons programs and the rest by commercial power reactors, said a spokesman for the Department of Energy. The United States has resolved to use storage caverns in supposedly impermeable geologic formations far beneath the ground. But even if the Energy Department surmounts political and legal hurdles that still bar the use of such permanent burial sites as the planned excavation under Yucca Mountain, Nevada, scientists say that a site of this size would fill up in thirty years at the present rate of waste production. Moreover, the rate may increase. Since the 1970s no new nuclear power plants have been ordered by United States utilities, but some energy experts believe this hiatus may soon end.

The construction of new reactors of the kind most widely used in America, "light-water" reactors, would add to the flow of high-level radioactive waste.

Proponents of transmutation say it would not only reduce the volume of waste requiring burial, but would greatly reduce the time such waste would remain dangerous. Transmutation, they say, can transform waste that would otherwise remain dangerous for up to 10 million years into waste that would become no more dangerous than natural uranium ore in as little as 300 years. It is much easier to ensure the safety of an underground storage system, they point out, if its contents remain dangerous for only a few decades—or even a few centuries—rather than for a period longer than mankind's existence. All the proposed transmutation schemes share another advantage: they would produce electric power that would partly defray their operating costs.

The various transmutation methods under consideration, which involve complex chemical processing as well as bombardment of radioactive waste with neutrons, are promising enough so that in 1991 the Department of Energy commissioned a study by the National Academy of Sciences and Engineering. The panel is expected to report its conclusions in 1992.

Two federally supported laboratories, Brookhaven National Laboratory on Long Island, and Los Alamos National Laboratory in New Mexico, have proposed different types of particle accelerators for the job; a third, Argonne, is working on a new type of reactor that would simultaneously consume dangerous waste while producing electric power. Dr. William H. Hannum, a research director at Argonne, says that the laboratory's planned Integral Fast Reactor not only would consume dangerous nuclear waste, but would produce plutonium fuel that could be safely and securely processed at or near the reactor plant. Although such a reactor resembles the "breeder" type used in this country to manufacture plutonium for nuclear warheads, the variant designed by Argonne would produce a mixture of plutonium and other materials that would be very difficult to convert into explosives.

Breeder-type power reactors were abandoned in the United States because of fears that nuclear explosives they produce could fall into terrorist hands. But for lack of breeder reactors to consume the waste from conventional uranium reactors, the United States has been forced to stockpile vast amounts of dangerous waste. If the Argonne design was adopted for future reactors, the rate of growth of waste would fall dramatically, proponents say. If America was supplied with such reactors, supplies of uranium fuel needed by conventional reactors could be made to last one hundred times as long.

Critics of the Argonne reactor and of all transmutation schemes argue that they could create as many problems as they solve. Dr. Thomas H. Pigford, a nuclear engineer at the University of California in Berkeley and a member of the new academy panel, believes that the electric power industry is not willing to build reactors that would burn their own waste or existing stockpiles of nuclear waste. "To gain acceptance by the utility industry, new reactors must be more economical to run than conventional light-water reactors," he said. "And that simply won't be the case."

Los Alamos already possesses an accelerator that scientists consider particularly suitable for transmuting radioactive waste. Protons from the accelerator would crash into a lead target, which would spew a dense shower of neutrons in all directions. Some of the neutrons from such a device would hit the nuclei of dangerous atoms in the waste, making these atoms unstable and forcing them to split into safe substances or radioactive atoms with short half-lives. The half-life of a radioactive material is the period in which half of it will decay into other atomic forms. Longevity is measured in half-lives, because a given amount of a radioactive substance will never completely decay.

Dr. Edward D. Arthur, the program manager at Los Alamos, said in an interview that transmutation of nuclear waste has been suggested from time to time in the last twenty years, but that neither funds nor adequate equipment was available. Now, however, two factors are prompting renewed study. The first is mounting public and political opposition to underground waste disposal at both a test site, the Waste Isolation Pilot Plant near Carlsbad, New Mexico, and the permanent site selected under Yucca Mountain, Nevada. Some scientists and officials believe this would wane if the public could be assured that the waste would become relatively safe after some reasonable period of time.

A second reason for renewed interest in transmutation at Los Alamos, Dr. Arthur said, is the availability of a powerful linear accelerator, built for the "Star Wars" antimissile research program, that could be used for rapid transmutation.

Dr. Gregory J. Van Tuyle, who heads Brookhaven's transmutation study, said that although spent reactor fuel contains many dangerous isotopes, only a few have half-lives long enough to cause problems when buried for thousands of years. One of these is plutonium, a byproduct of reactor operation and the metal that fuels nuclear explosions. Plutonium is extremely poisonous and has a half-life of 24,000 years.

Efficient chemical methods already exist for separating plutonium from the waste, along with three other man-made radioactive elements—neptunium, americium, and curium, all of which could be used to help fuel a transmutation system Brookhaven has dubbed "Phoenix." Four other reactor by-products have top priority for elimination from stored waste. Two of these, strontium 90 and cesium 137, have half-lives of only about thirty years, but are so radioactive they cause heating problems in storage and must therefore be removed. Two others, technetium 99 and iodine 129, have half-lives of 21,300 years and 16 million years, respectively, however, and could easily outlast the seals designed to confine them safely.

Both iodine 129 and technetium 99 are good candidates for transmutation. When iodine 129 is placed in an intense neutron beam and is hit by a low-energy neutron, it becomes iodine 130. This isotope decays in less than one day to xenon gas, which undergoes further transmutation to become a harmless xenon isotope. Bombarded by neutrons, technetium 99 is similarly transmuted to a nonradioactive form of ruthenium.

In Brookhaven's Phoenix scheme, a high-energy particle accelerator, which has yet to be built, would send a beam of neutrons into an array of large cells containing some 2,500 tons of waste. This array would hold a "subcritical mass" of fissionable material; that is, it would be incapable of spontaneously generating enough neutrons to start or maintain a nuclear chain reaction. A beam of neutrons from the accelerator shot into the waste could make up this deficit, however, and a chain reaction would then begin to "burn" the dangerous radioactive material into shorter-lived isotopes. After supplying its own needs, this "subcritical reactor" would produce 850 megawatts of electric power—an output comparable to that of the abandoned Shoreham nuclear plant built by the Long Island Lighting Company.

A major safety feature of both the Brookhaven Phoenix and its somewhat similar Los Alamos counterpart would be "subcriticality"; a chain reaction could never get out of control because the instant the accelerator sustaining it shut down, the nuclear reaction would stop. A variant of this approach, called CURE (for Clean Use of Reactor Energy), has been proposed by the Westinghouse Hanford Company, operator of the Department of Energy Hanford Site at Richland, Washington. A recent Hanford report concluded that "destruction of the bulk of the long-lived radioactivity rather than geological disposal would greatly reduce uncertainties in the long-term performance assessment."

An important part of all schemes for processing nuclear waste is chemical separation of the various types of elements in the mixture. The best known of these systems, called the Purex (for plutonium-uranium-extraction) method, has been used for decades by many nations to separate plutonium from other reactor products. Most of this plutonium has been used to make nuclear warheads, but some has been used as fuel for a type of power reactor some experts predict will eventually replace conventional uranium-fueled reactors. A newer chemical separation system, called the Truex (for trans-uranic extraction) process, uses the waste from the Purex process to extract residual plutonium, uranium, neptunium, curium, and technetium—all of them dangerous. Once isolated from the nuclear waste produced by Purex, these substances could be conveniently targeted for transformation by neutron bombardment, or even used as fuels in subcritical accelerator-driven reactors.

Are any of these ideas practical? Replies vary according to points of view. Dr. Clyde Frank, director of environmental and waste management for the Department of Energy, opposes anything likely to delay permanent underground storage of high-level radioactive waste. "Transmutation may be feasible for part of the waste," he said, "but if the necessary chemical processing ends up increasing the overall volume of waste by tenfold, where's the point?" Dr. Van Tuyle of Brookhaven and other proponents of nuclear waste treatment see the issue differently. "Transmutation is practical. No one really disputes that," he said. "Of course there are difficulties in applying it to a full-scale operation. But the problem of high-level radioactive waste won't go away. We are obliged to find and implement long-term solutions. We have to think of our remote descendants as well as our children and grandchildren." [MWB, OCTOBER 1991]

WEANING FARMERS FROM PESTICIDES

A MERICAN farmers have long maintained that using fewer pesticides would result in greater crop losses and increased food prices. But a comprehensive analysis of the benefits and costs of the present heavy dependence on chemical methods of pest control strongly suggests otherwise. Cornell University researchers have concluded after reviewing data on crop yields and pesticide use from hundreds of scientists at university laboratories and government agencies, that yields would not decline and food prices would rise less than 1 percent if half the chemicals now applied to crops were replaced by other control techniques. The findings support growing consumer concerns about pesticide pollution and underscore suggestions that a more organic approach to agriculture would be beneficial.

A thirty-page summary of the study, directed by Dr. David Pimentel, was published in 1991 in the *Handbook of Pest Management in Agriculture*, a three-volume, 2,300-page handbook. Dr. Pimentel, an entomologist and ecologist at the New York State College of Agriculture and Life Sciences at Cornell, worked with ten graduate and undergraduate students who compiled and analyzed nearly 300 scientific references. Dr. Robert Metcalf, an entomologist at the University of Illinois, said that "if anything, Dr. Pimentel's estimates are conservative," adding, "Large-scale pest management studies have shown that pesticides could be reduced by half, three fourths, even 90 percent in some cases without adversely affecting yields or the cost of food." But John McCarthy of the National Agricultural Chemicals Association, which represents the pesticide industry, said: "We think Dr. Pimentel has drastically underestimated the impact on the price of food of reducing pesticides by 50 percent. The assumption that yields wouldn't decrease needs to be critically examined. Most people who've looked into this have reached a different conclusion."

The Cornell study suggests that a net economic benefit would result from a 50 percent reduction in pesticide use because there would be less damage to fish, wildlife, crops, trees, water supplies, and human health. Currently, for example, about 45,000 people each year report accidental poisonings by pesticides, and the Environmental Protection Agency estimates that 6,000 Americans, most of them farm workers, are afflicted with pesticide-induced cancers. Government efforts to monitor and control pesticide pollution cost at least $150 million a year, the report states. Furthermore, the findings suggest that heavy dependence on chemicals to control weeds, crop diseases, and insect infestations long ago reached the point of diminishing returns. Since the 1940s, there has been a thirty-three-fold increase in the amount of pesticides used and at least a ten-fold increase in their potency, but 37 percent of crops are now lost to pests, up from 31 percent in the 1940s.

Currently 700 million pounds of pesticides are used annually in American agriculture at a cost of $4.1 billion, and nearly another $1 billion is spent to counter environmental damage and public health effects of pesticides, the analysis found. Dr. Pimentel and his collaborators advocate a return to practices that in some cases can increase yields while decreasing pesticide use. These include rotating cash crops to prevent a buildup of destructive pests. For example, corn might be grown in alternate years with soybeans.

"In 1945, when all corn was grown in rotation and no insecticides were used, only 3.5 percent of the crop was lost to insects," Dr. Pimentel said in an interview. "But today, corn is the largest user of pesticides in the nation, and 12 percent of the crop is lost to insects, which indicates that the loss of crop rotation has been counterproductive."

The study also indicated that by combining crop rotation with the planting of insect-resistant varieties of corn, only one fifth of the insecticides now used would be needed and less of the crop would be lost to insects. Other well-tested alternatives to spraying pesticides on a set schedule, as is usually the case, include "scouting" systems to detect pest problems early and analyses of weather forecasts to help farmers predict more precisely when chemical treatments are needed.

Dr. Pimentel said that modern methods of pesticide application have worsened the problem of environmental contamination. He explained: "Airblast sprayers used in orchards and vineyards spread 35 percent of their chemicals into the environment. Even under ideal conditions, only half the chemicals sprayed on crops from aircraft lands on the target area. And with the new ultralow-volume spraying,

only 25 percent hits the target; 75 percent goes into the environment."
The low-volume technique uses concentrated pesticides that have
been broken into minute particles, which drift badly when sprayed
from crop-dusting planes.

Instead, he suggested spraying under umbrella-like units that
drape over vines and row crops and that collect and recirculate excess
chemicals. For weed control, rope-wick applicators can deposit herbicides directly between rows of crops.

Other recommendations to reduce dependence on chemical pesticides include denser planting patterns to crowd out weeds, the use of
lures to trap insects and "insect vacuums" to remove insects from
crops, and the planting of varieties that resist disease or mature before
pest populations are ready to attack. The Cornell researchers urged
increased use of biological weapons and called for changes in government regulations that set cosmetic standards so high that pesticides
must be used to keep foods marketable. "People are already eating
insect parts in their fresh and processed foods," Dr. Pimentel said,
adding that the amount of these contaminants would increase only
slightly if fewer pesticides were used.

The most controversial suggestion in the report is a revision of
the government's price-support programs for several crops. These
income guarantees have generally limited what farmers in the program can grow and have enabled crops to be produced in areas where
they are subject to heavy pest attack and require costly control measures. A revision of the price-support program could save billions
in government payouts without reducing farmers' net income, Dr.
Pimentel said.   [JEB, APRIL 1991]

SEWAGE SLUDGE AND
THE SEA FLOOR

OCEANOGRAPHERS are debating whether sewage sludge and other
wastes can be safely deposited on the deep sea floor. At an
international meeting at the beginning of 1991, some argued that

deep sea dumping of sewage sludge should not be ruled out, despite the concerns of environmentalists and statutory retraints. Others expressed doubts about the long-term effects of such dumping.

A variety of proposals for delivering waste to the deep sea bottom were discussed, some of them seemingly exotic. In one scheme, an eighteen-inch hose several miles long with a forty-ton nozzle at its lower end would be lowered from the sludge ship to deliver its load close to the bottom. Another proposal would link fifty-five-gallon drums of waste into trains with a heavy "nose cone" on the bottom drum. The train of drums, dragged downward by the heavy cone, would sink at fifty miles per hour, penetrating deep into the bottom ooze, which in many areas is thousands of feet deep.

The meeting, at the Woods Hole Oceanographic Institution in Massachusetts, was organized by Derek W. Spencer, a marine chemist on its staff. Citing the growing crisis in waste disposal, he urged that the deep sea not be ruled out. More than half the earth's surface, he noted, is under the oceans at depths of several miles. Dr. Spencer cited advantages of the proposals for controlled delivery of the waste to the sea floor without contaminating the upper levels of seawater. He said he had discussed with European investors a joint academic-industry venture in which the government would be asked to permit a ten-year pilot program. In it 1 million tons of waste would be channeled to the deep sea floor each year. According to one proposal, instead of using a long tube, two ships would participate, with an "enclosed elevator" to lower the waste. The system using a giant hose has been proposed by Maersk, a Danish shipping company. While the fermenting sludge would probably deprive the bottom area of oxygen, this test, Dr. Spencer said, would make it possible to assess such an effect and resulting faunal change in one or more areas, including the time for each spot to return to normal.

Some argued that too little was known about the fate of dumped sewage sludge to predict its long-term effects. Evidence was presented that deep-water fish were being contaminated hundreds of miles at sea off the Hudson River Canyon, presumably by sewage swept down the canyon from the river. Such deep-dwelling fish are not harvested for food. Sewage residues also appear to be accumulating on the bottom of a dump site 106 miles off the coast of New Jersey. This site, where processed sludge from sewage plants in New York and New Jersey is being dumped, is near the outer edge of the slope from the continental shelf to the deep sea floor. Frederick Grassle of Rutgers

University said some sludge was reaching the bottom immediately west of the site, as predicted from bottom currents. The sludge's presence has been shown by analysis of bottom samples for trace metals and more than normal spores of the bacterium *Clostridium perfringens*, a sewage indicator. Mike Bothner of the United States Geological Survey found silver in the sediment to be a good indicator of contamination. Silver is discharged in quantity by photographic laboratories and development of medical X-ray films.

At the end of 1991, such sludge dumping will become illegal, initially incurring a fine of $600 a ton, followed by annual increases, though the fines are not entirely punitive, since the money will partly be set aside to help dumpers develop alternative strategies.

Much public opposition to the dumping stemmed from episodes in the 1980s when syringes and other medical supplies washed up on New Jersey beaches and also when dumping of sludge close to shore poisoned local waters. Furthermore, there were sea mammal deaths from causes that at first were mysterious. None of these, the oceanographers say, were related to the dumping of sewage sludge in water thousands of feet deep and more than a hundred miles from shore.

At the meeting, as in the past, it was argued that the sludge, a prime natural fertilizer, can have a beneficial effect. Dr. Marvin V. Angel of the Institute of Oceanographic Sciences in Wormley, England, told of a hundredfold improvement in fisheries over a shallow-water dump off the Clyde River in Scotland. Samples of the fish showed some toxic heavy metals in their guts, he said, but virtually none in their edible parts. Such shallow-water dumping, however, might introduce disease-causing agents into the food chain and has "effectively destroyed" the British shellfish industry, Dr. Angel reported. Britain is now dumping 10 million tons of sludge into the sea each year, half of it into deep water off the Thames estuary. From there it is washed into the English Channel, and within 210 days it has reached Scandinavia. Unless the law is changed, Dr. Angel said, by 1998 Britain will outlaw all ocean dumping.

The present dumping method depends on scattering of the material as it sinks thousands of feet through coastal currents. The largest particles sink directly to the bottom; the tiniest, it is now believed, may drift from the site off New Jersey almost as far south as Cape Hatteras before they sink. If the sludge was delivered directly to the bottom of the deep ocean, it would bypass shallower depths where most organisms live. In the view of James R. Ledwell of Woods Hole, however, before such a test is conducted, more should be learned of bottom currents from the 106-Mile Dump Site and other tests.

[WS, JANUARY 1991]

THE REEMERGENCE OF MERCURY

Two decades after the government thought the problem had been put to rest, mercury is accumulating in fish in thousands of lakes across the United States and Canada, poisoning wildlife and threatening human health. Twenty states, including New York and Connecticut, have warned people to limit or eliminate from their diets fish they catch in certain lakes because of dangerous levels of mercury. Canadian scientists have found elevated levels of mercury in fish caught in 95 percent of the lakes tested in Ontario. Scientists say the principal source of contamination is rain containing traces of mercury from coal-burning power plants, municipal incinerators, and smelters. Other contamination comes from lake and ocean sediments previously polluted by mercury. States and the federal government have taken almost no action to reduce releases of mercury, in part because recognition of the problem is recent—and because federal energy and state environmental policies are actually part of the problem.

There have been few studies of the extent to which Americans might have been harmed by mercury poisoning, and state health officials say there is no evidence yet of damage to human health in this country. But mercury has been confirmed as the cause of deaths of panthers and loons in Florida and is suspected in the reproductive failures seen in eagles, minks, otters, and other animals in the Great Lakes region. Contamination is generally not an issue for store-bought fish, which do not come from the lakes most affected, the authorities say. "It's a very messy pollutant," said John Bachmann, an engineer in the Office of Air Quality at the Environmental Protection Agency (EPA). "It's a liquid metal that becomes a gas even at mild temperatures. That makes it difficult to control. We need to know more."

But state environmental officials and a top government mercury researcher disagree, saying that enough is known to begin halting mercury's spread. Delays, they say, are a result not of inadequate information but of conflicts. Federal energy policy encourages power plants that burn coal, which contains small amounts of mercury. Meanwhile, the states, faced with dwindling landfill space, are encouraging construction of incinerators. Since mercury is used to make batteries, paints, electrical switches, and hundreds of other products, incineration of these discarded items releases mercury.

"Solving this problem means changing our ways and spending money to control emissions—a lot of money," said Dr. Gary Glass, a chemist at the EPA Environmental Research Laboratory in Duluth, Minnesota, who is a leading government researcher and has been studying mercury since 1987 with state support. "It's going to take a very focused effort to cut back on consumer products that contain mercury." The Edison Electric Institute, a trade group for utilities, estimated that power plants with equipment to remove mercury from emissions could cost $5 billion nationally. Incinerator builders say curbing mercury emissions could cost $10 million to $30 million per plant.

Some steps, much less costly, are already being taken. Disposal methods that keep discarded batteries and paint from incinerators help reduce mercury in the atmosphere. Battery manufacturers, concerned about possible new regulations, have cut the use of mercury to 250 tons in 1989, from almost 1,200 tons in 1984, the EPA says. In 1990, the agency outlawed mercury in interior latex paints. But there are still hundreds of millions of batteries and many old paint cans. And wood that has been covered with latex paint containing mercury still emits mercury when burned.

Mercury has been a valuable raw material from the earth's crust for 3,500 years and a recognized hazard for nearly as long. Romans used the bright red sulfide ore of mercury for pigments, and at least one Roman naturalist, Pliny, described how mercury miners died in large numbers. In the nineteenth century, fur that was used in the manufacture of felt hats was dipped in mercuric nitrate solution. Many felt workers absorbed so much mercury through their skin that they became known for slurred speech and uncontrollable shaking.

In the twentieth century, mercury's disinfecting ability makes it indispensable to the paper and paint industry in controlling slimes and molds. Chemical companies incorporate mercury in some reactions as a catalyst. Historically, industrial plants poured their mercury waste into rivers or lakes, where it collected in sediments and passed up the food chain, from plankton to minnows to large fish to birds of prey and large mammals—and human beings. In the 1950s and early 1960s, more than one hundred people developed tremors, fell into comas, and died in Minamata, Japan. Fish caught in Minamata Bay had mercury levels that measured an average of 11 one-thousandths of a gram for every kilogram (2.2 pounds), comparable to a speck of pepper on a 36-ounce steak. The Food and Drug Administration (FDA) considers eating a single meal of fish containing one-thousandth of a gram of mercury per kilogram to be dangerous, and bars commercial sales of fish that contain more. The events in Minamata spurred a global investigation that yielded evidence in the 1960s of rising mercury levels in game fish caught in American waters. In 1972, Congress passed the Clean Water Act, requiring paper companies, smelters, paint factories, and other plants to install equipment and prevent mercury from being released into water.

Before the law, Minnesota sampled its rivers and found adult fish containing a mean mercury level of about one-thousandth of a gram per kilogram in their flesh—the amount judged by the FDA to be too dangerous. By the late 1970s, the mean mercury levels in fish taken in Minnesota rivers dropped to 0.38 thousandth of a gram per kilogram, a level then considered safe. But prompted by reports from Sweden of persistent and widespread mercury contamination in fish caught in remote lakes in that country, the Minnesota Department of Health in the 1970s began sampling the state's lakes, particularly those along the wild border with Canada. In 1978, the agency identified mercury at levels of more than one-thousandth of a gram per kilogram in large walleye and northern pike caught in Crane Lake, 130 miles north of Duluth and miles from any industry. The discovery prompted sampling by scientists in Minnesota, Wisconsin, Michigan, and in Ontario, which turned up similarly high levels and spurred renewed efforts to identify the sources.

Scientists now believe they know the culprits. They say mercury is being swept into the upper atmosphere from cement and phosphate plants as well as power plants and incinerators. Mercury also is evaporating from contaminated lake and ocean sediments and falling back to earth as toxic rain. "There is a lot of very nasty, unpleasant stuff in rain coming at us from everywhere," said Dr. Terry A. Haines, a fishery research biologist for the United States Fish and Wildlife Service in Maine who has documented evidence of fish contaminated with mercury in the wilds of that state. Eliminating mercury and the other compounds from rain is an enormous technical and political problem. For one thing, like the air pollutants that cause acid rain, mercury is released into the atmosphere hundreds of miles from where it is doing the most damage. How far mercury can travel is not known, but in its gaseous form it can linger in the atmosphere up to two years before it falls back to earth. Swedish scientists estimate that 930 tons of mercury is circulating in the world's atmosphere at any time, enough to taint rain at levels that average 10 to 50 parts per trillion. That amount, while minuscule, is enough to cause problems.

In each of the last two years, the Minnesota Legislature rejected legislation that would have made it the first state to enact strict controls on mercury emissions. Industry argued that it would increase the cost of doing business without lowering mercury levels in fish, since most of the mercury falling on Minnesota was coming from outside the state. "In a sense, they're right," said Willard Munger, the chairman of the state House Environment and Natural Resources Committee, who proposed the measure. "It's going to take national legislation to solve this problem. But we have to start somewhere."

Crane Lake in northern Minnesota is a stepping-off point to one of the largest wilderness regions left in the continental United States. Packs of timber wolves roam the pine forests, otters sun themselves on the rocky shoreline, bears forage for berries, and eagles soar across blue skies. Yet studies by Dr. Glass and his colleague Dr. George R. Rapp, Jr., a researcher at the University of Minnesota in Duluth, have found that mercury levels in large adult walleye and northern pike from Crane Lake range from 0.9 to 1.1 thousandths of a gram per kilogram, and that they are rising 3 percent to 5 percent a year. Younger, smaller fish have less mercury.

The Minnesota Department of Health has set a limit for mercury in fish, 0.16 thousandth of a gram per kilogram, that is thought to be the nation's strictest. New York's limit is one-thousandth of a gram per kilogram, the same as the FDA's. In almost every case, walleye and pike, even young fish five inches to fifteen inches long, that are caught in Crane Lake and in neighboring Sand Point Lake exceed the state limit. The Minnesota Department of Health has warned Crane Lake anglers not to eat more than one eight-ounce serving of pike or walleye a week. Pregnant women, nursing mothers, women thinking of becoming pregnant, and children under the age of six are advised against eating any fish.

Businessmen and lodge owners from Crane Lake say the limits are so stringent that they may ruin summertime lodging and fishing. Large fish are recognized as having the most mercury and they are rarely eaten, say homeowners and fishing guides. But smaller fish are staples of the meals that guides prepare, and the guides say they are harmless, especially to visitors who spend only a few days in the region. "I've been eating fish here my whole life, and I'm fine," said Arthur (Butch) Eggen, a thirty-eight-year-old fishing guide. "The small fish aren't going to hurt you."

But businessmen recognize that rising levels of mercury in fish in northern Minnesota lakes represent an economic problem, especially if people conclude that families seeking refuge from city pollution face a greater risk of exposure to a dangerous toxic compound while on their vacations. "We just have to tell people who come here what we know," said David K. Dill, the economic development director in Orr, twenty-eight miles southwest of Crane Lake. "Yes, mercury is here. Yes, it's in the fish. But nobody in Minnesota has ever been diagnosed with mercury poisoning. And as far as the local people are concerned, it's a pressing issue only because if people get scared and go someplace else, it's pressing our pocketbooks."

Perhaps most distressing about mercury pollution, say scientists, is that even if every industrial source of mercury were shut down today, the problem could get worse in some areas before it got better. First, more than a hundred years of reliance on mercury has helped to produce some 45 million tons in the soil, the oceans, the sediment of lakes and rivers, and the atmosphere. Second, scientists have found that other pollutants affect how mercury behaves.

Mercury is most dangerous when it is converted in the environment from its elemental form to methyl mercury, the organic form readily absorbed by fish. One of the disturbing recent findings is that acid in lakes and in clouds, and ozone pollution from cars and power plants, more quickly converts elemental mercury to methyl mercury. Environmental agencies in Minnesota, Wisconsin, and New York have noted that the highest levels of mercury were found in fish taken from the most acidified lakes.

Thomas C. Jorling, the Commissioner of the New York Department of Environmental Conservation, said mercury contamination "can't be solved by one state acting alone, which makes it an appropriate place for the federal government to act." The Edison Electric Institute estimates that the amount of mercury released from burning coal in the United States each year is 100 tons, a small fraction of the 3,000 to 5,000 tons of mercury that pours into the atmosphere from burning coal around the world. The group argues that, like the destruction of the earth's ozone shield, the mercury problem will be solved only by an international treaty. "Maybe we'll decide to go to new ways of generating power," said Dr. Donald B. Porcella, an ecologist at the Electric Power Research Institute, the utility industry's research arm. "Maybe we'll put more controls on incinerators. Maybe we'll cut back on using, or even eliminating, mercury in industry. But it's a very complicated problem, and we better understand it before we start making decisions." [KS, AUGUST 1991]

THE POLITICS OF DISPOSABLE
DIAPERS

T HE war over how to cover American baby bottoms has ended in a rout. Exhausted by their failure to convince parents that the nation's landfills have turned into reeking mountains of disposable diapers, many of the most zealous environmentalists have simply stopped trying. The signs of surrender are everywhere. In 1989, twenty-two states considered taxing or banning disposables. None has succeeded. In 1990, New York nearly passed a law requiring hospitals to distribute pamphlets about cotton diapers to all new parents. In 1992, a similar effort died in a day. Even the Environmental Protection Agency seems to have run up the (reusable) white flag. In its major new guide to reducing waste, the word *diaper* never even appears.

"You know Freud was right about us," said Allen Hershkowitz, a solid waste expert at the Natural Resources Defense Council in New York, and a man who has long been plagued by his own ambivalence over the diaper debate. "Civilization has its costs." Clearly one of those costs is disposable diapers. There has never been a more potent symbol of the national conflict between convenience and conservation. More than 17 billion disposable diapers were sold in the United States in 1991, and every child who uses them goes through about 4,500 during infancy. Cotton diapers, by comparison, which have swaddled babies at least since Alexander ruled Macedonia, can be used hundreds of times—then recycled.

For years environmentalists fumed about the waste caused by disposables, arguing that each diaper tossed onto the rubbish heap furnished fresh evidence that Americans would rather plunder nature than spend the effort necessary to preserve it. "Let's deal with the big-ticket items before we ask millions of mothers to torture themselves," said William Rathje, an archeologist and director of the Garbage Project at the University of Arizona. "There are so many ways we are wasteful in this country that are not at the absolute core of modern American behavior. Let's start there. After all, convenience is something we should consider."

At first, the debate seemed one of stark contrasts: disposable diapers waste trees, often include plastics that can't be broken down, and account for a numbing amount of unnecessary garbage each year. Cloth diapers, on the other hand, which now account for less than 15 percent of the American market, seem environmentally benign. But closer scrutiny suggests the facts are less one-sided. Many of the trees used for disposables are planted just for that purpose. Excavations of representative landfills—including Fresh Kills on Staten Island, the world's largest dump—have revealed that discarded diapers take up from 0.5 to 1.8 percent of landfill space. Compared with old newspapers (which can account for as much as 40 percent of space at landfills), construction debris, or food waste, diapers are about as big a problem as used sheets and towels.

Reusable diapers have their problems, too. They can require large amounts of water and detergent to clean. Diaper-service delivery trucks burn gas-wasting energy and cause pollution. In some Western states, like California and Washington, where droughts have presented major problems in recent years and landfill space is relatively easy to find, disposable diapers seem to many people not only more convenient but better for the environment as well. "This is not a simple issue," said a senior official at the Environmental Protection Agency, who insisted on anonymity due to the "sensitive nature" of the debate. "There are environmental consequences, health considerations, and issues of lifestyle that all matter. And the right answer is not always the same for everyone. But it certainly is not something one should resolve based on ideology alone."

It takes only a few brief conversations with harried parents to appreciate the overwhelming freedom that disposable diapers can offer. Even the most aggressively "green" parents seem to have ways to rationalize their use of such an obvious symbol of the throwaway society. Stricken by fear, guilt, and conscience, some have even been caught hiding their Pampers when friends come to visit. "I hate to admit what a chicken I was," writes a confessional Patricia Poore, editor of the quintessentially environmentally correct publication, *Garbage* magazine. Ms. Poore came out of the closet as a user of disposables in 1992. "I let myself be bullied by image," she wrote, explaining her initial view that cloth diapers were the only permissible route for someone in her position. "How else to explain that the disposables bought for travel days were locked in the glove compartment or hidden in my luggage?" Yet, eventually, convenience had its way with her, as it has with millions of other parents. Disposable diapers are easy to find, easy to use, and easy to get rid of. They almost always cost more—about $0.25 each compared with as little as $0.07 each for cloth diapers washed at home—but the washing takes time that many people are not willing to spend.

Of course there are some die-hard devotees of cotton. Services that provide cotton diapers have scrambled to make their product competitive. Cotton diapers have come a long way since the days when their rigid edges and flat pins brought tears to the eyes of mothers and babies alike. "In the next year you are going to see a revolution in the diaper industry," said Anne Beaudry, an environmental consultant who frequently works for the National Association of Diaper Services. "You'll see the soft inner lining, the outer plastics, the snap closures, and plenty of Velcro. The only thing that will be different is that you can you use them again."

Ms. Beaudry concedes that disposable diaper fans have overwhelmed the cloth contingent, and that legislation to limit the use of disposables has become a waste of time. But she and others say that millions of dollars worth of advertising from companies like Procter & Gamble—which dominates the industry with Pampers and Luvs—has had far more to do with the shift than any fair discussion of environmental priorities. They also contend that ignoring the waste caused by disposable diapers because it represents "only" 1 percent of municipal refuse is foolish and shortsighted. "Because there is no overwhelming conclusion to draw from most of the studies that have been done on this issue, people think they can ignore it," said Richard Dennison, a senior scientist at the Environmental Defense Fund, which, like most similar organizations, takes no official position on whether disposable diapers are acceptable baby wear. "One percent of billions of tons is worth worrying about. And if we don't think about how to address that 1 percent, which 1 percent will we address?" Mr. Dennison argues that nobody can make proper assessments of waste by looking only at what fills garbage dumps—or in what quantity. "These are renewable resources that are used once. And we can do better than that, even with disposable diapers."

Many advocates for cotton diapers now say the only way to limit disposables is to begin charging more for all garbage. Led by Seattle, many cities are now doing just that—the more a family tosses out each week the bigger the bill they must pay for sanitation. If garbage costs increased sharply—and many economists argue they should—people might begin to take another look at the issue. Until that happens, however, the diaper wars appear to be over. "It's funny," said Judy Enck, a senior environmental associate at the New York Public Interest Research Group, who is a strong supporter of cloth diapers and proud of it. "I've seen backlashes before, but I never saw one this powerful." [MIS, OCTOBER 1992]

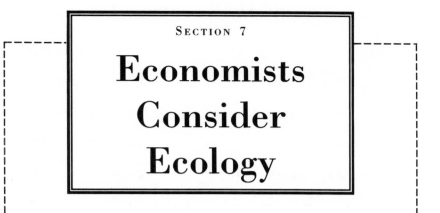

SECTION 7

Economists Consider Ecology

HARNESSING REGULATION TO MARKET FORCES

ENVIRONMENTAL REGULATIONS impose enormous costs on industries targeted for clean up, and economists have long been concerned by the inefficiency of the usual legislative approach that requires everyone to meet the same standard of cleanliness.

Plants that burn coal to generate electricity, for example, may differ widely in their ability to avoid emitting sulfur dioxide, a potent contributor to acid rain. Everyone would be better off if the plants that could curb sulfur dioxide most efficiently undertook most of the required cleanup, letting their less efficient brethren chug out more of the pollutant gas. But how could that be arranged?

Easy, said the economists who took an interest in environmental matters. Set an overall target for the amount of sulfur dioxide that all power plants may emit in a year; create emission permits to emit that amount of gas; and allot a quota of permits to individual plants. Then let the trading begin.

The cleverness of the system is that it gives plant operators a choice of either reducing sulfur dioxide emissions by more than they need and selling their surplus permits, or of reducing less and buying extra pollution permits. The more each plant pursues its own best course, the less will be the overall cost of controlling sulfur dioxide.

In a further refinement, some coal mines that produce high-sulfur coal have been buying up pollution permits and packaging them with their coal. That builds the cost of polluting right into the price of the coal.

A different scheme, even more imaginative, is the debt-for-nature swaps, which in essence reduce a country's foreign debt in exchange for an endowment to protect its tropical forests. The leverage built into these cunning financial instruments enables one dollar to buy many times its worth of forest protection in terms of the local currency.

Economists may not share the environmentalist view of the world in many respects, particularly in their general preference for free-market solutions over command regulation. But, as the articles in this section make evident, their very different perspective has much to contribute to the efficient solution of almost all environmental problems.

TRADING DEBT FOR RAIN FORESTS

COULD foreign debt be the lever that moves poor countries to save their rain forests? The Bush White House apparently thought so, and backed a bold program to channel billions of dollars that Latin American governments owe Washington into local conservation projects. "Debt-for-nature" swaps are not new. Private groups are already busy raising cash to buy up foreign debt, trading the IOU's back to the financially troubled debtors in return for commitments to acquire parks and conserve environmental resources in eight countries. What is new is the possible addition of vast quantities of government money to the pot—and the prospect of a systematic, well-financed defense of tropical forests, which serve as a natural sink for greenhouse gases and shelter the lion's share of the world's plant and animal species.

William Reilly, the Bush administration's chief administrator of the Environmental Protection Agency and the program's most influential champion, believes that a successful reshuffling of some $12 billion in foreign aid loans by the United States would mobilize $100 million a year for conservation projects. The approach could also serve as a model for European and Japanese governments, which carry another $38 billion in Latin American debt. No less important is that the plan requires the participation of local environmentalists, who have often been excluded from decision-making. John Sawhill, the head of the Nature Conservancy, an active promoter of debt-for-nature swaps, argues that the resulting public-private partnerships could tilt local interests in favor of environmental protection.

Thomas Lovejoy, an ecologist now at the Smithsonian Institution, dreamed up the idea of linking foreign debt relief to the financing of environmental projects in debtor nations in 1984. At the time, crushing foreign debts had led most poor countries to cut back on environmental protection. Why not wipe out part of the debts denominated in dollars and yen for commitments to spend cruzeiros and pesos on conservation? But it was private organizations, not governments or commercial banks, that turned theory into practice. In the very first swap in 1987, Conservation International, an American group, paid $100,000 for an uncollectible $650,000 that Bolivia owed to Citicorp. The group then agreed to wipe out Bolivia's $650,000 debt in return for its promise to protect a 3.7-million-acre buffer around the Beni Biosphere Reserve and to spend the equivalent of $250,000 in local currency to manage the reserve. Since then, fourteen other debt-for-nature swaps have been carried out, reducing external debts and protecting forests in Ecuador, Costa Rica, the Philippines, Madagascar, Zambia, the Dominican Republic, and Poland.

Clever financing arrangements, along with the enthusiastic cooperation of environmentally sensitive governments, have magnified the effects of the $16 million investment far beyond initial expectations. But as Mr. Sawhill of the Nature Conservancy points out, dependence on charitable donations has limited the overall impact on the global environment to "peanuts." That is why environmental groups, led by the World Wildlife Fund in Washington, worked hard to make a case for federal intervention. They struck pay dirt when Mr. Bush included debt-for-nature swaps in his "Enterprise for the Americas" initiative, a broad effort to pare debt, liberalize trade, and stimulate investment in Latin America and the Caribbean. In October 1990, Congress authorized swaps for some $1.7 billion in debts incurred in the sales of subsidized food. Bush asked that the swaps be extended to loans made by the United States Agency for International Development, as well as Export-Import Bank and Commodity Credit Corporation loans originally used to subsidize United States exports.

To be eligible, debtor countries have to pass muster on a number of criteria—what one environmental lobbyist calls the "flaming hoops." They must be actively working to make deals with their other big creditors, in particular the World Bank, the International Monetary Fund, and the commercial banks. And they must open their borders to foreign investors on reasonable terms. The carrot is substantial debt relief. The Bush administration targeted a 50 percent write-off. Payments forgiven by the United States Treasury would be converted to local currencies and deposited in a national environmental fund. The money could be used for anything from conservation training to restoration of the world's oceans and atmosphere. But outlays would be planned and supervised by boards that included private citizens nominated by the United States Government.

Many a slip is still possible. While environmental interests played a major role in passing the legislation, "different people in the administration have different priorities," Mr. Sawhill noted. Jamaica, Chile, Bolivia, and Costa Rica all reportedly have advocates in the administration, and will probably be the first to cut Enterprise for the Americas deals. But if the United States takes a hard line on debt arrears or foreign investment rules, environmentally critical countries like Brazil and Peru will not qualify anytime soon.

Another worry is the host nations' receptivity. Debt-for-nature swaps on a large scale will require countries to reorder economic priorities. Unless governments cut back on other spending when they agree to spend more on the environment, the arrangement will be inflationary. Outright rejection of swaps as an impingement on sovereignty, the position taken by Brazil's former president, José Sarney, is no longer fashionable in Latin America. Indeed, Latin American politicians seem more inclined to follow the lead of Costa Rica, which has touted debt-for-nature as a way to sustain jobs in tourism and develop agricultural techniques that will allow sustainable development.

It is still not clear, though, whether elected officials will buy the idea of independent boards, which could compete with established interests. "Will they really allow anybody outside the government to have guaranteed funding?" asked Lamond Godwin, a vice president at the American Express Bank who has served as an adviser on a number of private debt swaps. Perhaps the most serious obstacle to swaps is the issue of how they will be treated in the federal budget. The Bush administration expected to arrange deals that maintain the level of payments to Washington that would otherwise be expected. Debtor countries would come out ahead, since they would no longer need to reschedule unpaid debts each year and would be able to liquidate their debts in a reasonable time frame. But since there would be no real loss of income to Washington, the administration contended that there ought to be no effect on budget accounting.

If, for example, a country is now paying $1 million in principal plus $4 million in interest each year on an $80 million debt, it would go on writing annual checks to the United States Treasury for $5 million. But all the $5 million would be declared repayment of principal, allowing a far faster liquidation of the debt balance. The $4 million annual interest, converted to local currency, would go into the national environment fund. This socially redeeming sleight of hand does not, however, sit well with the professionals who keep the books for Congress. Some want the Treasury to treat debt reduction the way a private creditor would write off a bad loan, taking a loss in the year the deal is signed. Congress would be obliged to appropriate funds to cover the paper loss, adding to the budget deficit.

That is not a problem in principle: if debt-for-nature swaps are worth doing, the logic goes, they are worth paying for. But as a practical matter it would probably torpedo large-scale swaps. "If there is a single budget item less popular than foreign assistance," said one senior Bush administration official, "I'm not aware of it." Environmental groups are nonetheless optimistic. Many of their leaders believe the administration is committed to their cause and is eager to offset any image as a proscrastinator on the problem of global warming. Moreover, there is no serious opposition to debt-for-nature swaps in Congress, and there probably will not be unless the plan runs afoul of the budget process. Once off the ground, they believe, the initiatives will be imitated in Europe and Japan. Debt-for-nature provisions could also be routinely integrated into the rescheduling of hundreds of billions of dollars in debts owed to the World Bank and the International Monetary Fund. If the optimists are right, the only practical limit on their scale will be good ideas for making conservation compatible with economic development.   [PP, JANUARY 1991]

THE MARKET IN POLLUTION PERMITS

EVER searching for new ways to make markets and money, commodity exchanges have broadened their horizons from familiar products like soybeans and wheat to concepts, like Eurodollar futures contracts, that only a business school graduate could love. Now the nation's largest commodity mart has gone a step further, approving trading in government permits to pollute. The Chicago Board of Trade voted in July 1991 to create a private market for rights to emit sulfur dioxide. The rights are to be issued to electric utilities by the Environmental Protection Agency (EPA) as part of Washington's strategy to reduce acid rain. Besides providing a service to the electric power industry, such a market would allow trading by individuals, letting them stake investment money on a rise or fall in the value of pollution rights, much as they now speculate on stocks and bonds.

Such a market was made possible by the Clean Air Act of 1990. In a departure from traditional regulatory practices, Congress gave polluters the right to meet sulfur emissions standards by buying and selling allowances that the Environmental Protection Agency will allot to individual plants. Although federal officials are unwilling to comment on the Board of Trade initiative before they examine the details, there is every reason to be optimistic.

Free-market proponents say they think the new market will make it cheaper and easier for utilities to do their part in reducing acid rain. "We are anxious to establish a bona fide private market," said William G. Rosenberg, an assistant administrator at the EPA. Initially, no government approval is required for the trading.

Many environmental analysts say, moreover, that the new market could serve as a model for least-cost controls on other pollutants—notably the smog-producing chemicals that bedevil most American cities. And it could presage a far more ambitious effort to limit emissions of gases that are widely thought to be warming the earth's atmosphere. The Clean Air Act limits total emissions of sulfur dioxide gas from 110 power plants in 1995. Five years later, a much more stringent limit will force the industry to reduce emissions to less than half of the 1991 level. Dan Dudek, an economist at the Environmental Defense Fund who helped to draft the rules, argues that by allowing polluters to trade their emissions allowances, individual utilities in different markets with different types of power plants will not be locked into a single cleanup strategy.

One company may find that it pays to install smokestack scrubbers on aging coal-fired boilers, bringing its emissions below the requirements, and then sell the surplus allowances. Another may leave untouched a heavy sulfur polluter that is otherwise efficient and will buy allowances to cover the excess emissions. Still another may subsidize customers' purchases of energy-efficient appliances and lighting equipment, thereby cutting electricity demand and permitting it to shut down its offending boilers. But Richard Sandor, an executive managing director of Kidder, Peabody & Co., Incorporated, notes that the freedom to buy and sell allowances will not yield the maximum possible benefits unless utilities have an easy way to exchange them at a price that reflects the lowest possible cost of removing sulfur from the air.

That is where the Chicago Board of Trade's initiative fits in. Under the plan, the exchange would begin trading "cash forward" contracts in 1993—simple agreements to deliver allowances after they are issued in 1995. It will also ask the Commodity Futures Trading Commission for permission to establish a continuing "futures" market, permitting anyone to gamble on emissions rights in standardized twenty-five-ton allotments up to three years in advance.

A utility might, for example, buy 100 contracts due in 1997, thereby nailing down the right to spew an extra 2,500 tons of sulfur dioxide that year. The seller might be another utility that is planning to close down an old coal plant in 1997. Or it might be a mutual fund run by a brokerage house, whose manager thinks the price of allowances will fall, and is prepared to risk clients' money on the bet. Mr. Sandor estimates that contracts will initially trade at about $400 a ton and will fluctuate with factors ranging from the demand for electricity to the state of scrubber technology. The price could not rise above $2,000 because utilities always have the option of exceeding their legal emissions and paying a fine of $2,000 a ton.

Not everyone is convinced that the plan will work smoothly. John Palmisano, the president of Aer-X, a Washington firm that is a pioneer in the private trading of local pollution allowances for smog-creating chemicals, says he thinks the market will be hard to establish. Most of the exchanges in sulfur allowances, he suspects, will be made directly between utilities, in large blocks. He worries, moreover, that some state regulators will balk at allowing utilities to participate in a national market for pollution rights.

The volume of trading may be light by the standards of the Board of Trade, acknowledges Mr. Sandor, who drafted the proposal along with Philip Senechal, chief executive of the Bellefonte Lime Corporation in Bellefonte, Pennsylvania. On a typical day, futures representing 200,000 bushels of corn and 150,000 bushels of soybeans are traded on the exchange. But computerized trading could be used to match buyers and sellers at low cost. And in any case, notes Jim Thompson, the former governor of Illinois, who, along with Mr. Sandor, served as cochairman of the exchange committee analyzing emissions allowances, noted that "the Board of Trade has social benefits as well as members' profits in mind." Those benefits could spill into market-based approaches to environmental regulation that are just now reaching the public agenda. Southern California regulators are pondering the wisdom of creating a computerized market for business permits to emit volatile organic chemicals. Dozens of other cities, hard-pressed to meet federal air quality standards, will also be seeking the least intrusive ways to regulate emissions of these smog-producing gases.

Mr. Sandor said the Board of Trade's venture might prove invaluable both in designing these local markets for emissions permits and gaining legitimacy for the concept with local regulators. It would also give them a head start in producing computer software for operating such markets cheaply and fairly. The experience could pay even greater dividends, should Washington decide to limit emissions of greenhouse gases as part of a global commitment to slow atmospheric warming. The principal greenhouse gases—carbon dioxide, methane, and refrigeration chemicals—are emitted in large quantities by thousands of businesses. The possible means of mitigating their effects—everything from energy conservation to planting trees that trap carbon—are many and varied. Mr. Dudek of the Environmental Defense Fund says that strategies for controlling greenhouse gases that try to second-guess private efforts are bound to be wasteful. His group is now pressing for legislation to limit utilities' emissions of carbon dioxide—which could become more fodder for the Board of Trade.

[PP, JULY 1991]

TRADING THE RIGHT TO FOUL THE AIR

Two utilities hundreds of miles apart announced on May 12, 1992, that they had signed a contract that calls for one to buy from the other the right to emit a chemical that causes acid rain, freeing the dirtier one from having to clean up its own plants as stringently. In the first such deal to be publicly disclosed, the Tennessee Valley Authority (TVA) bought the right to emit 10,000 tons of sulfur dioxide, the main cause of acid rain, from Wisconsin Power and Light. The Wisconsin company will reduce its emissions to a level 10,000 tons below what federal law requires, and the TVA will gain additional time to install smokestack scrubbers or replace high-sulfur coal with cleaner fuels. The price was not disclosed but is believed to be around $2.5 million to $3 million. The deal was made under a system established in the Clean Air Act of 1990 and will be regulated by the Environmental Protection Agency. Acid rain, which is believed to be responsible for damage to lakes and perhaps to forests, is a principal target of the Clean Air Act. Other targets include smog and toxic chemical emissions.

Economists and some environmentalists have long called for a "market-based" system that encourages deals like the one between the TVA and the Wisconsin utility. They say such a system reduces the cost to the economy of cutting sulfur emissions, compared with a "command and control" system of ordering each utility to comply. The goal of the Clean Air Act is to reduce such emissions nationally by 10 million tons a year; the TVA is buying "emission allowances" because it believes that at least in the short run the purchase price is less than what it would cost to clean up its own plants enough to be in compliance with the act. For its part, Wisconsin Power can turn a profit by "overcomplying" with the federal law and selling the allowances.

The idea of trading emission allowances has generally won praise as creating a "win-win" deal, in which costs are minimized and everyone benefits. Some authorities estimate a savings of 20 percent compared with making each utility comply. Such deals create the possibility that sulfur dioxide emissions will fall more in some locations than in others. In most cases, a local group that opposed plans by a utility to buy emission allowances rather than cut emissions could presumably contest the decision before state regulators, but in this case opponents, if they emerge, would appear to have few options because the TVA is not subject to such state regulation. But the 10,000 tons represents only a small fraction of the reduction required at the TVA, and the authority anticipates meeting the rest of it internally. In fact, experts say that most utilities that buy allowances will meet only a portion of their needs that way.

Utilities have thus far been slow to strike such deals. Since the first phase of the law takes effect in 1995 and scrubbers usually take three years to build, some appear to have decided to forgo the market.

But this deal could lead the way for others, said John S. Palmisano, president of Aer-X in Washington, a subsidiary of Electronic Data Systems, which is seeking to broker similar arrangements. "It's like going to a church dance, with the boys on one side and the girls on another," he said. "Sooner or later, somebody's going to walk into the middle." This deal will form a benchmark, he said, with other potential buyers and sellers wanting to peg their prices against this one.

John B. Henry 2d, the president of Clean Air Capital Markets, a small Washington-based investment banking firm that arranged the contract, said it was important because it was the first and because the price was low. "It sends a clear signal to the industry that allowances can be purchased below the cost of most scrubbers," he said. Mr. Henry said scrubbers would become financially attractive on a wide basis if the cost of allowances rose to $300 to $350 a ton.

In addition, Mr. Henry said, buying allowances could be easier for utilities than relying on cleaner fuels that would have to be shipped from far away. A utility that bought allowances, he said, would often, in effect, be buying the benefit of the seller's having switched to cleaner fuels available locally.

But for the moment, the terms of this contract, which was signed on May 1, 1992, are not clear. Mr. Henry refused to discuss its terms, and neither would top officials of the two utilities. But William F. Malec, the senior vice president and chief financial officer of the TVA, said that a May 1992 report in *The Wall Street Journal* that first disclosed the deal said the price of $250 to $300 a ton was "in the ballpark." Such a price would be on the low end of what experts had expected. But Mr. Malec and Erroll B. Davis, Jr., the chief executive of Wisconsin Power, pointedly refused to say when the money would be paid— now, in 1995, or later. If it is not paid now, the cost of money would have to be figured in, and the value could be less.

When the Clean Air Act was signed by President Bush, some had estimated that a single allowance, or the right to emit one ton of sulfur dioxide, would be worth about $1,000 on the open market, but with improving technology for lowering such emissions, along with other factors, recent estimates have been lower. If the cost of removing a ton of sulfur dioxide from the air is in fact lower than expected, that is good news for electricity users because it means the total cost of compliance with the Clean Air Act will be lower. But it may be bad news for companies that invested heavily in expensive pollution-control hardware, expecting to recoup the cost through sales of allowances.

The limits are set in terms of pounds of sulfur dioxide per unit of heat produced in utility boilers, keying them, in effect, to electricity production. The limit is set at one level from 1995 to 1999, and a stricter level beginning in 2000. In addition, new plants will have a limit of zero, meaning that for each ton of sulfur dioxide they produce, they must buy an allowance from the owner of an older plant who is willing, for a price, to clean up.

In the case of the deal to be announced, Mr. Davis said, "these prices are going to come out eventually, as we go into regulatory proceedings." But his company does not want to divulge the number now, he said, because "we're hoping that the market is a bit more robust" and prices of allowances will rise. Establishing the market price is important, according to another expert, Robert D. Conley, the president of Pure Air Inc. of Allentown, Pennsylvania, because utilities that are considering buying pollution allowances are weighing that option against installing pollution-control hardware or switching to lower-sulfur fuel, or both. Likewise, a company that is considering making the investment to "overcomply" wants to know what the allowances would sell for. If this deal and others that will presumably follow do not establish a price, then the industry will probably have to wait for an auction of extra allowances that the Environmental Protection Agency is planning to hold. Mr. Conley said that the TVA-Wisconsin deal was probably small by the standards of those that will follow. Utilities typically need tens of thousands of tons of allowances, or more than 100,000, each year, he said.

The Clean Air Act is meant to cut acid emissions roughly in half, but the trading system also has the potential to shift the emissions geographically, if buyers are concentrated in one region and sellers in another. Mr. Henry, the investment banker, described the establishment of the trading system as "like a magic legal wand was waved, and all utilities in the country became one utility for purposes of acid rain control." Most environmentalists consider acid rain a national problem, not a regional one, unlike smog, for example, which is more local in nature. The emissions trading system was passed largely at the impetus of the Environmental Defense Fund, a nonprofit environmental group.

Acid created in power plants can be deposited hundreds of miles from the source by rain or snow. Some state regulators, however, have proposed limiting allowance trading to within their borders, instead of allowing utilities in their jurisdictions to clean up their stacks and sell the allowances to utilities upwind, with the resulting pollution coming back to the original state. But experts yesterday said no state had yet instituted such restrictions.

Mr. Malec and others involved in the deal said it should not be construed as the sale of the right to pollute. He stressed that the sum of emissions by the TVA and by Wisconsin Power and Light would be equal to the total permitted by the new law. The 10,000 allowances, a small fraction of the reduction the TVA will need, will give the authority some breathing room in case modifications to boilers or fuel switching arrangements are delayed, he said. It is also a small fraction of the allowances that Wisconsin has available to sell. Under a state law, it has been held to stricter standards than those set by Washington, and passage of the act turned that "overcompliance" into a salable asset.

Generally, however, sellers have been held back in part because state regulators have not ruled on the question of who benefits from the proceeds, the stockholders or the electric customers. Thus utilities have been reluctant to take the risk of investing in scrubbers or other equipment to create "overcompliance" because their shareholders might not benefit, and if the sale of the allowances does not recoup the costs, their shareholders might actually suffer. Wisconsin regulators have not decided how the sale proceeds will be treated.

[MLW, MAY 1992]

PROTECTING NATURE WITH TAXES, NOT LAWS

COULD the exploding cost of environmental protection, widely seen as part of America's productivity problem, become part of the solution? A new generation of environmental researchers, as comfortable with the theories of Adam Smith as they are with those of Darwin or Mendel, thinks taxes that penalize polluters could make the economy fitter and leaner, even as it makes the environment cleaner. Their case is outlined in a report from the World Resources Institute, by no coincidence released in November 1992 to gain maximum attention from the nascent Clinton administration.

The institute could hardly have picked a more propitious moment to advance "green taxes" as the cure to ailments ranging from global warming to traffic congestion to the scarcity of places to dump garbage. President Clinton is likely to be attracted by environmental strategies that minimize the cost to consumers while yielding tens of billions of dollars in revenue. So, too, are recession-battered state and local governments, which are under the gun to sustain services and improve the quality of life without raising income, property, or sales taxes. Even conservatives, who worry that more government revenue will mean more government, soften at the prospect. After all, notes William Niskanen, the head of the Cato Institute, a free-market research organization in Washington, "it's better to tax 'bads' than to tax goods."

The idea of green taxes has been kicking around university seminars since it was proposed in the 1920s by the English economist Arthur Pigou. He warned that prices determined by competitive markets would not reflect the full cost of making goods if some of those costs were not borne by producers. If, for example, smoke from a steel mill fouled the paint on nearby houses, steel would sell at a price below the true cost to society. Pigou argued that the problem could be remedied by imposing a tax equal to this "externality." Once polluters were charged for their mess, they would have incentives to raise prices and reduce production or shift to less polluting technologies. Either way, producers (and thus consumers) would pay the full cost to society.

What works on a blackboard, however, may not work as well in practice. Externalities are often hard to measure (how much damage did that car horn cause by waking the baby in Apartment 2C?). And they can be even harder to assess (just jot down the license plate number and have the city mail out a bill . . .). That explains, in part, why the political impulse is to regulate away externalities rather than to ask offenders to internalize the cost—and why horn blowing is usually illegal in cities, except in emergencies.

More important, pollution is rarely viewed as simply a sin that can be erased by the payment of the secular equivalent of an indulgence. If it is bad enough to worry about, the reasoning goes, it can hardly be made socially acceptable by offsetting it with fees. Indeed, hardly anything makes traditional environmentalists madder than the idea that businesses should be allowed to pay to pollute. It should not be surprising, then, that America's sweeping environmental laws governing air, water, solid waste, and wildlife preservation leave little room for market-based environmentalism. Standards are generally set according to what is deemed safe, aesthetic, and technologically feasible. And they are enforced with civil and criminal sanctions intended to deter, not to offer the polluter a chance to pay and play.

Why, then, the born-again enthusiasm for environmental regulation that puts a price tag on pollution? One reason, argues Paul Portney, an economist at Resources for the Future, a Washington research group, is that scientists are growing more sophisticated about the implicit trade-offs between cost and risk in modern life. It is surely worth a few thousand dollars to save a child from lead poisoning or to prevent a case of lung cancer from radon gas. But just as it doesn't pay to reduce highway deaths by lowering the speed limit to twenty-five miles per hour, it may not be worth billions of dollars to prevent every possible death from, say, airborne toxic chemicals.

Another reason, suggests Robert Hahn of the American Enterprise Institute in Washington, D.C., is that the enormous costs of "command and control" environmental regulation are beginning to hit home. A study published in the March 1992 issue of *Environment Magazine* estimated the current cost at $120 billion a year. And by almost everyone's reckoning, the number is bound to grow far more rapidly than the economy for decades to come.

The Clean Air Act of 1990 mandates the outlay of billions of dollars annually to curb acid rain, brighten urban skies, and wipe out emissions of toxic industrial gases. Tens of billions have already been spent on the cleanup of toxic waste, and the process has hardly begun. Note, too, that Clinton pledged to roll back carbon emissions to 1990 levels by the year 2000—a promise that may force spectacularly expensive shifts in industrial technology and in the mix of fuels consumed.

Although environmental goals may eventually be scaled back to meet cost concerns, there will surely also be pressure on government to get more bang for an environmental buck. And that is where Robert Repetto, the chief economist of the World Resources Institute, thinks green taxes fit in. Take the big enchilada of environmental challenges: the limitation of carbon emissions to slow or stop global warming. Environmental strategy-as-usual would require a bureaucratic redesign of energy use, dictating which fossil fuels could be burned in what industrial processes, subsidizing nonfossil energy sources like windmills, and setting efficiency standards for everything from cars to power plants. The environmental economists' alternative is to charge fees that discourage carbon emissions, raising the prices of fuels according to their carbon content. This is obviously easier in administrative terms: the taxes could be collected from producers and importers. And however tough the goal, the carbon tax route is likely to be less of a drag on the economy because carbon emitters themselves are in the best position to calculate the least-cost fix.

Or consider what Mr. Niskanen of the Cato Institute calls the "biggest externality of modern life," traffic congestion. America (and the rest of the world, save Singapore) rations scarce space on roads at rush hour the way the Soviet Union used to ration sausage: with lines. The World Resources Institute report notes that the technology now exists for charging vehicles according to their location and to the time of day. And it cites estimates that by the year 1999, fees ranging from $0.01 to $0.36 a mile could induce enough drivers to stay off the road at rush hour to save some $21 billion annually in time, fuel, and accidents.

Not everyone, though, is convinced that green taxes are unalloyed virtue. Lynn Scarlett, director of research for the libertarian Reason Foundation in Los Angeles, argues that they could prove to be "a fast train in the wrong direction"—a seductively efficient means for achieving goals that may not be worth achieving. That argument hardly applies to traffic congestion, where the waste in time and fuel is obvious. But it certainly raises questions on global warming, where scientists are still arguing about the likely consequences of carbon emissions.

Those who are sure they know which direction the train should be heading still worry about how far it should go: a green tax, after all, is no better than the estimate of the "externality" it is meant to offset. And all too often, says Dale Jorgensen, an economist at Harvard, "the practical problems of estimation are enormous." Once again, global warming illustrates the problem. William Nordhaus, the Yale economist whose article in the November 20, 1992, issue of *Science* is probably the most sophisticated integration of the climatology and economics of global warming ever attempted, estimates that the optimal carbon tax would start at about $5 a ton and gradually rise to $20. But he also estimates that the tax required to meet Mr. Clinton's campaign promise would exceed $200 a ton by the middle of the next century, with a cumulative cost of $5 trillion in lost economic output.

Another concern is who pays. James Poterba, an economist at the Massachusetts Institute of Technology, found that a carbon tax is likely to take a relatively bigger bite out of the living standards of the poor. By the same token, taxes on traffic or household garbage or pollutants from auto exhausts could also prove regressive. But Mr. Repetto counters that a disproportionate share of the benefits of a cleaner environment are likely to go to those smaller incomes. "Only poor people," he points out, "live near landfills and busy highways." And in any case, revenues could be recycled in ways that offset the maldistribution.

Whereas there may be some muddle over the incidence or appropriate magnitude of green taxes, it is no mystery why politicians are attracted to them. Like any other taxes, green taxes would meet certain resistance from groups and regions most adversely affected. Lester Lave, an economist at Carnegie Mellon University in Pittsburgh, notes that a carbon tax would add roughly $0.04 to the price of coal for every penny it added to the price of oil or natural gas. And judging from past donnybrooks over curbing sulfur emissions from coal-fired power plants, the coal lobby in Congress would not go gentle into that dark night.

But unlike most taxes, green taxes can be sold as user fees that advance environmental goals that would otherwise have to be met with direct regulation—regulation that could prove far more costly to consumers. Commuters might initially be furious about paying an extra five dollars to get to work. But their anger might quickly dissipate if the commuting time were cut in half, or if the congestion fees were presented as the alternative to mandatory car-pooling. What's more, green taxes could prove to be terrific cash cows. The World Resources Institute estimates that congestion fees set at efficient levels could have generated a whopping $98 billion for states and localities in 1989. A relatively modest $30-a-ton national carbon tax (about $0.10 per gallon of gasoline) would bring home $35 billion.

How one views this potential flood of revenue depends on what one expects would be done with the dollars. The World Resources Institute sees green taxes as substitutes for income taxes that undermine incentives to work and save, and they could thus increase measured output as well as cleanse the environment. That also seems to be the thrust of Mr. Clinton's thinking: his campaign pamphlet on the economy called for "revenue-neutral market incentives" to "penalize polluters and energy wasters."

But Mr. Hahn, a former adviser to President Bush on environmental economics, worries that it could presage an unwanted growth in government. When he left the White House, he left behind a memo on the revenue potential of green taxes—a memo he titled "Pandora's Box." [PP, NOVEMBER 1992]

ECONOMISTS START TO FRET AGAIN ABOUT POPULATION

J UST when you thought it was safe to procreate, the population bomb is back. Two decades ago, mainstream economists brushed aside the vision of a future chronically short of food and fuel. Now some are having second thoughts, prompted by new concerns about possible global warming and other strains imposed by population and economic growth on the planet's ecology. Most economists remain confident that the conventional analysis of the population problem is substantially correct: a steady flow of new technology that uses resources ever more efficiently will offset any scarcity of minerals and arable land, at the very least dampening the tendency for commodity prices to rise.

But few ever bought into the more-the-merrier approach to population growth that became fashionable during the Reagan years. And a general unease with the academics' defense of laissez-faire population policies is now coalescing around new fears that the environment will not easily support a larger population at a decent living standard. "Simply allowing every Chinese family to have a refrigerator and a television will swamp painful efforts in the West to limit global warming," argues Paul Portney, a researcher at Resources for the Future, a nonprofit research organization in Washington.

The gloom-and-doom school of population theory, founded two centuries ago by the Reverend Thomas Malthus, held that continuing population growth virtually guaranteed falling living standards as more mouths tried to feed off increasingly marginal land. Economists came to understand that Malthus had underestimated the capacity of technology to enhance productivity. But biologists and others were not so well persuaded. The Malthusian dilemma reached a high-water mark of popular acceptance in the early 1970s. Paul Ehrlich, a Stanford University biologist who wrote *The Population Bomb,* raised the prospect of mass starvation by the end of the century as too many people tried to subsist on too little land. "The Limits to Growth," a 1973 report from the Club of Rome, a group of business leaders and academics, forecast a more general hard landing as the world ran out of resources. But neither history nor contemporary events confirmed the neo-Malthusians' predictions. Scarcity of resources has always been overcome in the past by the discovery of ways to wring more output from a declining resource base. Coal, for example, was substituted for charcoal in iron smelting when nineteenth-century industrialists ran out of accessible forest. And as both the "green revolution" in agriculture and the broader decline in commodity prices in the 1970s suggested, technology was having no trouble staying ahead. Even the exception—the massive runup in energy prices after the Arab oil embargo in 1974—seemed to prove the technological optimists' rule. The energy shock stimulated a combination of new oil production and energy-saving investment that drove the real cost of fuel back to precrisis levels by the mid-1980s.

This is not to say that the critics of the unreconstructed Malthusian view were entirely sanguine about population growth. The dominant view of the relationship between population and economic welfare remained as simple as it is intuitive: more people meant less land and less capital per person, which in turn meant lower living standards than would otherwise be possible. And as David Bloom, a Columbia University economist, points out, population-driven poverty can be self-perpetuating. The more mouths to feed, the less families can set aside for savings; the more babies in need of education and medical care, the lower the proportion of savings available for productivity-enhancing investment.

But this drag-on-productivity model was forcefully challenged in the 1980s by Julian Simon, an economist at the University of Maryland. Drawing on the ideas of economists like Simon Kuznets and Esther Boserup, he noted that population growth could also stimulate productivity. More people, he speculated, would mean more heads to invent good ideas for improving technology. Similarly, higher population density would allow scale efficiencies in production. More intensive farming, for example, would make it economical to extend roads and rail to rural areas. And a large population of consumers would generate a natural internal market for mass-produced industrial goods. "Does anyone seriously doubt," Mr. Simon asks, "that Europe is more prosperous with a population of hundreds of millions than it would be with a population of hundreds of thousands?"

Mr. Simon's revisionism had no difficulty drawing converts. Many economists, notes Dan Dudek at the Environmental Defense Fund, were attracted by its libertarian implications: if population growth did not interfere with development, there would be no need to interfere with the procreative choices of consenting adults. And while it stopped short of endorsement, a prestigous panel of experts assembled in 1986 by the National Academy of Sciences gave population revisionism a respectful review.

Traditional conservatives also liked the idea. If population growth is not a social ill, governments need not spend money in support of family planning or abortion—and there would certainly be no rationale for Chinese-style coercion. At the 1984 World Population Conference in Mexico City the Reagan Administration broke ranks with other affluent countries, abandoning Washington's long-held position that economic development would hardly be possible in the third world unless population growth was contained. The revisionist message also meshed neatly with the cause of more open immigration policies: if more people would not retard prosperity in Africa or Asia, it certainly would not harm the American economy. Even the political left liked what it heard. Marxists have never had much truck with population worries; Friedrich Engels explicitly dismissed the Malthusian dilemma as an artifact of capitalism.

The worm is now turning. David Bloom, writing with Richard Freeman, a Harvard economist, found no statistical relationship between population growth and changes in output per person—a conclusion that would not surprise Julian Simon. But Mr. Bloom believes that generalizations from past experience are dangerous. He noted, for example, that Kenya managed to achieve a reasonable 2 percent annual improvement in living standards during the last quarter century even while it was experiencing the highest rate of population growth (4 percent) in sub-Saharan Africa. But that happy coincidence was probably only possible, Mr. Bloom argued, because the country had plenty of good land on which to extend agriculture. Future population growth, he suggested, will be far more problematic.

Kenya's predicament may apply elsewhere, and with a vengeance. In the last twenty years, Mr. Bloom points out, some 1.3 billion people have been added to the third world—more than the entire population of the developed countries.

By the same token, Mr. Bloom rejects Julian Simon's broad-brush claims for economies of scale in poor countries. There may be circumstances in which high population density makes it easier to develop local markets for industry or to support an efficient transportation system. "But wouldn't Bangladesh be better off with 5 million fewer people?" he asks. "The answer is certainly yes."

Once population has raced past some reasonable level of density in poor countries, rapid population growth is surely a drag on living standards. That is music to the ears of George Zeidenstein, the head of the Population Council in New York, who is frustrated that less than 1 percent of all development aid now goes to family planning. Even as American intellectuals backed away from population control, he notes, poor countries have been pushed toward it by the accumulating weight of health and education obligations. "They have been convinced," Mr. Zeidenstein said, "by their own realities."

But the decisive tilt in the intellectual debate is coming from a newer source: fear of global ecological instability. Emissions of so-called greenhouse-effect gases—primarily carbon dioxide, methane, and refrigeration chemicals—are widely believed to be warming the earth's atmosphere. Computer models project that higher temperatures would raise ocean levels and flood low-lying areas. Weather patterns would also be likely to change, disrupting agriculture and creating new deserts. Though rapid population growth, notes Daniel Hamermesh, an economist at Michigan State, may bear little relation to the pace of global warming. Greenhouse emissions are more closely related to the level of economic activity than the numbers of emitters. Thus the average American generates nineteen times as much carbon dioxide as the average Indian. And it is entirely possible that, say, an economically vibrant Brazil with slow population growth would burn down its tropical forests more rapidly than an impoverished Brazil with rapid population growth.

The problem of preventing atmospheric warming without consigning a substantial fraction of the world to permanent poverty is daunting enough, but it could be immensely complicated by excessive population growth. By United Nations estimates, the population of poor countries will rise by almost 3 billion in the next thirty years.

Even if carbon dioxide emissions from third world economies can be held to the current per capita rate—an unlikely prospect if they are to become more prosperous—global emissions would rise by 30 percent. Julian Simon is not perturbed by such arithmetic. People used to worry about running out of copper, he notes; now they worry about running out of atmospheric resources. It is already technically possible to beat the greenhouse effect with a mix of conservation and power generation from nonfossil fuels like solar and nuclear energy, he says. The real question, then, is how costly the fix will be. And if history is any indicator, he asserts, it will be far cheaper than now expected.

Many economists, however, are no longer prepared to put all their chips on the assumption that technology will again come to the rescue, offsetting the effects of the projected doubling of world population in the next century. "In the absence of certainty," argues David Bloom, "the responsible position is to act conservatively." Hardly anyone is laughing at Malthus anymore.   [PP, DECEMBER 1990]

ECONOMISTS' IDEAS ABOUT ECOLOGY

C OULD biologists, ecologists, and other natural scientists have more to say about the economics of the environment than economists themselves? Researchers calling themselves ecological economists are challenging traditional economics on its own turf, accusing economists of mismeasuring development, underestimating the intangible costs of pollution, and ignoring society's responsibilities to future generations.

Although many economists dismiss the ideas of their fellow scientists and critics as both unoriginal and loosely reasoned, these notions are finding a respectful audience in bastions of the establishment, particularly those that deal with the third world. The rebels' ideas have special application for countries that depend heavily on their natural resources. The United States Agency for International Development and the conservative Pew Charitable Trusts underwrote a conference on ecological economics in May 1990 at the World Bank, which drew some 370 participants. And the Jessie Noyes Foundation in New York is supporting one of the ecological economists' favorite projects, an effort by the United Nations to incorporate environmental factors in the basic accounts used to measure national output.

If the rebels succeed in the goal set by Robert Costanza, a biologist at the University of Maryland and a founder of the recently formed International Society of Ecological Economists, they will persuade governments to give the "sustainability" of natural "life support systems" priority over conventionally measured economic growth. That could mean radical changes in policy, sharply reducing efforts to improve living standards through investments in land-intensive agriculture and resource extraction. But succeed or fail, they will almost certainly force economists to acknowledge that traditional analysis tends to undervalue environmental resources. They may also kindle public debate on some very uncomfortable questions, from the need for population control to the compensation owed by the present generation to those who will inherit radioactive reactor wastes in the year 3000.

Economic science long ago filed "environment" under N for natural resources. Breathable air, mountain scenery, and edible marine life were categorized as inputs of production or goods for consumption, like machine tools or wheat or copper ore. The right decision on how much to use, explains Allen Kneese, an economist at Resources for the Future in Washington, depends on the "opportunity cost," what society would lose later by consuming the resource now. Sophisticated resource economists—among them, Mr. Kneese—are sensitive to the practical limitations of the framework. Markets alone cannot be depended upon to weigh, say, the cost of damaging a marsh that serves as a breeding ground for birds. But "conceptually, such values are not hard to incorporate," says Robert Repetto, an economist at the World Resources Institute in Washington. A determined economist could tote up the losses associated with filling in the wetland and compare them to the benefits of the shopping mall that would replace it. All too often, though, argues Dan Dudek, an economist at the Environmental Defense Fund in New York, "economists tend to ignore such intangible benefits, effectively setting their value at zero."

Another limitation is the economists' dependence on "discount rates" to account for the dimension of time in measurements of value. Discounting works fine for showing, say, that a ton of steel delivered today is worth more than the same ton delivered a year from now; the difference is an extra year's worth of use from the products made from the steel. When economies are working efficiently, the discount rate is equal to the interest rate; a year's delay in receiving that ton of steel would make it worth about 8 percent less. But the choice of discount rates becomes increasingly problematic in the long time frame of environmental resources. A town council might decide it is worth sacrificing a grove of 300-year-old spruce to save $100,000 on road construction. But what of future town residents, whose pleasure in seeing very large, very old trees will not be considered? Mr. Repetto notes that decisions affecting many generations can be even stickier. Carbon dioxide emissions may eventually force people to live indoors, protected from perpetual desert summer by air-conditioning. But what point would there be, asks Mr. Repetto, in discounting the loss of free access to the outdoors to future generations who have never known, and thus may never miss, the pleasure.

Mr. Repetto and his colleagues at the World Resources Institute have been widely applauded for an attempt to correct a common distortion introduced by conventional economics practices: the failure to include natural resource depletion in national income accounts. When economists measure a nation's net output, they subtract capital depreciation, the loss of machines, vehicles, and buildings in the ongoing production process. But they rarely account for gains or losses of less tangible forms of capital, like human skills. Equally important, they neglect changes in reserves of natural resources, which are typically large (and negative) in poor countries.

The Repetto team used the example of Indonesia to show how important this omission can be in gauging national development. Losses from soil erosion due to deforestation, they calculated, reduce the net value of crop production by about 40 percent, actually exceeding the value of timber harvests. Moreover, from 1980 to 1984 depletion of oil fields reduced the value of Indonesia's reserves base by about $10 billion annually, roughly 15 percent of national income. In industrialized countries, where total output is much larger relative to natural resource depletion, similar extensions of conventional accounting methods have been used to calculate the impact of environmental degradation. Japan, Germany, and France all have ambitious projects under way. And the United Nations Statistical Office is working on a general framework for environment and natural resource accounting.

But ecological economists are not ready to permit researchers like Mr. Repetto, who accept the basic tenets of modern economic theory, to be the profession's toughest critics. What economics needs, they argue, is a whole new framework, one that fits economic production into ecological systems, rather than the other way around. To Herman Daly at the World Bank, David Pearce at the University of London, and Paul Ehrlich at Stanford University, the key goal is the achievement of "sustainability"—adjusting economic activity so it does not damage the natural systems that underpin all functioning economies. Too many economists, they argue, simply assume that the biosphere can roll with any economic punch and bounce back for more.

But sustainability is proving hard to define and even harder to measure. One approach, now popular among ecological economists, is to calculate energy balances on the assumption that energy supplies represent the ultimate constraint on human activity. Mr. Costanza, for example, measures the amount of energy absorbed by swampland in order to compute the swamp's value. Economists have been down this road before. Nicholas Georgescu-Roegen, an eccentric Romanian economist who is now retired, spent a career mulling the relationship between economics and the laws of thermodynamics. The amount of energy in the universe is constant, but the amount available for work in a closed (economic) system is limited and constantly in decline. Energy is indeed critical to human activity, agrees William Nordhaus, an economist at Yale University. However, only a tiny fraction of the fuel consumed is actually used to sustain life. Technology for efficient processing of inputs—among them energy—is thus the real, long-term constraint. And ecological economists are not any better at predicting how these limits will impinge than garden-variety economists.

Mr. Daly, an economist by training who long ago defected to the enemy, approaches sustainability from another angle. He constructed an "index of sustainable economic welfare," adjusting conventionally measured output for environmental damage, resource depletion, the availability of leisure, even the degree of income equality. The index suggests that Americans' sustainable welfare peaked more than a decade ago, that "economic development" as contrasted with economic growth has stopped.

Mr. Nordhaus and the Nobel Prize–winning economist James Tobin put together a less ambitious "measurement of economic welfare" in the early 1970s in response to Marxists, whose claims to be creating more livable societies were then taken seriously. The two economists found that the output omitted from regular income accounts—like the fruits of household labor—roughly offset the unmeasured costs, like pollution. Thus growth in economic welfare (in advanced industrialized economies, anyway) roughly tracked the growth in conventionally measured output. At the heart of the sustainability question, Mr. Nordhaus argues, is the issue of endowing future generations with at least as much productive capacity as this generation inherited. Current levels of economic activity may deplete valuable resources and degrade ecological systems in irreversible ways, he acknowledges. But this generation will also pass on precious new technologies, cures for fatal diseases, incredibly efficient means for processing information, for example. Who is to judge whether our resource-stripping, environmentally stressful ways may more than offset this technological bounty?

Robert Hahn, an economist at the American Enterprise Institute, offers another way of parsing the question. Traditional economics implicitly assumes that as a practical matter no wasting asset, whether it be oil or the atmospheric ozone layer, is absolutely critical to economic growth or human welfare. Ecological economists, by contrast, are technological pessimists: if nations are not careful, they will make the planet uninhabitable.

No one really knows who is right. And to Mr. Hahn, the appropriate response to uncertainty is not agnosticism. It makes sense, he argues, to err on the side of caution where the penalty in output forgone is not high. The ecological economists thus score most tellingly, Mr. Hahn suggests, in their criticism of traditional economists' live-and-let-live approach to population issues. Traditional economics, with its focus on the welfare of individuals, has generally been indifferent to the overall scale of economic activity. But for any given living standard, it is virtually certain that more people mean more damage to ecological systems, whose carrying capacities are poorly understood. Thus it may matter critically whether the world's population stabilizes at, say, 10 billion rather than 20 billion. It is not yet clear whether the ecologists will establish a beachhead in the economists' carefully constructed intellectual empire. What they have already demonstrated, though, is that environmental economics is too important to be left by default to economists.   [PP, NOVEMBER 1990]

THE COSTS OF CLEANUP

DOES environmental protection hurt the economy or help it? The question was under hot dispute in the 1992 presidential campaign. The vice president–elect, Senator Al Gore, argued that environmental protection boosts the economy and creates jobs; former Vice President Dan Quayle, whose White House Council on Competitiveness sought to reduce environmental regulations, claimed the Democrats' environmental policies would cost jobs. But the answer to the economy-versus-ecology question, says an emerging group of environmental economists, is far more elusive.

An Environmental Protection Agency analysis, for example, puts the cost of controlling and cleaning up pollution under federal regulations at more than $100 billion a year, or about 2 percent of the nation's total annual output of goods and services. But like a number of other analyses, the study does not take into account the economic benefits of cleaner air and water. An analysis of benefits is under way, but not yet complete. Nor does the study include protection measures that do not involve pollution control, like conserving the ecosystems that underlie all economic activity, such as water, soil, forests, fisheries, wetlands, wild plant species, and the complex biological web that supports life itself. Gauging the costs and benefits of such measures is hard but essential.

Environmental economists argue that the economy is merely a subsystem of the planet's ecology, on which it depends for materials, energy, and general sustenance. "To me it's just as plain as the nose on your face," says Herman Daly, an economist at the World Bank and a proponent of the view that economies can flourish in a steady state, without growth. Traditional economists, he and others contend, ignore this relationship, and with it the economic cost of depleting natural resources, degrading soils, and otherwise insulting nature. Until these "external" costs are reflected both in company balance sheets and calculations of national wealth, say Mr. Daly and his allies, the benefits of environmental protection will be seriously underestimated and the basic health of the economy will be overestimated.

This line of thought is starting to make some headway, as both the United Nations and the United States Department of Commerce move to include the costs of natural resource depletion as an adjunct to conventional accountings of national wealth. Also, regulatory commissions in New York and other states are starting to require electric utilities to factor in the cost of emitting heat-trapping carbon dioxide when deciding how to generate energy. Including such external costs favors Mr. Gore's side of the argument. But economic studies in general are not so clear-cut. A number of economists say the value of environmental protection measures can be assessed only on a case-by-case basis.

"I don't think you can make a broad, sweeping conclusion" about the economic value of environmental protection, said Dr. William Nordhaus of Yale University. "There are some net pluses and some net minuses." Among the "good buys" are the air pollution controls enacted in the first Clean Air Act of 1970, according to a cost-benefit analysis by Dr. Paul R. Portney, an economist at Resources for the Future, a Washington research institute. The act placed the first limits on air pollution from smokestacks and motor vehicles. Dr. Portney found the benefits of the Clean Air Act have exceeded the costs. His preliminary estimate suggests that the same is not true of the 1990 amendments to the Clean Air Act, designed to curb acid rain and air pollution in urban areas. Costs will be $29 billion to $36 billion a year by the year 2005, but benefits will probably range from $6 billion to $25 billion, he found. Since the analysis is preliminary, Dr. Portney does not rule out a different final result. Another good buy, in Dr. Portney's view, is the phasing out of chlorofluorocarbons that destroy the earth's protective ozone layer, which he calls "a small price to pay for insurance against what could be a pretty serious problem." Bad buys, in his book, include some toxic waste sites that pose little risk but will require tens of millions of dollars apiece to clean up.

The issue of economy versus ecology is also complicated by the fact that environmental regulation distributes both costs and benefits unevenly. On costs, for instance, Dr. Dale W. Jorgenson of Harvard University and Dr. Peter J. Wilcoxen of the University of Texas estimate that all federal environmental regulations adopted before 1990 will reduce the national economic output by 2.5 percent by the year

2000. But the economy does not suffer uniformly, they found; the burden is being borne disproportionately by the chemical, coal mining, motor vehicle, refining, primary metals, and paper industries. Dr. Jorgenson and Dr. Wilcoxen calculate, for instance, that the long-run output of the automobile industry has been cut by about 15 percent as a consequence of controls on motor vehicle pollution. "The flip side of that is that some industries are going to benefit," Dr. Jorgenson said. An example is companies that produce pollution-control equipment and services, a market estimated at more than $100 billion a year.

Mr. Quayle argued during the campaign that thousands of autoworkers could be thrown out of work if automobile fuel-efficiency standards are raised, as Bill Clinton favors, to 40 miles per gallon, from 27.5 miles, to reduce emissions of carbon dioxide. Dr. Jorgenson agrees that achieving the standard would impose substantial costs and thereby cause industry employment to shrink. But this does not take into account whatever environmental and economic benefits might result.

Another difficulty in drawing up an economy-versus-ecology bottom line is that there may be different answers for the short term and the long term, said Dr. H. Ronald Pulliam, an ecologist at the University of Georgia. "In the short term, there are certainly job losses" in some cases of environmental protection. "But in the long run, decades, there is probably very little conflict between maximizing economic goals and ecological goals." For instance, he said, some jobs would be lost if logging was prohibited in the old-growth forest habitat of the spotted owl in the Pacific Northwest. But if the old-growth forest is clear-cut "those jobs are going to be lost anyway in a decade or two," he said, while limiting logging so that biological diversity is preserved over the long haul "is going to provide for the needs of both the local economy and biodiversity."

In a study of the costs of global warming, Dr. William R. Cline of the Institute for International Economics finds that costs would roughly match benefits for the first twenty to thirty years but would then far outstrip them after the easy ways of abating carbon dioxide emissions had all been exploited. But in time, Dr. Cline found, the benefits would begin to outweigh the costs—in the second half of the next century if the predicted warming was severe, a century later if it fell in the middle range of the predicted warming. Politicians, of course, do not generally look too far beyond the next election, a predilection that may be shared by their constituents. In a recent study by Resources for the Future and the University of Maryland, researchers asked people in 1,000 households which of two pollution-control programs they preferred, one that saved fewer lives now or one that saved more lives in the future. The researchers found that the respondents considered six lives saved twenty-five years in the future and forty-four lives saved a hundred years in the future equivalent to one life saved today.

Economists find that it is especially hard to assign dollar values to some benefits of environmental protection—for instance, saving a threatened species or ecosystem. They are trying but "I don't think anyone is particularly comfortable with how far they've gotten," Dr. Portney said. Environmental benefits have often been portrayed as harder to measure than costs. But Dr. Portney says: "Economists have been much too glib about how easy it is to nail down the cost; there are some economists who make it seem like there's nothing out there that we can't slap a dollar value on. We're making progress on some things, but there is a whole range of things that we're never going to be able to express comfortably in dollar terms."

Dr. A. Myrick Freeman 3d of Bowdoin College, an expert on measuring environmental benefits, acknowledges the difficulties. But, he said: "We have methods that are able to measure within an order of magnitude, or within a factor of two, the benefits of many environmental improvements, and plus or minus 25 percent in some cases. The errors, the bounds, around cost estimates are arguably just as large." Dr. Freeman notes a philosophical objection raised by some critics to the use of cost-benefit analysis: it values the environment only in terms of its usefulness to people without giving "independent weight to nonhuman species or ecological systems" in their own right. Nevertheless, he said, there is some information that says something about policy, imperfect as it is. "And it's better than making policy in the dark, without any reference at all to costs and benefits," he said. [WKS, SEPTEMBER 1992]

ENVIRONMENTAL RULES
AND INNOVATION

Do strict environmental standards enhance or harm America's ability to compete in the global economy? Conservatives typically insist that the standards hurt. Environmentalists and their allies argue that the standards force companies to develop more efficient practices and technologies, thereby gaining an edge in the worldwide marketplace. Some economists say neither point of view is wholly correct. Environmental regulation can spur innovation and enhance competitiveness, they say, but only when regulations provide the right incentives. "Regulation can trigger innovative activity that may not only nullify the cost of a cleaner environment, but may also go beyond that and create a competitive advantage," says Dr. Michael E. Porter, the leader of the Harvard Business School's Competition and Strategy Group. "But if that kind of win-win outcome is to happen, you have to be very careful about how you structure your regulations." The key is to set goals without prescribing the means. If this is done, Dr. Porter said, companies will choose the most efficient technology. Too often, he said, Washington has set specific remedies, like scrubbers for reducing air pollution from coal-fired power plants, which have thwarted the search for innovative solutions.

In an era when environmental regulation appears here to stay, some economists and even some businessmen contend, companies that are able to reap maximum profits while using few resources and producing little pollution will benefit. Companies and countries that are unable to do this "will soon lose competitive advantage to their more ecoefficient rivals," says Stephan Schmidheiny, a Swiss industrialist who is the chairman of an international business group, the Business Council for Sustainable Development. At the Earth Summit in Rio de Janeiro in June 1992, Mr. Schmidheiny predicted "a coming environmental shakeout for business and industry."

Environmentalists argue further that regulation creates new markets for companies that make pollution-control equipment and provide environmental services, and that the United States is in danger of conceding the export-market advantage in this area to Japan and Germany. But again, Dr. Porter says, American regulations must be carefully written to achieve maximum effect. If they are too much stricter than those of other countries, he says, American companies may end up making equipment that the other countries cannot use. But if American regulations "are on the strict end but still in sight of other countries," he said, "it may enable them to leapfrog their competitors abroad." The key is for the United States to be "a little bit ahead but in sync with the way international standards are evolving."

[WKS, SEPTEMBER 1992]

OZONE CLEANUP MAY NOT BE WORTHWHILE

F AR from being ruinously expensive, efforts to head off a feared global warming could actually save money or even turn a profit in the long run, environmentalists, government analysts, and even some business leaders and economists say. The view is contrary to that of the Bush administration, which in international talks resisted placing limits on emissions of carbon dioxide, a heat-trapping gas. The administration found support from studies indicating that the costs of ultimately reducing emissions could run to tens of billions of dollars a year.

But now the opposite view is being pressed with increasing insistence. Citing studies of their own, advocates argue that reducing the emissions would force the economy to use energy more efficiently and at less cost in the long run, would free up large amounts of capital for expansion if the right governmental policies were followed, and would make American business more competitive internationally. "To ignore the economic opportunities is to fail to seize the moment, to become paralyzed by exclusive focus on one side of the economic ledger," Dr. Robert N. Stavins, an economist at the John F. Kennedy School of Government at Harvard University, said at a recent conference on the subject at the Smithsonian Institution in Washington.

A recent study by four environmental groups, coordinated by the Union of Concerned Scientists, concluded that aggressive action to lower carbon dioxide emissions by 70 percent over the next forty years could cost the economy about $2.7 trillion. But it could also save consumers and industry $5 trillion in fuel and electricity bills, the study found, for a net saving of $2.3 trillion. And unofficial studies by Environmental Protection Agency analysts conclude that the gross national product would rise, not fall, over the next twenty years if emissions were reduced through a "carbon tax" on the extraction of coal, oil, and natural gas—and the tax revenues were "recycled" back into the economy through investment tax credits for industry, thus spurring capital investment. Competing studies consider different factors and operate on different assumptions, and no consensus on the net economic effect of reducing carbon dioxide emissions has emerged. But the economic debate has been joined, and its outcome could be critical in the attempt to deal with a global environmental concern of the first magnitude.

Carbon dioxide and other gases, chiefly methane, trap heat in the atmosphere much as glass panes trap it in a greenhouse. An international panel of scientists convened by the United Nations has predicted that if current emission rates continue, the earth's average surface temperature will rise by 3 to 8 degrees Fahrenheit by the end of the next century. Many scientists believe this could have a catastrophic effect on climate. Global warming and energy are inextricably linked because carbon dioxide, the most abundant and important greenhouse gas emitted by industrial society, is produced by burning fossil fuels like coal and oil. The United States, which lags behind other industrialized countries like Japan and Germany in energy efficiency, is the world's leading emitter of carbon dioxide. Thus greater efficiency of energy use in this country is viewed as essential in trying to stabilize or reduce carbon dioxide emissions. Analysis by the Environmental Protection Agency (EPA) suggests that modest energy-efficiency measures already under way will allow American per-capita emissions of carbon dioxide to stabilize at 1990 levels by the year 2000, at little or no cost to the economy. The European Community has called for overall emissions to be stabilized at 1990 levels by 2000; although the United States has opposed such a target and timetable, the EPA's analysis suggests that as a practical matter, it will be close to compliance anyway.

Many scientists believe that sharp reductions in carbon dioxide emissions—not just a stabilization—will ultimately be necessary. They say that at 1990 rates of emission, atmospheric concentrations of carbon dioxide would still grow. And in this context, the debate on the economic effects of reducing emissions takes on even greater importance. Answers will be needed if it becomes clearer in the next few years that the threat of warming is indeed serious. One major study made public in December 1991, commissioned by Congress and carried out by the Department of Energy, concluded that reducing carbon dioxide emissions by 20 percent from 1990 levels would cost $95 billion a year in 2000. In general, its conclusions are consistent with those of a number of other government and private studies. But the study is based on the assumption that the economy is already using energy in the most efficient way possible, said Alden Meyer, an energy analyst with the Union of Concerned Scientists. "That assumption is flat-out false," Mr. Meyer said. He said the market contained many barriers to the adoption of more efficient practices and technologies. For instance, a landlord may have no incentive to install more energy-efficient appliances or windows because tenants pay electricity bills. If the landlord was offered a subsidy to do so, the barrier could be overcome.

Electric companies in a few states are indeed paying customers to install more efficient lighting, cooling, and heating systems, for example, in lieu of building new emission-producing power plants. The companies are allowed to recover the money by increasing rates. The saving to the economy comes in the form of lower electric bills for the building's owner. The restraint on emissions comes from lower energy use, and the power company gains by not having to build a new power plant. The study coordinated by Mr. Meyer found that if an aggressive policy to expand energy efficiency and switch to clean, renewable energy sources were pursued, the economy would reap a net saving of $2.3 trillion over the next forty years, and carbon dioxide emissions would be reduced by 70 percent. Participating in the study along with the Union of Concerned Scientists were the Alliance to Save Energy, the American Council for an Energy-Efficient Economy, and the Natural Resources Defense Council, all nonprofit organizations that advocate greater efficiency of energy use.

But an analyst at the Department of Energy, who spoke on condition of anonymity, said that although the department favored the removal of barriers to greater efficiency, consumer behavior was more complicated than the environmentalists' study assumes. That could make the barriers more difficult to remove, he said. He said the environmentalists' study assumed that the economy would continue to shift away from manufacturing as it has in the past, which he called a questionable assumption. He said the study also assumed a lower basic growth rate for the economy: 2.5 percent a year as compared with 3 percent in the Department of Energy study. A higher growth rate means emission reductions are more difficult and costly to achieve. Mr. Meyer criticized the administration's projected 3 percent growth rate as unrealistically high, a view that is shared by many private economists.

Analysts for the Environmental Protection Agency say the Energy Department study does not reflect the ways in which, according to the unofficial study by their agency, the proceeds of a carbon tax could be recycled through the tax system to spur economic growth. The analysts found that if the tax revenues were used to reduce personal income taxes or the federal budget deficit, this would barely offset, if at all, the negative effect of the tax. That negative impact would come when the coal and oil industries passed on the carbon tax to their customers in the form of higher prices. But if the revenue was used to encourage business investment through tax credits, they found, the effect of the carbon tax would be more than offset, producing a net gain for the national economy. A combination of investment tax credits and personal income-tax reductions—to make the tax more acceptable to consumers—could achieve substantial reductions in carbon emissions at no cost, according to the analysis. Market-based solutions of this sort could also make the price of American goods and services more competitive with those of the more energy-efficient economies of Europe and Japan, said Dr. Stavins. Although the current anti-tax mood of the United States discourages the adoption of a carbon tax, at least for now, the European Community is seriously considering it as the centerpiece of its efforts to reduce emissions.

Relatively cheap energy in the United States has made this country less efficient and therefore less competitive worldwide, Stephan Schmidheiny, a Swiss industrialist, told the Smithsonian conference. Mr. Schmidheiny is the principal adviser for business and industry to Maurice F. Strong, the secretary-general of the United Nations environment meeting. Shakeouts are painful, and the move to an energy-efficient market would undoubtedly produce some transitional pain, even if the end result is a more robust economy. Coal and oil producers and their employees, for example, could be heavily hit by a carbon tax, even if other sectors benefited from the recycling of the tax.

Beyond all this, another question arises: what would be the cost of not taking action if serious global warming occurs? Few economists have addressed it. One, Dr. William D. Nordhaus of Yale University, has published a "best guess" estimate that a doubling of atmospheric carbon dioxide would reduce this country's gross national product by one fourth of 1 percent. But Dr. Nordhaus notes that many important factors are not included in economic accounts. These include "human health, biological diversity, amenity values of everyday life and leisure, and environmental quality," he wrote in a 1990 monograph. It may be impossible to place monetary values on some of these big factors, even though they are clearly valuable. Biologists, for instance, fear that global warming will catastrophically speed a steady loss of biological species that is now occurring worldwide. They also believe that the world's forests harbor untold billions of dollars' worth of biological riches that could be exploited for pharmaceuticals and other products without harming the environment. But their worth has not been gauged.

The effort to do so is "low on the totem pole of what is of interest to our discipline," Allen Sinai, chief economist of the Boston Company, Inc., said recently at a debate on development and the environment held in Cambridge, Massachusetts, under the sponsorship of Earthwatch, a Boston-based scientific research and education organization. Some scientists believe economists should refrain from even making the attempt until more is known about the biological world. The tropical forests, for example, are mostly unexplored and only a fraction of species with economic value have been identified. Pending more knowledge, Dr. E. O. Wilson, a conservation biologist at Harvard University, said at the Cambridge debate, economists "should avoid fruitless and dangerous exercises in cost-benefit analysis which is far beyond their reach and join in the ethic of saving every scrap of biological diversity possible." [WKS, MAY 1992]

PROFITS IN PREVENTING GLOBAL WARMING

THE health benefits of cleaning up a widespread urban air pollutant, ground-level ozone, may not be worth the price, two economists argued in a 1991 study. The economists at Resources for the Future, a respected nonadvocacy research institute in Washington, compared the costs of plans for Los Angeles and the nation as a whole to meet national air quality standards for ground-level ozone with their potential health benefits. In both cases, the most optimistic estimate of the costs fell far short of the most optimistic measure of the health benefits.

They chose to look at ground-level ozone because it is one of the most difficult air pollution problems to solve. They also said they believed they could effectively apply cost-benefit analysis to it. According to cost estimates based on 1989 government data, they found the cost for the nation to meet the standards would be $8.8 billion to $12.8 billion through 2004, while health benefits would be $250 million to $1 billion. They estimated that the cost of a more ambitious 1989 Los Angeles plan would be $13 billion through 2010, but that it would yield only $3 billion in health benefits.

The economists, Alan J. Krupnick and Paul R. Portney, writing in the journal *Science*, concluded that air should be cleaned up in the most polluted areas but that an investment of billions of dollars directed toward encouraging people to quit smoking, control radon gas, and provide better prenatal and neonatal care might contribute much more to public health.

Mr. Krupnick and Mr. Portney used laboratory and epidemiological studies linking improvements in air quality to improvements in human health. They then combined those data with a number of studies that have sought to determine how much people would be willing to pay to avoid loss of income and medical costs associated with illness or some symptoms. For example, they used a value of $25 for each asthma attack prevented. They did not include crop damage or reductions in chronic illness, they said, because those changes had not been linked convincingly to reductions in ground-level ozone, though many scientists believe such a connection exists.

The economists readily acknowledged in interviews that their analysis was based on educated guesses and data from the past. They said new pollution control technologies and studies linking other health benefits to reductions in ground-level ozone might make the costs and benefits more equal. But they said they did not believe their conclusions would change if new technologies or benefits were discovered. "I don't expect people to like the conclusions," Mr. Portney said. "But this is not a justification for not cleaning up the air. It just says maybe we could get more health benefits for our money if we spent it someplace else."

Environmentalists familiar with the study strongly disapproved of its cost-benefit analysis technique and its conclusions, though they agreed that the most cost-effective means must be used to control pollution. "This study's Achilles' heel is that it cannot capture the nonmonetizable aspects of cleaner air," said Dr. Michael Oppenheimer, senior scientist at the Environmental Defense Fund. He said it was impossible to get people to put a dollar figure on how much they wanted or benefited from cleaner air. He added that the study did not consider the aesthetic benefits of cleaner air nor did it include possible damage from chronic exposure to high levels of ground-level ozone.

Industry representatives were more sympathetic. "They are daring to ask the questions that need to be asked," said William D. Fay, former administrator of the Clean Air Working Group, a coalition of 2,000 businesses that worked on the recent changes to the Clean Air Act. "I'm not sure the public knows the trade-offs of focusing on clean air."

In the face of such uncertainties over costs and benefits, the recent amendments to the Clean Air Act were written to provide flexibility, said Rob D. Brenner, the director of the Air Policy Office at the Environmental Protection Agency. He said the areas with the most severe air pollution problems had to reduce emissions of complex hydrocarbons by 3 percent a year. In this way, he said, the least costly things can be done first, and Congress can decide later if laws need to be changed.   [WKS, FEBRUARY 1991]

PUTTING A PRICE TAG ON NATURE

How much is a Pacific sea otter's life worth—not someone's pet, but a wild animal that will never be studied by scientists or frolic in front of tourists? Could the government find out by asking people in Plattsburgh or Peoria how much they would voluntarily fork over to keep the otter safe from unnatural hazards? Until recently, such abstract questions have mostly been grist for academic debate. But now federal regulators are under orders from Congress and the courts to figure ways to measure losses to people not directly affected by environmental problems like oil spills or haze in national parks. The first set of guidelines, from the National Oceanic and Atmospheric Administration, is widely expected to support the use of survey-based techniques. So with little fanfare, "contingent-value" measurements of "passive uses" of the environment are on the verge of becoming an accepted tool in the making of public policy. They may also become a potent weapon in large pollution-liability suits.

For three decades, scholars and environmentalists have suggested that failure to account for benefits for "nonusers" could lead to systematic underprotection. If passive uses are ignored, said Alan Randall, an economist at Ohio State University, it would encourage "the riskiest enterprises in the most pristine environments." What is new is the ambitious use of opinion surveys to measure passive-use benefits. In 1989, a federal appeals court ordered the Department of the Interior to rewrite regulations for assessing damages under the Clean Air Act and the Superfund toxic-waste cleanup program. The loss of passive-use value, the court said, was to be included if it could be "reliably calculated."

The subsequent drive to bring survey-based measurement into the corridors of power is drawing praise from environmental groups and has even gained the cautious imprimatur of some prestigious scholars. "You can learn quite a lot from a well-done contingent-value study," said Robert M. Solow, a Nobel Prize–winning economist who is advising the National Oceanic and Atmospheric Administration on the use of such studies. But the approach has bitterly divided professionals. "Economists just don't want to admit there is stuff that cannot be measured," argued Zvi Griliches, a teacher of statistical methods in economics at Harvard University and a consultant to the Exxon Corporation. Such surveys are anathema to industries that produce, use, or transport toxic substances. If damages are measured by contingent-value surveys, warned Charles J. DiBona, the president of the American Petroleum Institute, "junk science will gain a companion—junk economics."

But plaintiffs in big environmental-damage suits suspect that a pot of gold is waiting under the contingent-value rainbow. The State of Alaska commissioned a $3 million study of what Americans who will never visit Prince William Sound lost from the *Exxon Valdez* disaster, teasing out the numbers by asking more than 1,000 people in a random sample how much they would pay to avoid a similar accident over the next decade. When pressed, the typical respondent put the figure at about $30. The state thus inferred that Americans would collectively be willing to pay about $2.8 billion. If that was true, Alaska argued, Exxon should be liable for $2.8 billion beyond the billions spent to restore oil-soiled beaches. Although the survey drew praise from some quarters—Paul Portney, an economist at Resources for the Future in Washington, called it "far and away the best contingent-value study I've seen"—Alaska's tactic was never tested in the adversarial setting of a courtroom; Exxon settled the liability suit for $1 billion before the survey was introduced as evidence. But the sums at risk focused businesses' attention on the threat posed to them by such surveys.

The oil industry, in particular, is sparing no effort to get across its message that contingent value is at best a gravy train for consultants, at worst a legal bomb that will blow apart the Great American Prosperity Machine. "If you applied this methodology to any human activity, you could stop it dead," Mr. DiBona said.

Are the critics right? Most economists are indeed inclined to look at contingent value with a jaundiced eye. They have traditionally relied on market transactions to reveal value, and for an obvious reason: anyone who buys bananas at thirty-nine cents a pound must think they are worth at least thirty-nine cents a pound. Survey techniques, by contrast, are inherently limited by the fact that the conclusions are based on what people say they would do—not on what they have done. To demonstrate that contingent value does not reveal what courts and policymakers want to know, Exxon hired an army of brand-name economists to test its mettle. Although the sponsor's bias must be kept in mind, the newly published research certainly does touch on a variety of widely acknowledged pitfalls in the technique.

Peter Diamond and Jerry Hausman of the Massachusetts Institute of Technology point to the public's inclination to be overly generous with hypothetical outlays. They note, for example, that a mail survey found 6.6 percent of fishing-license holders in Montana would be willing to pay to protect healthy water flow in two rivers. But just 1.1 percent selected randomly from the same group actually responded to a request for donations. Another flaw is the extreme sensitivity of the results to the way the questions are asked. In particular, people seem willing to pay implausibly large sums if they are not carefully reminded of the broad range of possible environmental damages and the practical limits of their own incomes. Walter Mead of the University of California at Santa Barbara points out that one major study pegged the nonuse value of saving old-growth forests in the Pacific Northwest at $119 billion to $359 billion. Sparing the whooping crane from extinction was valued at $51 billion to $715 billion.

Still another pitfall is the apparent irrationality of survey respondents. If a little preservation is worth something, both economic theory and common sense suggest that a lot ought to be worth a good deal more. Yet William Desvousges and a team of colleagues from the Research Triangle Institute in North Carolina found the public's willingness to pay to save 2,000 migratory birds from oil-coated ponds—a well-documented pollution hazard—was as great as their willingness to save 20,000 birds or 200,000. "No matter how you skin this cat, you get incredible anomalies," Mr. Hausman concluded.

But practitioners are not about to fold their tents. "There are good contingent-value studies and bad contingent-value studies," insisted Raymond Kopp, an economist at Resources for the Future who worked on Alaska's study of Prince William Sound. "The technique works as well as any other empirical methodology." And fans of contingent value got a big lift in 1993 from a blue-ribbon panel of economists with no financial stake in the issue—a lift that assures the technique will be treated with respect by the courts.

Acting under the Oil Pollution Act of 1990, which requires the National Oceanic and Atmospheric Administration to write damage-assessment rules for oil spills, the agency invited six economists, including two Nobel Prize winners, to advise it on contingent value. Their January 1993 report lays out tough standards for credible surveys—standards virtually no survey to date would meet—and urges the government to conduct benchmark studies of its own. The economists concluded, however, that "contingent-value studies can produce estimates reliable enough to be a starting point for a judicial process of damage assessment." The regulators are not obliged to adopt the panel's recommendations when they issue rules. But it would be the bureaucratic path of least resistance. And if, as is widely expected, the agency does follow the recommendations, the Interior Department would probably adopt parallel standards for damage assessment on toxic waste and air pollution violations. Indeed, the failure of either agency to defer to the panel's expertise would open it to legal challenges from one side or the other.

The impact of the new rules is anyone's guess. Opponents take heart from both the heavy burden of credibility imposed by the panel and the reluctance of federal courts to carve out precedents. Where big money is involved, moreover, defendants will have every incentive to hire experts to punch holes in the evidence. "I believe that no contingent-value study will ever meet the courts' standards," said John Seddelmeyer, associate general counsel of Exxon USA. But Mr. Seddelmeyer may be whistling in the wind. "I see great potential for mischief here," conceded Mr. Portney of Resources for the Future, who was a member of the blue-ribbon panel and, in principle, supports the contingent-value approach.

Mr. DiBona of the petroleum institute is not shy in speculating about the potential consequences. While the chances of getting hit hard with a damage award for lost passive use may be low, he argues, the sums involved are so large that they are bound to affect commerce. At the least, the legal exposure would raise insurance premiums, he said, and the risk might well render it impossible for some industries to obtain insurance. That might lead Congress to rethink the very idea of linking damage awards to the pain felt by Americans when they learn that a wilderness has been sullied or a species endangered. But then again, maybe not.

"I can think of no instance in which Congress has relaxed environmental regulation," said Robert Hahn, an economist at the American Enterprise Institute. "It's just not politically correct."

[PP, SEPTEMBER 1993]

RECONCILING INTERESTS
IN THE EVERGLADES

"THE river of grass has been given a new lease on life," Interior Secretary Bruce Babbitt exulted, announcing the 1993 pact in which Florida's sugar and vegetable farmers joined with a host of government agencies to defend the Everglades from the ravages of civilization. The pact may not, in fact, assure the survival of this uniquely fragile marsh, for no one knows for certain why it is deteriorating into a garden-variety swamp. But Mr. Babbitt should be excused a touch of hyperbole. For the deal does promise a relatively happy ending to a bitter war between farmers and environmentalists that might otherwise have been fought into the next century. As important, it could set a precedent for resolving some heavy-duty environmental struggles to come. "The failure to deal with runoff from land is America's most glaring, unaddressed pollution problem," says Paul Portney, an economist at Resources for the Future, in Washington.

Until the 1920s, much of the southern shank of Florida was a flat, pale-green wilderness that was underwater a part of each year. Roughly half of the great marsh has since been drained for farms and suburban home sites, with 1,400 miles of canals and hundreds of pumps to buffer the annual seasons of dry and flood. The rest is state and federal park and conservation areas. But all is not well in this remaining chunk of humid Eden. Water pumped into the Everglades contains a dose of chemical nutrients, a combination of farm runoff, treated urban waste, and acidic rain that nurtures alien plants and is probably upsetting the ecology of the grasslands. Perhaps as threatening, the artificial plumbing has disrupted the slow, even seepage of water through the Everglades, a process called sheet flow.

In 1988, a coalition of local environmentalists persuaded the United States Attorney in Miami to sue the state to clean up its act. And in 1991, a sympathetic Democratic governor, Lawton Chiles, consented to a plan to set aside some 35,000 acres for "stormwater treatment areas"—filtration marshes filled with plants that would absorb the offending phosphorus nutrients. The $400 million or so needed to build the system, it was assumed, would be levied against the farmers.

That set the stage for what everyone expected to be the mother of all legal battles, with the farmers using their ingenuity and financial muscle to delay implementation. But U.S. Sugar, the largest of the landholders and a company that had gone a long way to atone for the sugar industry's legendary abuse of itinerant labor, preferred to deal. And the agreement the industry cut with the state of Florida and the Interior Department contains more than a little something for everyone. The environmentalists get their filtration marshes, a cleanup method the farmers believe will cost far more than alternative technologies. But the growers will get credit against their part of the bill for removing up to 45 percent of the phosphorus on their own. This will allow—indeed, almost guarantee—the creation of a system of tradable antipollution credits not very different from the one now being set in place nationally to remove sulfur from power plant smokestacks. The farmers will divide the responsibility for removing phosphorus, then pay the most efficient among them to refrain from polluting. Robert Hahn, an economist at the American Enterprise Institute, thinks the farmers can remove phosphorus at less than half the cost of the marsh solution.

What J. Nelson Fairbanks, the president of U.S. Sugar, calls an "environmental peace plan" goes further than defining the farmers' responsibilities for runoff. It also includes a framework for dividing rights to Florida's water and a technical plan for re-creating something akin to sheet flow for the grasslands south of the sugarcane fields.

There is plenty of offstage grumbling about the deal. Growers do not see why they should be obliged to discharge water that is purer than the water entering their fields. By the same token, environmentalists who have been waging guerrilla warfare against the farmers for a decade are smarting about two compromises. The pact puts a clear limit on the farmers' responsibility for the cost of the filtration marshes, and it decrees that a portion of the marshes will be built on public land.

For their part, many economists are dismayed the farmers will not be given the chance to show they could get the whole cleanup done more cheaply on their own. But the agreement will prevent the lawyers from fiddling while the Everglades chokes on cattails. And it is a high-profile precedent for meeting a high-priority environmental challenge—the protection of lakes and rivers from "non-point source" pollution. For the easy part of cleaning the nation's water is almost done. Most of the gunk still entering public waterways comes from thousands of storm sewers, tens of thousands of farms, and millions of lawns. One way or another, government is going to have to identify the sources and create incentives for cost-effective abatement.

[PP, JULY 1993]

Priorities and Reassessments

SOME THREATS ARE WORSE THAN OTHERS

THE laws that now protect America's earth, air, and water were not conceived as a coherent framework but were built up piece by piece over many years and after many political skirmishes. Not surprisingly, the edifice, to one who looks back on it, is a ramshackle structure that is nowhere very even.

Critics have pointed out the mismatch between the seriousness of various threats to the environment and the amount of money that Congress has decreed be spent on them. Thus there is an enormous bill due for cleaning up abandoned dumps of toxic chemicals, yet these dumps, in fact, have caused very little illness so far.

Besides the reordering of priorities, many environmental hazards are being reassessed in the light of new evidence and second thoughts, as the articles in this section describe. Fortunately, these assessments are usually downward, since the proponents of environmental laws rarely understate the magnitude of the hazard they seek to control. Thus the radon that leaks into basements from the ground beneath seems less serious than was at first thought, since the data set used as the standard of comparison—uranium miners who had died of lung cancer from breathing radon—no longer seems so pertinent. Acid rain cannot be good for the environment, yet the number of acidified lakes and streams in the United States has turned out to be fewer than feared, according to a large-scale survey that was reported in 1991 just before Congress took action to abate acid rain.

That environmental hazards should require reassessment is not a matter of scandal but a routine scientific procedure. Dangers are usually responded to on the basis of imperfect knowledge, which may change after refinement. Nonetheless, some of the skepticism expressed by critics of global warming is an attempt not to refine the theory but to debunk it altogether. Such skepticism can be healthy, especially if it makes the proponents refine and strengthen their ideas.

RANKING RISKS

ARE Americans preoccupied with relatively modest environmental threats while neglecting big ones that could unleash catastrophe? To a large extent, some scientists and government officials believe, the answer is yes. William K. Reilly, then administrator of the Environmental Protection Agency (EPA), told a Senate committee in Washington at the start of 1991 that in many cases, the public and Congress are at odds with scientists over which environmental threats are the most serious. He has begun a campaign to reassess those priorities, and he leaves no doubt that his money is on the scientists. "Sound science is our most reliable compass," he says in speeches calling for the nation to establish environmental priorities.

Mr. Reilly's campaign is intended to stimulate a national debate over environmental goals. And at a time when many of the most obvious and clear-cut environmental threats, like air pollution and water pollution, have been addressed and more subtle, complex problems are coming to the fore, the campaign may usher in a new, more complicated, and more contentious phase in the national environmental struggle.

There seems little doubt of a mismatch between public perceptions of environmental risk and those of the scientists. Oil spills, hazardous wastes, underground storage tanks, and releases of radioactive materials, for instance, have aroused high emotions, generated reams of reports, and prodded Congress to spend billions of dollars. Opinion surveys place them in the front ranks of public concern about the environment. But in terms of the actual magnitude of risk they pose, scientists advising the EPA rate them near the bottom of a broad array of environmental threats. This, the scientists say, is because their effects are relatively limited or short-lived or both.

At the same time, global warming and the destruction and alteration of natural habitats rank relatively low in public perception, polls show. But the scientists place them among the top risks because their potential consequences appear to be so damaging in the long run and their effects so widespread and difficult to reverse. Federal environmental laws "are more reflective of public perceptions of risk than of scientific understanding of risk," the EPA Science Advisory Board said in a report on environmental risks, which was the basis for the 1991 hearings. Mr. Reilly and others say environmental problems are addressed unevenly, usually on the basis of episodic, momentary public anxieties about problems that, while frightening, represent a relatively limited threat: contamination of a local waterway by hazardous wastes, for example.

No one is suggesting that these problems should be ignored. Oil spills and other low-ranking risks can cause "real damage where and when they occur," Mr. Reilly told the senators. But, he said, "they are in a different league compared to some of our other problems, such as stratospheric ozone depletion and climate change, which have the potential to affect life everywhere, and for many years to come." The advisory board identified four environmental threats to health that it said were in the front rank: outdoor air pollution, exposure of workers to chemicals, indoor air pollution, and pollutants in drinking water.

It established three categories of risk for threats that humans pose to the environment. Relatively high-risk problems of this nature included the global warming that many scientists predict will result from an increase in heat-trapping atmospheric gases produced by human activity; depletion of the ozone shield that protects the earth from the sun's harmful ultraviolet radiation, and destruction and alteration of natural habitats and the extinction of species, with an accompanying loss of biological diversity. A middle rank includes herbicides and pesticides, pollution of surface waters, acid precipitation, and airborne toxic substances. Relatively low risk was assigned to oil spills, escape of radioactive materials, acid runoff to surface waters, and pollution of groundwater.

Risks were assigned largely on the basis of how many people a problem affects, how wide a geographical area is involved, and how serious and long-lasting the harm might be, said Dr. William Cooper, a zoologist and aquatic ecologist at Michigan State University who headed the board's panel on ecological risks. On that basis, oil spills, for example, ranked low because their effects on coastal areas are relatively short-term and local. "The public doesn't perceive it that way," Dr. Cooper said, "but those ecosystems bounce back real fast."

By contrast, he said, the loss of natural habitats and the disappearance of species are top risks because they affect the economic welfare of future generations worldwide and because the loss is "virtually irreversible." Similarly, ozone depletion and global warming were placed in the top rank because they are worldwide problems and because their effects are potentially catastrophic and reversible only over decades.

Given the substantial cost of environmental protection, Mr. Reilly argues, it is all the more important to set sensible priorities as the next phase of environmental protection begins. The EPA estimates the United States will spend nearly 3 percent of its gross national product on environmental protection by the end of this decade. The nation "can probably afford to spend 3 percent," Mr. Reilly said, "but we're not rich enough to spend it in the wrong places."

Although many environmentalists and politicians say it is a good idea to set priorities, doubts and possible points of dispute are cropping up. Environmentalists who have devoted themselves to causes ranked low on the priority list are unlikely to stop pushing their interests. Others resist anything that might look like an effort to practice environmental triage, concentrating on some problems to the exclusion of others. "I don't quarrel with the conclusion that global warming is the number one threat," said David Doniger, a senior lawyer with the Natural Resources Defense Council in New York. "But I don't think the only way you can tackle global warming is by not tackling hazardous wastes. We can and should, and can afford, to do it all."

The Science Advisory Board acknowledged that assessing relative risks was an imprecise science, since much was unknown about some environmental threats. The board noted in its report that environmental policymaking "necessarily embodies subjective values" and that policymakers should take both science and public perceptions into account. As more complex and challenging environmental threats dominate the discussion, the debate will probably be complicated by increasing uncertainty about the nature of environmental risks, noted Sen. Daniel Patrick Moynihan, the New York Democrat who presided over a hearing in January 1991. Science, he said, is a matter of complexity and probability, not simple certainty.

What this means is that when science is invoked as a guide to priorities, as Mr. Reilly and others believe it must be, clear-cut answers are harder to come by. As science investigates an issue, it often tends to raise as many questions as it answers. In the eyes of the public, this could weaken the claim of science as an arbiter of priorities. But on the biggest risks, some scientists argue, uncertainty must not become cause for inaction. Much is uncertain about the magnitude and effects of global warming, for instance. By the time scientists know whether they are right or wrong about predictions of climatic catastrophe, Dr. Cooper said, it will be too late to do anything. This requires "a whole different mind-set," Dr. Cooper said. "You don't care about being right," he said. "You just don't want to be wrong. Once the cost of being wrong gets too high, you go into a risk-aversion mode. You avoid the risk no matter what the cost."

What's a Serious Hazard?

Experts Rank Risks

Relatively High-Risk Ecological Problems:
Habitat alteration and destruction (soil erosion, deforestation)
Species extinction and overall loss of biological diversity
Stratospheric ozone depletion
Global climate change (greenhouse warming)

Relatively High Risks to Human Health:
Ambient (outside) air pollutants
Worker exposure to chemicals in industry and agriculture
Air pollution indoors
Pollutants in drinking water

Relatively Medium-Risk Ecological Problems:
Herbicides and pesticides
Pollution of surface water
Airborne toxic substances

Relatively Low-Risk Ecological Problems:
Oil spills
Groundwater pollution (hazardous wastes, underground tanks, etc.)
Escape of radioactive materials

Acid runoff to surface waters
Thermal pollution

Source: Science Advisory Board, Environmental Protection Agency

The Public Perceives Risks

Ranked as very serious risks by at least 20 percent of people
    polled, in descending order:

- Hazardous waste sites (in use)
- Hazardous waste sites (abandoned)
- Worker exposure to toxic chemicals
- Destruction of protective ozone layer
- Radiation from nuclear power plant accident
- Industrial accidents releasing pollutants into air, water, or soil
- Radiation from radioactive wastes
- Underground storage tanks leaking gasoline and other
    substances
- Pesticides harming farmers, farm workers, and consumers
    who work with them
- Pesticide residue on foods eaten by humans
- The greenhouse warming effect
- Nonhazardous wastes, like trash disposal
- Radiation from X rays

Source: The Roper Organization

[WKS, JANUARY 1991]

ASSESSING LOW-LEVEL RISKS

DIOXIN, once thought of as the most toxic chemical known, does
not deserve that reputation, according to many scientists. But
electric blankets may be dangerous. And cyclamates, banned from
diet soda twenty-one years ago as a cancer risk, may be coming back
because more recent research casts doubt on the original suspicions.

In nearly every aspect of modern life—in food, fuel, even building materials—there are ingredients suspected of causing cancer or organ damage, and the list is growing. New threats, like catching AIDS from a doctor, arouse public concern, often far out of line with their statistical probability. And the commonly used method to determine whether something is dangerous over long periods and in low doses is little trusted even by those who use it.

Whereas knowledge of chemistry and cancer is growing, by many counts the certainty of life is not. "The number of chemicals about which we know little is increasing faster than the number of chemicals about which we know much," said Brooks B. Yeager, a lobbyist with the Audubon Society in Washington.

And apart from the growth in the number of chemicals is growth in the ability to detect them. Technology has become the enemy of stability. "We are better and better at finding small quantities of a chemical, but no better than we were at assessing the risk," said Dr. Peter M. Sandman, director of the Environmental Communication Research Program at Rutgers University. "When the concentration is small, it used to be we couldn't find the concentration and didn't have to ask about the risk. Now we can find the concentration and can only ask about the risk."

In fact, scientists do more than ask, but their investigations raise still more questions. At the heart of much of the uncertainty is something called a "linear, no-threshold" model, a way of looking at damage in rats or mice from a large, quick dose of a chemical and deciding what that means to a human who gets a small dose over a long period. The model has been in wide use for more than thirty years, but no one is sure it is valid for most chemicals. But most researchers are afraid to abandon it, because it seems to offer the safest course. The model says that as doses get smaller, damage declines proportionately, but that any dose has some harmful potential. For example, if 10,000 people had to cross a river ten feet deep and 1,000 people drowned, this model would predict that if the same group crossed a river half as deep, or five feet, then half as many people, 500, would drown. If the river was one-tenth as deep, or one foot, then 100 people would drown. And if it was one one-hundredth as deep, or just over one inch, then 10 people would still find a way to drown.

"The presumption exists, in the absence of better information, that there is no threshold below which a carcinogen will not induce cancer with some probability in humans," said Michael H. Shapiro, deputy assistant administrator of the Environmental Protection Agency

(EPA). Obviously, he said, it is hard to drown in one inch of water, but since scientists do not understand in most cases how the cancer or other ill effect is produced, it is "prudent" to assume that dose and risk are in lockstep. Scientists have been pushed into this assumption because the nature of the threats from dioxin, which is a benzene and chlorine combination that is a by-product of various chemical reactions, or those from food additives: low doses over the years, almost a slow-motion attack on the body. The usual scientific approach is to study a phenomenon under controlled conditions, but the results to be measured from these chemicals—cancer, birth defects, abnormal development, and organ damage—are hard to differentiate from the same maladies when they occur from other causes. In fact, with some hazards, scientists state explicitly that although the cancer rate may rise, identifying the particular cases that are due to exposure to a particular agent is impossible.

Kenneth Rogers of the Nuclear Regulatory Commission said techniques are available for distinguishing subtle patterns, like extra cancers, against a background of naturally occurring cancers. But proving that there is no pattern is nearly impossible. For example, in the last few years, scientists have studied whether electromagnetic fields, which originate in devices from power lines to electric toasters to electric blankets, cause cancer. But the devices are so ubiquitous that proving a pattern will be difficult.

Giving chemical or radiation doses to a sample human population is out of the question. And although people are naturally exposed, Mr. Shapiro of the EPA said, "It's very rare we have enough data on human populations to address directly the nature of the concern and the relationship of exposure to the substance to the chance of getting cancer or some other health effect." Another approach would be to figure out the mechanics of how a chemical causes cancer in an animal, rather than simply observing that it does, and then determine whether it could do the same in people. But that requires more understanding of chemistry than is available for most suspect substances.

The current, guilt-by-analogy system is clumsy in part because the linear, no-threshold model does not take into account processes by which the human body may handle small insults, Mr. Shapiro said— for example, the way it produces enzymes that can eliminate small quantities of some toxins. At the Food and Drug Administration, Dr. Robert J. Scheuplein, director of the office of toxicological sciences, said "a linear estimate is probably hugely wrong" in most cases. But

he added, "How do you distinguish from those that are truly carcino-
genic at low doses?" One solution would be to feed small doses to
many animals, but if a chemical compound causes one fatal cancer in
1,000 people, he said, then in a test on 100 animals "you've got almost
no chance of finding it." Increasing the dose produces a cancer rate
far easier to measure, he said, "but if you treat humans with doses
you gave to rats, they'd probably get cancer, too."

Environmental advocates agree that the government is operating
on assumptions that may someday be proven wrong. But David Doniger, an air pollution specialist at the Natural Resources Defense Council, said the assumption behind the linear, no-threshold model is one
position to be cherished. "If you don't really know, if you have a wide
range, the only prudent thing to do in public health is to be safe rather
than sorry," he said.

Dr. Sandman of Rutgers says that even if risk assessment techniques were perfect, they would still be inadequate to determine where
society's resources should be spent. What concerns people, he says, is
not so much the likelihood of a given harmful effect as what he calls
"outrage," something not based on statistics. For example, he said,
many people are concerned about dying from an AIDS infection that
comes from an infected doctor. The probability is much higher that
a person will die as a result of some other hazard. But what dominates
thinking, he said, is outrage, not hazard. "You'd be a very weird
person if you didn't think it was particularly evil for a doctor to infect
a patient," Dr. Sandman said. "Statistics don't capture how we feel
about getting AIDS from our doctor." Both victims would be just as
dead, he said, but in this comparison, "a pound of feathers and a
pound of lead have a different weight."   [MLW, AUGUST 1991]

SPECIES LOSS: CRISIS OR
FALSE ALARM?

RATS, weeds, cockroaches, and other hardy, ubiquitous "tramp"
species may never inherit the earth. But some scientists say they
could make a run for global ascendancy if humans, as many biologists

fear, precipitate a mass annihilation of less adaptable creatures. In this scenario, the actions of an exploding human population are sundering the ecological webs that support life by setting off a worldwide wave of extinctions comparable to the one in which the dinosaurs perished some 65 million years ago.

But is the scenario accurate? A minority of dissenters says that while wild habitats are indeed disappearing because of human expansion, and species with them, the supposed magnitude and rate of the extinctions are unsubstantiated by hard evidence and have probably been exaggerated. In possibly overstating the risk, some critics say, conservationists may harm their own cause by setting themselves up for the charge of crying wolf.

The argument over the seriousness of the threat has surfaced in a 1991 issue of the journal *Science*. In one of six articles on biological diversity and extinction of species, two prominent biologists, Dr. Edward O. Wilson of Harvard University and Dr. Paul R. Ehrlich of Stanford University, assert that if tropical rain forests continue to be cut down at the present rate, a quarter or more of all the species on earth could be exterminated within fifty years. For the first time in geological history, they say, plant species are becoming extinct in large numbers.

The tropics, and most of all the rain forests, are the richest repositories of biological diversity on earth, and the two biologists point out that many tropical species exist only locally and are subject to immediate extinction with the clearing of a single tract. They say that although conservation efforts are needed, the only way to head off the crisis in the long run is to reduce the scale of human activities.

Since the *Science* article was prepared, Dr. Wilson has further estimated that 50,000 species a year, or about 6 every hour, are being doomed to eventual extinction. The estimates are based on a mathematical model of the observed relationship between habitat area and number of species and on the observed disappearance of rain forests. Coral reefs, dry tropical forests, and other tropical habitats are also being destroyed. The resulting mass extinction, Dr. Wilson said, is likely to compare with the largest extinctions in geological history and to take place in a much shorter time: decades, perhaps, instead of centuries or millennia. "It is a genuine holocaust," he said. "That sounds alarmist," Dr. Wilson conceded. "But I invite anyone to check through the figures."

The skeptics have not yet had a chance to examine Dr. Wilson's latest assessments in detail, but they have attacked earlier, similar assessments made by him and other scientists. The critics say there simply is not enough information on which to build a reliable assessment.

Although species constitute a "valuable endowment" and should be protected, there is "a total lack of evidence" of a biological holocaust, said Dr. Julian Simon, a University of Maryland economist. He is perhaps better known for arguing that the world's resources, coupled with human ingenuity, can support a surging population. "We're being asked to take the entire scenario on faith" and on the judgment of those who advance it, he said. The warnings of mass extinction, he said, "seem like guesswork and hysteria."

Other dissenters say there is a problem, but that its dimensions simply cannot be known at the moment. No one even knows the true number of species in the world, they say. This is acknowledged by Dr. Wilson and others who share his view.

Only 1.4 million species have been identified worldwide, but estimates of South American species alone range from 5 million to 50 million, and estimates of global species range up to 100 million.

"When you deal with that kind of error, it's hard to say what's happening," said Dr. Michael A. Mares, a zoologist at the University of Oklahoma who is an expert on neotropical habitats. Likewise, he said, it is difficult to come up with a rate of extinction when the geographical distribution of organisms is not known. "Most of them are invertebrates," he said. "We really don't have a good handle on whether or not they're going extinct and how rapidly. The problem is data right now." More should be known, he said, before the poor countries of the world are asked to make large sacrifices to preserve tropical forests. For his part, Dr. Mares believes that the wolf is not yet at the door. "The wolf is coming," he said, "but he's coming later."

It is "understandable that there's disagreement," said Dr. Jared Diamond, an ecologist at the University of California at Los Angeles who has examined the problem. "What people are arguing about is what's going to happen in the future." Predicting the stock market, with its well-known variables and wealth of data, is a far more certain pursuit than predicting the future of species, he said. Dr. Diamond has concluded that, even taking into account all the uncertainties, "something like half the species that now exist will go extinct or will be on the verge of going extinct in the next century" if current trends continue.

Geological history is filled with mass extinctions. The most famous is the wave of extinctions in which the dinosaurs vanished 65 million years ago. Three quarters of the species on earth were wiped out in that event, paleontologists say. Extinctions of similar scope took place about 208 million, 367 million, and 439 million years ago. An estimated 96 percent of all species disappeared in a mass extinction 245 million years ago in the most extensive wipeout of species in the geological record. Most recently, an estimated 35 percent of species disappeared in an extinction 35 million years ago.

Scientists argue about the causes of such events. Species become extinct in the natural course of evolution, but this "background" rate of extinction is very low, said Dr. David Jablonski, a paleontologist at the University of Chicago. Some scientists have tried to assign a single cause, like an impact of a meteorite or comet, to the mass extinctions. Others say changes in climate, sea level, ocean currents, or ocean oxygen content could do it. In any case, some great environmental disruption, or combination of disruptions, is believed to be responsible in each case.

Writing in *Science*, Dr. Jablonski says that according to fossil studies, widespread species are more likely to survive a mass extinction, whereas specialized species adapted to a smaller area are especially vulnerable. This, he wrote, suggests that disruption and fragmentation of habitat caused by humans are likely to result in the increasing appearance of "widespread, weedy species—rats, ragweed, and cockroaches." The weedy species, he said in an interview, "are biologically prepared to cope" with environmental change and are "capable of using a lot of different kinds of resources," like disturbed roadside habitats and human waste.

Coming at it from a different perspective, Dr. Terry L. Erwin, an entomologist at the National Museum of Natural History in Washington, wrote in *Science* that if the disruption of ecosystems continues, "we can expect the evolutionary process as we know it to become degraded and retarded." If current trends continue and are pushed to their extreme, he wrote, "within a few hundred years this planet will have little more than lineages of domestic weeds, flies, cockroaches, and starlings evolving to fill a converted and mostly desertified environment."

The big question is whether the disruptions caused by human activity will be enough to create this bleak landscape and to bring about a mega-extinction like those of the distant past. "That's the

$10,000 question," said Dr. Jablonski. "We have no idea how many species are out there and how many are dying. My own personal feeling is that if the destruction goes unchecked, we will reach an extinction level unmatched since the end of the Cretaceous" period, when the extinction of the dinosaurs took place. "Under any circumstance, we're going to have a big loss," he said.

Dr. Simon has argued since the mid-1980s that there is no evidence of extinction rates of the magnitude advanced by Dr. Wilson and others. In an article in 1986, to which he says he still holds, he wrote that "there is no prima facie case for any expensive policy of safeguarding species without more extensive analysis than has so far been done." He says that the only scientifically observed extinction rate in this century is one species a year.

On the contrary, says Dr. Wilson, "the observed extinctions of species in this century have been massive and worldwide." Although "our very incomplete knowledge" makes it difficult to monitor extinctions, he said, "in the small minority of groups of plants and animals that are well known, extinction has been found to be proceeding at a rate hundreds or thousands of times above prehuman levels. That has been spread prominently on the scientific and public record." Although no comprehensive global survey has been taken, he says, there are hundreds of separate examples of serious recent extinctions: for instance, 90 plant species whose only habitat was a single mountain ridge in Ecuador, and half the 280 freshwater fish species in peninsular Malaysia.

Dr. Wilson bases much of his case on calculations employing a mathematical model that describes the effect on the number of species when the geographical area in which they exist is reduced. The model, which he says has been tested for validity against field studies and observations "over and over again," calculates that when species' habitat in a given area, such as an island or a continent, is reduced by 90 percent, the number of species eventually declines by about half. Worldwide, he said, tropical rain forests are being lost at the rate of nearly 55,000 square miles a year, a loss roughly equivalent to the land area of Florida. This figure, he said, was derived recently from satellite reconnaissance and from surveys by governments and scientific teams. At that rate, Dr. Wilson calculated, the world's rain forests would be reduced by half in thirty years. Applying the area-species model to this finding, he calculated that 10 percent to 22 percent of the rain forest species would be "doomed" in the next three decades.

As used by ecologists, *doomed* means that extinction might take some time, but that it is a foregone conclusion. Although they cannot be sure, scientists believe that more than half the world's species, from bacteria to big mammals and trees, live in the rain forests.

The mathematical model used by Dr. Wilson "is based on nothing but speculation," said Dr. Simon. "If scientific models are to have any validity, they must be based on some solid data." He said he has been unable to find such data. Critics also say that deforestation statistics can be misleading, that in the Amazon, for instance, more than a third of the region that is considered tropical forest is not rain forest but savanna and semidesert. They say also that some of the forest is not virgin forest, which is richest in species, but secondary growth. In reply, Dr. Wilson says that his calculations involve rain forest only, and apply globally, and that secondary forest is included as well. To observations that not enough is known about the number of species in the world, Dr. Wilson says that this is "completely true," but that it makes no difference: whatever the number, it is the proportion by which the species total is reduced that is important, and this is calculable.

Dr. Mares notes that there was no widespread extinction of species in the eastern United States after its forests were cleared. "While there were quite a number of changes in distribution patterns of many species," he said, "we haven't had massive die-offs." Dr. Wilson said that in the temperate zones, species tend to be distributed over a wider area than in the tropics, where it is common for a given species to be confined to one mountainside or one river basin. Temperate-zone species, he said, are consequently better able to survive habitat destruction. Dr. Mares acknowledged this, but said that "when you look at mammals" in the tropics, in which he specializes, "I don't think this is the case. Many have extensive distributions."

Some dissenters have also said that the experience of Puerto Rico casts doubt on the doomsday scenario. There, they say, there are as many species now, or more, than before the arrival of Columbus. Yet the island was largely deforested at the turn of the century. "That's probably true," said Dr. Wilson, "but it has been loaded up with tramp species, cockroaches, weeds, and so forth. Everywhere you go, you get them, and they're the same ones you get in Caracas and Lagos and Miami." Meanwhile, he said, some of the local species have been lost, and those are "gone from the global roster." That, he said, is the direction in which the world is going, "as we wipe out very rich assemblages of local, endemic species that have taken millions of years to build up, in many cases wiping them out before we have put scientific names on them."   [WKS, AUGUST 1991]

EUROPE'S FORESTS THRIVE DESPITE POLLUTION

C ONTRARY to a commonly held view, the forests of Europe have grown substantially despite a chronic assault by air pollution, according to a study by scientists in Finland. Pollution is indeed causing harm, the study says, and could lead to a future long-term decline. But after analyzing a range of recent studies, the Finnish scientists concluded that from 1971 to 1990, the rate of tree growth on the Continent increased by 30 percent and the total volume of wood in tree trunks increased by 25 percent. "A decline of forest resources in Europe is a threat for the future, not a historical fact," the Finnish investigators wrote in the journal *Science*. The study was conducted by Dr. Pekka E. Kauppi, Dr. Karl Mielikainen, and Dr. Kullervo Kuusela of the Finnish Forest Research Institute in Helsinki.

The conclusions on the rate of forest growth were based on detailed studies from Finland, France, and Sweden, and those on total forest volume on data from Austria, Finland, France, Germany, Sweden, and Switzerland. These intensive surveys were supplemented by less detailed assessments from the rest of Europe. Some forestry experts, including the authors themselves, say that the lack of definitive data from all but about a third of Europe is a drawback. To extrapolate from a few countries to the rest of the Continent "may be a bit tenuous," said Dr. Peter Duinker, a forestry expert at Lakehead University in Thunder Bay, Ontario, who is familiar with the European situation. Moreover, he said, many important signs of pollution-induced forest decline would not necessarily be revealed by simple surveys of forest growth and forest mass because "the complicating factors are enormous." Still, he said, he could not dispute the evidence so far as it goes.

Dr. Kauppi and his colleagues cited a number of possible reasons for what they say is the forests' growth, including a warming climate;

the fertilizing effect of airborne nitrates; and an increase in atmospheric concentrations of carbon dioxide, which is the basic raw material that plants use, in combination with sunlight and water, to manufacture food. Both nitrates and carbon dioxide are produced by the combustion of fossil fuels like coal, oil, and natural gas. Potentially, Dr. Kauppi and his colleagues say, these positive influences could lead to similar increases in growing stock and growth rate in other parts of the world. But they also said that ultimately the positive factors could be outweighed by the harmful impact of pollution. They found that deposits of airborne pollutants from the burning of fossil fuels have changed soil chemistry on the Continent in ways that could have long-term adverse effects. Because entire forest environments change on a time scale of decades, however, the upward growth trend of the last two decades cannot be reversed in fewer than five to ten years, guaranteeing that forest resources will be plentiful for the next ten to twenty years, the authors wrote.

Some of what they say appears to be consistent with some recent findings in the United States. A federal study ordered by Congress, completed in 1990, concluded that acid rain could stunt forests in the long term by altering soil chemistry, that red spruce at high altitudes was being damaged, and that acid rain might be contributing to a decline of sugar maples in Canada. But it found no evidence of an overall forest decline. Similarly, preliminary studies by scientists at the New York Botanical Garden have indicated that uncut old-growth forests at the garden's site in the Bronx have continued to function efficiently despite some of the worst pollution in America. The New York scientists warned, however, that such insults could lead to ultimate decline.

The Finnish investigators reported that more than 15 percent of Europe's trees were moderately to severely defoliated, though they noted that this does not always indicate decline in a forest stand. Defoliation often takes place naturally in a fast-growing forest as some trees outcompete others. The scientists calculated that about 3,100 square miles of forest, or about half a percent of the Continent's total, had been killed by pollution. As a particularly extreme instance, they cited the vicinity of the Montshegorsk smelter at Kola, near Murmansk, in northwestern Russia. Emissions of sulfur compounds and heavy metals from the smelter have killed all trees within a radius of three miles, according to the report. The destruction is the most extensive in the immediate area of any single source of pollution in

Europe, the report said. But severe decline like that at Montshegorsk is rare, the scientists concluded.

Among the factors not included in the Finnish analysis, said Dr. Duinker, is the fact that since World War II, Europe has been engaged in a deliberate effort to build up forest resources to meet the wood demands of a resurgent economy. European foresters also remove a lot of unhealthy-looking trees so that they can be salvaged alive for commercial use, a fact acknowledged by Dr. Kauppi and his colleagues. This "may be masking our ability to detect pollution-induced decline by going in and getting out the trees in worst shape," Dr. Duinker said. He also suggested that less severe forest decline than in the 3,100 dead square miles "could be a real phenomenon." There may be ten times more forests in moderate decline and a hundred times more in slight decline, he said. "It's like a boxer," he said. "Minor punches could put the guy on the floor after fifteen or twenty bouts."   [WKS, APRIL 1992]

DOES IT PAY TO SAVE OIL-DRENCHED OTTERS?

T HE dark-eyed sea otters that were slathered with oil in the *Exxon Valdez* tanker spill in Alaska quickly came to represent innocent wildlife befouled by people, and no expense was spared to save them. Now that emotions have died down, a biologist at the United States Fish and Wildlife Service is raising questions about the value of such rescue efforts. "There is a general feeling that a lot of otters were saved," said the biologist, Dr. James A. Estes. "But very little was accomplished, despite all the money that was spent." Depending on such rehabilitation efforts to conserve wildlife populations is unrealistic, Dr. Estes wrote in a recent issue of the journal *Science*, adding, "planning of this kind tends to lull the public and policymakers into a false sense of readiness."

Sea otters in California, Oregon, and Washington are listed as a threatened species by the Fish and Wildlife Service. The Alaska population of otters, about 150,000 animals, is not considered threatened or endangered, however. In the weeks after the March 1989 oil spill in Prince William Sound, 357 live sea otters were captured and delivered to rehabilitation facilities. Most of them were coated with oil, but a few healthy animals were inadvertently captured. Nearly 900 dead otters were also collected. By August, 222 otters, or 18 percent of the total number picked up, had survived the spill and the rehabilitation process and had been released to the wild or placed in aquariums. Dr. Estes, who is also an adjunct professor of biology at the University of California at Santa Cruz, said, however, that of all the otters affected by the spill, the percentage that were successfully rehabilitated was even lower than 18 percent because only one fifth of the otters that died immediately were ever found.

With just 222 of the otters surviving, Dr. Estes wrote, rehabilitation cost more than $80,000 per animal. Exxon USA paid all the expenses. Lance Lamberton, an Exxon spokesman, said, "We regret that we weren't able to save all the otters, but are pleased that the program did successfully result in saving large numbers of them. In this particular case we felt we did what was appropriate." Dr. Estes said scientists should consider several points before the next crisis. The first step, he said, is to assess wildlife populations beforehand. "How many otters were lost in Alaska is anybody's guess," he said. "That became painfully evident as the agencies tried to prepare substantive litigation against Exxon." Second, he said, it is important to evaluate just how effective intervention will be, and whether the wildlife population is truly threatened by the loss of some individuals. "Should the time, money, and anguish be put forth to save a few individuals?" he asked. "I have no illusion that the same thing wouldn't be done if we had another spill," he said. "But it's important to think about, from a conservation perspective, just what good it does. More often than not, there is a sort of panic response, with very little thought given to why we are doing what we are doing."

To try to head off that panic response, federal and state agencies and private groups are now formulating rehabilitation plans for the next oil spill. With the help of Dr. Randall Davis, a biologist who ran the otter rehabilitation effort in Prince William Sound and is now chairman of the marine biology department at Texas A&M University, California is setting up a permanent rehabilitation center to protect the state's 2,000 sea otters. Other centers are being established in Texas and Alaska, with the support of nonprofit organizations, Texas A&M, and the oil industry.

Dr. Davis said the experience in Alaska would enable the centers to be much more cost effective and to produce a higher survival rate than was once possible. "If we'd had advance planning and training, and facilities in place, our efforts in Alaska would have been more effective, and it would have cost a heck of a lot less," he said. "We've learned an incredible amount about how to do it better in the future. What we learned was worth every cent."

But Dr. Estes expressed concern that these facilities would lull people into a false sense of security. "People will think, well, now we have taken the protective measures that are necessary, and things are taken care of," he warned. "I don't support these facilities as effective conservation measures. I don't think they are going to do any good. We're doing it for the people, not for the animals," he added. "As a long-term strategy for conservation, we need to look toward prevention rather than cure."

The regional offices of the Fish and Wildlife Service are also drafting contingency plans to deal with the effects of spills. "We are trying to identify the areas of biological activity that are very significant, such as pupping centers and feeding grounds," said Ron Britton, the service's oil and hazardous substance spill response coordinator in Alaska. He said the agency was trying to set priorities for response efforts. "If we had a spill in an area where the effect on populations or individuals might not be high, we might decide to take no rehabilitative action," he said. "Each spill scenario is different."

Sarah Chasis, a senior lawyer for the Natural Resources Defense Council, an environmental group in New York, said: "It's best to err on the side of protecting the animals. It does make sense to step back over time and figure out the best way to restore and replenish the population. But in the case of another spill, how will you know if it might have occurred during a key period of migration?"

Many people will always vote on the side of protecting individual animals, perhaps at any cost. "Those animals were in so much pain, gouging their eyes out, chewing their paws off," recalled Nancy Hillstrand, a seasonal fisheries biologist for the Alaska Department of Fish and Game and one of the first people to volunteer for otter rehabilitation. "The otter losses wouldn't cause a problem in the population, but I believe in the individual animal. When you are listening to an otter scream, you can't look into its eyes and say, 'There's a lot of you around, so I'm not going to do anything.' I did whatever I had to do." [CD, DECEMBER 1991]

REASSESSING THE RISKS OF RADON

R ADON, described as the nation's most damaging cancer-causing pollutant and the second leading cause of lung cancer, may be less of a hazard to the average American than is generally believed, a number of critics contend. A natural, odorless, colorless, inert gas, radon is one breakdown product of an isotope of uranium, a solid, radioactive element naturally present in tiny amounts in rocks. Radon's breakdown products, in turn, include two isotopes of polonium that emit high-energy alpha particles. If inhaled, they can bombard lung cells, ultimately causing cancer. But study after controversial study has failed to document an epidemic of disease and death traceable to radon. With direct evidence of a hazard meager at the most, scientists have begun to challenge the basis for the high level of concern that the Environmental Protection Agency (EPA) and other organizations have tried to generate about this radioactive pollutant, which can seep into homes from the earth.

The agency estimates that 8 million American homes are dangerously contaminated by radon. It has also projected from preliminary data that radioactive particles from radon inhaled over a lifetime may cause up to 20,000 deaths from lung cancer each year. "We're trying to convey the message that if you're concerned about environmental risks, this is a serious problem," said Margo T. Oge, director of the EPA's radon division. "All we're asking people to do is spend ten to twenty dollars to find out if they have a problem, because we have no way of identifying the 8 million homes at greatest risk." The highest concentrations in homes are nearly always found in the crawl spaces, basements, and lower floors closest to contaminated rocks and soil. Short-term tests using charcoal canisters set beneath living areas for several days give a rough idea of levels. If the reading is over four picocuries, officials advise EPA-approved instrument tests lasting several months to one year in one or more main living areas before remedial measures are taken.

But several reputable scientists say that the extent and seriousness of radon contamination have been greatly exaggerated. In one of the studies that diverge farthest from the assumption of serious risk, covering 170,000 households in nearly 1,000 counties across the country, Dr. Bernard L. Cohen, professor of physics and radiation health at the University of Pittsburgh, found that counties with high radon levels tended to have low rates of lung cancer, and vice versa. Further, "the EPA surveys exaggerate the number of people living at or above the agency's action level of four picocuries per liter of air," said Naomi Harley, environmental radiation specialist at New York University's Institute of Environmental Medicine. A picocurie is a unit of radioactivity, and the EPA has recommended measures to lower radon levels in homes that are above the four-picocurie level. "EPA has literally tried to hit the public over the head with a hammer to get people to pay attention to radon," Dr. Harley said, adding that she does not think the approach is warranted. She contends that every time the agency issues a warning, the companies that test for radon "get inundated and don't process the tests properly."

Thus far, however, the public has been hard to arouse; according to the federal agency, fewer than 5 percent of American homes have been tested for radon. The critics are not giving radon a clean bill of health. No one questions its ability to cause lung cancer, a disease that used to kill half of uranium miners, who inhaled large amounts of radon breakdown products every workday. And in extrapolating from the experience of hard-rock miners, various expert groups, including the National Research Council and the National Council on Radiation Protection, have come up with radon-induced cancer estimates within the EPA's range of 5,000 to 20,000 a year.

In studies of the public to date, however, it has not been possible to tease out an effect of radon apart from the far more extensive lung disease caused by smoking and perhaps other air pollutants. Of the 140,000 deaths from lung cancer among Americans each year, about 120,000 are the consequence of cigarette smoking, which may be swamping the effects of radon in studies involving only hundreds of cancer victims or studies like Dr. Cohen's that do not carefully assess smoking habits. For example, no significant difference was found in radon exposure between 433 women with lung cancer and 402 similar women free of the disease, all of whom lived in New Jersey, one of the nation's radon hot spots. Although the researchers, headed by Janet B. Schoenberg of the New Jersey Department of Health, maintain that a statistically significant trend suggested an increased cancer risk associated with higher exposure levels, this observed trend was based on very small numbers. A study in Shenyang, China, where lung cancer is a prominent cause of death in women, found no difference in radon exposure over a year among 308 women with lung cancer and 356 healthy women. Here, smoke from indoor fires or some other unidentified factor may be masking any effects of radon.

Scientific critics of what they call "radon hysteria" are not suggesting that all American homes are free of danger from radon. Rather, they object to the across-the-board warnings to all Americans living in private homes or on lower levels of multiple dwellings when in fact only a small fraction of homes are likely to be dangerously contaminated. Dr. Anthony V. Nero Jr., a physicist at the Lawrence Berkeley Radiation Laboratory, said that perhaps 100,000 homes, not millions, as suggested by the EPA's "action level" of four picocuries or higher, had radon levels high enough in the rooms where people live to increase their cancer risk significantly over a lifetime.

Even those scientists like Dr. Harley, who generally support the agency's position on radon, take serious issue with the agency's advice to test for radon in basements and crawl spaces. They say radon levels at or below ground level of a house are likely to be far higher than on the floors where people live and thus may greatly exaggerate actual exposure. Some researchers have also questioned the applicability to the public of the studies of miners. The team that conducted the Chinese study, including four researchers from the National Cancer Institute, concluded that "projections from surveys of miners exposed to high radon levels may have overestimated the overall risks of lung cancer associated with levels typically seen in homes." The exposure of most miners was far more intense, and the dusty conditions in mines helped carry radon products into miners' lungs. So even if radon levels in home air are the same as in a mine, damaging particles may be less likely to find their way into householders' lungs. However, as physicians learned from the experience of miners, smoking significantly enhances the damage radon can cause, not just among smokers but probably also among those who inhale environmental smoke.

The EPA has vigorously defended its alarm call, pointing out that "radon risks are far higher than those associated with most environmental health hazards" that the agency regulates. The federal warnings have been supported by other health organizations, most notably the American Lung Association.

Although Dr. Nero said he had "substantial difficulty with what

EPA is doing," he and other critics concede that they understand the agency's concern. "EPA is accustomed to regulating environmental pollutants that perhaps place 1 person in 100,000 at risk of an adverse outcome," Dr. Nero noted. "Here the projected risk is maybe 1 person in 1,000 to 1 in 100" for those exposed to high radon levels in indoor air. This estimate of risk presumes that the experience of home-dwellers will parallel that of miners. Yet Dr. Cohen of Pittsburgh said his data and similar data gathered in England, Sweden, and Finland challenge the assumption that radon risk follows a straight line in extrapolating from danger at high levels to risks at low levels. He concluded: "My interpretation of the data is that low-level exposure is essentially harmless; there is no effect at very low levels, as are found in most homes." He added, "If this is true, we could save billions of dollars a year now spent trying to protect people from low-level radiation."

While Dr. Nero still believes that radiation in any amount carries some risk, he maintains that for an overwhelming majority of Americans the radon risk is no greater than hundreds of other risks Americans take every day. By the reckoning of the New Jersey Department of Environmental Protection, indoor radon exposure risk is about the same as that from home accidents and half that from car accidents.

Leonard Cole, a professor of political science at Rutgers University, said, "Many studies have shown that the general public is much more fearful of radiation than any other risk, yet few people have done anything about radon." He said he believed homeowners avoided radon tests because "they don't want to hear bad news" and because the full cost of reducing radon levels "comes out of the homeowner's pocket." Dr. Nero said that instead of trying to test every home for radon, measurements should be confined to known radon hot spots like parts of New Jersey and Pennsylvania. "Many people in these areas are living in homes with radon levels above twenty picocuries, levels greater than the occupational limit for miners," he said. "There are about 100,000 such households, and these people really do need help. There should have been a program long ago to find and fix these homes instead of scaring people into thinking 20 to 30 percent of houses have high levels."

Dr. Oge of the EPA countered that neither Dr. Nero nor any other scientist has come up with a way of zeroing in on the homes at greatest risk. She defended the agency's call for testing of all homes, explaining that neighboring homes can have greatly different radon levels in living quarters. "We're in the business of protecting the public health," Dr. Oge said. "We're not interested in panicking anybody. The public is apathetic about radon. Even when homes were tested and found to have a radon problem, most people haven't done anything to rectify it."

Dr. Nero, Dr. Harley, and others also take strong issue with how radon measurements are taken. "A test that monitors radon levels for two to seven days is not enough, even if it is done in rooms where people live," Dr. Nero said. "Monitoring should last for months, and ideally for a year."

The EPA defends its testing recommendation as an initial inexpensive screening method to pick up homes where radon levels in living areas might be undesirably high. Although the agency would prefer that every home in the country be tested, it is studying a proposal to make testing mandatory before selling a home, already a requirement in some states. But under the pressures of a pending sale, sellers are apt to use a short-term and hence less accurate test. And at the rate that houses turn over, it would take fourteen years to obtain tests on half of American homes.   [JEB, JANUARY 1991]

ACID RAIN LESS WIDESPREAD THAN FEARED

A TEN-YEAR, half-billion-dollar federally sponsored investigation is concluding that acid rain causes some significant environmental damage but far less than initially feared. "The sky is not falling, but there is a problem that needs addressing," James R. Mahoney, the director of the National Acid Precipitation Program, said as about 700 scientists from more than thirty countries gathered at a 1990 conference in Hilton Head, South Carolina, to digest, pick apart, and argue about the results of hundreds of recent studies. "Acid rain does cause damage," Dr. Mahoney said, "but the amount of damage is less than we once thought, and it's much less than some of the characterizations we sometimes hear."

Some of the program's findings are riddled with uncertainty. Some scientists at the Hilton Head review, moreover, criticized the assessment as prematurely concluding that acid rain is causing little harm to American forests. And Canadian scientists charged that the assessment understated the problem in their country, a problem to which, it is generally agreed, the United States greatly contributes. But Dr. Mahoney said that whereas there is "a great deal of room, still, for debate and interpretation," the extremes of the debate—the view that acid rain represented an imminent environmental disaster and the opposite view that it was not a problem—have now been eliminated.

The federal research program, created by Congress in 1980 to provide the government with a definitive study of acid rain, has engaged the efforts of hundreds of scientists. The Hilton Head meeting was meant to be the last major critical scientific review of the findings, among them these major ones:

In the United States, close to 1,200 lakes have become fully acidified. Little can live in them, and acid rain is mostly responsible. This is about 4 percent of all lakes in areas where acidification might be expected. Earlier, it had been feared that thousands of lakes would be fully acidified by now. In the Northeast, where most of the concern has focused, those lakes that are going to become acidified have already done so. An additional 5 percent of American lakes on which acid is thought to fall, while not necessarily fully acidified, are acidic enough to threaten some species of aquatic life.

Except for red spruce at high elevations in the Eastern mountains, there is no evidence that acid rain has caused a general decline of American forests. But a sizable minority of scientists at Hilton Head argued that because this part of the research effort is relatively young, and because new, provocative, but unevaluated data are still coming in, the door was being closed too soon. Furthermore, they argued, the report on forests had given short shrift to the possibility that over the long term, acid rain causes nutritional deficiencies in trees by altering soil chemistry. However, no evidence was presented that acid rain in the United States harms crops.

Acid rain and dry acid particles in the atmosphere could pose a health risk to asthmatics, people with heart or lung disease, children, and the elderly, either alone or in concert with other pollutants such as ozone. Symptoms include wheezing, shortness of breath, and coughing. But, citing uncertainty surrounding the issue, the study report said the health risk was speculative at this time. The study found also that acidic deposition might cause the chemical release in the environment of enough lead to affect health.

In the Eastern United States, sulfates of the kind borne by acid rain are the dominant cause of haze and reduced visibility, accounting for half the degradation of light. Acid rain also damages such construction materials as marble and limestone and causes a number of metals and alloys to corrode more rapidly. At particular risk are an estimated 35,000 historic buildings and 10,000 monuments in the Northeast.

Congress is debating proposed amendments to the Clean Air Act. Acid rain is one target of legislation, introduced by the Bush administration, to amend the law. Industries, electric utilities in particular, would be required to reduce emissions of sulfur dioxide and oxides of nitrogen by 10 million tons and 2 million tons a year, respectively, by the year 2000, at a cost estimated by the Environmental Protection Agency as $22 billion over the next decade.

Sulfur dioxide and nitrogen oxides, produced by the burning of coal, oil, and natural gas, are the precursors of acid rain. In the atmosphere, they react with water and other chemicals to form sulfate and nitrate compounds that can be carried hundreds of miles by air currents before they are deposited on the earth by rain, snow, sleet, mist, fog, or clouds. Dry sulfur dioxide and nitrogen oxides also sometimes fall to earth nearer the point of origin.

In broad perspective, say Dr. Mahoney and some others associated with the federal study, acid rain cannot be seen as ranking at, or even near, the top of a present-day priority list of environmental issues that also includes urban air pollution, destruction of tropical forests, depletion of the earth's ozone layer, and the possibility of global climate change. "I completely disagree with that," Deborah A. Sheiman of the Natural Resources Defense Council, an environmental advocacy group in New York, said as the conference was ending. Not least, she and others said, this is because in one respect, there are more reasons, not fewer, to be concerned about acid rain today than there were ten years ago. Then, the concern focused on damage to lakes and streams in the Northeast. Now it involves lakes and streams in other regions as well, along with forests, human health, atmospheric visibility, and damage to materials.

Ten years ago, Dr. Mahoney recalled, some environmentalists predicted that within a decade, acid rain would increase by tenfold the acidity of thousands of lakes in the United States. In fact, the research shows, the acidity actually increases by up to fivefold over twenty to fifty years, and far fewer lakes are involved. (Tenfold is equal to 1 point on the 14-point pH scale, which is the standard measure of acidity and alakinity. A pH of 0 is totally acid; of 14, totally alkaline. A pH of 7 is neutral.) Damage to aquatic life begins to take place below a pH of 6, according to findings presented at Hilton Head. The federal study found that 9 percent of lakes in areas of the United States known to be targets for acid rain had acid levels below pH 6, and that 4 percent were totally acidified. These lakes, though a small fraction of the national total, were concentrated not only in the Northeast, as had long been suspected, but also in Appalachia, on the mid-Atlantic coastal plain, in northern Florida, and in contiguous parts of northern Wisconsin and the Upper Peninsula of Michigan. The survey also found that 2.7 percent of streams in areas where acid rain falls from the sky were acidic, and that many streams in the Appalachians were vulnerable to future acidification.

"I'm not saying there's no problem," said Dr. Mahoney. "But we don't have very rapid decay of large numbers of lakes." Although many lakes will recover once no more acid falls into them, he said, the recovery will take some years.

The federal study incorporates data from Canada showing that 5 percent of a sample of 8,500 Canadian lakes were acidified. If that is an accurate sample of the whole, it would mean that perhaps 14,000 Canadian lakes are fully acid. And about a quarter of the Canadian lakes sampled had a pH of 6 or less. Canadian scientists say that perhaps 150,000 lakes could fall in this category. By treating these findings separately, burying them in the body of the study, leaving them out of the summary, and generally underplaying them, the scientists "greatly diminished" the extent of the Canadian problem, contended Tom Brydges, a lakes expert from Environment Canada, his country's environmental agency.

Lawrence Baker of the University of Minnesota Water Resources Center, who was the chief author of the lakes report, said that ideally, the Canadian data should be integrated with the overall study. But he said that it was unclear whether the Canadian sample was a true random sampling, and that the two studies did not examine the same variables. "I'm not exactly sure if it can be resolved, scientifically speaking," he said. Patricia Irving, the associate director of the federal study and its science coordinator, said a major purpose of the Hilton Head meeting was to uncover and ventilate concerns like Canada's before the final report.

At the levels at which acid is now being deposited in North America, the study found that with the exception of Eastern red spruce at high elevations, there is "no evidence of widespread forest damage." Moreover, it found that acid rain "is not associated with crop damage." The real villain is ozone, which "is capable of regional-scale crop growth and yield reduction."

Beyond that, the reports on forests and vegetation generated considerable contention. There is wide agreement that to the extent acid rain does harm forests, it is just one of many stresses, including natural ones like drought and cold. Scientists say it is extremely difficult to sort out cause and effect. Moreover, critics at Hilton Head said that data collection on forests was still going on and not that much information was in hand. The study was also criticized for drawing a sweeping conclusion that hardwoods like the sugar maple are not harmed by acid rain. Some studies in Canada suggest the opposite. And in one of the biggest reservations on the forest issue, a number of scientists said that there was much evidence that acid rain changes the balance of nutrients in forest soils and that the issue would have to be reevaluated before a final report.   [WKS, FEBRUARY 1991]

A MISDIRECTED CAMPAIGN
AGAINST SMOG

A NEW study by the National Academy of Sciences has found that smog is so poorly understood that much of the nation's effort to control it may be misdirected. The study was required under the Clean Air Act passed in 1990. It said progress in meeting standards for smog "has been extremely slow at best," in part because of measurement problems. Among these problems, it said, is properly accounting for variations in weather.

Smog is formed when two classes of chemicals react together in sunlight: one class is volatile compounds from oil and gasoline, and the other is nitrogen oxides, often a by-product of burning fuel. Both classes of chemicals are emitted by automobile tailpipes. Air pollution control officials have been concentrating on organic compounds; the study strongly suggests that they should also have been concentrating on nitrogen oxides. The study raises the possibility that although billions of dollars have been invested at refineries and gasoline stations and in the hardware of cars to reduce organic emissions, not nearly enough money and effort have been aimed at reducing nitrogen oxides.

Overall, the study tends to affirm the contentions of lobbyists for the oil and auto industries that smog formation is not yet understood well enough to require large-scale changes in cars or fuel. Of particular interest to the oil industry is a finding that whereas new substitutes for gasoline could help clean the air in cities, the uncertainties are so great that "requiring the widespread use of any specific fuel would be premature."

An expert on air pollution, Michael Bradley, who is the executive director of an organization of eight Northeastern states working on air pollution issues, said the report pointed in the right direction. "It's just a matter of how alarmingly you want to put it," he added. Mr. Bradley, who reviewed the study in advance of publication, said, "It tells us we have a lot of work to do and that all the available controls we're aware of have to be implemented."

Another air pollution expert, David G. Hawkins, who was assistant administrator for air at the Environmental Protection Agency in the Carter administration and is now a senior lawyer at the Natural Resources Defense Council in New York, said: "It's saying we've been doing the wrong thing in neglecting nitrogen oxide control. It's not that we should do less volatile organic control."

But another expert, Terry Yosie of the American Petroleum Institute, said that in light of the report, the pollution control measures now in place or proposed "may also be significantly flawed." The report shows that policymakers now have "a fundamental lack of knowledge about ozone and its formation," he said, and even over how much progress is being made. "If the National Academy of Sciences is concluding we're flying blind, why trust the pilots in charge of the aircraft now?" he said.

The two-year-long study cost $430,000 and was cosponsored by the Environmental Protection Agency, the Department of Energy, the American Petroleum Institute, and the Motor Vehicle Manufacturers Association. An academy spokesman, Stephen P. Push, said it was not unusual for the academy to accept money from outside the government. The petroleum institute, which is the oil industry's main trade association, has been fighting a losing battle against the air pollution control standards adopted by California for its cars. Eleven Eastern states have announced their intention to adopt the same standards. Mr. Yosie also pointed to a conclusion of the report that smog problems differ from region to region. In contrast, he said, what the widespread adoption of the California standard amounted to was "a one-size-fits-all" approach. The study, he said, shows that in some locations reducing volatile organic emissions would not help air quality.

Smog is known to pollution experts as ground-level ozone, which is not connected with the stratospheric ozone that filters harmful rays from the sun. Atmospheric scientists say that the volume of ozone formation depends on the ratio of volatile organics to nitrogen oxides. That ratio is an important factor in choosing methods to fight smog. According to the academy's report, when the ratio of volatile organics to nitrogen oxides is ten to one or less, control of volatile organics "is generally effective," and reducing nitrogen oxide may be counterproductive. But if the ratio of volatile organics to nitrogen oxides is twenty or more, the opposite is true. The report says that to reduce smog, officials should try to reduce nitrogen oxide, not volatile organics. The problem, according to the report, is that for years officials have underestimated the amount of volatile organics. The report found that cars emit volatile organics at levels double to quadruple the amount previously estimated. The estimates may be too low because the cars tested on laboratory treadmills are not a fair sample of the ones on the road, or because the test procedure does not reflect actual driving, the study said.

In any case, the study found, concentration on reducing emissions of volatile organics in cities over the last two decades has not led to the substantial reductions in ozone that were predicted. Reductions in volatile organic compounds are probably far smaller than those claimed by state and federal air pollution officials. And even if they are correct on an absolute basis, they are wrong on a percentage basis, the study said, because the total amount of man-made volatile organics is higher than previously believed. Perhaps even worse, from the point of view of state air pollution control officials, is a finding that in many areas even if man-made volatile organic chemicals are eliminated, naturally occurring volatile organic chemicals given off by plants, combining with man-made nitrogen oxides, may push ozone concentrations over the national standard. [MLW, DECEMBER 1991]

THE BACKLASH ON GLOBAL WARMING

D ESPITE the Clinton administration's plan to control waste industrial gases that trap heat in the atmosphere, conservatives and industry groups have mounted a renewed assault on the idea that global warming is a serious and possibly catastrophic threat. In a drumroll of criticism, they have characterized the thesis of global warming as a "flash in the pan," "hysteria," "scare talk," and a ploy by socialists to justify controls on the economy. The rhetoric is the mirror image of some that was heard at the height of the 1988 North American heat wave, when some environmentalists and politicians warned of climatic apocalypse on the basis of assertions by a minority of scientists that global warming was already under way.

The evidence that warming or harm from warming will occur in the foreseeable future is "ludicrously small," argues a 1993 book published by the Cato Institute, a free-market research organization in Washington. Reining in global warming "will require a degree of bureaucratic control over economic affairs previously unknown in the West," wrote Ben W. Bolch and Robert D. McCallum, professors of economics and chemistry at Rhodes College in Memphis, in a book, *Apocalypse Not: Science, Economics and Environmentalism*, edited by Harold Lyons.

Dr. Dixy Lee Ray, the former governor of Washington and a former chairwoman of the Atomic Energy Commission, called carbon dioxide "an unlikely candidate for causing any significant worldwide temperature changes" in another 1993 book, *Environmental Overkill: Whatever Happened to Common Sense?* And a number of newspapers, including *The Washington Times* and *The Wall Street Journal*, have published articles debunking global warming. In the July 1993 issue of *Commentary*, Jeffrey Salmon, executive director of the George C. Marshall Institute in Washington, stated categorically that there is "no solid scientific evidence to support the theory that the earth is warming because of man-made greenhouse gases."

In the midst of this revisionist onslaught, whom is the public to believe? Global warming is not a cut-and-dried issue, and scientific experts are still debating most of its aspects. But few scientists are to be found at either of the extremes that have characterized the political debate. A substantial number of highly regarded climate researchers have long believed that global warming set off by industrial and automotive emissions is a real possibility that could have serious consequences sooner or later. But they cannot say exactly how severe the effects of the warming will be or when it will come. And very few climatologists are ready to declare that global warming has begun. Most believe that no clear sign of human-induced change has yet made itself apparent amid the wide natural fluctuations of the earth's climate.

There are two undisputed facts about global warming: first, carbon dioxide, the waste gas produced by burning coal, oil, and wood, has been accumulating in the earth's atmosphere over the last century; and second, the gas traps heat that is produced when the sun's energy is absorbed by the earth and then re-radiated. Given those physical facts, the practical question of interest is how much the earth's climate will heat up after injection of a given amount of carbon dioxide. Since no experiment can answer that question, other than the global one now in progress, scientists have turned to their next best method, which is to simulate the earth's climate system in a series of equations that are run on a supercomputer. This exercise, known as computer modeling, is somewhat contentious because the models are far from perfect and represent a simpler, stripped-down version of the earth's real climate.

After examining results from the best computer models, a scientific advisory committee to the United Nations concluded in 1990, and again in 1992, that a doubling of atmospheric carbon dioxide—expected to occur by the year 2100 without remedial action—will raise the average global temperature by 3 to 8 degrees Fahrenheit. In comparison, the earth has warmed by only 5 to 9 degrees since the last ice age.

The United Nations panel and various committees of the National Academy of Sciences, made up of leading experts in the field, have consistently found merit in the global warming theory. Still, the issue is far from settled and critics of global warming continue to attack the models' predictions on various grounds. One, Dr. Richard Lindzen, a meteorologist at the Massachusetts Institute of Technology, argues that the computer models fail to account accurately for the role of water vapor, a heat-trapping gas which by its sheer quantity exerts a far stronger greenhouse effect than carbon dioxide. Most climatologists believe carbon dioxide is pivotal because the warming it induces, though quite small in itself, causes more water to evaporate from land and sea. The water vapor in turn traps more heat, thus amplifying the effect of the carbon dioxide. Dr. Lindzen denies that this amplification takes place, and if he is right, then a doubling of carbon dioxide would indeed cause little or no greenhouse problem. But other climate researchers dismiss his argument as speculation, whereas the amplifying role of water vapor is well documented, in their view.

Critics of global warming say that the computer models cannot be trusted, because they fail to reproduce the exact pattern of warming actually experienced over the last century. The models predict that in response to a 25 percent rise in atmospheric carbon dioxide over the last century, average global temperature should have risen by 2 degrees. In fact the climate has warmed by 1 degree. Defenders of the models counter that with an extra refinement—taking into account the fact that industrially emitted sulfate aerosols reflect sunlight—the models' forecasts match the historical record much better.

Besides the imperfections of computer models, critics point out an apparent anomaly in global warming theory: that over the last century the chief rise in global temperature occurred before 1940, though most of the carbon dioxide has been spewed out since then. Defenders respond that the climate is an erratic system and that a neat, constant relationship between gas input and temperature rise should not be expected. The critics go on to say that the small temperature spike seen so far could easily be nothing but another jiggle in the zigzag course of the climate's normal variability. Climatologists almost universally agree that this is indeed possible. The United Nations panel said it was equally possible, however, that a natural cooling trend could be masking an even larger greenhouse warming than has been observed.

Conservative columnists and industry groups have jumped on another apparent discrepancy: the models predict greater warming in the arctic than seems to be the case. Defenders say the measurements were not made in places where the warming would be most manifest, and that many observations have borne out the greater warming predicted for northern latitudes.

The models appeared to gain some important empirical support in December 1992, when Martin I. Hoffert of New York University and Curt Covey of Lawrence Livermore National Laboratory reconstructed two ancient climates, one much warmer than today's and one much colder. Since they were able to estimate temperature changes and prevailing carbon dioxide levels from evidence in the geological record, they were then in a position to answer the critical question— at least for those two periods—of how much warming is produced by a given rise in carbon dioxide levels. Their answer was that when carbon dioxide levels double, the temperature of the atmosphere rises by about 4 degrees. This figure agrees well with the best estimate from the computer models, which is, in the view of the United Nations panel, that a doubling of carbon dioxide induces a 4.5-degree rise in average global temperature. Some scientists believe the Hoffert-Covey findings rule out a warming in the lower end of the panel's broader range of 3 to 8 degrees. A climate system that responds so sluggishly to external forces could not have produced the great temperature swings of the past, they say.

Dr. Lindzen, on the other hand, questions the Hoffert-Covey study's utility in predicting future climate change on the ground that the climate may have behaved differently in the remote past. Critics note that evidence for the observed global warming trend of the 1980s depends on ground-based measurements of temperature, which amount to only a sampling of the whole earth. These measurements are also suspect, in the critics' view, because many of the measuring sites are near cities, which are warmer than the surrounding countryside. Satellite observations that started in 1979 failed to see any warming trend. Defenders say the satellite measurements could be distorted by atmosphere factors, that their record is too short to support any generalization, and that the ground-based temperature measurements have been correctly calibrated to discount warmth from cities.

Some critics contend that even if the atmosphere does heat up, the warming will be benign. Dr. Patrick J. Michaels, a meteorologist at the University of Virginia, points out that the warming seen so far has made itself evident mostly at night and in winter. If that continues, he argues, global warming will be a boon, not a catastrophe. Growing seasons will be longer, winters less harsh, and plants invigorated by rising carbon dioxide will grow faster. But Thomas R. Karl, chief of the global climate laboratory at the National Climatic Data Center in Asheville, North Carolina, responds that the warmer nights may have other causes, possibly natural, quite apart from greenhouse gases. James E. Hansen, a climatologist at the National Aeronautics and

Space Administration's Goddard Institute for Space Studies in New York, notes that the warmer winters, far from being welcome, could disrupt the chilling that many plant seeds must experience to germinate properly in the spring. Botanists have found that carbon dioxide does spur plant growth, but also the plants can then outgrow their nutrient supply, making them less nutritious as food.

As for other effects of the predicted warming, the United Nations panel estimated that an average global warming of 4.5 degrees would cause sea levels to rise two feet by the year 2100 and would make heat waves more frequent and cold spells rarer. Model simulations have suggested that although average global rainfall would increase, the interiors of continents would become drier, droughts more common, and tropical storms more violent. Some climatologists also believe that climatic zones would shift and regional weather patterns would be dislocated, disrupting agricultural production and natural ecosystems. But these effects are regarded by climatologists as being uncertain.

Where does all this leave the debate? Issues in science are not decided by taking votes, but polls of climate researchers show that most believe there is a better than even chance that the climate will warm by at least 3.5 degrees over the next century. Climatologists also know that once in the atmosphere, carbon dioxide stays there for centuries; whatever climatic effect it has will not be reversed in several human lifetimes. This may partly explain why the weight of opinion among climate scientists, as measured by polls, is that lack of certainty should not stand in the way of prudent steps to control greenhouse gas emissions.

Indeed, a panel of the National Research Council—the government's chief source of scientific advice—concluded in 1991 that "despite the great uncertainties, greenhouse warming is a potential threat sufficient to justify action now." How much action, what kind, and how soon is an economic and political issue of great consequence in a world that runs on the burning of fossil fuels. Proponents of the greenhouse theory therefore need not be surprised at the intense fire now being rained on their ideas.   [WKS, OCTOBER 1993]

AN EDEN IN ANCIENT AMERICA?
NOT REALLY

CONTRARY to widespread belief, evidence is mounting that pre-Columbian America was not a pristine wilderness inhabited by people who lived in such harmony with nature that they left it unmarked. Instead, many scientists now say, the original Americans powerfully transformed their landscape in ways both destructive and benign—just like modern people.

In the latest piece of evidence, British investigators have analyzed sediments from Lake Patzucaro in the highlands of central Mexico and found that ancient farming practices around the lake caused "staggeringly high" rates of soil erosion, which were unsurpassed even after the Spanish arrived. The study "shatters the myth of pre-Columbian America as an Eden in which people were 'transparent in the landscape,'" Dr. Karl W. Butzer, a geographer at the University of Texas, wrote in a commentary on the study in the March 4, 1993, issue of the British journal *Nature*.

The question is of more than academic interest, since ancient and traditional forms of agriculture have lately been held up as an ideal alternative to present-day practices that degrade the landscape. Although some of what ancient farmers did was ecologically friendly, much of it was not, scientists warn, and great care must be taken in deciding what models to follow. "It's not true that only in modern times have people begun to abuse the environment," said Dr. Daniel J. Hillel, a professor of soil physics at the University of Massachusetts. "We're doing it more intensively and on an ever-larger scale than before," he said, but he added: "It's wrong to say the ancients knew best and that we're stupid. It's also wrong to say that the ancients were always stupid."

It is becoming abundantly clear to geographers, ecologists, and archeologists that, whether for good or ill, ancient people had a heavy and widespread impact on their environment. Some scientists are convinced that a number of early civilizations were brought down by environmental degradation of the land. The brilliant cultural centers of ancient Mesopotamia, for instance, are widely thought to have collapsed because of over-irrigation, which forced water tables to rise and carry salt to the surface, where it made land unfit for farming. And some scientists suggest that erosion brought about by overclearing of forests undermined the Maya of Central America. In antiquity, as today, people were making decisions aimed at gaining a living in the short term without always considering the long-term effects. "People did what made sense to them and sometimes that was destructive," said Dr. Charles Redman, an anthropologist at Arizona State University.

In the Western Hemisphere, pre-Columbian people changed the landscape nearly everywhere from the Arctic to Patagonia, according to a 1992 review of the literature by Dr. William M. Denevan, a cultural ecologist at the University of Wisconsin at Madison. In some ways, in fact, the pre-European landscape may have owed its essential character to humans. When the glaciers retreated from the upper Midwest at the end of the last ice age, for instance, there was no vegetation at first. But humans were there, Dr. Denevan said in an interview, and as grasslands and forests returned, the Indians shaped the vegetation by setting frequent fires to clear land for farming, better hunting, visibility, and security. Many fire-resistant grasses, flowering plants, and trees consequently flourished; the ecosystem in effect evolved partly as a result of human action.

Although climate plays a major role in shaping ecosystems, Dr. Denevan and others argue that the pre-Columbian forests of Eastern North America, for example, were more open and parklike as a result of burning than they were in 1750, after the Indian population of the Western Hemisphere had been reduced by about 90 percent as a result of diseases imported from Europe. The thick primeval forests of colonial times, Dr. Denevan argues, represent a recovery from the impact of the Indians at their zenith. In attacking what he calls "the pristine myth," Dr. Denevan's September 1992 review, published in *The Annals of the American Association of Geographers*, said: "By 1492, Indian activity throughout the Americas had modified forest extent and composition, created and expanded grasslands," and rearranged topography through "countless artificial earthworks. Agricultural fields were common, as were houses and towns and roads and trails. All of these had local impacts on soil, microclimate, hydrology, and wildlife." Even mild impacts and slow changes, Dr. Denevan wrote, add up to dramatic long-term effects. Although the impact was not as extensive as that of modern people, he wrote, the paradise that Columbus thought he had found "was clearly a humanized paradise." He concluded that pre-Columbian Indians changed the landscape more than the Europeans and their descendants did in the 250 years after Columbus landed, and in some cases in the 500 years since.

At Lake Patzcuaro, west of Mexico City, Dr. Sarah L. O'Hara of the University of Sheffield and two British colleagues took twenty-one samplings from the lake bottom. The lake has no outlet and therefore acts as a trap for sediments that have washed into it from surrounding slopes over thousands of years. By analyzing the radio-carbon content of charcoal and small animal shells trapped in the sediments, the investigators were able to calculate how much sediment was deposited in the lake during various periods in the past. The results, published in the British journal *Nature*, showed that there had been three distinct periods of soil erosion before the Spanish appeared in Mexico, coincident with the rise of three early human occupations. The first erosion episode, between about 3,900 and 3,250 years ago, was minor. The second, from about 2,600 to 1,350 years ago, coincided with the classical Mesoamerican civilization of the Maya period. The third and most destructive came between A.D. 1200 and the arrival of the Spanish in the sixteenth century, when the land around the lake was occupied by a post-classical civilization called the Purepecha, and continued thereafter. It was Dr. O'Hara who characterized the later pre-Columbian rates of erosion, amounting to about 85 tons of soil per acre per year, as "staggeringly high." The finding, she said, "explodes this sort of myth that the indigenous peoples of central Mexico lived in harmony with the environment and didn't practice environmentally damaging agriculture."

Although the findings indicate the arrival of the Europeans "was not the watershed event in the environmental degradation that people make it out to be," Dr. Redman said, they make another, perhaps more interesting point as well: that in some periods the occupants of the lake watershed pursued more benign practices than in others. "There are some centuries where it was better than today and some centuries where it was hellacious, where they were stripping the land and gullies were forming everywhere," said Dr. Redman.

Methods may make a major difference. Dr. O'Hara attributes the long episodes of high erosion partly to classic slash-and-burn agriculture, in which the land is denuded of trees to create cropland and erosion often results. But at other times and places in ancient America, less damaging methods were employed. These included terracing, a practice called agroforestry, and the use of what are called raised fields. In one form of agroforestry, still practiced in the Amazon, agricultural plots are managed so that over a period of years they evolve in preplanned phases from cleared farmland back into thick forests. The farm plots move through stages in which conventional crops predominate at first, but then wild species of useful plants and trees are encouraged to encroach gradually. These yield medicines and pesticides. Eventually the forest reclaims the plot. Other plots are meanwhile in different phases, with the result that the forest continually renews itself while sustaining the farmers.

In raised-field technology, employed by ancient peoples from Mexico to Peru, crops were grown on rows of end-to-end rectangular platforms, about a yard high, created by digging the dirt from areas between the rows. These dug-out areas became canals that harbored fish and turtles. Each year silt from the canals was placed on the platforms as fertilizer. This eventually sound and highly productive system flourished for thousands of years before mysteriously dying out, apparently before the Spanish appeared. But archeologists in Bolivia and Peru have resurrected it experimentally, and it has been held up as a low-cost alternative to modern agriculture.

Traditional methods like these might well be adapted to local conditions at minimum cost and maximum ecological benefit, said Dr. Butzer, who wrote the *Nature* commentary, and in fact are preferable to what he calls "technodevelopment"—the attempt to force high-technology, high-cost agriculture on social systems unprepared to use it. But they are not a panacea, he said. On slopes steeper than about 5 degrees, for instance, "there is virtually nothing you can do" to stop erosion if the slopes are farmed. The lesson of the O'Hara study, he said, is that some traditional farming knowledge can be "profitably applied, but it has to be applied with care."

There is also a question as to whether the ecologically sound but essentially small-scale, labor-intensive traditional methods are adequate to the demands of a surging population. Some experts suggest that the Mayan system, for example, initially depended on a combination of agroforestry, raised fields, and terracing, but the Mayan population outgrew these methods and resorted to extensive forest clearing that led to erosion. Dr. O'Hara suggests that the erosion she has documented at Lake Patzcuaro resulted simply from too many people trying to live off too little land. But even that explanation does not universally apply, says Dr. Hillel, because "some densely populated societies did live in harmony with the environment, and some sparsely populated ones destroyed their environment." [WKS, MARCH 1993]

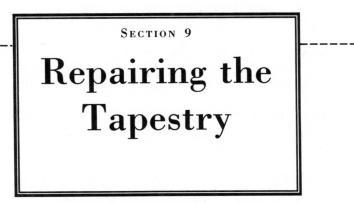

Repairing the Tapestry

SOME DAMAGED ECOSYSTEMS CAN BE RESTORED

NATURE IS resilient, but when the breaking point of an ecosystem is reached, collapse is often complete and permanent. Yet permanence need not always mean forever. A new school of ecologists has resolved to learn how to restore lost and damaged habitats.

Wetlands are one object of their attention. Federal laws encourage developers who pave over wetlands to restore others that are damaged. But the science of reviving wetlands is far from complete, and many experiments are still under way.

Even more challenging is the restoration of nearly

vanished American ecosystems like the oak savanna and the prairie. By trial and error, with much study and labor, pioneers have found that these lost glories can be brought back. For the American prairie to flourish, the vital ingredients were Indians and bison; Indians to set fires that only the prairie species could survive, and bison to graze and to fertilize the soil. In the culmination of many years of effort, the Nature Conservancy has returned a herd of bison to roam free on a tract of restored prairie in Oklahoma.

Protecting threatened species is an important endeavor, but even more vital is preserving the larger systems of which they are part. The peregrine falcon is being successfully restored to much of its former range in the United States, but that is possible only because the pesticides like DDT, which fatally thinned its eggshells, have long since been banned.

Restoration of an ecosystem like the prairie or oak savanna gives new life to dozens of rare or threatened species. So intricately are nature's assemblages put together that the pioneers restoring the oak savanna found that once they had planted certain species, others began to appear spontaneously.

Restoration ecology holds out the promise of reversing the last century's steady impoverishment of the American landscape. Not for a century has a bison herd roamed free and wild in a prairie. From this unexpected rebirth, others may follow.

RESTORING THE VANISHED SAVANNA

HUMANS can never return to the Garden of Eden, and vanished ecosystems may never be totally restored. But a surprising degree of recovery can be achieved, as recent ventures in ecological restoration by green-thumbed amateurs and scientists attest. The restoration projects are showing just how much remains to be understood about nature's complexities. One pertinent insight yielded by some of the experiments is that after certain key species have been successfully reintroduced, other species seem to return almost as if by magic.

An outstanding example is an effort by the Nature Conservancy, a leading ecological preservation group, to resurrect a long-lost savanna ecosystem in Northbrook, Illinois, outside Chicago. The group says that the savanna ecosystem, essentially grasslands punctuated by oak trees, is composed of a distinctive mixture of plants and animals that make it different from both prairie and forest. Few if any prime examples of oak savannas are believed to exist anywhere. Through arduous detective work, restorationists tracked down certain species of savanna plants, some rare or endangered, that were said to have flourished in the area originally but were barely clinging to existence in scattered nooks. Exotic brush and weeds introduced by human activity had crowded them out, all but obliterating the natural ecosystem. The restorationists destroyed the intruding plants by fire. Seeds of the original grasses and flowers were sown on the bare ground, and within two years a rich, evolving savanna ecosystem was well on its way to reassembling itself under the oaks. Uncommon species of butterflies, like the Edwards' hairstreak and the Appalachian brown, appeared as if from nowhere to feed on the plants. A pair of Eastern bluebirds, long absent from the area, returned in 1989 to establish a family in what had become, for them, an ideal habitat. The resurrected ecosystem is "so strikingly beautiful," says Steve Packard, the science director of the Illinois Nature Conservancy, who directed the project.

"It was like finding a Rembrandt covered with junk in somebody's attic."

Similar tracts of savanna have subsequently been restored in other parts of the Chicago area. On one of them, rare and endangered plants like the prairie white-fringed orchid, the small yellow lady's slipper, and the pale vetchling, a legume, popped up; and the silvery-blue butterfly, which had not been seen in the state for decades, suddenly reappeared to feed on the vetchling.

At first, some academic scientists scoffed at the notion that the Northbrook site could originally have been anything but a prairie ecosystem and advised the experimenters to cut down the oaks if they wanted to succeed. Others told them to leave the project to expert ecologists. Now, although Mr. Packard's findings about the nature of the ecosystem remain to be confirmed, his advice is in demand. And some ecological theorists cite his results in support of the contention that ecosystems assemble and develop not haphazardly, as if by accident, but in special patterns and sequences, according to specific affinities. If even a few key species are missing, according to this idea, the ecosystem will not function.

Increasingly, ecologists are coming to see restoration not only as a true acid test of their ideas but also as a powerful research technique that in turn will lead to more effective restoration. Although intriguing connections between theory and practice are starting to be made, however, restoration ecology remains largely a matter of trial and error and the intuition of its practitioners. Evocative as its results may be, they have yet to be tested with scientific rigor. Restoration offers the hope not of just halting or slowing ecological damage, but of ultimately reversing it. One goal is to help replace the steady loss of habitat that is leading to the gradual disappearance of plant and animal species. Scientists rank this loss of biological diversity as one of the world's most important environmental threats. Prairie and savanna ecosystems lend themselves particularly well to restoration ecology because they can be re-created quite quickly.

One of the more illuminating restoration projects is unfolding on a 1,000-acre expanse of prairie inside the ring formed by the circular four-mile tunnel of the Fermi National Accelerator Laboratory at Batavia, Illinois, near Chicago. Restorationists have brought to life a functioning prairie ecosystem supporting some 125 native plant species. Previously missing prairie fauna like meadowlarks, falcons, bobolinks, coyotes, and foxes have turned up to make the tract their permanent habitat. But as successful as the project has been, it also illustrates the considerable difficulties of restoration.

The Fermilab experiment shows that an ecosystem unfolds and develops in a precise fashion and order, beginning with what Dr. Robert F. Betz, a prairie ecologist at Northeastern Illinois University, calls a few "matrix species" of plants. "You cannot put a prairie in backwards," said Dr. Betz, who has been instrumental in the Fermilab project. "It appears that you have to start with some basic plants that prepare the way for the others." The matrix plants, principally two six-foot-tall grasses called big blue-stem grass and Indian grass, prepare the ground by changing the soil, adding antibiotic chemicals and organic matter that in turn nourish successive waves of flowering plants. Prairies, it appears, "return to their native condition by steps, over years and decades, once the pioneers prepare the way," said Dr. Betz. "You don't get [them] all at once." This means that humans have to tend the ecosystem until it runs on its own, beating back invading nonprairie plants, continuing to plant desired ones, and contending with invading animals like deer and imported pheasants. Eventually, it is hoped, humans will be able to leave the cleansing process to natural fires and native grazing animals like bison.

Restoration ecology is still a matter of controversy. Developers are sometimes allowed to destroy wetlands if, in accord with the federal government's "no-net-loss" policy, they make up for the destruction of one tract of wetlands with the restoration or creation of another. Conservationists who doubt the success of wetlands restoration say it is no substitute for preservation. Restorationists agree. "Any of us will tell you that," said Dr. William R. Jordan 3d of the University of Wisconsin arboretum in Madison. "This is a healing art. The first rule is to do no harm." Dr. Jordan is a founder of the Society for Ecological Restoration, an alliance of theorists and practitioners that has grown to nearly 1,700 members since its inception in 1988. He has coined the term *restoration ecology* for the new scientific discipline. He also operates a sort of intellectual clearinghouse for the movement and edits its journal, *Restoration and Management Notes*.

The restoration effort is spearheaded mostly by nonacademic practitioners working for reclamation or parks agencies, conservation groups, and private companies engaged in wetlands or landscape restoration. "The people on the front line with spade and seeds have a lot to teach the theoreticians, and we as theoreticians may well have some things to tell them," said Dr. Stuart Pimm, a theoretical ecologist at the University of Tennessee. "You can't just throw these ecological communities together and expect them to work."

Restoration projects are under way in coastal and freshwater wetlands, on prairies, in forests, in lakes and streams, and on mountaintops, and "people have even tinkered a little with coral reefs," Dr. Jordan said. But since the discipline is still in its infancy, he said, "the success rate is not clear to anyone."

Is full restoration of ecosystems really possible? "Strictly speaking, you can't get everything back just the way it was," said Dr. Jordan. Primarily, he said, this is because ecosystems are not static but rather are dynamic, continually evolving entities. "You're not making carbon copies, you're putting it back in motion," he said. The key, he and other scientists say, is to restore essential ecosystem functions—the mutually supporting relationships that sustain the community's inhabitants. And that, many scientists agree, is feasible.

But it is not easy, as Mr. Packard and his colleagues found out in their efforts to restore the savanna ecosystem outside Chicago. At first, in a largely futile effort to restore what he mistakenly believed was a prairie ecosystem, Mr. Packard watched while the prairie plants he tried to reintroduce died out in the partial shade of the oak trees. At the same time, a handful of other miscellaneous grasses and plants, including thistles, cream gentians, and yellow pimpernels, popped up under the oaks.

"They weren't what I was looking for and I sort of wrote them off," Mr. Packard said. In time, it dawned on him that these might be specially adapted to a savanna habitat. He confirmed his suspicions when he discovered the upstarts in an 1846 listing of plants found in the Illinois "barrens"—that era's everyday term for the oak savannas. It was, says Mr. Packard, like finding the Rosetta stone. Pursuing the ecological puzzle to its end, he dived into an 800-page book of the Chicago area's plants and identified more than one hundred "associated" species that grow together with the savanna plants. This led him to search the area for savanna plants that once flourished but had almost died out. He found "pitiful, patchy remnants" of them in odd places like railroad rights-of-way and cemetery nooks. Collecting the seeds of these "oddball species," he and his colleagues planted them in the ninety-acre Northbrook tract. The result, two years later, was a flourishing community of savanna flora and fauna.

"It's not a piece of cake," said Dr. Pimm, the theoretical ecologist. "It didn't work until he got everything just right." The oddball species, he said, were almost magic ingredients, suggesting that "plant and animal communities may indeed fit together in special ways." Among theorists, he said, that idea has always been controversial, with some arguing that the assembly of ecosystems is essentially haphazard. Both the Northbrook and Fermilab experiments, he said, also suggest that the sequence in which species become established is critical. This coincides with the results of independent studies Dr. Pimm has made with theoretical models.

Many of the difficulties facing restorationists have surfaced in widespread attempts in the United States to restore or create wetlands to replace those that are taken over for farming or development. A 1990 assessment commissioned by the Environmental Protection Agency found that these attempts often failed for lack of expertise or knowledge. Dr. Joy B. Zedler, a wetlands ecologist at San Diego State University, studied a restored salt marsh in California and found that after five years of effort, the ecosystem was functioning half as well as had been expected. "Evaluation of success is often made on the basis, 'So let's go out and look and see if it's green,'" she said. "The marsh is green. It does grow some plants. But it's not enough to be able to support an endangered bird population."

Some ecologists wonder whether ecosystems that took centuries to evolve can be restored in any less time. This is an important consideration if restorationists hope, as some do, to help reverse the destruction of forests and grasslands on which many people in the third world depend for their livelihoods. "It's no good to just say, let's take away the cattle and wait" for the ecosystems to regenerate naturally, said Dr. Anthony Bradshaw of the University of Liverpool in England, an expert in restoration ecology. "Meanwhile, two or three generations of people will have no firewood or will die because they've got no food." But "in trying to do it fast," he said, "we discover what we don't know."

Some scientists say that most attention has focused on the restoration of the plant portions of ecosystems—ecological restoration as agriculture or gardening, as it were—and not as much on animals. "Restoration has been dominated by the horticulturalist, you might say," said Dr. Stanley A. Temple, a wildlife ecologist at the University of Wisconsin. And although fauna are obviously as important to ecosystems as flora, he said, animals greatly compound the difficulties of restoration. Many animal populations, for instance, demand much more space than plants if they are to survive, Dr. Temple said. But since practical considerations now tend to limit the scale of restoration projects, he said, many ecosystems may never be able to function entirely on their own, independent of human managers.

[WKS, OCTOBER 1991]

SEED BANKS AS A SAFEGUARD AGAINST EXTINCTION

T HE Malheur wire lettuce, an unprepossessing but rare plant that grows only in hot, dry central Oregon, appeared to have lost its struggle for survival. The few existing populations of the plant that managed to cling to life in its inhospitable ecological niche were gradually erased by the hoofs of cattle, foraging by jackrabbits, fire, and an invasion of Asian cheat grass. By the early 1980s there were no plants of the species known to be alive. But Dr. Leslie D. Gottlieb, a professor of plant genetics at the University of California at Davis who discovered the plant in 1968, had stored a large number of its seeds. They were propagated at the Berry Botanic Garden in Portland, Oregon, and the seedlings were planted on land managed by the Bureau of Land Management there. The extinct plant was returned to life.

The resurrection of the Malheur wire lettuce is one of a growing number of successes of a nationwide cooperative effort among scientists, botanical gardens, state and federal governments, the Nature Conservancy, and other private conservation groups to preserve the nation's endangered flora. Don Falk, executive director of the Center for Plant Conservation, one of the groups leading the effort, said he believed that there need be no further losses of native plants. "We have set as a realistically attainable goal preventing from this point on any further extinctions of American flora," Mr. Falk said.

Saving every American plant would be a formidable task. There are about 25,000 native plants, of which 3,000 are considered in some danger of extinction. The Center for Plant Conservation has estimated that more than 700 plants will disappear in the next ten years if strong measures are not taken to save them. More than a third of these could be wiped out in five years. Although there are many sources of danger, the chief cause of extinction is the destruction of the plants' limited habitat by housing, industry, or other human activity. "We are talking about protecting plant diversity on a continental scale and that is not a trivial exercise," said Mr. Falk. But he added: "This is not something we have any choice about. The consequences of not attending to the diversity of plant life would be felt fairly quickly as ecological communities deteriorate."

Little is known about most of the rare endangered plants, but many of them are genetically related to food crops, including grains, vegetables, and fruits. Many could have pharmaceutical value and many others should be saved for their beauty, Mr. Falk and others engaged in the rescue effort contend. As an example of the value of saving rare plants, Mr. Falk pointed to a Texas wild rice, *Zizania texana*, whose habitat is now reduced to a single stream in Central Texas. The genetic characteristics that enable it to live in a hotter, drier climate could be used to extend the growing range of wild rice in the United States, where it is now generally limited to the North Central states.

Even more important, he said, is the value of the wild rice's genes as insurance against a significant warming of the earth over the next century as a result of the greenhouse effect. If, as many scientists expect, rising global temperatures make the nation's interior hotter and drier, crops that can grow under such conditions would be urgently needed. "We are talking about a survival issue for *Homo sapiens*," Mr. Falk said.

In October 1990, the Center for Plant Conservation announced that to strengthen its efforts to preserve species, it was moving from Boston to St. Louis to affiliate with the Missouri Botanical Garden, a leading institution for plant research. The botanical garden is coordinating the preparation of a twelve-volume *Flora of North America*, which will be the first comprehensive listing and description of the plants of the United States, Canada, and Greenland. Peter Raven, the director of the Missouri Botanical Garden, said his institution's wide and growing storehouse of information about native plants would fit directly into the Center for Plant Conservation's efforts to identify and collect plants that are in danger of disappearing. The next step after finding and collecting those endangered plants, he said, is reintroducing them into the wild. Preserving seeds or a few plants in botanical gardens does not permanently protect plants, because their survival depends on money and continuing care by people that could be cut off. Only reestablishing plant communities in their natural setting can save them over the long run, he contended. Mr. Falk agrees. "A botanical garden is a holding pattern—an ark," he said. "We have to find a place for the ark to land. Plants need to live in an ecological community with pollinators and symbiotic organisms such as fungi. Our objective is to restore species to a fully functioning existence in their ecological setting so that they can continue on their evolutionary pathway."

But before endangered plants can be reintroduced into the wild, they must be found and collected. This task is shouldered in large part by natural heritage programs run by state governments in cooperation with scientific institutions and cultural groups. The Nature Conservancy, a private nonprofit group based in Arlington, Virginia, plays a major role in this program, providing technical support and a database for state programs. Members of the state programs meet at least once a year with the Center for Plant Conservation, representatives of botanical gardens, university scientists, federal land managers, and private conservation groups to discuss the status of the most critically threatened species and to determine which must be collected to assure their safety.

Plants identified as being in trouble are collected, their seeds stored, and individual plants propagated and studied. "If you have only a few populations of a plant left, you don't dare mess around with it," said Robert E. Jenkins, vice president for science programs of the Nature Conservancy. "You have to study it in the greenhouse to find out how much sun it likes, whether or not it should be fertilized and watered. Only then can you think about reintroducing it into the wild."

Not all botanists think the goal of saving all native flora is realistic. Dr. Gottlieb of the University of California, for example, called the notion of zero losses of American plants romanticism. It would be a mistake to try, he said. "We must save those species we know are very important and, if we have the time and the money, save the rest," he said, adding that there is not enough money or scientists or other workers to save every plant in danger of extinction. He recalled that he had urged the California Fish and Game Commission, which decides which plants and animals to list as threatened or endangered, to try to save a plant called *Oryctes nevadensis*, a small annual herb in the tomato family that grows only in a few populations in the Owens Valley of California.

The plant belongs to a family "of supreme economic importance" because its genetic structure is related to that of tomatoes, potatoes, tobacco, and petunias, Dr. Gottlieb said. But the commission turned down his petition and spent its resources on what he said were much less important plants. At the time of the commission's action in 1989, one member of the panel was quoted by the local paper, *The Sacramento Bee*, as saying, "Here's a very weedy looking plant, and what I'm really wondering is, why are we worrying about it?" The paper did not identify the member.

Although Dr. Gottlieb calls for scientists to be selective in deciding which plants to rescue, many say virtually all native plants could be saved. "It is a lot easier to save plants than it is to save, say, spotted owls," said Bruce MacBryde, a botanist for the United States Fish and Wildlife Service. Mr. Falk says he is confident that his goal can be achieved. "Like any good doctor, I should never say never," he said. "But I really think we can pull it off—that we will not lose a single native plant. We have a system now we believe will enable us to prevent anything from slipping through the cracks." [PS, NOVEMBER 1990]

GIVING A RIVER BACK ITS MEANDER

ORIGINALLY the Kissimmee River meandered among 43,000 acres of wetlands, says Lou Toth, a senior environmental scientist with the South Florida Water Management District. It had a floodplain one to two miles wide embracing shrub and forest habitats filled with a wide variety of species. But in the early 1960s the Army Corps of Engineers made it into a poker-straight canal called C-38. Turning it into a straight channel drained or destroyed most of the wetlands. As Mr. Toth aimed his boat upriver, he pointed out alien wax myrtles that had displaced the willows that once lined the riverbanks. Turkey vultures circled overhead. "Turkey vultures are not normally found in a wetlands ecosystem," he said. "This river might not look so bad, but biologically it is very degraded." Mr. Toth and the water district are part of an alliance that now hopes to do what once seemed impossible: turn C-38 back into the twisting Kissimmee River, re-creating the habitat that once supported thousands of wading birds, waterfowl, and fish.

To restore the river to something even close to its natural state has been a dream of environmentalists almost since the canal between Lake Kissimmee and Lake Okeechobee in central Florida was completed in 1971. Now the state of Florida is behind the restoration, as are the Corps of Engineers and the Sierra Club, two organizations that clash more often than not. If Congress approves, a fifteen-year project sponsored by Florida and designed and managed by the Corps of Engineers would restore 29,000 acres of the ecosystem. It would be the largest restoration in the United States undertaken solely for environmental reasons, and would cost $368 million for construction and land acquisition.

It was the Kissimmee's own tendency to flood that originally led to its demise. In the 1940s, the growing population of central Florida, including ranchers and farmers who had moved onto newly drained wetlands, demanded protection from floods. In response to their pleas, Congress authorized the Kissimmee River Flood Control Project in 1954. Although control measures that would have been less environmentally destructive were considered, for economic reasons the Corps decided to dredge the river, turning 103 miles of meandering river into 56 miles of dirt-lined canal. Protests by environmentalists began almost as soon as the canal was completed. In 1983, Bob Graham, then the governor, began a program to save the Everglades that included the Kissimmee, which through Lake Okeechobee provides much of the water to the Everglades.

A demonstration project conducted by the water district in 1984 began to show that restoration was technically feasible. Heading toward the demonstration project, Mr. Toth stopped at a remnant river bend to show how the ecosystem had been changed. "The canal acts like a sink," he explained. "It draws water into it no matter what you do." The bend was choked with vegetation because it received little water from the canal, he said. As a result the wetlands disappeared, and alien plant species tolerant of dry conditions moved in. Low dissolved oxygen levels in the water, from the diminished flow, reduced fish populations. Many wading birds, including great blue herons and snowy egrets, disappeared, along with more than 90 percent of the thousands of waterfowl. A few minutes later, Mr. Toth nosed the boat into one of the three bends in the demonstration project. Here, steel barriers placed across the canal had diverted water into the bends. The water was relatively free of vegetation, and the sandy bottom was visible. A few willows were growing on the banks. "We found that restoring the flow of water can lead to restoration of the environmental values," Mr. Toth said. "The species that left did come back." A large flock of ibis, wading birds that were once abundant in the area, rose into the air near the boat. Before the water was put back, he said, "I could count the number of ibis on one hand." The weirs, however, were not able to restore all the original water-flow characteristics. "The Kissimmee was a slow-moving river, "Mr. Toth said. "Weirs produced a high velocity of flow. That leads to an unstable environment."

To find the most effective way to re-create the hydrology and physical structure of the river, the state turned to Hsieh Wen Shen, a professor of civil engineering at the University of California at Berkeley. Based on field data, Professor Shen built a 100-foot-by-100-foot model of a typical section of the river. Biologists provided the hydrological criteria, like flow rates and flooding frequency, and the rates at which water drains from the floodplain. Professor Shen then tested three water-diversion schemes being considered by the state.

He recommended a plan to fill the entire canal, which is now navigable, with dirt, removing several concrete locks and building eleven miles of new channels to add to the sixty-eight remaining miles of the river's original twisting course, now largely stagnant.

The plan would be combined with changes in the headwater lakes near Orlando that feed water to the Kissimmee. "We operate those lakes for flood control by regulating the amount of outflow, just like the stopper in a bathtub," said Stu Applebaum, chief of flood control and floodplain management for the Corps of Engineers office in Jacksonville, Florida. "In the spring we draw the lakes down, so we have storage available for the rainy season. But historically, spring is a dry time of year, and if you release water then, you disturb nesting birds. Changes in the storage scheme will allow us to more closely approximate a natural system." Flooding would still be controlled, he said, primarily through the purchase of about 65,000 acres of floodplain.

"The project is absolutely feasible," said Andre Clewell, president of A. F. Clewell, Inc., an environmental restoration company in Florida that has done restoration in several states and nations but is not involved in the project. "It will be a darn close approximation of what it once was." If the restoration goes as planned, it is expected that almost 200 species of birds, 33 species of mammals, 35 species of reptiles, 48 species of fish, and numerous invertebrates will reinhabit the area. The tally includes several endangered species, like wood storks, bald eagles, and Florida panthers.

"There is broad support in the state for the restoration," said Estus Whitfield, an environmental adviser to Governor Lawton Chiles of Florida. "The decision to purchase the land that will be reflooded, and not condemn it, allayed a lot of the fears people had." Not everyone agrees. The Florida Farm Bureau Federation, a nonprofit association representing 80,000 ranchers and farmers, opposes the project. "It is going to have a big impact on our landowners," said Mike Joyner, the federation's director of local governmental affairs. "A lot of the land that they have been running cattle on for years may be taken out of production."

The Sierra Club, which pushed for the restoration for many years, now finds itself in the unusual position of endorsing a Corps of Engineers project. "We generally try to block public works projects," said Theresa Woody, the club's associate field representative in the Southeast. "Now here we are, hat in hand, saying yes, we can trust the Corps. We are giving them the opportunity to truly show that they are the environmental engineers of the 1990s, which has been their rhetoric for the last couple of years."

The Corps, in fact, was somewhat reluctant to get involved until the 1986 Water Resources Development Act for the first time gave it the authority to act on existing public works projects solely for the benefit of the environment. American Rivers, another environmental organization, based in Washington, is not quite as enthusiastic as the Sierra Club. "I think there will be some improvement in fertility and productiveness," said Kevin Coyle, president of the Washington-based organization. "But this is the only project of its type. I worry that the Corps' public relations machine will be telling everyone how wonderful they are and pointing to the Kissimmee. In reality, you can't do this everywhere. It is too costly. We need to find lower-cost ways to restore destroyed natural areas."

Nancy Dorn, the Assistant Secretary of the Army for Civil Works, said: "This is perhaps the biggest environmental restoration project that we've been involved in, but it is by no means the only one. We have a number of smaller projects that involve the restoration of fish and wildlife values at existing Corps projects. We are going to proceed cautiously and establish parameters for how the federal government and states interact on a project like this. The Corps is no longer just a construction agency. The Corps has changed its attitude much as the American people have changed their attitude about the importance of the environment." [CD, MARCH 1992]

BRINGING BACK LOST WETLANDS

SPRINGY peat soil seemed to quiver underfoot as Ed Garbisch led a small inspection party out of a stand of towering loblolly pines and onto the bank of one of the innumerable fingers of Chesapeake Bay that meander through Maryland's Eastern shore near St. Michaels, Maryland. "Does this look like a wetland to you?" Dr. Garbisch asked. It certainly did. Occasional flights of Canada geese honked by overhead. White feathers and an empty crab shell marked the spot where an egret or gull had enjoyed a shoreline lunch. Along the shore itself, stands of six-foot-high greenish-yellow cordgrass, a premier marsh plant, marched out into the water, while ranks of finer, darker salt-marsh hay backed them up just inside the high-tide line. When no humans prowl the site, blue herons and white egrets patrol it in search of baby fish that use the marsh as their nursery.

This was no marsh made by nature, however. In 1984, in an act that has become increasingly common, it was literally re-created—the eroded bank filled in and the cordgrass and salt-marsh hay planted from nursery stock—by Dr. Garbisch and workers at the nonprofit restoration company that the former chemistry professor founded twenty years ago, Environmental Concern, Inc. As the nation steadily loses marshes, swamps, and bogs to development, a relatively young movement to restore lost wetlands and even create new ones has gained momentum and begun to make a small dent. With some 350 successful wetlands restoration projects under his belt, Dr. Garbisch is one of a handful who have been in the business long enough to learn from mistakes and build up expertise in a tricky, exacting discipline.

But as federal and state governments belatedly require developers and farmers to compensate for or "mitigate" any loss of wetlands they cause, inexpert, inexperienced, often incompetent practitioners are rushing into the field. More often than not, according to proliferating studies made by and for federal and state governments, their efforts are ending in failure. The failures not only threaten to undermine a highly advertised federal and state goal of achieving no further net loss of wetlands, they also jeopardize the hard-won credibility of wetlands restoration itself.

"The problem is that there are too many people getting their hands on it who shouldn't be in it," said Dr. Garbisch, who has been called on to repair some of the failures. "It's giving mitigation a bad rep." Worse, he and others say, it is beginning to convince regulatory agencies charged with overseeing wetlands mitigation that restoration does not work. As a result, some experts say, the goal of no net loss of wetlands appears a long way off. "We're not even close; that's a joke," said Robin Lewis of Tampa, Florida, a private practitioner who has re-created more than 125 acres of wetlands.

In the enterprise of wetlands restoration as a whole, "we have relatively high success rates in creating some wetlands functions in some contexts and abysmally low success rates in others," said Dr. Jon A. Kusler, executive director of the Association of State Wetlands Managers, a national technical group based in Berne, New York. Dr. Kusler was the coeditor of a comprehensive and authoritative 1990 study of the status of the science of wetlands creation and restoration commissioned by the Environmental Protection Agency (EPA). Restoration seems to be most successful, he said, when it is undertaken by people who make a long-term commitment to managing the recovering wetlands. Some state wetlands agencies and conservation groups display such commitment, he said, whereas many developers "don't want to go in and create something and manage it for a long time, keeping exotic species from crowding in, and the like. They want to get in and get out. It's understandable."

Wetlands fulfill a number of functions. Not all wetlands provide all functions, but depending on their type and landscaping, they can provide essential habitat for countless species of mammals, birds, fish, and invertebrates; serve as breeding grounds for the nation's commercial fisheries; reduce the severity of floods by slowing and storing flood waters; and filter impurities out of water. Their plants can also protect shorelines from erosion.

An estimated 200 million acres of wetlands existed in what is now the contiguous forty-eight states when European settlers first arrived, and federal agencies estimate that more than half are gone. Those that remain are concentrated especially in the Southeast, the upper

Midwest, and the Northeastern coastal states. The rate at which wetlands are now disappearing is a matter of argument, but federal estimates place it between 200,000 and 400,000 acres a year. Creation of new wetlands is much more difficult than restoration of old ones, for the simple reason that if a piece of land were suitable for a wetland, nature would probably have put one there in the first place. For this reason, said Dr. Kusler, "we're not real excited" about creation of wetlands in general.

But restoration is another matter, many believe. Dr. Garbisch, an optimist in the small community of wetlands restorers, believes that many kinds of wetlands can be restored in their essential functions and in some cases made to function even better than they did originally. At the other end of the spectrum is Dr. Joy B. Zedler, a wetlands ecologist at California State University at San Diego, who says that in California, where more than 90 percent of the state's original wetlands have been lost, the remaining ones are so degraded that there is serious doubt that their original functions can be brought back.

Dr. Mary E. Kentula, acting technical director of the Environmental Protection Agency's wetlands research program at Corvallis, Oregon, said, "I know of nobody who has proved scientifically and unequivocally that they have created or restored a fully functioning ecosystem; on the other hand, in some parts of the country, things look very hopeful." Dr. Kentula was coeditor, along with Dr. Kusler, of the 1990 state-of-the-science study for the EPA. The most widespread restoration activities have taken place, and the most knowledge and experience have been developed, along the Eastern Seaboard, according to the Kusler-Kentula report. Estuarine marshes like those where Dr. Garbisch has done much of his work are among the easiest to restore because tides make water levels predictable and dictate which marsh plants should be planted and where. Results are usually apparent in about a year, and any midcourse corrections can be made then. But in forested wetlands and bogs, water fluctuations are much subtler and harder to detect; and in wetlands that depend on underground water, they can be nearly impossible to pin down. To add to the difficulty, it may take forty years, as trees mature, to determine whether the project in forested wetlands is succeeding.

Much of the argument over whether restoration can succeed depends on how success is defined. If it is defined as restoring a wetland to its pristine condition, then some will not succeed for thousands of years: that is how long it takes soils to evolve to a "mature" condition.

But if it is defined as fulfilling a few limited but essential objectives—providing a critical wildlife habitat in one case, or a clean-water filter in another—then restoration becomes more feasible.

Restorationists have yet to develop a common set of standards for restoration and creation, though they are working on it. But some are coming to believe that a restored or created wetland's success should be measured according to how it should be expected to behave at any given stage of development: one year into the project, five years in, and so on. And many say the ultimate standard should be how well a wetland functions over the long term. Looking good for one year, or two, or three, is not enough, they say.

At the heart of wetlands restoration is hydrology—the behavior of the water that makes the wetland what it is; its depth, its flow, its seasonal variations. In other respects, wetlands restoration is much like gardening: figure out the right plants, plant them, and weed the plot, if necessary, to keep unwanted species from taking over. If this is done properly and the plants thrive, in theory, wildlife will return and the wetland will function naturally. Dr. Garbisch maintains an extensive nursery of wetland plants here, from which he draws the raw material for restoration projects along Chesapeake Bay, up to Maine and out to Ohio.

"If the hydrology is on the button, you can't fail," he said. But if the water is too deep or too shallow or is not there at the right time of year, the project is doomed. He had early failures, he said, but only 7 or 8 total ones in some 350 restoration and creation projects that he has undertaken since founding his nonprofit enterprise twenty years ago. "Ed is the granddaddy of the field," says Dr. Kusler.

Another course may offer a bigger immediate payoff in progress toward the no-net-loss goal, at least in the aggregate. This is the simple expedient of returning to nature some of the millions of acres of wetlands that have been drained to provide farmland in the last 200 years. Bringing these wetlands back sometimes simply requires plugging ditches and culverts that were originally installed to drain them. By October 1991, nearly 118,000 acres of farmland had been restored in eighteen months as waterfowl habitat under a 1986 federal law; and since 1987, another 140,000 acres of farmland have reverted to wetlands under voluntary agreements between the Fish and Wildlife Service and private landowners.

Mitigation was not a factor in these restorations. Whenever it is, studies of projects in a number of states all point to a common conclusion: failure is common. Dr. Kentula cites studies by consultants and academics in Florida, Connecticut, and Oregon that found that many projects were improperly designed and were undertaken with no clear goals. Improper water levels and otherwise flawed hydrology were widespread. Many of the projects were dominated by deep, open water rather than by shallower water with the vegetation necessary to wetland functions. "What we typically saw were steep-sided ponds," Dr. Kentula said. Sites would be 90 percent open water and 10 percent vegetation, she said, whereas the proportion in a natural wetland might be 75 percent vegetation and 25 percent water.

A recent study for the South Florida Water Management District found that of 1,058 acres of wetlands required by permit to be created or restored to replace those destroyed by developers, only 530 acres had actually been constructed. Most of the forty projects were improperly designed, the study said; twenty-three were located where surrounding land uses—parking lots and housing, for example—might prevent the wetlands from fulfilling their intended functions. Twenty-five of the projects displayed hydrological flaws. In one project, for instance, water control to protect a nearby housing development kept water from the wetland. It also found that the wetlands had been colonized by undesirable plants, but that in most cases no corrective action had been taken. Often the situation was not even being monitored.

One problem, said Robin Lewis, the Tampa restorationist, is that it is easier and cheaper to hire, say, a landscaper who will design and build something that looks green and wet until the developer is out of the picture than to hire a restoration expert. "There are no wetland police," he said. "The development industry knows that." And some restorationists contend that some state regulators themselves are inexpert. For all of these reasons, many restorationists are concluding that "no-net-loss" has a better chance of succeeding when pursued outside a regulatory context by conservation groups and others whose goal is restoration rather than by developers whose goal is to build houses and shopping centers. Moreover, they say, most mitigation projects are small and do not offer the opportunity to affect entire ecosystems or to make major progress in reversing long-term wetlands losses. "We'll end up with something that looks like a checkerboard" if mitigation is the sole strategy, said Kevin L. Erwin, the consulting ecologist who did the Florida study. The result: "a lot of green islands surrounded by inhospitable terrain, and a loss of biodiversity."

Rather than merely reacting to the actions of developers and others, a number of experts say, a more deliberate effort is needed to set restoration objectives over whole watersheds and ecosystems. That effort has barely begun, and the same can be said of wetlands restoration in general. "But," says Dr. Garbisch, "I think the potential is fantastic." [WKS, OCTOBER 1991]

HATCHED AND WILD FISH: CLASH OF CULTURES

To millions of true believers, there is nothing more beautiful in all of nature, nothing to make the heart beat faster, than the aristocratic trout and its royal cousin, the salmon. Brilliantly spotted, pink-flanked, or simply and elegantly silver, they linger in the mind's eye as paragons of sleek grace and primitive power. In pursuit of that vision, and to replenish commercial salmon stocks, fisheries biologists over the last half century or so have released billions of hatchery-reared fish in American streams, rivers, and lakes. For years, no one thought much about the ecological and genetic consequences of turning them loose. But now it is clear that fish-stocking programs have transformed the nation's trout and salmon population and may even be threatening the long-term survival of wild fish.

When adult hatchery trout are suddenly thrust into a stream where wild trout have already established a stable social order, "they run around like a motorcycle gang, making trouble wherever they go," says Dr. Robert A. Bachman, a behavioral ecologist who directs Maryland's freshwater fisheries division. The new arrivals charge about the stream in a tight school, something the wild fish would never do, provoking fights everywhere. The conflict and chaos, Dr. Bachman has found, eventually result in fewer fish of either kind. Other studies have also found that stocking tends to reduce the number of wild trout. The hatchery trout dwindle, too, since they are generally more easily caught and less adept at feeding on wild fare. The outcome is often an impoverished fishery dependent on periodic fixes of stocked fish.

Of more serious concern are the genetic risks posed by stocking programs. The genetic integrity of some wild strains, and at least one species, is being threatened by interbreeding and hybridization. Meanwhile, hatcheries in some cases have produced populations of trout and salmon with less genetic variety than is found in the wild. As these fish breed with wild trout, scientists say, they erode the natural gene pool and may impair the ability of wild fish to adapt genetically to environmental changes.

Awareness of these dangers is encouraging fisheries biologists to preserve and bolster populations of wild fish and is prompting a shift in fishery practices. Some states have imposed strict limits on killing trout, thus limiting the need for restocking. Hatcheries and "put-and-take" stocking programs, in which adult fish are planted in streams only to be caught almost immediately, are being reexamined and assigned a reduced role in many places.

In one sense, stocking from state, federal, and private hatcheries has enriched the nation's fisheries, giving millions of anglers the chance to go after trout and other game fish. Nearly 40 million Americans, about 12 million of them trout and salmon anglers, spend more than $20 billion a year on freshwater sportfishing. The widespread introductions have also helped put a delectable and healthful food on many tables.

The ranges of the major species of stream-dwelling trout have been greatly expanded. Brown trout originally were found only in Europe; rainbow trout, in Western North America; brook trout, in Eastern North America. Now all are established in cold waters across North America—in many cases crowding out the original denizens. Other fish, especially bass, have been widely propagated as well. But trout and salmon account for most hatchery and stocking activity.

In the typical trout or salmon hatchery, scientists say, fish are reared under conditions that cause them to act differently from wild fish. They grow up in concrete tanks where they are usually segregated by size class, in dense concentrations, under unnatural light and temperature. They eat "fish chow," specially prepared pellets of fish meal and other ingredients that resemble dry pet food, and grow used to the humans who cast the pellets into the water.

Under these conditions, fish that rush to the food fastest, disregarding the presence of humans, survive and prosper. In the wild, survival depends on just the opposite response. Besides avoiding fishermen and other predators, wild fish in streams must capture the insects and crustaceans they feed on while expending as little energy as possible in fighting the current. Positioning becomes critical. A fish that uses more energy than it takes in will waste away and die.

When brown trout raised in a hatchery were placed in a stream with wild brown trout, Dr. Bachman found in a study in Pennsylvania, they would "throw caution to the winds," rushing around in search of food. But they spotted wild food less skillfully and swam farther than wild fish to get it. Their energy equations did not balance and they tended to get thin and die.

While they lived, they thoroughly disrupted the ecology of the stream. Wild trout jealously guard their prized feeding and resting stations. But because hatchery trout do not easily recognize body-language signals used by wild trout to warn away interlopers, they readily antagonized the established residents. Exhausting fights ensued, and the wild trout were often ousted from their preferred spots, disrupting their feeding patterns. The upshot, said Dr. Bachman, was that after two years the stream contained fewer trout, both hatchery and wild, than there were wild trout when the experiment started.

Trout from genetically different local strains, subspecies, and even species often interbreed after fish are introduced from one range to another. A dramatic example concerns the rainbow trout and the cutthroat trout, both native to the Northwestern United States. In Montana, one of the nation's trout-fishing meccas, the commonest fish is now a rainbow-cutthroat hybrid, said Dr. Robb Leary, a fisheries geneticist at the University of Montana. This hybridization, he said, is probably the main cause of widespread loss of the native cutthroat population. "That's genetic extinction right there," he said.

Regional authorities in the Pacific Northwest are undertaking a new program in which hatchery salmon will supplement wild populations that are declining because of overfishing and habitat loss. As part of an attempt to avoid inadvertent genetic damage, four kinds of genetic risk posed by hatchery operations have recently been identified by a scientific panel of the Northwest Power Planning Council. This is an organization established by Congress to protect wildlife in the region. These are the risks:

- Local extinction of wild fish populations. This can happen when a declining population is reduced even further by the need to obtain wild fish whose eggs can be used in hatcheries. "The hatchery can increase the risk of extinction if you're continually mining the wild parents and if the hatchery fish don't do well and don't contribute to the wild population," said Dr. Anne Kapuscinski, a fisheries geneticist at the University of Minnesota who heads the team of scientists examining the problem.

- Loss of genetic variability. Some important genes can be lost as a result of hatchery operations if, for example, the operators rely on too few parent fish for eggs or if sperm comes from too few males.
- Loss of population identity. This can happen if hatchery fish whose parents came from one stream are introduced into another stream with a different environment. Because of the environmental difference, the local fish populations will have developed different genetic adaptations. The introduced fish may not perform well in the new river. But they will interbreed with the natives, and the resulting hybrids may not perform well, either.
- Domestication of hatchery fish. Hatcheries inadvertently select for characteristics that are inappropriate in the wild. They may also promote an unrepresentative section of the wild gene pool, for example by taking brood stock from fish that spawn just in the first part of a weeks-long spawning run. If the early spawners then predominate in the wild, the population may be less able to survive a poorly timed spell of bad weather or flooding.

Genetic changes become "more of a problem over a long period of time as you increase the number of hatchery fish that are surviving and returning to reproduce," said Dr. Harold Kincaid, a research geneticist at the National Fisheries Research and Development Laboratory, an agency of the Fish and Wildlife Service, at Wellsboro, Pennsylvania. "We gradually lose genetic material," he said, as genomes are "basically broken up" by the modified hatchery population. This, he said, is already happening: "I'm sure it's widespread, no question about that." How serious this will be, he said, remains to be seen.

Alerted to all these dangers, many fisheries biologists have begun thinking wild and changing their practices.

Increasingly, the role of hatcheries and put-and-take stocking is being reduced. A number of states have allowed prime trout water to return to the wild state, with no stocking, while permitting anglers to keep one or two fish a day, or none. In Maryland, for instance, this type of fishing has been expanded. In Maryland streams where natural reproduction is insufficient but the habitat is otherwise favorable, hatchery trout are introduced as small "fingerling" fish and allowed to grow up essentially wild. Put-and-take angling for adult hatchery-raised trout is being restricted to waters that for much of the year are too warm for trout to survive.

"By and large," said Dr. Bachman, "what you're seeing across the country" is a recognition that "where one can manage streams for wild trout, you're better off doing so."

In the Pacific Northwest salmon fishery, commercial fishing will continue to make some stocking necessary. But in a new approach, stocking is considered strictly supplementary and the hatcheries are managed to minimize genetic differences with the wild fish. "It's a pretty hot topic out here; all the states are going into it in a big way," said Dr. Craig Busack, a geneticist with the Department of Fisheries in Washington State. Dr. Busack was one of the first to delineate the genetic threats posed by hatcheries.

One way to reduce the mismatch between wild and hatchery fish is to make hatcheries more natural. There are some precedents for this. At the Connetquot River State Park Preserve on Long Island, which contains a surprisingly pristine spring-fed trout stream, trout are bred in a hatchery section of the stream itself. The trout are screened from human contact as much as possible. As a result, "our fish swim away from you," said Gilbert Bergen, the park manager for the environment. "At every other hatchery they come and crowd at your feet. We're trying to raise these fish as close to natural fish as possible."

That may or may not become widespread, given the large investment in traditional hatcheries. But more and more fisheries experts are convinced that going wild, with hatcheries secondary, is the wave of the future.   [WKS, JULY 1991]

CONSERVATION, TEXAS STYLE

THE ecological heart of Texas consists not of desert and dust, but of deep, spectacular wooded canyons where eagles soar and rare songbirds nest and thousands of crystalline springs bubble from the forested hillsides. Beneath the surface lie vast, honeycombed formations of limestone where strange creatures whose kind have not seen the light of day for millennia live in subterranean rivers, caves, and flooded crevices. This is the Texas hill country, and a grand experiment in what might be called the New Conservation is under way to save its distinctive assemblages of flora and fauna.

In an area almost twice as large as New Jersey where 2.5 million Texans live, including the cities of San Antonio and Austin, the Nature Conservancy is brokering a pioneering effort involving dozens of public agencies and private interests. The goal of the Conservancy, a nonprofit organization that operates the world's largest system of private nature preserves, is to help the economy and ecology of the hill country flourish together.

The principle, a sharp departure from traditional conservation, is to focus on the entire inhabited landscape, not just individual species or even habitats. That requires humans, too, to be treated as part of the ecosystem. Conservationists have historically ignored and excluded humans as somehow separate from and antagonistic to the rest of nature. They have tried to set aside nature preserves, keep people out, and let nature take its course, reckoning that this was enough. The results have been less than satisfactory. Natural ecosystems have become increasingly fragmented, and even in the preserves, native species have often been pushed toward extinction by plants and animals introduced from elsewhere. "For too long we have behaved as if conservation could be achieved merely by separating nature from people, with detrimental effects on both," said Dr. Robert E. Jenkins, Jr., the Conservancy's vice president for science.

Consequently, conservationists increasingly seek to integrate human activity with natural ecosystems. The plan in the case of the Texas hill country is to stitch together a quilt of healthy natural habitat and settled areas, saving as many species as possible while preserving economic vitality. In attempting to execute the plan, the Conservancy is working with local state and federal authorities, environmentalists, and landowners in a three-pronged strategy:

- Setting aside a few highly protected and carefully managed "core" reserves for native fauna and flora, in addition to existing parklands.
- Surrounding the core reserves with ecologically friendly buffer zones. These would consist, for instance, of ranches that maintain wild habitat for tourists to visit, as well as undeveloped areas of military installations.

- Creating ecologically healthy islands of wildlife habitat on the outskirts of cities while allowing development to proceed around them.

The strategy assumes that when conservationists can plan for an entire ecological region, preserving the most essential tracts of land, it becomes less necessary to protect every scrap of habitat. The hope is that fewer knockdown fights will develop between environmentalists and economic interests, and that fewer wild species will wind up on the endangered list.

The Nature Conservancy and its allies here are not insisting that "every little-bitty bug, every little-bitty tree" be protected, said Beryl Armstrong, the manager of a 9,300-acre guest ranch west of here where an extensive habitat protection program is under way. This moderate path, he said, opens a welcome middle road between "the screamers on the far right, who say this is my damn land and I can do anything I want with it, and the screamers on the far left, who chain themselves around every tree they come up on."

Experimenters in the New Conservation are still feeling their way, both here and in other parts of the country, and how their efforts will turn out remains to be seen. Not least in Texas, with its highly developed sense of bow-necked, don't-tread-on-me landowner independence, the potential for conflict remains high in the best of circumstances. The fate of some aspects of the hill country project is touch and go. But a general shift in philosophy is clearly taking hold among conservationists, and in the hill country the challenge is more than matched by the grandeur of the opportunity.

The hill country's most distinctive feature is the Balcones Escarpment, a 200-mile-long crescent of limestone stair steps crosscut by rivers and streams that have carved out the region's characteristic ravines and canyons. Rainwater cascading off the stair steps runs into millions of tiny openings in the limestone and collects underground in a reservoir, one of the biggest and purest in the country. In the crevices of the aquifer dwell many species of insects, crustaceans, salamanders, and small fish, many of them unpigmented and blind. The aquifer, the region's sole source of drinking water, depends for its quality on the integrity of the natural ecosystem above, which buffers it from pollution.

Oak and Ashe juniper, locally called cedar, set the vegetational tone of the region. Its green hills, canyons, and tablelands are a biological crossroads for species from grasslands, deciduous forests, and deserts. The hill country is host to seventeen major plant communities, each with its own special assemblage of animals and microorganisms. One measure of the region's biological variety is the 158 species of birds that have been sighted on the Prade Ranch, managed by Mr. Armstrong, in the heart of the region. On a March day in 1991, three golden eagles wheeled in the sky above a mist-shrouded ridge, while an endangered golden-cheeked warbler, newly arrived after migrating from Central America, appeared in response to Mr. Armstrong's call. "My enchilada from Guatemala," Mr. Armstrong called the bird. Both the warbler, which nests exclusively in Texas, and the black-capped vireo, also endangered, depend on the hill country habitat.

Over all, some seventy species of hill country plants and animals have been identified as rare or threatened. They include plants like Hellers' false gromwell, the broadpod rushpea, and the Comal snakewood, and creatures like the Blanco blind salamander, the Bee Creek Cave harvestman, and the ghost-faced bat. So far, the hill country still supports most of the species that lived there before Europeans settled the country, and only a tiny fraction of the total are under threat. While the raising of sheep and goats has changed the landscape, it has been spared intensive development until recently. The population of the San Antonio and Austin areas is booming, and the beauty of the hill country is an increasingly strong magnet for urban expansion, retirees, and tourists. The population of the twenty-six counties that make up the conservation project grew by 27 percent from 1980 to 1990.

In the hill country, as in eleven other large, diverse geographical areas in the United States and Latin America, the Nature Conservancy has delineated a landscape-wide "bioreserve" planned to include as many of the region's species as possible. The 18,650-square-mile Texas bioreserve is to contain four to six core preserves. The first of which, through which the Devil's River runs, was purchased by the Conservancy in fall 1990. In the last forty years, the Conservancy has bought more than 5.5 million acres of ecologically important land in the United States and abroad, reselling 60 percent of its holdings to governments. It operates some 1,300 private nature preserves in the United States and abroad.

The Devil's River core preserve is a spectacular 19,000-acre tract in the relatively dry western part of the hill country. The river's source is the clear springs that flow from towering limestone formations streaked in colors of gray and rust. The centerpiece of the reserve is a lush but ecologically delicate oasis with a cataract called Dolan Falls. Cormorants and great blue herons fly above. Sycamores and oaks line the banks. Killdeer run along the flats. Spotted squirrels batten on acorns. Tiny rare fish swim in the crystal water. "This is so fragile," said Jeff Weigel, the Texas Nature Conservancy's director of stewardship. "This is what takes the highest level of protection. It couldn't take a lot of human use."

But neither the Conservancy nor any other group will ever be able to buy up entire landscapes. So the group is trying to work with landowners to promote land use that both turns a profit and is compatible with the ecosystem's health. These tracts would serve as buffers for core preserves. The prospects appear good in the hill country, since much of it is taken up by ranches rich in habitat, many of whose owners have long been concerned with preserving wildlife.

The Conservancy has identified several ranches to serve as examples that other landowners might be persuaded to follow. One is the Prade Ranch, whose 9,300 acres are a biological cornucopia. There, Mr. Armstrong tends a going enterprise based on limited cattle ranching; hunting, which prevents an exploding deer population from wreaking ecological havoc; the hosting of conferences and meetings; and nature study, especially bird-watching. "When I first came here I looked around and said to myself, 'I could keep this place full of binocular-toting people from New York all day long,' " he said. "People will pay big money to come and see golden-cheeked warblers. I got 'em, and I got more than anybody else, and I know where they are, and I known how to talk to 'em."

Making a go of the venture requires Mr. Armstrong to preserve intact the ecosystem on which it depends, and to manage it carefully. Marrying economics and conservation "is going to have to happen more and more and more," he said, because it is becoming evident that traditional ranching activities are not enough to sustain the high costs of maintaining a ranch. But there is some distance to go in convincing ranchers to embrace conservation values. Some, Mr. Armstrong said, "were raised on the idea that the Lord gave you dominion over all, and that it was not only your right but your responsibility to go out there and make America safe for domesticated animals and to eradicate anything wild."

The struggle between landowners' prerogatives and conservation values erupted with a vengeance in 1987 in the Austin area, and the result has been the birth of a pioneering conservation program for the burgeoning metropolitan area whose progress is being closely watched around the country. This is the front line of the hill country project, the place where urban development and nature meet head-on. The issue was forced in 1988 when developers came into conflict with the Endangered Species Act, under which the golden-cheeked warbler, the black-capped vireo, and five species of endangered bugs living in the Austin area are protected. Under the law, developers must comply with federal regulations protecting the species. Fearing legal chaos and economic paralysis if each landowner negotiated separately with the government, developers, environmentalists, and local agencies invited the Nature Conservancy to mediate in an attempt to come up with a coordinated, countywide plan that would allow development to proceed while protecting habitat. Such consolidations are permitted under the Endangered Species Act.

The result is a conservation plan for the Austin area, worked on since 1988, by a committee composed of parties on all sides of the issue. The plan aims to carve out 60,000 acres of the least fragmented habitat within the metropolitan area and establish it as a system of preserves. "Incidental takings" of habitat by developers are to be allowed, said David Braun, the director of the Texas Nature Conservancy. But the most important chunks of habitat, many of them contiguous, will be set aside as "a viable preserve system around which development can occur," he said. The land is being assembled in a variety of ways. The federal government is acquiring half the required acreage. The Conservancy has been taking options on other parcels. Some of the land will be paid for by local governments. Some is being purchased and donated by developers with the understanding that they will be allowed to pursue, uncontested, developments they plan elsewhere in the local area.

The locally financed portion of the plan is poised to go into effect if a bond issue to finance the city of Austin's share of the land acquisition, tentatively set for August of 1992, passes. But there is much contention. Although there is considerable support for the plan, some taxpayers balk at putting up the money. Some landowners argue that if anyone should pick up the tab, the public should. The general mood in Austin, a liberal university town, favors the plan, "but the details could kill it" said the mayor, Bruce Todd, who is also chairman of the project's executive committee. "It can pass, but not without some work."

As for the overall hill country bioreserve project, "they've got a good idea," said Dan Byfield, a lobbyist for the Texas Farm Bureau, which opposes what it sees as the Endangered Species Act's infringement of property rights. The Conservancy "got off on the wrong foot" with landowners by announcing the project without consulting ranchers, he said. And "once you put that line on a map," he said, "you have inadvertently put somebody in harm's way of the Endangered Species Act. You've said that land is environmentally sensitive." Nevertheless, he said, "what the Nature Conservancy is doing is probably a concept we've all got to turn toward."

[WKS, MARCH 1991]

A HANDS-ON APPROACH TO NATURE

CONSERVATION biologists are coming to realize that the common practice of letting nature work its course in a preserve often guarantees the ecosystem's decline. One reason is that even apparently pristine reserves have been widely infiltrated by non-native plants, animals, and microbes introduced by humans. Unrestrained by their natural predators or pathogens, these exotic species often crowd out the reserve's native species. Human actions have also distorted ecological functions. One such action is the policy of suppressing fire, once a periodic cleanser and regenerator of ecosystems. Another is the eradication of predators, in whose absence prey species like deer have proliferated and damaged the ecology.

So, with the overriding goal of preserving native species and restoring ecosystems to health, conservationists increasingly favor active intervention to eradicate invaders, reintroduce fire where appropriate, and compensate for the loss of predators. The Hutcheson Memorial Forest at Rutgers University has been cited by several ecologists, including Dr. Steward T. A. Pickett of the New York Botanical Garden and Dr. Daniel B. Botkin of the University of California at Santa Cruz, as an example of what can happen when the traditional conservation philosophy is followed. In 1955, what was thought to be a virgin patch of mature forest in New Jersey was set aside as a nature preserve on the assumption that, in Dr. Pickett's words, "protecting the forest, but otherwise leaving it alone, would be an adequate and appropriate conservation strategy."

Three decades later, exotic species from other continents, including Japanese honeysuckle, Norway maple, and Chinese tree of heaven, had become abundant in the forest. Many native wildflowers had become rare. And oaks, the backbone of the forest, were no longer regenerating. Ecologists believe that oaks, which, unlike other species, can survive fire, require it to flourish; they can withstand it, other species cannot. In the absence of fire, sugar maples were choking out the oaks. Though the ecologists say the forest still has considerable conservation and educational value, it has become partly a human artifact.

Similar alterations have affected ecosystems of varying kinds across the country, and conservationists are beginning to undo them. In Nebraska, for instance, the Nature Conservancy is conducting what it calls "prescribed burns" of the mixed-grass prairie. In the past, the grasslands were regularly swept by fires; the deeply rooted plants simply popped back up after the fire, while competing species were killed. Similarly, the long-leafed pines of the Southeast were the heart of a fire-dependent ecosystem that kept hardwoods from competing with the pines. Controlled burning is being selectively reintroduced to restore the original ecological community.

To keep up with demand, the Conservancy maintains a fire management and research program based in Tallahassee, Florida. Dr. Ron Myers, its director, said he supervised scores of burns, amounting to about 15,000 acres a year, mostly on small urban and suburban sites. Similarly, the Conservancy last year hired an expert on the identification and management of invasive and exotic species, Dr. John Randall, who is based in Galt, California, near Sacramento.

Managing plant communities is challenge enough, but compensating for human-induced distortions of wild animal communities has its own problems, not least the pause and soul-searching that often come when people realize it may be necessary to kill animals. But many ecosystem managers believe it is the only way. At the Prade Ranch in the Texas hill country, for instance, Beyrl Armstrong, the ranch manager, is plagued not only by out-of-control herds of native white-tailed deer but also by non-native animals, like Russian wild pigs and axis, sika and fallow deer. The exotic deer were imported by neighboring ranches as game, but they have escaped and invaded the Prade Ranch, where they upset the natural ecosystem.

Mr. Armstrong actively promotes the hunting of deer both to generate income and to contain the ecological damage posed by a runaway population. He sees it as compensation for previous human destruction of predators, like the mountain lion, that once kept the deer herds under control. "Preserves that aren't hunted turn into deserts for animal life," he said, so thoroughly does a burgeoning deer population strip the vegetation that is fundamental to Texas hill country habitat. As for the Russian swine, they are so destructive of habitat, digging plants up by the roots, that Mr. Armstrong said it "behooves us to smite them hip and thigh, like Samson smote the Philistines." [WKS, MAY 1991]

RESTORING THE MIDWEST'S OAK SAVANNAS

INTERIOR Secretary Bruce Babbitt's announcement that he would try to prevent endangered-species crises by promoting the long-term health care of whole ecosystems may signal a new era in federal conservation policy. But the concept is already built into a number of ambitious ecosystem protection efforts that have already been undertaken across the country. Almost as Mr. Babbitt spoke, in fact, scientists, conservationists, and government officials from throughout the Midwest gathered in Chicago for a long-planned three-day meeting to develop a recovery plan for one of the nation's largest and most threatened ecosystems: a vast expanse of oak-studded savanna that once intertwined with the open prairies in a diverse mosaic of biological wealth reaching from the Great Lakes to Texas.

Before Europeans arrived in America, the oak savannas carpeted some 30 million acres of the Midwest, including half the landscape in places like southern Wisconsin and northeastern Illinois. In many places, the savannas had the aspect of a tidy, open picnic grove; in others they were brushier, with hazel bushes much in evidence. Naturally occurring fires killed most trees, but enough tough young oaks survived over the years to provide the ecosystem with its keystone plant species. An unusually rich array of wildflowers and grasses, suited to partial sunlight and able to pop back up quickly after a fire, formed a thick green carpet under oak canopies. Butterflies that are rare today flocked to the plants. Both bison and deer, depending on location, grazed and browsed in the savanna-prairie mosaic.

The fires ceased with farming and development, and invading trees and alien plant species like European buckthorn filled in and choked savannas not plowed or covered by subdivisions. Now less than 1 percent of high-quality oak savanna remains, in fragments that biologists say are too small and scattered for many of the species that live there to survive in the long run. But hundreds of thousands more acres exist in degraded and biologically impoverished form, their ecological character destroyed and most of the many species that once lived there long gone. Scattered restoration experiments have shown that these choked and degraded tracts can be revived and that much of their biological diversity will then return, scientists say. The Chicago group worked out a preliminary plan for restoring sufficient acreage to assure the ecosystem's long-term health, and it is now turning to the task of working with public and private landowners to put it into effect. "We cannot preserve species unless we preserve the entire system which supports those species," Dr. Alan Haney, the dean of forestry at the University of Wisconsin at Stevens Point, an organizer of the savanna conference, told the participants.

This is the heart of the approach being advocated by Mr. Babbitt and pursued on a number of fronts, and Dr. Haney said the approach marks "a radical change in the way we look at our natural resources." The object of the approach is to practice preventive medicine on ecosystems and their entire array of species rather than wait until it is necessary to prescribe painful emergency treatment on a crash basis when a single species becomes endangered. By that time, according to the theory, an ecosystem has become so degraded that options for protecting species are narrow and there is little leeway for compromise between economic and conservation interests.

By intervening earlier on an ecosystem-wide basis, say proponents of the approach, it is easier to make acceptable trade-offs between the ecology and the economy while avoiding confrontational politics and lawsuits. In this way, Mr. Babbitt said, it might be possible to avert "national train wrecks" like the one that occurred when logging interests and conservationists collided in the spotted owl controversy in the Pacific Northwest. The ecosystem approach, said the secretary, is "clearly an idea whose time has come." But can the approach work in practice?

The results for both species preservation and economic health may not be seen for some time. Two initiatives similar in concept to the savanna plan, however, are encouraging conservationists to believe that diverse interests can at least band together in the cause of ecosystem preservation and recovery.

In California, state, local, and federal agencies are joining with landowners to preserve the coastal sage scrub ecosystem that stretches from Los Angeles to San Diego. This is a formerly extensive but now shrinking assembly of shrubby, chaparral-like flora and associated fauna. Many of its species, among them a bird called the California gnatcatcher, are approaching but have not yet reached federally endangered status. Some seventy private landowners and many local governments have formally enrolled 200,000 acres of land in the project; the ecosystem consists of 250,000 to 350,000 acres. The state hoped to put the plan, which will be legally binding, into effect in 1993. The project is the first concrete step undertaken under a new statewide conservation policy that divides California into ten contiguous bioregions. Each has its own ecological character and its own council of state, local, and federal representatives to coordinate long-term planning for both conservation and economic development. An explicit purpose of this arrangement is to promote preventive, ecosystem-wide conservation of multiple species.

A similar effort in Texas seeks to accommodate both the ecology and the economy of the biologically rich hill country region. In the Austin area, the Nature Conservancy has brokered a plan by various governmental and private interests to acquire and assemble ecologically rich tracts of the regional ecosystem into a 60,000-acre preserve around which development can proceed. In some cases, developers are giving up land in exchange for the right to build elsewhere in the country. The arrangement is part of a larger hill country strategy in which several large "core" preserves are being set aside and surrounded by buffer zones of ecologically friendly activity, including ecotourism ranches. The Nature Conservancy is also pursuing this general strategy in more than forty other places in the United States.

Mr. Babbitt, who describes the group's conservationists as "surely the leaders" in trying to balance biodiversity concerns with economics through the ecosystem approach, has conferred on the matter with

John C. Sawhill, the Conservancy's president. The secretary said he did not yet have a "good fix" on the fledgling Midwestern savanna plan, which in any case is being cosponsored by the Environmental Protection Agency. But he said he had been briefed in detail on the California project and considers it "an important, important demonstration of how these concepts might work."

Douglas P. Wheeler, California's Resources Secretary, suggested that while Interior officials were "taking a hard look" at his state's program, the Endangered Species Act needed to be modified to accommodate the ecosystem approach. "The whole notion of ecosystem planning is far more advanced today than when the law was enacted in 1973," said Mr. Wheeler.

The Endangered Species Act requires that a conservation plan be put in place for a single species already listed as endangered. But it does not require preventive programs for entire ecosystems with all their species. Other public and private organizations are pressing their own ecosystem recovery plans. The Chicago savanna conference in late February 1993 was a major example. The conference was sponsored by the Environmental Protection Agency, the University of Wisconsin at Stevens Point, the Nature Conservancy, and Northeastern Illinois University, and was attended by experts from many other agencies and groups.

Scientists argue about how the savanna should be defined. A broad rule of thumb is that the tree canopy covers 10 to 80 percent of the ground in a savanna, while the prairie is essentially treeless and the forest canopy is essentially closed. Some experts assign the term *woodland* to denser concentrations of savanna oaks short of closed forest. But whatever classifications people impose, there is no sharp demarcation; plant and animal species find their favored habitats along a prairie-to-forest continuum, with many making their primary home in the savanna by any definition. As they actually arrange themselves on the land, the savannas, prairies, wetlands, and sometimes even forests are so intertwined that it is virtually impossible to separate them. That complicates the conservation effort, as does the fact that changing climatic factors caused the savannas and prairies to shift their positions on the landscape. Both the mosaic aspect of the ecosystem and its dynamics, it was decided at the conference, require the conservation of large enough slices of the landscape to accommodate all the interrelated parts and the shifts they undergo; small, isolated remnants of savanna will not do the job.

The preliminary recovery plan, some features of which are still being refined as a result of the Chicago discussions, calls for identifying large acreages of overgrown savanna on public land that can be restored to something approaching their condition before European settlers arrived. These might serve as "core" reserves, said Steve Packard, the science director of the Illinois Nature Conservancy, another organizer of the conference. In addition, he said, many private holdings like farms and timberlands contain degraded savanna that could be restored as buffer zones without interfering with economic uses of the land. All these tracts would be stitched into a network containing perhaps 5 to 10 percent of the original savanna. That is thought by some scientists to be sufficient for long-term maintenance of the ecosystem.

The organizers of the conference are just starting to develop a mechanism for putting the plan into effect. It might consist of a regional "recovery team" of scientists, agency representatives, and conservationists negotiating land-use arrangements.

Once the arrangements are in place, the basic restoration strategy is to start to reintroduce burning on a controlled basis. In some types of savanna, experiments have already shown, this is sufficient to allow the savanna to reemerge. In others, like the classic tall-grass, black-soil savanna of northeastern Illinois, it is necessary not only to burn out invaders but also to resow the savannas with seeds from the past. When this is done, as a Nature Conservancy restoration project directed by Mr. Packard in the Chicago area has shown, the savanna can rebound spectacularly. But some savanna species have disappeared already. "We have no idea whether that number is a few dozen or a few hundred or even a few thousand," Dr. Haney said. As time passes, he said, continued development and invasion by exotic plants may cause more species to disappear, and it will become more difficult to restore the landscape. "This is the last decade or two when you can do this," Mr. Packard said. "The communities are disintegrating."

[WKS, MARCH 1993]

CLEANER WATER,
YET RIVERS SUFFER

Two decades of federal controls have sharply reduced the vast outflows of sewage and industrial chemicals into America's rivers and streams, yet the life they contain may be in deeper trouble than ever. The main threat now comes not from pollution but from humans' physical and ecological transformation of rivers and the land through which they flow. The result, scientists say, is that the nation's running waters are getting biologically poorer all the time and that entire riverine ecosystems have become highly imperiled.

Dams disrupt temperature and nutrient patterns on which organisms depend. Countless river and stream channels have been straightened, eliminating the meandering course on which rivers depend for their ecological variety. Repeated diversions of water from a river's floodplain can decimate populations of fish that spawn there. Sediments from farming run into streams and suffocate many small forms of aquatic life. Vacationers who cut down trees to improve the view in front of summer homes may erode stream banks. The stream then carries more sediment and becomes wider, shallower, and warmer, making the water unfit for many vital organisms. "If you take a drive out into pretty, rolling farm country, nobody thinks of the farming activity as habitat destruction," says Dr. J. David Allan, a freshwater ecologist at the University of Michigan. "But the transformation of the landscape by agriculture is taking its toll" on life in rivers and streams, as are urban and suburban development and the spread of exotic, disruptive species of aquatic life. The transformation, says Dr. Allan, is far more destructive to aquatic life than are spills of oil or toxic chemicals. For all the one-time harm they may cause, these spills have relatively little long-term impact. And because the transformation is so much a part of deeply entrenched patterns of land and water use, it is also far harder to deal with.

Dr. Allan lays out the threat to riverine organisms and ecosystems in an article in the journal *BioScience*. A 1990 study by Larry

Master of the Nature Conservancy found that in North America, 28 percent of amphibian species and subspecies, 34 percent of fishes, 65 percent of crayfish, and 73 percent of mussels were imperiled in degrees ranging from rare to extinct. The comparable figures were 13 percent for terrestrial mammals, 11 percent for birds, and 14 percent for land reptiles. In the West, where dams and the introduction of exotic species are common, the situation is particularly acute. Of thirty species of native fish in Arizona, twenty-five are listed as threatened or endangered, according to Dr. W. L. Minckley, a zoologist at Arizona State University.

The biotic impoverishment goes beyond the loss of individual species, however. Many rivers, Dr. Allan wrote, contain few or no endangered species, yet there are so few representatives of each species present that the ecosystem's functioning is impaired. Scientists do not know at what precise point this thinning of life causes an ecosystem to disintegrate. But "it's like an airplane wing," said Dr. John Cairns, Jr., an environmental biologist at Virginia Polytechnic Institute, explaining, "if you keep pulling rivets out, the wing is going to go." Among other benefits, riverine ecosystems create breeding grounds for commercial fisheries, carry nutrients to them, and support multimillion-dollar recreational activities. In concert with wetlands, they regulate the flow of water, releasing it more slowly in flood times so that more will be left for dry times.

Few if any major river systems are unaffected by the threat to ecological integrity. Sediment from farm fields, for instance, has clouded the mighty Mississippi, making it more hostile to many organisms. Levees prevent the sediments from settling out naturally on the Mississippi Delta. Instead, they are channeled directly to the continental shelf. This contributes to a sinking of the land in southern Louisiana and releases so many river-borne nutrients into the Gulf of Mexico that plankton growth is stimulated. The plankton use up oxygen when they decay and die, and scientists fear this oxygen depletion may harm Gulf fisheries. The Colorado River south of Lake Mojave has been so altered by disruption of water flow and the introduction of exotic fish species, Dr. Minckley said, that it has become the first major river in North America with no native fish left. Dams on the Columbia River have so interfered with salmon migrations that one variety of Columbia salmon has been listed by the government as endangered, another has been declared threatened, and five more have been proposed for listing.

All three of these watercourses appear on a 1992 list of North America's ten most endangered rivers compiled by American Rivers, a Washington-based conservation organization. Others include the Alsek and Tatshenshini river system in Alaska and Canada, the Great Whale River in Quebec, the Everglades, the American River in California, and the Penobscot in Maine. The list is rounded out by the Beaverkill and the Willowemoc, legendary Catskill trout streams where American fly fishing was born, and Montana's Blackfoot, the putative setting of the hit movie *A River Runs Through It*. Habitat in lower stretches of the Beaverkill-Willowemoc system is threatened by developers' cutting of streamside vegetation. The Blackfoot has become so degraded by timber cutting, agriculture, water diversions, and mining activities that the moviemakers were forced to move to another location.

Kevin Coyle, the president of American Rivers, describes "the four horsemen of river destruction" as dams, diversion of water, alteration of channels, and land development. Dams trap nutrients and keep them from flowing downstream. Perhaps more devastating, they alter the temperature of downstream water, making it either too cold or too warm, and thus annihilate whole populations of insects vital to the riverine food web. One dam might not be so bad, but many dams on the same river, as is common in the West, repeatedly interrupt the river's natural functioning. Diversion of water for human use, also widespread in the West, has simply dried up many rivers and streams for much of the year, with the result that their ecosystems are, in Mr. Coyle's words, "ghosts of what they used to be." The straightening, diking, and redirection of river channels, common across the country to control floods and convert floodplains to cropland, housing, and highways, reduce the variety of habitats critical to biological diversity. Land development often denudes stream and river banks of vegetation, eliminating the vital transition between the river and the uplands. Draining land for farming or development causes water to flow more rapidly into the river channel than it naturally would. This leaves less water to percolate into the river in drier times. If the river channel has been straightened as well, water draining from the land moves more efficiently, producing more powerful floods. These carry the increased sediments from farming and development farther, choking organisms and ecosystems well downstream.

On top of all this, legions of exotic species have been introduced into running waters. Some, like the zebra mussel slowly spreading across the country, have appeared by accident. Others, like fish imported to provide sport or to clean vegetation from the waters, have been introduced on purpose. Together, Dr. Allan said, they have significantly reduced biological diversity through predation, alteration of habitat, introduction of diseases or parasites, and interbreeding with native organisms.

Such ecological tinkering can unexpectedly cascade through the water, onto the land, and into the economy as well. In one instance, fishery managers in Montana introduced opossum shrimp into Flathead Lake and its associated river systems, hoping the shrimp would provide forage for kokanee salmon that were the basis of a thriving tourist industry. Instead, the shrimp consumed zooplankton that were the staples of the kokanee diet. The kokanee population collapsed. Bald eagles and grizzly bears that once congregated at the rivers to feed on salmon disappeared, as did tourists who had come to see them. Once invasive species have established themselves, said Dr. Allan, it may be impossible to eliminate them. The other main causes of biological impoverishment seem only a little less intractable. Even so, Dr. Allan, Mr. Coyle, and others say much can be done.

American Rivers advocates a three-pronged strategy: saving the headwaters of the major rivers, which for the most part are already publicly owned; protecting and restoring riparian zones by replanting green strips along rivers; and working with governments to regulate water discharges from dams so they disrupt ecosystems less. Federally controlled dams are also being examined for their environmental effects as their hydroelectric licenses come up for renewal.

A number of scattered efforts to restore rivers and streams are being undertaken. Restorationists have become expert at restoring streams for game fish like trout, Dr. Allan noted. What is needed now, he said, is a comparable effort to restore habitat for the full panoply of riverine organisms. An ambitious effort along these lines involves the Kissimmee River in Florida. To control flooding, the Army Corps of Engineers basically turned the twisting, 103-mile-long river into a straight canal, largely destroying the riverine-riparian ecosystem. Now, after a successful demonstration project, the state of Florida and the Corps hope to restore the river's twists and turns—and its ecosystem. Broader restoration of this sort is still in its infancy. But as fragile as riverine ecosystems are, Dr. Allan points out, they are also remarkably resilient. They tend to repair themselves once the causes of their impoverishment are removed. So, he says, all is not lost. [WKS, JANUARY 1993]

FARMING BUTTERFLIES
TO PROTECT THEM

W ITH a wingspan nearly half a foot across, banded in black and yellow with iridescent blue patches, the homerus swallowtail is one of the most spectacular butterflies on earth. But its beauty and rarity have brought the gorgeous insect to the brink of extinction as poachers and collectors prowl its last refuges in the remote mountain rain forests of Jamaica. Now, a team of conservationists working with the Nature Conservancy and the Xerces Society, a group that protects endangered insects and their habitats, is trying to rescue the last homerus colonies. Their plan is to discourage the illegal poaching of the wild butterfly by local people and instead to train them how to cultivate the insect themselves in butterfly farms. The homerus project is part of a growing effort by conservationists around the world to save the habitats of endangered species by setting up cottage industries, like butterfly farming, that rely on preserving resources such as the rain forest. Projects for raising exotic butterflies have already begun in Ecuador and China.

The new farms are modeled after the successful example of a butterfly farm in Papua New Guinea. This tropical island is home to butterflies known as birdwings, so called because they can be mistaken for birds. Since the 1970s, the farms in New Guinea have been helping to turn an epidemic of poaching and destruction into a profitable industry. Dr. Thomas C. Emmel, a professor of zoology at the University of Florida and a researcher on the homerus project, said the poaching problems that threaten homerus did not originate locally. "The dealers are from the United States and Germany, the two chief offending countries," he said. "Most of the customers are in Japan. The dealers go to Jamaica and they go to one of the towns near a classic collecting site and they put out the word that they are ready to buy. Maybe they bring in a few nets, give out their address, and offer $50 apiece for a butterfly that they can sell later for $1,500. The average annual wage of the people is $300. So a subsistence farmer

says, 'The heck with farming, I'm going to go collect these butterflies.' "

Many butterflies are wasted because dealers will pay the full price
of fifty dollars only for specimens in perfect condition. Homerus's
soft, fragile wing edges appear to get damaged in the first two or three
hours of flight through the forest, making most specimens caught in
the wild much less valuable than those raised and carefully killed at a
butterfly farm.

It might seem surprising that avid collectors, presumed butterfly
lovers, would go so far as to help drive a species to extinction and be
willing to break international law to do it. But for some the desire to
own the rare specimen is irresistible. "It's like buying a stolen Rembrandt," said Ron Boender, the founder of Butterfly World, a butterfly farm, research facility, and tourist attraction near Fort Lauderdale,
Florida. "You can't display it. You can't say you have it. I guess it's
like the drug trade—you're hooked." The drug trade analogy is particularly apt in Papua New Guinea, where the Coast Guard patrols the
northern shores of the island nation to keep out people seeking to
enter illegally to poach birdwings. "The Papuan government has inter-
cepted these boats," said Dr. Emmel. "They've arrested these people,
thrown them in jail, fined them heavily. Sometimes they stay in jail
for years. And yet they keep coming back." Because some birdwings
can bring $7,500 a pair on the black market, the incentive to take the
last of what is left remains strong. As the number of rare species
grows, the lure of the profits of rarity, or extinction, has increased.
Buyers present a potentially devastating threat to the endangered
species that they covet, and new reports of illegal collection of rare
butterflies are turning up all over the world.

In theory, butterfly farming is simple. Just cultivate the food plant
of the butterfly, near homes, on the outskirts of villages, in gardens,
and around the edges of the forest. Then let the butterflies do all the
work. One homerus female will drop down out of her flyway high in
the forest canopy to lay her eggs. The caterpillar will hatch, eat until
it is nearly the size of a full-grown mouse, and magically metamor-
phose into an adult homerus.

Butterfly farming has its complications, however, and these remain
to be worked out in the case of homerus. Most butterflies are extremely
fussy about where and when they lay their eggs, and their caterpillar
offspring can be quite demanding about what they eat and where they
live. Homerus is not likely to be any different. Before any butterfly

farms are in place, researchers will have to find out exactly what is necessary to bring the females in and keep their caterpillars alive.

Scientists are fairly sure that one problem homerus farmers will have to solve will be how to keep their farms as wet as the wettest rain forests. "The favorite habitat for homerus and its food plant, whose name means the water-filled tree, is along streams" in water-saturated areas that get 300 to 400 inches of rainfall a year, Dr. Emmel says.

In order to learn more about the secret habits of this rare butterfly, scientists will be enlisting the help of the experienced butterfly farmers at Butterfly World. Mr. Boender said it had enclosed flight areas full of tropical plants, complete with waterfalls and mist systems, where the initial experiments could easily be done.

Although he says that a butterfly farm could be crucial to the survival of homerus, Michael Parsons, a founder of the New Guinea farm project, warned that "to say that butterfly farms are the be-all and end-all of saving butterflies is nonsense." One lesson from New Guinea, he said, was that no amount of money spent on butterfly farms could keep a species safe unless it was part of a larger government-sanctioned project to preserve the rain forest.

Aware of the need for a variety of coordinated conservation projects, leaders of the homerus project are simply trying to find enough money to get the butterfly farms going before the homerus becomes extinct. The fate of homerus is very much in doubt, Dr. Emmel said. "It depends on the success of the fund-raising drive," he said. "It shouldn't cost more than $25,000 to set up. Think of the payoff. It's a modest investment." [CKY, APRIL 1992]

IN LOUISIANA, A CRITICAL WETLAND FOUNDERS

SHEA Penland, associate director of the Louisiana Geological Survey, eased a twenty-two-foot skiff out of its slip in Cocodrie, Louisiana, a small settlement deep in the bayous of Terrebonne Parish. He nudged the throttle forward and the boat picked up speed, clearing the harbor and skimming over the light chop of Terrebonne

Bay toward the barrier islands that protect the estuary and its fragile marsh from the Gulf of Mexico. From the boat, the marsh seemed vibrant, a sea of green and golden grass punctuated by occasional clumps of bushes and trees. Fish and even an occasional porpoise jumped in the water, egrets and herons fished at its edge, and flights of pelicans soared overhead.

But this is not a healthy marsh. Salt-tolerant grasses have moved in where freshwater plants once grew. The small clusters of trees and shrubs mark a landscape in decline. "An unhealthy marsh gets real clumpy and fragmented," Dr. Penland said. "It's dying." In about fifteen minutes, the edge of the marsh had receded into the distance. "You look out there and see open water," observed another passenger, Robert S. Jones, the parish engineer. "If you look on a state map, it shows as solid marsh." But the state's mapmakers are not keeping up with the marsh. For reasons still imperfectly understood, the wetlands here are disappearing; each year, up to forty square miles of Louisiana quietly sink underwater. If wetland loss continued at its present rate, Dr. Penland said, Terrebonne Parish would be gone in a hundred years.

More than the landscape is at stake. Louisiana has more than 41 percent of the coastal wetlands in the United States. It supports the nation's largest fin- and shell-fishery, producing 30 percent by weight of the country's commercial harvest each year. Almost every fish caught in the Gulf of Mexico spends part of its life in the Louisiana marsh. The wetlands are the wintering ground or vital refueling stop for most of the migratory waterfowl that travel the Mississippi flyway, as well as being vital in the production and transportation of much of the nation's oil and natural gas.

Fueled by industry grants, federal appropriations, and a new state trust fund financed by oil and gas royalties, scientists and engineers are struggling to save this critical resource, but they are only beginning to understand the host of influences that are combining to destroy it. Remedies like dikes, dams, and even old Christmas trees are still under study. The new research effort marks a profound change from the 1970s, when wetland loss and oil and gas development hit their peaks and the industry was accused of literally destroying the state. Today, while industry leaders acknowledge a share of the blame, there is wide agreement that the problem would continue even if the industry pulled out its rigs, filled its canals, and left the state without a trace. In fact, the industry has a strong incentive to protect the marshes.

Much of its equipment could not survive in open water and, under some conditions when wetlands give way to open water, "those water bottoms become the property of the state," Dr. Penland said. "If you're a private landowner you face the possibility of losing your mineral rights." But there is plenty of disagreement as geologists, ecologists, and engineers argue over how to solve the problem and whether it can be solved at all.

A principal cause of wetland loss in Louisiana is subsidence. The land is made of sediment laid down over centuries by the ever-shifting Mississippi River. So much has accumulated that its weight is actually warping the earth's crust. The thicker and fresher the sediment is, the more it subsides. In parts of Terrebonne Parish, the land is sinking more than one inch a year. In the past, the river would have made up the subsidence by adding new sediment in its spring floods. But by the 1950s, the dams built on its tributaries had sharply reduced its load of sediment. And the river itself has been walled off from the marshes by miles of levees constructed at huge expense to protect the land from the very floods that nourished it.

Besides subsidence, other forces are helping undermine the fragile wetlands:

- The sea level is rising.
- Hurricanes, tropical storms, and even passing cold fronts erode the delicate barrier islands that buffer the marsh.
- Access canals dredged by oil and gas companies disrupt the natural flow of surface and underground water. As they erode, they enlarge the area of open water.
- Removal of oil and gas accelerates subsidence, and the brine brought up with them and dumped nearby kills marsh plants.
- Nutrias, rodents introduced to control the water hyacinths clogging navigation canals, devour the roots of marsh plants.

The exact role of all these and other factors in wetland loss is now becoming a matter of intense study. "The only thing that's been done on wetland loss is we've measured how much has been lost," said Harry H. Roberts, a marine geologist who directs the Coastal Studies Institute at Louisiana State University. "People in Louisiana have this mind-set that everything has been studied and now we need action. But all that's been done is document how fast we're losing the land." Experts from the United States Geological Survey and the Argonne National Laboratory in Illinois launched a five-year effort in 1990 to classify and map sources of wetland loss. The Army Corps of Engineers and the Louisiana Department of Natural Resources began a three-year study earlier that year to evaluate possible ways of preventing or restoring marsh loss. "There are an awful lot of good ideas out there," said Col. Richard V. Gorski, who heads the New Orleans District for the engineers. "We're going to tie them together, establish some priorities, and recommend construction."

One method of saving wetland, on which many landowners are pinning their hopes, is marsh management. Landowners have built weirs, levees, and other structures that limit saltwater intrusion and scouring by tides. For example, the Louisiana Land and Exploration Company, an oil and gas concern, has built more than 400 weirs and other structures on its 600,000 acres. These "slow the exchange of salt water back into the fresh water," said H. Leighton Steward, the company's chairman. While they allow fish in and out, he said, they "prevent salt water in an extremely high tide from getting in there and killing the plants. We can look at our property where we've had water control structures in place for thirty years and look at adjacent property owners' property and see the difference," he said.

But others question the value of marsh management. "We can show you examples where they've been effective and where they haven't been effective," Colonel Gorski said. "It's very dependent on the local circumstances, the people involved." Few of these projects have been systematically monitored, said Donald R. Cahoon, a plant ecologist at Louisiana State University and chief of the environmental resources section of the Louisiana Geological Survey. "The vast majority of policies on marsh management in Louisiana have been set on a very limited database and in some cases no data at all," he said.

Dr. Cahoon and other researchers have just finished what he said was the first study to compare managed marsh areas with unmanaged controls. After surveying sixteen managed areas, they concluded that marsh management was not consistently effective in preventing wetland loss. Half of the managed areas were no better off than the unmanaged controls and only five of the sixteen showed improvement. The unmanaged areas even gained more sediment.

The United States Fish and Wildlife Service recently designed a four-year study in which researchers created four marsh-management sites of 75 to 400 acres and compared them to unmanaged sites. Investigators will monitor sediment flow, plant growth, and the amount of material plants add to the marsh. "We're trying to take an objective stance on marsh management," said A. Lee Foote, a research ecologist for the agency. "I have some genuine, heartfelt doubts about whether this kind of marsh management works." Dr. Cahoon says: "Marsh management is a question of trade-offs. You might have to trade off sediment, you might have to trade off some species of fish. You have to be careful what you're trading off for what."

A different approach to marsh management relies on putting the river back into the marshland rather than keeping the ocean out. The idea is to use a flood of fresh water to push back salt water and prevent it from poisoning the plants whose roots hold the marsh together. Enormous diversion structures would carry Mississippi River water through canals or spillways to the marsh behind the levees. The Corps of Engineers is designing a $76 million diversion project at the Bonnet Carre, a $41 million project at Davis Pond, both upriver from New Orleans, and a $26 million structure downriver at Caernarvon. In effect, these diversions will operate as giant gates, maintaining the integrity of the levee in floods, but allowing water through at most other times.

The Caernarvon diversion system will go into action whenever gauges indicate too much salt water in the marsh behind it. But experts disagree about whether restoring fresh water to the marsh will create new wetlands. Some say marshes are built primarily of heavy bedload sediment that moves along the river bottom, not the finer sediment suspended in the water. Getting bedload sediment up on land would probably require very deep cuts in the levees, elaborate pumps, and, as one engineer put it, "a vast amount of money." But others, like Dr. Roberts, say that is not necessarily the case. "Bedload is mostly quartz, which has little nutritional value" for a marsh, he said. "Most of the marsh plants are seeded on fine grain sediment, which include quartz and clays."

Another approach to reducing wetland loss is one that many experts think the state and the Corps of Engineers are neglecting: strengthening the barrier islands at the edge of the Gulf. Like everything else in southern Louisiana, the protective barrier islands are sinking. Dr. Penland estimates that some will survive only another decade. When they go, the winds and waves of Gulf storms will accelerate the destruction of the state's marshes. Ignoring these islands is particularly shortsighted, in his view, because they can be strengthened quite cheaply. That is what Mr. Jones, the Terrebonne Parish engineer, did on eastern Isle Dernieres, one of a line of islands whose few hundred yards of dunes is all that protects parish marshes from the full brunt of the Gulf's waters. The island was cut when a hurricane struck in 1974, and though the breach healed, parish officials feared their bulwark would fail again. When officials at the state capital did not act, Mr. Jones said, the parish decided to attack the problem itself. The result is a project that Dr. Penland says could serve as a model for low-cost barrier island restoration.

In effect, Mr. Jones raised the island. Lacking high-quality sand, he used material from the island itself to build dikes along the island's front and back. Then he filled the middle with inferior material dredged from a channel in back of the island. Finally, teenagers employed in a summer job program planted beach grass on the new dune. "We drug a stick to make a hole, used another stick with a Coke bottle with a hole in it to spread the seeds, and then a third guy came along shuffling his feet to cover them up," Mr. Jones recalled. The ultimate in low-tech, the 3,200-foot project was completed for less than $1 million and has survived five years of Gulf weather so far. "I'd call it a success," Mr. Jones said.

For Mr. Jones and others, the state's coastal wetland conservation and restoration plan is a source of continuing irritation in that it does not concern itself with barrier islands unless they actually have marsh on them. But other experts say marsh management and diversion projects have bigger potential payoffs and funds must be concentrated on them. "By preserving barrier islands, the greatest impact you'll have is maybe 10 percent," said David M. Soileau, who heads the state's Wetland Conservation and Restoration Task Force. "Salt water intrusion and subsidence are still real major problems, even if you were able to replace the barrier islands."

Federal guidelines require all Corps of Engineers projects to show direct economic benefit. When it comes to uninhabited islands, Colonel Gorski said, "we don't have a mechanism to accurately calculate those benefits. Intuitively we know that barrier islands are good and they help protect the interior from storm surges and erosion, but we haven't determined a dollar mechanism."

While state and federal authorities continue their studies, individuals and communities press ahead with their own small-scale attempts to save their marshes. Some set fire to the marshland's cypress trees and live oaks, a custom dating from the earliest European settlement. In theory, burning old vegetation helps newer, more vigorous plants to thrive. Others, encouraged by the Coalition to Restore Coastal

Louisiana, plan to donate their used Christmas trees to trap sediment. G. Paul Kemp, the coalition's executive director, says, "This year we have a goal to get a quarter of a million Christmas trees." Some scientists dismiss the idea as a gimmick, since the trees cannot trap sediment if there is no sediment to be trapped.

In coastal parishes, where roadways are often built on land so low and narrow that people pull over and fish the bayous from their pickup trucks, officials are considering mounting their own elaborate defenses, like surrounding their towns with levees. "The only way we're going to be able to survive down here is with levees," said Mr. Jones, the Terrebonne Parish engineer. "Eventually we'll all be living in a bowl."

While engineers and public officials debate the merits of this range of mitigation efforts, scientists are continuing their basic research into the geology and ecology of the delta. "This is a very complicated set of processes," said Dr. Roberts, the Louisiana State University marine geologist. "If someone asked me to map subsidence in the coastal plain I could not do it. And in order to control subsidence I have to know what I am up against." Mr. Soileau of the state's wetlands restoration force said he was optimistic that research and mitigation efforts could eventually create ways to replace or restore marshland as quickly as it is lost. "I predict perhaps even in twenty years we will have reached a static relationship between wetlands lost and wetland gain in Louisiana," he said.

But for most other scientists and engineers, this "no-net-loss" is an impossible dream. The most they hope is to slow the rate at which their state is disappearing. "If you look at the numbers—sediment in the river and the techniques and cost of getting that sediment out—the achievement of no-net-loss is not attainable," Dr. Penland said. "The river of today is not the river of yesterday that built the delta." [COD, NOVEMBER 1990]

SAVING BEACHES FOR SEA TURTLES

A DECADE ago, the slaughter of sea turtles along Brazil's 4,600-mile South Atlantic coastline was a saga familiar to defenders of endangered species in third world countries. Conservation went no further than a list of endangered turtle species kept on file at the nation's environmental protection organization, then called the Brazilian Institute for Forestry Development. "They only had the names in Latin, and they were spelled wrong," according to oceanographer Guy Guagni dei Marcovaldi. People here traditionally welcomed the annual arrival of egg-laying turtles to Brazil's richest concentration of turtle nests. "It was a big outing here—everyone would go to kill the turtles and collect the eggs," Mr. Marcovaldi said of the village of Praia do Forte, fifty miles north of Salvador. "They would eat the meat, eat the eggs, and sell the shells. Almost all the turtles that came to Brazil's coast were killed."

By some estimates, the world sea turtle population may have dropped in half in the last twenty years. Now, however, the five species of sea turtles that frequent Brazil's coast can come ashore without fear. Every morning during the laying season from September to March, 200 workers, largely fishermen, comb 620 miles of Brazil's top nesting beaches for sea turtle eggs. Collected in insulated boxes, the precious eggs are carried by a human chain until they arrive by dune buggy at one of eighteen coastal hatching centers. Last season 230,000 baby turtles were hatched and released to the sea.

In February 1991, Brazilians celebrated the one millionth sea turtle hatched in the eleven-year history of Project Tamar, short for *tartarugas marinhas*, or sea turtles in Portuguese. Funds for the project came from a newly reinvigorated Brazilian environmental agency and, rare for the developing world, local corporate sponsors. When Brazil's top soap opera actress, Cristiana Oliveira, posed in a sea turtle T-shirt, sea turtles even became chic.

"Tamar is a model for developing countries in sea turtle protection," said Dr. Karen A. Bjorndal, an American zoologist who directs the Archie Carr Center for Sea Turtle Research at the University of Florida at Gainesville. Because its shoreline provides one of the world's top five sea turtle nesting areas, Brazil is playing a key role in a worldwide campaign to put an end to poaching and avert the extinction of the eight sea turtle species known to man. Five species nest on Brazilian beaches: the loggerhead, the leatherback, the hawksbill, the green, and the olive ridley.

In 1990, Mexico banned the taking of sea turtles and Japan promised to phase out purchases of turtle shells and leather by the end of 1992. Feeding a cottage industry that made eyeglass frames, combs, belts, and shoes, Japan imported products from an estimated 2.25 million turtles during the 1970s and 1980s.

Now that Mexico and Japan are ending their trade in turtle products, the major countries that harvest turtles are Indonesia, Cuba, and several Pacific islands. Thousands of other turtles die annually when they are caught in nets set by fishermen or shrimp boats. A 1989 survey found that 55,000 sea turtles were drowning annually in shrimp nets in American waters.

Although a leatherback hatchling weighing less than 2 ounces can become a 1,500-pound adult, it is thought that only about 1 hatchling of 1,000 survives to adulthood, which takes at least twenty-five years. Estimates of their life span range as high as seventy years.

Sea turtles, whose existence dates back 150 million years, are creatures of habit. "We have tagged one turtle who came back to lay under the same coconut tree after an absence of two years," said Mr. Marcovaldi, who is national coordinator of Tamar. Over the last decade, a mile-and-a-half stretch of Praia do Forte beach has averaged 140 turtle nests a year. Between nestings, sea turtles often swim thousands of miles. In 1989, fishermen in the Azores netted a juvenile loggerhead sea turtle that, according to its stainless steel flipper tag, had been released three years earlier in Brazil, 4,000 miles southwest.

To discover the main reproduction and feeding areas on Brazil's shoreline, Mr. Marcovaldi and his wife, Maria Angela, a fellow oceanographer who is the president of Tamar, conducted a two-year survey. As a result, Tamar now concentrates its $800,000 annual budget on patrolling the 13 percent of Brazil's shoreline that accounts for 90 percent of turtle nests. To staff the eighteen stations, Tamar uses former poachers, who know where the animals land and nest. Tamar also works to raise awareness of entire fishing communities about the threat of extinction.

Beachfront development represents another worldwide threat. Unless beach lights are shielded during the nesting season, disoriented hatchlings move toward electric lights instead of toward light created by the sun shining on the ocean. Brazil adopted a shielding law in 1990.

To build up goodwill among adults, some of whom depended on turtles for extra income and nutrition, workers distribute free turtle T-shirts and posters, and offer jeep rides and radio communication. At seven of the beach hatcheries visited by tourists, Tamar shops hire local residents as salespeople and sell locally made souvenirs.

In an environmental education campaign, children dress up as sea turtles in "turtle carnivals," visit observation tanks at local hatcheries, and attend ceremonial releasings at which hatchlings race across the sand into the ocean. Using power from jeep batteries, Tamar workers show sea turtle conservation videos in villages without electricity. In a context of declining turtle populations, Brazil's program may play a key role in arresting a worldwide trend.

"If Brazil is turning out many hundreds of adult turtles, it will have a profound effect on a world scale," said Dr. Karen Eckert, a zoologist who edits *Marine Turtle Newsletter* in La Jolla, California. Noting that many turtle conservation efforts are limited to protecting nesting colonies of twenty or thirty adults, Dr. Eckert said: "Tamar really stands alone in its scale. There is no other project in the world that covers 600 miles of nesting beaches." In one measure of success, 30 percent of the eggs that Tamar workers once transferred to protected hatcheries are now left undisturbed in their nests. Praia do Forte is one of several beaches considered free of human poachers. Here, Tamar workers protect the shallow nests with steel screens to reduce poaching by foxes, lizards, and rodents during the fifty-day incubation periods. "No one fishes turtles around here anymore—they would be arrested," said a fisherman who was collecting crabs from a tidal pool one morning.

But traveling video shows, free T-shirts, and a fleet of thirty vehicles cost money. To guarantee government and private funds, Tamar has built a strong constituency among Brazil's wealthy and politically powerful urban elite. Working in Tamar's favor, most Brazilians consider the beach their native habitat. Indeed, 80 percent of the 150 million people of this continental-sized nation live within a hundred miles of the ocean. "If the project was to save some Amazon canary, no one would have bought as many T-shirts," said Luca Padovano, a former diver who in 1988 started merchandising a line of sea turtle T-shirts through his Aqualung beachwear boutiques. Tamar receives 10 percent of turtle clothing sales in Aqualung stores and 50 percent of sales in the stores at Tamar's seven beach stations. Mr. Padovano predicted that in 1991 his clothing line, available only in Brazil, would bring Tamar more than $250,000, about one third of the annual budget.

The project's goal for the 1990s is to prevent the fishing of turtles in their feeding areas. They have already prepared weatherproof yellow tags that show fishermen how to revive turtles accidentally caught in their nets. Aiming at commercial shrimp-fishing boats, Tamar plans to promote the use of turtle-excluder devices. These devices provide air-breathing turtles with a trapdoor to escape drowning in nets that are dragged across shrimp beds on the ocean floor. Looking to the future, Mr. Marcovaldi concluded: "The era of killing, eating, and selling sea turtles is closed." [JB, DECEMBER 1991]

VETIVER, PLANT BARRIER
TO SOIL EROSION

V ETIVER, a tall grass whose long, fragrant roots are commonly used in perfumes and soaps, could serve as an inexpensive and effective barrier against soil erosion, a panel of experts says. Considered a leading threat to the environment, soil erosion results when nutrient-rich topsoil is washed away by water or swept up by wind. Vetiver, when planted in rows across steep slopes, keeps soil and water from flowing past. Experts on soil erosion and specialists on the vetiver plant, who collaborated on a recent study for the National Research Council, said that vetiver's roots, which are six to ten feet deep, hold the grass barrier and soil in place from below while the plant's tall blades of grass form a barricade against runoff aboveground.

Able to grow in acidic or alkaline, fertile or infertile, waterlogged or parched soils, vetiver does not deprive crops of nutrients or space. Its sharp grass blades do not seem to harm livestock but do discourage them from eating or disturbing the vetiver hedge, said Dr. Noel D.

Vietmeyer of the research council, who directed the study. Vetiver, believed to be native to India, grows best in tropical and subtropical areas where rainfall is heavy but frosts are rare. The researchers said the grass hedge is able to grow in drier climates, like those in areas of Africa, and in cooler but not freezing climates, like those in areas in the Southern United States. The grass can take from a few months to a year to grow deep enough and tall enough to combat soil erosion produced by water. Generally, however, it is less effective against erosion caused by wind unless the grass is planted close together to form a dense wind barrier, the study said.

Some scientists say grasses were planted in various parts of the world to limit soil erosion as early as the 1920s. The new study, primarily financed by the Agency for International Development, was begun because vetiver has remained "unloved and unrecognized as a means of preventing soil erosion," said Dr. Vietmeyer. "It needed credibility." Other plants that have been used to prevent soil erosion, like the vine kudzu, grow so rapidly and wildly that they become uncontrollable nuisances. He said vetiver was a self-leveling grass that grows tall enough to block erosion but does not grow out of control and, in that way, interfere with crops the way that kudzu, weeds, and some other grasses do.

Vetiver is not effective in most of the United States, especially in parts of Iowa where the soil, among the richest in the world, is eroding at one of the fastest rates in the world, said Dr. David Pimentel, a professor of entomology at Cornell University, who was an author of the new study. He said the vetiver research findings should not detract from the importance of crop rotation and other erosion-control techniques that can be used alone in colder climates or in conjunction with vetiver in warmer areas. Dr. Pimentel said it takes 200 to 1,000 years to replace one inch of topsoil. "Once topsoil is lost, you cannot sit around and wait for it to correct itself," he said.

Dr. W. Doral Kemper, who directs the research unit on soil and water conservation for the Agriculture Department, is studying other methods to control soil erosion. He said rows of vetiver and other grasses should be planted more widely, because the method was described about fifty years ago and works well. He said he was looking for other grasses that would withstand colder climates, like those in the Northern United States and Canada.

The researchers said that since a simple row of vetiver could keep large amounts of water on crops longer, they grow faster and denser.

Dr. Vietmeyer said that in a poor economy when farmers tend to live hand to mouth, they see little incentive to protect the land from damage that might not become apparent for another decade. "Increased moisture in the soil makes the crops and trees grow better," he said. "To the farmer struggling to feed his family this year, that may be the only important reason to plant vetiver."

[ANON., FEBRUARY 1993]

RAGWEED TO MOP UP METALS FROM SOILS

A FOREST once grew here in the bend of the Delaware River. Now a multibillion-dollar plant where the Dupont Company manufactures 750 different chemicals sprawls under the span of the Delaware Memorial Bridge. After seventy-five years of manufacturing toxic materials like tetraethyl lead, an antiknock gasoline additive, at the Chambers Works, E. I. Dupont de Nemours & Company is trying to cleanse some of the contaminants from this now-barren land. Dr. Scott Cunningham, a Dupont researcher, has an idea for reclaiming it with plants. But Dr. Cunningham does not envision establishing another forest here. In order to remove substantial concentrations of lead from the ground, he is planting ragweed.

Dr. Cunningham is one of a handful of researchers around the world who are trying to use plants to clean contaminated soil. They are attempting to plant crops that will absorb metals, then harvest the plants, and, it is hoped, process them to recycle the metals that are reclaimed. The process, they say, offers cheaper, more environmentally sound possibilities for cleaning contaminated sites. "No one has successfully remediated a site with plants yet," Dr. Cunningham said. "But it just makes sense."

The researchers use varieties of plants, called "hyperaccumulators," that can build up in their cells higher concentrations of metal than exist in the soil where they are planted. They can be found thriving in areas that most plants, animals, and humans would find uninhabitable. Dr. Cunningham, for instance, tested the levels of lead in plants growing around a basin that used to contain the swill washed from water used in the tetraethyl lead manufacturing plants at the Chambers Works. Two types had large quantities of lead in their upper shoots, hemp dogbane and common ragweed. Now Dr. Cunningham and his associates have planted a small plot in the defunct tetraethyl lead plant. Amid the exposed brick, pipes, railroad tracks, and hard-packed gravel paths, the "garden" grows inside a fence marked with bright yellow tape. Although they are trying many varieties of plants, the researchers say the ragweed and hemp dogbane are accumulating the most lead. Samples of the ragweed after four months have shown a concentration of 8,000 parts per million lead, although the plot's soil has only 1,000 parts per million.

Another field project, the Woburn Market Garden Experiment at Rothamsted Experimental Station in Hertfordshire, England, has produced plants that take up 1 percent of their dried body weight in zinc. Researchers there, led by Dr. Steve McGrath, are also having success absorbing cadmium and nickel deposits, all left by earlier experiments that tested organic wastes as nutrients for plants. Dr. McGrath has calculated that the zinc could be brought to acceptable levels in thirteen croppings. That process could be speeded with manipulation of the soil, fertilizer, and plant species, he said.

Perhaps the most widely publicized field experiment is one that Dr. Rufus L. Chaney, a research agronomist at the United States Department of Agriculture, began in 1991 with Mel Chin, a conceptual artist. The project, called "Revival Field," uses a variety of plants to clean a Superfund site in Minnesota.

The goal of all these projects is to produce a genetically altered plant and proper soil conditions to allow plants to amass 2 percent or more of their dried body weight in metals, Dr. Cunningham said. If the plants were large enough, a harvest could produce a substantial quantity of the metal, which could possibly be smelted from the plants. The plants would need to be dried, like hay, burned, and then smelted as a type of "bio-ore." This would avoid the need to return the metals to the ground. If smelting was not practicable, the researchers say, the burned plants could still be placed in a landfill. The volume of waste from placing the ashed plants in a landfill would still be thousands of times less than that produced in current procedures for reclaiming contaminated soil, the researchers say.

One of the reasons that this technology, called "green" remediation or phytoremediation, has attracted attention in the last few years is

that there are few alternatives for cleaning metals from soil. Bio-
remediation does not work, since the types of microbes that eat metals
are very hard to remove from the soil once they are done. So companies can vitrify the soil, pouring in a compound that traps the metals
to keep them from spreading, or "wash" the soil with an acidic compound, which leaves metal-contaminated acid and soil with impaired
abilities to support growth. The third and most widely used method
is to dig up the contaminated soil, mix it with cement, and bury it.
"The only technology now is to dig the stuff up and bring it someplace
less politically sensitive," said Dr. Paul Jackson, a biochemist at Los
Alamos National Laboratory in New Mexico. " 'Suck, muck, and
truck,' they call it. That's not going to hack it for long."

More traditional forms of soil reclamation are also more expensive.
Dwight Bedsole, business director for remediation, safety, and environmental services at the Chambers Works, estimated that the company would spend $75 million to $100 million a year for the next five
years for remediation at the site. Dr. Cunningham said that if his
research was successful, it could be used as an inexpensive way to
slowly clean the land around small companies, urban roads, or even
farmhouses that used lead paint. It cannot be used to clean highly
contaminated sites, however, like those with more than 1 percent lead
in their soil.

One of the biggest puzzles of phytoremediation research is why
and how some plants accumulate such high levels of toxic metals.
Although researchers have been studying plants' potential for reclamation for only a decade, evidence that plants absorb metals has
been collected for hundreds of years. Botanists, metallurgists, and
archeologists discovered early that the presence of certain plants indicated deposits of metals. Miners in Africa found copper, miners in
Russia found uranium, and miners in the United States found gold
using this method. In addition, archeologists have used plants to pinpoint ancient mining sites and civilizations in Latin America.

Dr. Alan Baker, a geobotanist from the University of Sheffield in
England, has traveled to remote climes to test and retrieve plants that
survive in highly contaminated soils. He began his research twenty-
one years ago in an effort to discover how the plants withstood such
high-metal soils. Most plants exclude the metals, storing them in their
roots where they will not affect the mechanisms of the plant. But a
very few accumulate the metals, detoxifying them and storing them
in their leaves. Dr. Baker has given cuttings of these plants to Dr.

McGrath, with whom he works on the Woburn Market Garden Experiment. "These plants seem to have magical properties," Dr. Baker said. "There has got to be something we can do to exploit that. We have got to find a way to harness this ability and put it to use cleaning soils."

The same mechanisms that allow plants to take up metals from soil may be used to solve other environmental problems. Some researchers are trying to clean other types of waste, like radionuclides. And some are examining the possibility of breeding plants to exclude toxic wastes rather than take them up. Dr. Jackson, for instance, has been using cells from Jimsonweed to clean plutonium from nuclear sludge. He grows the cells, packs them in a resin that he places in a column, and then pumps the sludge through the column. The plutonium binds with the plant cells, removing the radionuclides from the liquid. Dr. Jackson has also used plant cells in resin to clean metals like copper, selenium, and uranium from water or other liquids. His research for the last ten years has focused on the mechanism by which plants absorb metals and other toxics. "Of course these metals combine with biological organisms," he said. "That's why they're toxic. If they didn't affect the environment, they would not be considered harmful. We are just taking advantage of that property."

Dr. Jackson is also looking for ways to alter plants so they do not take up toxic metals from the ground. Such alterations would be especially useful for crops like tobacco, tomatoes, and potatoes that easily absorb cadmium. At Rutgers University, Dr. Ilya Raskin is beginning another effort to exclude metals. He will be coordinating an effort to help clean up the waste from the accident at the Chernobyl nuclear power plant in Ukraine in 1986. One priority is to breed forage grasses that exclude all radionuclides, so locally grown meat and milk are not contaminated. Dr. Raskin is also experimenting with the accumulating properties of mustards, which come from the same cabbage family as the plants Dr. McGrath is using in England. Dr. Raskin is testing the ability of mustards to take up radionuclides as well as chromium, a substantial pollution problem in New Jersey.

[EMB, SEPTEMBER 1992]

RETURNING BISON TO THE PRAIRIE

I N the most ambitious attempt so far to revive one of America's formerly vast and robust but now moribund ecosystems, 300 bison galloped headlong onto 5,000 acres of unobstructed tallgrass prairie—there to live free, eat their fill, and play a major ecological role, as their ancestors once did. Nervous at first in the presence of nearly 1,000 humans who had come to northeastern Oklahoma to see them resume their ancient place in nature, nudged along by a phalanx of pickup trucks, they moved balkily from their small holding pasture toward the narrow end of a fenced-in chute that led to freedom. Once through it, with nothing ahead but wide-open spaces, they dashed pell-mell for the horizon. In no time, they became dark brown specks amid the tawny swells and swales of prairie autumn, and a scene incomplete for more than a century was suddenly whole once more.

For at least 10,000 years, the triple forces of climate, fire, and the grazing of bison created conditions favoring maximum richness and diversity of plant life in the continent's midsection. The array was richest and most colorful in the eastern part of the mid-continent, where the climate was wetter and the open lands mixed with the forests of the East. This was the realm of the tallgrass prairie, where seas of grass rose taller than a man's head and hundreds of species of wildflowers graced the landscape in brilliant profusion. Before European settlers and their descendants arrived, the tallgrass ecosystem covered more than 220,000 square miles and stretched from Canada into Texas and from Nebraska to the Great Lakes. Today more than 90 percent of it has vanished under the plow and the bulldozer, and most of the rest is so fragmented and degraded that it scarcely resembles its former self. As a result, the prairie and its attendant oak savannas have become the rarest of North America's major biomes.

But during 1993, on a 36,600-acre tract north of Pawhuska, Oklahoma, owned by the Nature Conservancy, fire periodically began sweeping the landscape once again, and legions of fire-adapted prairie plants—with names like jointed goatgrass and rattlesnake fern, ebony spleenwort and lady's tresses—have sprung up naturally in its cleansing wake. And with the reintroduction of the buffalo, all the ecological forces are now in place for the nation's first attempt to re-create and maintain the tallgrass prairie. "We are basically putting the train back on the tracks and restarting the engine," said Bob Hamilton, director of science and stewardship for the Conservancy's Tallgrass Prairie Preserve. The reason the conservation group is doing this is that preserving an ecosystem's parts and setting them back in motion is considered the best way to preserve the most species in a condition in which evolutionary processes can play themselves out.

The 300 bison released into the wild are the first of 1,800 that will eventually roam the preserve, and their liberation was accompanied by more than a modicum of ceremony: a black-tie-and-blue-jeans dinner; an Osage Indian ceremony making an honorary chief of Norman H. Schwarzkopf, the retired Army general and a member of the Conservancy's board of governors; a Western swing band to entertain the pre-release crowd; and speeches paying tribute to the cooperation of environmentalists, cattlemen, Indians who own the mineral rights, and local residents who hope to see a tourist bonanza in creating the preserve. Tourists are clearly expected. "Loose bison," reads a big sign on the gravel road cutting through the preserve. "Bison are dangerous. Keep your distance." But the bison and the ecosystem itself, both imperiled in this century, were the real stars of the day. "This is sacred land; it is time for the bison to come home," said Mary Barnard Lawrence, whose family once owned the cattle ranch on which the preserve is situated.

No other animal, perhaps, so symbolizes and evokes America's past as the plains bison, or buffalo as it has long been popularly called. Nor has any other big American animal so strikingly and visibly been driven to the brink of extinction. Within a mere fifteen years, from 1870 to 1885, hunters wiped out most of the 60 million bison that had roamed the plains. By 1900, fewer than 1,000, and possibly as few as 300, remained in the country. Thus dawned the era of the buffalo as conservation object. Today their population in the United States has rebounded to 130,000 to 150,000, mostly on private ranches, and the buffalo is no longer in danger. It is flourishing so well, in fact, that its meat, which tastes much like beef but is low in fat, has ushered in another phase: the buffalo as a health-food delicacy. Now conservationists hope to cast it in yet another new role—the buffalo as an ecological restorationist.

Ecologists believe that fire and bison worked together to shape the presettlement tallgrass ecosystem in this fashion:

Each year, fires randomly burned over many separate patches of prairie. In the dry season of midsummer, most of the fires were probably caused by lightning. In spring and fall, most were probably caused by Indians—the Osage in this part of the country—whose ancestors had already appeared on the scene 10,000 years ago.

Early settlers' accounts have made it abundantly clear that the Indians routinely and liberally set fire to the prairie. They did it for a number of reasons: to stop pursuing enemies and deny forage to their horses, for instance, and to attract game.

The game, including buffalo, came because a profusion of succulent green plants sprang up after the fires. Prairie plants have deep roots, and when dead top growth is destroyed, new green growth springs up almost immediately. It is no accident that these disturbance-loving, fire-adapted plants dominate the prairie. Scientists believe they proliferated there expressly because of the fires.

The buffalo concentrated on the tender new grasses, moving on when these were gone and allowing dry, dead grass and wildflower stalks to accumulate, making ideal fuel for the next round of fires. As the vegetation returned, plant species reappeared in a specific order of succession, with different species combinations characterizing each stage. Myriad patches were in different stages of succession at any given time, creating a sort of ecological crazy quilt. This, the ecologists believe, is what gave the prairie its biological richness and diversity.

"Where the bison were currently grazing, it might look like your front lawn or like a putting green," said Mr. Hamilton. "At the other end of the scale, where the patches hadn't been burned or grazed for years, there might be a lot of standing dead vegetation." Agriculture, development, and the slaughter of bison erased this elegant ecological dynamic. Even in the few unplowed prairie remnants large enough for the dynamic to function, much of the original vegetation was suppressed by invading trees and brush that fire once held at bay and by grazing cattle that kept the prairie plants effectively cropped. As a functioning ecosystem, the tallgrass prairie was essentially a memory.

Controlled burning was recently reinstated on a number of small restored prairie remnants in the upper Midwest, especially in Illinois. The Nature Conservancy has also reintroduced fire and bison on preserves in Nebraska and the Dakotas. But until now the elements of the presettlement ecosystem have not been reunited on an unrestricted tract of land large enough for the system to function naturally and unfettered. The preserve here in northeastern Oklahoma fills the bill, restorationists believe. The 36,600 acres that so far make up the preserve (acreage is still being acquired) was once part of Oklahoma's sprawling Osage reservation. Most of the tract later became a cattle ranch. The Conservancy bought the ranch in 1989. Although the tract was mowed and grazed so much that it was in effect a pasture, it had never been plowed. This meant that although the plant composition on the site had been greatly altered, hundreds of original prairie plant species still grew there. This relieved the restorationists of having to reseed the land, as is commonly done on plowed and heavily degraded prairie restoration tracts farther north.

After letting the land rest for two years, some 26,000 acres were burned in spring 1993 in eleven separate controlled burns, the largest of which blackened 6,000 acres. Prescribed burning, as it is called, has become a standard conservation management tool in fire-dependent ecosystems across the country. The Conservancy probably does more burning than any other organization, and the tallgrass burn was one of the largest yet undertaken. In the summer of 1993, the prairie greened and bloomed spectacularly. More than 500 species of grasses and wildflowers have been identified by Conservancy scientists so far. In the fall, their season of bloom over, they created a carpet of soft browns and near-russets and somber grays over the undulating landscape. Marveling visitors walked among dead grasses eight feet tall.

In preparation for introducing the bison, fifty miles of fences that had broken up the tract into pastures were removed from the 5,000-acre tract where the big beasts—dark brown to black with lighter brown woolly coats over their shoulders, like shawls—will initially roam. As the herd grows to its full size of 1,800, a size that biologists believe will make it genetically viable, more fences will come down and the unrestricted prairie will be enlarged. The bison were donated by Kenneth and Diana Adams, who had them on their ranch at nearby Bartlesville.

It is estimated that the bison will eat about 25 percent of the vegetation that grows each year on the 5,000-acre plot, Mr. Hamilton said. That is a conservative estimate that may result in grazing that is too light, he said, and it may become necessary to readjust the size of the grazing tract in relation to the density of the animals. Since the frequency of fire in a given prairie patch probably was two to ten years, the restorationists will essentially split the difference and burn each of five, 1,000-acre segments every five years on a staggered schedule. All of this is subject to adjustment as the experiment proceeds, for that is just what the venture is—"a grand experiment," Mr. Hamilton called it.

"It's going to be a lot of fun," he said, "and a little challenging."   [WKS, OCTOBER 1993]

INDEX